It's Marty!

It's Marty!

MARTY MORRISSEY

SANDYCOVE

an imprint of

PENGUIN BOOKS

SANDYCOVE

UK | USA | Canada | Ireland | Australia
India | New Zealand | South Africa

Sandycove is part of the Penguin Random House group of companies
whose addresses can be found at global.penguinrandomhouse.com.

First published 2021
001

Copyright © Marty Morrissey, 2021

The moral right of the author has been asserted

The picture credits on p. 497 constitute an extension of this copyright page

Set in 13.5/16pt Garamond MT Std
Typeset by Jouve (UK), Milton Keynes
Printed and bound in Great Britain by Clays Ltd, Elcograf S.p.A.

The authorized representative in the EEA is Penguin Random House Ireland,
Morrison Chambers, 32 Nassau Street, Dublin D02 YH68

A CIP catalogue record for this book is available from the British Library

ISBN: 978–1–844–88567–1

This book is dedicated to my late wonderful dad, Martin Morrissey, who was always positive and taught me how to smile.

And to all who love the Marty Party!

Contents

CONTENTS

Prologue

It was September 4th, 2011. Twenty-two years and seven months since I did my first ever commentary for RTÉ, and here I was in the radio commentary position in Croke Park about to describe the first All-Ireland hurling final of my career.

Twenty-two years and seven months. Hardly an overnight success.

This was the first final without Mícheál Ó Muircheartaigh for three decades or more. How do you replace a living legend? A national treasure?

I looked at my watch: 2.30 p.m., an hour to throw-in. I watched some of the minor final between Galway and Dublin, but it was a bit of a blur. My mind was elsewhere.

Mícheál's retirement brought a change of attitude in RTÉ. At that time, they decided that no one broadcaster would dominate the radio airwaves on big matches as he had done. Ger Canning would continue to be the main TV commentator for both finals, while Darragh Maloney and myself would share the finals on the radio. It was a huge responsibility, but one I relished.

Ryle Nugent, then group head of sport, was the one who gave me this opportunity. He suggested I write a few bullet points, maybe even a few paragraphs, to help me get over any nerves and find my rhythm. I took his advice. It was now almost 3.25 p.m. The Kilkenny and Tipperary teams were shaking hands with the President, Mary McAleese, in the company of GAA President Christy Cooney.

81,214 people had taken their seats. The upper and lower Hogan, the upper and lower Cusack, the upper and lower Davin were packed to capacity. Thousands more stood in the Nally and Hill 16 terraces. Go on. Close your eyes. Can you see it? Can you feel it? It's special, isn't it?

Croke Park was awash with colour. Black, amber, blue and gold the dominant colours all around. The atmosphere was tense, anxious, but tinged with excitement.

The Artane Band, in tight formation, stood to attention before the Hogan stand, capes blowing gently in the autumn breeze. The Tipperary and Kilkenny teams lined up behind the band, and it began. One beat of the drum, just one beat, and the crowd reacted immediately, roaring their approval as the band, with the teams marching behind, began their circuit of the pitch. Now the decibel levels rose higher, as did the tension in the packed amphitheatre.

I stood on the lowest level of the upper tier of the Hogan stand with my headphones tight on my ears, a microphone extending from the headset covered in the black furry sponge-like material that protects it from excessive wind. The sound engineer, the great Mick McLoughlin, was stationed away to my right, surrounded by sound faders and flashing lights. He gave me the thumbs-up and grinned. 'Don't fuck it up,' says he.

To my left, surrounded by clipboards and paperwork, was my great friend, former Limerick hurler David Punch. Affectionately known as 'Punchy', he had been down there on the pitch when Limerick lost to Galway in the 1980 final, the day Joe Connolly made his famous speech. Punchy had been doing the statistics for me for years. We had developed our own system of communication, a complicated sign language that only we could understand. We gave each other a hug. We both knew how much this meant.

Jacqui Hurley and Con Murphy, who were presenting the radio programme, were sitting above and behind me in the Hogan stand. They ended their pre-match analysis and got the final verdicts from the panel as the Artane band and the players passed the Davin and marched on towards the Cusack stand. They looked down at me and said, 'Your match commentary team for this year's All-Ireland final is Donal Óg Cusack and first, Marty Morrissey.'

Right, here goes . . .

'Good afternoon, and wherever you are in the world right now, let me welcome you to Croke Park . . .'

For the next five years I was both delighted and privileged to be assigned the radio commentary for the All-Ireland hurling finals by RTÉ group head of sport Ryle Nugent. As it turned out, that was a total of nine finals because, amazingly, the 2012, 2013 and 2014 deciders all went to replays.

In the RTÉ sports department there has always been a subliminal attitude that TV is the glamour gig and that radio is well, *grand*. It's not really a criticism, just a fact of life, and is based on audience stats and so on. But from my own perspective as a commentator, radio is where it's at.

On TV, you're there to supplement and enhance the pictures. On radio, the listener is depending on you to describe the scene, capture the moment and appreciate what the event means. It's your words and your passion for the game that draw people in. The relationship between broadcaster and audience is far more intimate on the radio.

So why didn't I stick with radio, then? It really wasn't my choice. Management makes those calls. In the world where I work, the ultimate honour is to be assigned the TV commentary on an All-Ireland final. I had done the 2000 football final on TV – the drawn match between Kerry and Galway – as a substitute for Ger Canning, who was away at the Sydney Olympics. On Ger's return from Sydney, he was assigned the replay. I was heartbroken, but I understood and respected the reason why. I still wanted the job in my own right, and I would have felt I'd failed if I never achieved that in my career. It was that simple. And so I kept asking and asking and eventually, in 2017, I was assigned the All-Ireland hurling final on TV, and every one since then. Mission accomplished. It's an honour I appreciate every day of my life.

But where do I get the biggest reaction? Radio. No question. It's the best medium of them all. When I finally got the gig after Mícheál retired, I knew I had to do it differently. Mícheál was and will always be a legend in the best possible sense of the word. Nobody will ever compete with him. For any of us following in his footsteps, all you can do is do it your way. Put your own stamp on it. Just be yourself. Let it come from your heart and soul. Mícheál came from West Kerry. I come from New York via Clare.

Some people don't get what it's like to be abroad, either by choice or by necessity, on All-Ireland final days. I know what that feeling is like because it's part of me, part of my existence, part of my DNA. Being abroad on the day of All-Ireland finals – like Christmas and New Year – can be truly heartbreaking for our diaspora. I spent the first eleven years of my life in New York. I got my love of Gaelic games, our great heritage, our beautiful Irish language and our culture thousands of miles from home, because like so many others at the time, my parents emigrated in the 1950s when they had no jobs and no future here in Ireland.

I remember my father climbing out the sitting-room window of our one-bedroom apartment on Bainbridge Avenue in the Bronx and standing out on the fire escape, twisting and turning the radio with the antennae stretched to the last, trying to hear Michael O'Hehir describe the action 3,000 miles far away across the Atlantic Ocean. I have friends and relations who emigrated to Australia and New Zealand. They would be fine for 364 days of the year but would bawl crying when they heard or saw the match on that one day.

I wanted to reach out to those people – our people – who couldn't be with us physically but were with us spiritually and emotionally. And that is why these introductions became part of my performance on All-Ireland final day.

In the week leading up to the 2016 final, I asked on Twitter, 'Where will you be listening to the All-Ireland final this Sunday?'

One guy wrote back, 'In my kitchen.'

Another: 'In bed after I make love to my woman.'

Too Much Information!

So I tried again and asked a more specific question. 'Where in the world will you be listening to the All-Ireland final on Sunday?'

The replies were overwhelming. There were thousands. Sadly, I only had time to mention a few on the day.

I got an amazing reaction to my introduction to the 2016 All-Ireland hurling final:

Just in case you're walking on 5th Avenue in New York, jogging around the Corniche in Abu Dhabi, late night dining in Shi-buya in Tokyo or just chilling out on Long Street in Capetown South Africa, let me tell you: this is Croke Park on the north side of Dublin City. It's September 4th, 2016. It's 3.25 p.m. in the afternoon.

We are calling out to you from the 7th floor of what is lovingly known as the Hogan stand. Proud Corkman Donal Óg Cusack, three times an All-Ireland medallist and Clare selector, is standing right beside me. To the left, the Nally stand and Hill 16 are full. No seats across the way in the Cusack stand and to my right. Every seat has been sold out for a week at the Davin end. There is no venue in the world right now that has over 82,000 people gathered in what is undoubtedly one of the greatest stadiums in the world. Croke Park. Can you hear their voices? Can you hear the Artane band march across the green field of GAA headquarters with thirty warriors behind them? Shane Prendergast from Clara leads the men from Kilkenny, black and amber jerseys clinging to their muscular bodies.

To their left are fifteen Tipperary soldiers, hurleys held firmly in their grasp, with captain Brendan Maher from Borrisoleigh leading them into yet another battle with Kilkenny, their neighbours and arch rivals.

2016 has already been a remarkable year on the international stage. The music world lost David Bowie and Prince. In sport, the greatest of all, Muhammad Ali, passed away. He too graced this fabulous Croke Park arena on July 19th, 1972, when he boxed Alvin Lewis. The GAA lost the brilliant handballer Michael 'Ducksy' Walsh, and two former presidents, Jack Boothman from Wicklow and Joe McDonagh, who sang 'The West's Awake' after his county, Galway, won the All-Ireland hurling title on this very day thirty-six years ago. We remember them all today, and the many volunteers in the GAA who have passed away but who left a legacy of love and affection.

As you know, we are an island on the periphery of Europe, but we are a great people. We are unique and thank God for it.

The Olympics from an Irish perspective was a mixed bag of emotions but we should rejoice in the wonderful exploits of the men from Skibbereen, the brothers Gary and Paul O'Donovan who won silver in the men's double sculls – the first Olympic rowing medal Ireland has won. The West Cork men were a breath of fresh air.

We salute too on this day the incredible exploits of Annalise Murphy, who won a silver medal in sailing. We are proud of you.

While the world changes, some things in Ireland never change. Back on dry land here in Croke Park, the parade continues. It's Tipperary versus Kilkenny. But here is a change. Whoever wins will get an All-Ireland medal with a special added inscription of '1916–2016' to celebrate the centenary of the Rising.

Listen to the noise, listen to the heartbeat of the people of Ireland. All-Ireland hurling final day should be, in my humble opinion, a national holiday. There is no game in the world like the game of hurling. Can you feel the sense of pride of the people of Kilkenny and Tipperary? Black and amber against blue and gold. It's traditional, it's spiritual, and the more things change around us, the more they stay the same. Men, women, children in different coloured jerseys, over 82,000 here. No matter where you are now, stop, listen. Surely you can feel it? I've said it before but I want to say it again. If you had to leave home because of unemployment, or you just wanted to see the world, don't feel left out because you are with us today in spirit and in mind. We are thinking of you. We are Irish. We are Family.

I know Denise O'Keeffe from Jenkinstown, Co. Kilkenny, is listening in Perth, Australia. Damien, Ann and Clare Carney are beside the pool in Lanzarote, while Patrick Murphy from Cork is in York, Maine, USA. Stephen Kelleher and Paul Carty from Nenagh are listening to us in Hanoi, Vietnam. Hello to John Reaney in Capetown, South Africa. Mike O'Dwyer is enjoying the sunshine in Maui, Hawaii.

Gerry Bermingham is tuned in to us from the Czech Republic, Phily Englishby is with the Irish Defence Forces and listening to the wireless in the Golan Heights, Syria. We salute you and all your colleagues for what you are doing for peace.

Vivian Doyle is in Chicago, Illinois, Derek Ryan has found RTÉ Radio 1 in the Furancungo village in Mozambique, Niamh Burke is in Melbourne, Australia, and so too is Stevie Kelly. A. D. Morgan is in Tasmania while Eoin Hayes and Kate McDonald are in Muscat, Oman.

*Good morning, afternoon or evening to each and every one of you
and welcome to Croke Park.*

I have had more than my fair share of rejections and refusals,
but all the heartache, all the disappointments, are washed
away when your boss tells you that RTÉ wants you to commentate on the All-Ireland final. And for the record, Ger
Canning is a brilliant broadcaster, a superb commentator and
an absolute gentleman. We have always gotten on. I have
always respected his position and was honoured to be his
No.2 for, well, you could nearly say twenty-eight years. I first
started commentating – on a freelance basis – in 1989, and
was eventually appointed on my own merit to do the TV
commentary for the 2017 All-Ireland hurling final between
Galway and Waterford. It was Ryle Nugent, group head of
sport, who finally said, 'Yes, you got the gig.'

I have never found anything easy, believe it or not. Everything has always taken time. Being an only child can be lonely,
and that was exacerbated by the fact that my parents were
also only children, so no brothers, no sisters, no aunts, no
uncles, no first cousins, though I am close to my second

cousins in Tramore, Co. Waterford. I rely on great and loyal friends, and I am lucky I have them.

Going from playing on the streets of the Bronx to playing in the fields of Mullagh in West Clare, when we returned to Ireland for the first time when I was six, was all a bit confusing. We would return for good a few years later. Attending a massive school with 800 boys when I was just eleven years old was an intimidating experience, especially since I spoke with a different accent.

Like most teenagers, I hadn't a clue what I wanted to do with my life. I drifted from wanting to be a bus driver, a priest, an airline pilot, a doctor and a teacher to finally wanting to be a broadcaster. Losing a parent in that close family infrastructure can be devastating. It hasn't been that easy since my father died in 2004.

You deal with what God has lined up for you. You just get on with it. And I know there are so many people that have had it a lot tougher than me, so I appreciate what I have every day.

I knew nobody in RTÉ when I started applying. Not a soul. Nobody pulled a stroke to get me in. I just kept knocking on doors and kept making telephone calls. In hindsight I must have been the biggest pain in the ass that you could imagine. But I met some kind and wonderful people who obviously must eventually have said: 'Give him a chance.' At the beginning, I only wanted to commentate, but as time went by, I got the urge to diversify and experience everything. I still have that hunger.

On reflection, I've probably given too much of myself to my career, and indeed to RTÉ. Rejection, I think, has that impact on you. It leaves an indelible impression. You're afraid it won't work out. And if it doesn't, it's so goddamn public.

So you allow work to envelop you, to *be* you. While I love it, I don't want to be just a sports commentator. Being put into a box has always annoyed me. That's why I have diversified and evolved, and, in many ways, RTÉ have been good to me and allowed that to happen. But I want a lot more now.

I have loved every minute of my journey and hope that there's a lot more to come. I have regrets and I don't have regrets. Does that make sense?

This is me, my story.

It's Marty.

1. And So It Begins

My grandfather Paddy Morrissey fought in the War of Independence, and was involved in an incident at Rineen, Co. Clare, in which the IRA ambushed a Royal Irish Constabulary (RIC) lorry. The story goes that either at that time or in a related action, he was grazed by a bullet. Like so many others, he headed to America after the war, and like so many others, he worked on the railways. He returned home to Cooraclare in West Clare, and met and married my grandmother, Alice O'Doherty, who came from the neighbouring parish. They moved to the townland of Clonadrum near Mullagh, to live and farm thirty acres of what could only be described as poor land. They lived in a thatched cottage on a narrow country road which would, generations later, become the Wild Atlantic Way.

Their seaside parish was comprised of the two tiny villages, Quilty and Mullagh, and the townland of Coore. There was a creamery and two small stations on the narrow-gauge West Clare Railway. The villages lay a mile and a half apart, while the town of Miltown Malbay was about five miles northwards as one travelled towards Ennistymon, the Cliffs of Moher and the Burren. They had three priests in the parish, no fewer than eight schools, a Garda barracks but no doctor. He lived four miles away in Spanish Point. It was an era when priests were respected, masters admired and the guards feared.

Farming and the land meant everything to my grandfather.

He would get up every morning at 4 a.m. to milk the cows. He would tackle up his beloved horse, Grey Fanny, place the milk churns on the trap and secure them with ropes. Most mornings, it was either freezing cold or drizzling rain. He would sit on the right-hand side of the trap and wrap a blanket around his legs before motioning to Grey Fanny first to walk, then to trot . . . then to gallop.

Paddy and his two neighbours, Joe Flynn and Michael Lynch, each with his own horse and trap, would race each other down the hill, then up through Micheál O'Doherty's Cross and past O'Connor's pub to see who would make the creamery at the Annageeragh River first. This daily competition led to great slagging and banter between the three men.

During the 1940s, my grandmother operated a little shop out of the cottage. From what I gather, she sold only cigarettes. Rationing was a way of life at the time; everyone was issued with a ration book full of coupons which entitled you to buy particular items. The 'Small Woodbine' was an open-ended paper packet of five cigarettes which cost two old pennies and was the great favourite. News of the arrival of a fresh supply to a local shop spread like wildfire. Smokers from miles around would converge on the shop to beg or cajole the shopkeeper to let them buy a few fags. Each cigarette was good for two or three smokes; just a few drags before it was topped and pocketed for the next time. When real desperation set in, homemade cigarettes were assembled from brown paper, tea leaves or – if things were really tight – turf dust. There was a black market, of course, which introduced some unfamiliar names: Player's Weights, Capstan, Craven A, White Horse and even a few Turkish brands. My father used to often say the latter were not the most popular.

'Sure you'd need the jaws of an ass to knock a pull out of that fag.'

My father smoked from an early age and by all accounts made a few bob from his mother's shop. He used to swipe a handful of Woodbine to sell on his way to school on the West Clare Railway. He travelled every day from the Kilmurry Station to Ennistymon, where he attended the Christian Brothers School. Everything was taught *as Gaeilge*.

I was often told that my grandmother was way too kind for her own good. She used to give half her stock away for free, or 'on the book', which meant on credit. The other story told about her was that when my grandfather couldn't find a shirt he intended wearing, it eventually came out that Alice had given it to somebody that she thought needed it more.

Believe it or not, when my father did the Leaving Cert, the results of every student in the county were published in the *Clare Champion*. Martin Morrissey had nothing to fear, however. He was a very intelligent man; a lot smarter than his son. If you did well enough in your state exams back then, you could go straight into teaching without the need for university. So, within a few months of finishing school, he took his first teaching job in the Patrician Academy in Mallow, Co. Cork.

He rented a room from the Barrett family in a house near the Mouse Trap Bar in Mallow and settled into a new and exciting life away from home. The Barretts had cousins up the road called the Twomeys. They had one daughter, Margaret, whom everyone called Peggy, and judging by the photos I've seen of her at the time, she was a bit of a babe. She was educated in the convent in Doneraile by the Presentation Sisters and when she left, she became a hairdresser. It was at her cousins' house that she met my father, and so began a new relationship and a new adventure. Martin and Peggy got married in the Church of the Nativity of the Blessed Virgin Mary in Doneraile, and as soon as they were married, they set off to New York in search of a better quality of life.

My grandfather didn't take the news of his only son's departure very well. Forsaking the land for some daft notion of following your dream? The idea was completely alien to him. There was no phone in my grandparents' house, and of course this was long before smart phones and emails and texts. There were only letters back and forth across the Atlantic. My grandmother wrote regularly but there was silence between father and son.

Four years into the marriage, when it looked as though there would be no children, my mother became pregnant with me. Both my parents wanted me to be born in Ireland, but shortly before I was born, my father landed a new job and so couldn't make the trip. Cost was also a factor. They simply didn't have the money for the two of them to fly home. My mother has always hated flying, but to her very great credit she took a flight back across the Atlantic Ocean on her own so that I could be born at the end of October in the Mount Alvernia Hospital in Mallow, Co. Cork. I weighed in at 8 pounds and 2 ounces. Let's say I made an impression.

A month later, she was back on a plane again, this time heading to New York with yours truly in her arms. At the time, it was a fourteen-hour flight, made more uncomfortable by near-constant turbulence.

My father's first job in New York was with Cook Travel. From there, he moved to Aer Lingus, then Fairways Travel, before eventually setting up his own business, Morrissey Travel, on Bainbridge Avenue in the Bronx, where he rented a dingy office. He worked long hours, including weekends, while my mother held down two jobs. She worked with an insurance company in downtown Manhattan by day and was a receptionist in Fordham University by night. These were tough times for them, which is why they asked my Cork

Visiting my mother at work in New York

grandparents to come to America to look after me. My grandfather on my mother's side, Tom Twomey, or Pop Twomey, as I called him, was great fun: full of Cork wit and charm. He played ball with me on the streets of New York by day and worked as a security man in a bank at night. So you see where I get my work ethic.

I had a wonderful relationship with my father. You couldn't but like the guy. He was bright, witty, kind, easy-going and was nearly always in a good mood. He loved the travel business. In the days before the internet, if somebody wanted a holiday in Florida, or needed to come home to Ireland, they would book their trip with somebody like my dad. I loved going to Kennedy airport with him on the subway, or by taxi if the trip had to be made at night. We went so often that in time, I came to know JFK like the back of my hand. I particularly loved the TWA building because of its unusual design, but the most exciting thing was watching planes take off and land. I would run up the escalator and park myself at the big windows, outside of which the planes would park nose-first, so I could see right into the cockpit. I would sit there for hours watching them, though we never told my mother; she would kill Dad for leaving me alone. But it was

a different time. I knew my father was just downstairs. I imagined myself as Captain Marty Morrissey. *Fasten your seatbelts, we will be departing shortly for Hawaii.* The big treat, when he finished work, was a delicious hot dog, served with onions and ketchup.

Throughout those early years in New York, we came back to Clare regularly for our summer holidays. This was a rare luxury for the times, and was only possible because Dad worked in the travel business and could get cheap flights. Both my mother and himself wanted to keep that strong connection with home, not least because their long-term plans were to return to Ireland

I always remember my grandmother's great kindness. One time, we had only just arrived and she gave me a big glass of milk which I downed in one massive gulp. Being an American kid, I didn't know that this was unpasteurized milk,

straight from the cow. I threw up all over the place and haven't touched a glass of milk ever since.

If we were going off in our rented car to Kilrush or Ennis to do some shopping, my grandmother would grasp my hand, push money into my jacket pocket and whisper, 'Don't tell your mother or father I gave you that.'

I remember my grandfather's hobnail boots clattering across the kitchen floor. There was no television and nor do I remember any radio. But I do remember the smell of porridge in the morning and bacon and cabbage on a Sunday.

One thing I really loved about coming home on summer

holidays to Ireland was my grandfather's horse Fanny, or Grey Fanny if you want her official name. She was born on the farm and was so gentle and affectionate, even as a foal, that she was treated as a pet from the very beginning.

So picture this.

An American kid coming home to West Clare to visit his grandparents on his summer holiday, finding a beautiful grey mare with her head in the half door of the cottage, looking around and taking everything in, and her arse out the door with her tail swishing away the flies and the summer bees. It was the picture of utter happiness and I thought I was in dreamland.

The relationship between my grandfather and his horse was truly extraordinary. If I hadn't seen it myself, I wouldn't have believed it. Grey Fanny brought the turf home from the boglands of Shrea near Doonbeg and trammed the hay every summer in the five meadows, each of which had its

own name: Shan Gort, the Red Gate, Connell's Meadow, the Cross Meadow, which was at the back of the house, and the Long Meadow in the valley by the stream. Tramming was simply gathering together smaller haycocks or grasscocks into a massive pile. I loved climbing up to the top when it was finished.

But time has moved on. Modernization and baling has made the ancient art of tramming a thing of the past. Tramming the hay used to be a great communal thing, bringing together all the neighbours to help each other out. The Flynns, the Lynches, the McCarthys, the O'Dohertys and the Murrihys all arrived in to Morrisseys for the tramming, and Paddy Morrissey would do the same for his neighbours when their turn came. Simple days but great days.

My grandfather always wore a wide-rimmed flat hat, to save his balding head from the sun in the summer and from the Atlantic winds and rain in the winter.

The hat was part of his whole being.

'Paddy,' my grandmother would often say, 'will you please take off your hat coming into the house?'

One day, he and I were strolling up the road from the cow cabin to the house. My grandfather was holding the big grey mare's reins lightly between his fingers and the horse strolled behind him. I was talking at about ninety miles per hour. And then it happened, just as my father had described.

Grey Fanny grabbed my grandfather's hat from his head with her teeth, and held it in her mouth until she got to the half door. Then, sticking her head into the kitchen, she tossed it gently to my grandmother.

Grey Fanny would grab his hat in just the same way in the middle of ploughing or tramming the hay if she felt my grandfather wasn't giving her enough attention.

I loved back then the smell of fresh-cut hay and still do passionately to this day. The photos I have up on the trams of hay with my grandfather are very dear to my heart. I'll never forget those summers.

Back in New York, I remember my father coming home very upset one day. He had gotten a call to say that my grandmother in Clare was very ill and that he should come home immediately. We almost made it. We were in Mullagh, only a mile and a half away, when Alice Morrissey passed away. It was St Patrick's Day, 1964. My dad was heartbroken. He did not want to go back to New York, which is why we stayed in Ireland for the rest of that year. He got a job in the Shannon Industrial Estate and I went to school in Mullagh, where I made my First Holy Communion with my new friends.

One amazing thing happened during this period. My mother won a car, a top of the range Simca, in the weekly 'Spot the Ball' competition in the *Sunday Independent*. A

picture showed a goalmouth scramble or some other kind of action shot, but with the ball removed. You had to put your X wherever you thought it should be. And on this occasion, my mother got it exactly right. The picture of the family taking delivery of the new car appeared in the paper the following week, and that created a fantastic buzz around West Clare.

My grandfather was clearly lost without Alice. He continued to work the farm and I was sent down the road every afternoon after school to keep him company. He seemed to smile a little more when I was around, and for a while my dad and his dad seemed to get on a little better.

But the poor man was suffering from a broken heart and on 1 November 1964 – All Saints' Day – just over seven months after my grandmother had died, Paddy Morrissey joined his darling Alice. He was found leaning back on his trap while Fanny stood unmoving outside the hay barn.

Many years later, my father's first book was published: *Land of my Cradle Days – Recollections of a Country Childhood*. He tells the story of what happened next with Grey Fanny far better than I ever could.

For the first few days after my father passing, Grey Fanny grazed peacefully in her field. After about a week I noticed she was standing at the gate looking up the road towards the house with her head erect and her ears pointed forward.

Just to be sure I asked my cousin Jerry O'Connor, a local vet, to examine her and he found her to be in excellent physical condition. The watching from the gate continued. Then the loud whinnying began.

It continued at intervals day and night. She began to gallop around the field, head erect, eyes searching every nook and cranny. Everybody was convinced she was looking for my father.

What was even more amazing to all who knew her was the fact that she now began clambering over high walls and jumped lower ones, something that was totally out of character for her. The whinnying and searching continued for another week. I tried everything I could think of to calm her down, rubbing her white coat, talking to her, but to no avail. By the end of the week I was becoming desperate. I discussed the problem at length with Jerry who finally turned to me and said . . . 'Let's try something non-medical.' He went to the old house and got one of my father's battered old hats. Coming back to the gate, he held it out to Grey Fanny. She sniffed it a few times and grabbed it between her teeth as I had seen her do so often, many years before. She turned and galloped back into her field. The whinnying and galloping stopped. She began to graze peacefully. We watched for a long time. 'That's one very lonely horse,' Jerry remarked. 'She's got feeling.'

We left her in her field, happy in the knowledge her distress had disappeared and she seemed to have returned to normal. Early the following morning I went down the road to see her. I found her lying dead in a corner of the field, the old hat beside her outstretched head. The last link lay broken on the ground. It marked the end of an era.

Unfortunately, the land that my grandfather loved and worked so hard was ultimately sold a few years later. Dad didn't want to sell it, but he was reported to the Land Commission for not using it, and so, with a heavy heart, he put it up for sale.

With my grandfather gone, there was nothing really keeping us in Ireland. It was quite clear too that living so near to where he had lost both parents so quickly was making my father's grief harder to bear. Nor had he finished with New York and the opportunities it offered, so by Christmas, we were back in the Bronx. I went to school in St Ann's at 3511 Bainbridge Avenue, New York 10467. It was a Catholic school with a very wide student demographic: Hispanics,

African Americans, Native Americans and, when I was there, two Irish boys. Myself and Denis Murphy from Wexford.

Every morning, come hail, sleet or snow, we all stood together in the school basketball court and swore allegiance to the American flag that blew gently in the New York breeze:

> *I pledge allegiance to the flag of the United States of America and to the Republic for which it stands, one Nation, under God. Indivisible, with Liberty and Justice for all.*

The school was directly across the road from the Montefiore Hospital – which was huge. All day long, the sirens of ambulances and police cars never really stopped, which is why,

after a while, we stopped noticing it altogether. I really liked St Ann's and considered myself lucky to have a lovely Dominican nun – Sr Thomas – as my first teacher. She had Sligo blood, and loved me because I was Irish. My next teacher was Miss Seitler. A great teacher but a little sterner; the Irish charm I was developing didn't work on her at all.

Every Wednesday afternoon the alarm would sound and all 230 students would walk in orderly fashion down the stairs and out on to the basketball court. The teachers told us it was fire drill practice, but when the fire brigade, police and even a TV crew arrived in dramatic fashion one afternoon, it began to dawn on us, and our parents, that something else was going on.

It emerged that a public school a few blocks away had a half day every Wednesday, and that some of the students, for craic purposes, would call St Ann's and tell the principal that there was a bomb in our school and that they had ten minutes to get everybody out.

Every Sunday, like thousands of other Irish people, we travelled by subway to Gaelic Park, which is on West 240th Street and Broadway in Riverdale, Bronx. Gaelic Park has been the venue for Gaelic games in New York since 1926. When I was a kid, the place was run by a man called John 'Kerry' O'Donnell, who leased it in 1941. It was a very special place back then, and not just for GAA people. It was a meeting place for the Irish emigrant, to share news from home or meet a potential boyfriend or girlfriend. Above all, however, it was an unofficial employment exchange, where people sought contacts for jobs for themselves or their sister or brother who would be arriving in the Big Apple the following week.

My father and mother were always on duty here – drumming

up business for wherever he worked at the time. I couldn't wait for half-time, when I played football and hurling in the sand- and dust-filled goalmouths with all the other boys and girls. I used to imagine one day playing there myself.

When I was around nine years old, my parents saw an advertisement in the *Irish Echo*, which could be bought weekly in a store on Bainbridge Avenue. If Dad didn't manage to get it there, there was another place on Jerome Avenue that also sold papers from different countries. I also remember going downtown on the subway to Manhattan with my father, where he always went to a store on Broadway which carried the previous week's *Clare Champion*. Anyway, the ad was for the sale of a house containing a pub and grocery store, a dance hall and another pub, all to be sold as one lot and all located in Quilty.

I can remember the photo clearly: Martin Casey's Pub dead smack in the village. Would they have enough money to buy it? Probably not. What did they know about running a pub? Absolutely nothing.

But they were both adamant that I would have my secondary schooling in Ireland, not least because conscription was still in force in the States. 'The Draft', as it was known, meant that I would have had to give military service to the US armed forces once I finished high school.

So that was it. The Morrisseys were leaving New York.

2. Coming Home

There must be a seam of luck running down through the female side of my family because my grandmother Alice had a sister, Molly O'Doherty, who won the Sweepstakes way back in the 1930s. No less than £300, which was of course big money at the time.

She was married to a man called Egan, and having no children themselves, they adored her nephew – my father. When they died, they left the house and land they bought with their winnings to my father. Hillcrest, as it's called, is across the road and up the hill from my grandfather's home, and became our home for the few weeks before we moved into the house over the pub and grocery shop in Quilty.

Quilty itself is dead smack in the middle of the Clare coast, between Lahinch and Kilkee, just a few miles south of Miltown Malbay. Traditionally, it was a small fishing village, where lobster, salmon, bass, herring and mackerel were caught and landed at the nearby pier at Seafield. At one time there were twenty boats, but now there are just four left. Tommy Galvin is one of the few fishermen left there today; others include Alan Dickenson, Martin Kelleher, and Anthony and Finbarr Murrihy. As the fishing dwindled, so too has the Irish language. Quilty was once part of the West Clare Gaeltacht, but no more.

The Star of the Sea Church in Quilty is the most prominent building in the village. Its round tower is visible for miles around. It was built in remembrance of the French sailing ship *Leon XIII*, which plays a major role in our local history.

On Saturday April 20th, 1907, the ship left Portland,

Maine, carrying twenty-two men and a cargo of wheat bound for Limerick. The *Leon* met her end five months later in a week that changed Quilty for ever. By Monday September 30th the ship had reached the Shannon Estuary, but the following day a sudden storm blew her northwards towards Quilty, damaging her sails and rudder. Soon after dawn on October 2nd, the ship struck rocks off Sugar Island at Emlagh Point. Her hull broke and the stern sank, forcing the crew to cling on to the bow and rigging. Quilty people immediately tried to reach the stricken Frenchmen but the storm prevented all rescue attempts that day. At nightfall, every home had a lighted candle in the window, as a symbol of hope for the desperate sailors.

The following day, Thursday October 3rd, the weather was as bad as ever and the Seafield coastguard boat would not stay afloat. The Frenchmen built and boarded a raft, but it drifted out to sea, leaving many in the water. At this point, the Quilty fishermen launched their currachs. One capsized immediately and its three occupants were hurled overboard. They were picked up, thankfully, and the rescue attempt continued until all thirteen French sailors had been plucked from the sea. Captain Lucas, with his leg now broken, stayed on board with the other eight sailors for another horrific night.

On Friday October 4th the *HMS Arrogant* from Berehaven made it to the stranded vessel and the remaining nine sailors were rescued. Remarkably, no man lost his life, and nor were there any serious injuries. The people of Quilty looked after the sailors as they recovered from their ordeal and in time they all returned safely to France. The story of the brave fishermen of Quilty made international headlines, and many follow-up stories in the press highlighted the poverty of the people. A fund-raising initiative was begun in the aftermath of the incident, both to alleviate the poverty and to build a chapel. In 1911, the Star of the Sea Church was opened as a lasting memorial for the heroes of Quilty.

The French didn't exactly cover themselves in glory in this episode. They promised much but delivered little. Later on, however, they did send the original bell from the *Leon XIII*, and to this day, it is rung at every mass in the Star of the Sea Church.

For the first eleven years of my life, I was back and forth across the Atlantic on holidays, but once we made the move to Quilty, all the travelling stopped. I was home. I fell in love with my own area, with the smell of the sea, the sound of the seagulls, the beat of the music and the heart of the people. It was an intoxicating cocktail; I immediately felt a sense of belonging. These were my people and I was proud to be one of them. Those connections were first forged the year we spent in Ireland when my grandmother and grandfather died. I made friends easily and most of the neighbours had children I could play with.

One of my first and best friends was the lad next door, Michael King. We hit it off immediately. We did everything together, starting off with cowboys and Indians (though Michael would never die even though he had very clearly been shot). We balled up coats as goalposts and played football goal to goal in the small field at the back of our house. You had to play either with the hill or against the hill, at the top of which the old West Clare Railway line used to run.

After watching John McEnroe and Björn Borg in Wimbledon, we'd cycle over to John and Maura Daly's Clonmore Lodge in Kilmurry, hoping that there would be no guests on the tennis court. These games would be highly competitive and since Michael is not here to say otherwise, I can tell you I won every single game!

Standing behind the bar or the grocery shop counter was a whole new experience for all of us. At the beginning, trying to keep track of who was who was not easy. You see, in Quilty, everybody is related to everybody else. I remember my father explaining it all to me.

'The Moloneys are related to the Hickeys, who are related to the Considines, who are first cousins of the Murrihys, who are married to the McCarthys, who in turn are related to the Considines. Now, the Considines are . . .'

'Stop!' I said, clamping my hands over my ears. 'My head can't take this. I'll figure it out myself!'

And I did over time.

All my new friends went to school in Ennistymon CBS, my father's old school, but there, everything was done, as it was in his time, *as Gaeilge*. That unfortunately ruled me out, because Irish had not been on the curriculum back in the Bronx. There was no alternative but to send me to St Flannan's College in Ennis. I was only eleven years of age. In hindsight, a year in Quilty or Mullagh National School would have done me no harm, but the decision was made and off I went to Ennis. It was also decided that despite being exempt from Irish, I would now start learning the language. I can tell you that I found that very difficult, and in all my years in Flannan's, I was always that bit behind in Irish.

I'll never forget my first day. I didn't know a soul. Nobody. Almost 1,000 boys and everybody seemed to know everybody else. The corridors were full of talking and laughing and slagging. I felt intimidated by it all.

Then in English class, Mr O'Meara – affectionately known as Micko – asked me to read and what a reaction! Laughter rippled across the classroom. This was the moment that I realized I had an accent. Not just an American twang, but a full-blown New York accent. The smartarse comments came flying in from all round the room.

'Hey, Yank! Say it again!'

But I rolled with the punches and somehow by the end of my first week, I'd gotten used to being called 'Yank'.

Amazingly, however, the nickname never stuck. I put that down to the GAA. The late Fr Ollie O'Doherty was in charge of football in the college at the time. He organized the annual first year league. Because I could move fairly fast, I wanted to play wing forward in hurling but in football I only had one ambition. To be a goalkeeper. So I went into goals and let's just say I surprised my classmates with how well I played. 'Yank' was gone and Marty was in.

Back home in Quilty, my bedroom was the room right over the grocery shop in the middle of the house. The view from my window was truly spectacular. Across the road and over the dry wall, as it was called, lay the broad Atlantic Ocean, with Mutton Island just offshore and the Aran Islands about fourteen miles out in the wide blue water. At night, there was a solitary street light outside the pub entrance downstairs. Many a night, when I couldn't sleep, I'd watch the horizon and count the thirteen seconds it took for the lighthouse on Inis Oírr to complete its circle between flashes. In those early days, I often said to myself: 'We left the buzz of New York for this?'

But any longing for the bright lights quickly died away. On a Friday evening, the Quilty boys would arrive home on the CIE bus, a ball would be produced and a game would start. The goals were the doors of the Carrageen shed at the bend in the road at the centre of Quilty, where Beatrice O'Dwyer now has her shop and her brother John has the chipper.

Every now and then you'd hear an almighty wallop as the ball crashed against the door, quickly followed by a wild cheer. If a tractor or a car came down the hill from Kilrush or Kilkee, somebody would shout 'Stop! Car coming!'

My father might not have been a publican before, and indeed he never drank himself, but he had great ideas and was very culturally aware.

Big Tom and the Mainliners, Doc Carroll, Dermot Hegarty and the Plainsmen, Mick Delahunty and his orchestra, Ray Lynam and the Hillbillies and Margo and the Country Folk all performed at one time or another in the dance hall, which had a big sliding door as its front entrance.

The main pub adjoined the grocery store, both of which were part and parcel of the house. The dance hall stood next door, across the yard, while the Leon Bar was situated down the road as you headed towards Miltown Malbay. It was a lovely old-fashioned bar that only opened on bank holiday weekends and other special occasions. Sadly, it's gone now, but when I close my eyes I can still hear the music. Trad was the order of the day here: hornpipes, reels, jigs and slow airs. All the legends played in the Leon: Willie Clancy, Michael Falsey, Junior Crehan, Paddy Galvin, to name just four, all dressed in Sunday suits with caps on their heads. Set dancing was a big part of the culture. Many a night the locals battered out the steps on the stone floor with great style and gusto. It was a magical time, one that in many ways I didn't really appreciate properly at the time.

In our second year, RTÉ came to visit and asked my father if they could film some traditional music in the bar. The late and beautiful Áine O'Connor was part of the production team. Her arrival drew more attention than the local musicians performing. The black and white footage is still shown occasionally, and even now the set dancing is truly magnificent. Oh, the battering!

My father got the idea of transferring the pub licence from the Leon up the road to the dance hall, and thereby converting it into a huge pub. It was a big gamble. He built the bar counter more or less the length of the hall. My only concern with this innovation was the risk it posed to the soccer games myself and the lads played in the hall every Sunday morning during the winter months.

He renamed the revamped hall the Caledonian Lounge. There was lino on the floor, a galvanized roof overhead and the chairs were hard plastic and bright orange in colour. It was bog basic, but the gamble paid off. Thousands poured into the place night after night, and you'd often see the floor heaving under the ferocity of a Clare set.

Health and safety? Health and safety my arse.

RTÉ came a second time. This time Cathal O'Shannon was the reporter. He interviewed my father, and there was more dancing: the Caledonian set and the plain set. This footage has been seen many times on Pat Shortt's *Music from D'Telly*. Pat was kind enough to name check Dad, and to link me to him. I appreciated that.

The big pubs at the time were Mickey Wilson's and Friels in Miltown Malbay, and in the surrounding area you had Johnny Burke's Armada in Spanish Point, the Crosses of Annagh and ourselves in Quilty. Pub licensing laws meant you could get an extension which allowed you to stay open until one in the morning on nine nights of the year, including Christmas Eve, St Stephen's night, New Year's Eve, St Patrick's night and public holiday weekends in June and August. You opened Sunday morning but closed between two and four in the afternoon.

The Caledonian Lounge as it is today

Our music now became more traditionally focused and the Caledonian Lounge was packed at least three nights a week, with people travelling from Cork, Limerick, Tipperary and Kerry to savour the atmosphere.

The Bannermen were a huge local attraction, as were Noel Shine and the Dickie Linnane Band. Alfie Marrinan from Kilkee played the accordion while literally bouncing on the chair. The great Michael Falsey often played with him, while Tommy Boland, who had been in New York with Dad, was on drums. Sell-out crowds were guaranteed if either the Golden Star Band, the Kilfenora Ceili Band or P. J. Murrihy and the Bannermen were performing.

We had great characters in Quilty. Sis McGannon was a lovely lady with a quick wit and a sharp tongue. I remember a friend of mine, J. J. Cronin from Doneraile, was staying with me during the summer and we started a pillow fight in my bedroom. As the fight intensified, I stumbled backwards and crashed against the lower pane of glass, breaking it into smithereens. Sis was entering the shop at that precise moment and so was showered with glass. She never complained but simply looked up and said, 'Marty darling, you have a lovely arse.'

Plunkett Boyle was the organist in Quilty church for years. One Sunday morning, right in the middle of the mass, the organ broke down. Plunkett calmly got up from his seat, walked down the middle of the church and moments later returned with a stepladder. He strode back up the middle aisle and placed the stepladder under the main light which dangled from the centre of the ceiling. He climbed the ladder, took out the bulb, plugged the flex from the organ into the socket, and returned to the instrument just in time for the next hymn. The congregation had of course completely lost interest in anything the priest was doing up on the altar, and as Plunkett launched into the first chords, they treated him to a warm round of applause.

Another local man, Joe Cuneen, was in a wheelchair all his life. He managed to get wherever he needed to go despite the lack of aides or anything like the right facilities. Every single day – without fail – he would wheel his way down the road from his mother's house in Seafield to the pub, and there he would remain all day long. He would play the tin whistle for any visitor that called in and they would usually buy him a pint or two in appreciation. I don't know if he was pulling my leg, but one time he confided in me that he only knew four tunes, and adapted them to the circumstances to make them sound different. Later, a few of the local lads made him a special wheelchair with pedals which he could operate with his hands. But the adaptations never extended to a set of lights, so travelling home at night was always a risk.

This will make Quilty in the early seventies sound like the

dark ages, but at the time, the telephone system was not exactly state-of-the-art. In New York, you used the phone just as you see in old TV programmes like *Kojak* or *The Rock-ford Files*, by placing your finger in each numbered hole and dialling in sequence. It wasn't that straightforward in Quilty. To make a call you had to give the handle at the side of the phone a right good twirl, pick up the receiver and wait for somebody in Quilty post office to answer. You would then ask for whatever number you wanted and hope that the post-master would be able to put you through.

If I remember correctly, the post office was Quilty 01, our number was Quilty 04, Dr Michael O'Connor was Quilty 05 and Jerry O'Connor, the vet, was Quilty 06. To get the curate, you dialled Quilty 12 and the parish priest was Quilty 14. You could argue that the numbers reflected the order of importance of the particular individuals and institutions, with the pub owners well ahead of either doctor, vet or parish priest!

My father had a great friend in New York, Fr Sam Winters. He was originally from Co. Limerick and was a big burly man with a booming voice. My father rang him one day from the pub in Quilty, and as the conversation turned to sensitive matters – how the pub was doing and whether or not we liked our new lives – my father noticed what sounded like heavy breathing on the line.

'Sam,' he said, 'we won't discuss anything confidential on this line, if you don't mind.'

'Why?' asked Fr Sam, who then picked up the unidentified sounds. He roared down the phone: 'Whoever is on this line, get off it now!'

There was a pause, then a third voice spat, 'There's nobody else on this fucking line now!'

This was followed by an abrupt *click*, the line improved

dramatically and the two pals on either side of the Atlantic roared laughing.

The only things that matter in Quilty are traditional music, set dancing and football.

I organized football matches on our lawn at Lynch's Cross, or Mullagh Cross as it was sometimes known. Lads cycled from near and far to play these games. I had discovered that two hayforks made great goalposts, but to make sure we had enough, some lads brought their own. We played until it was pitch dark, and so home they would go on their bikes, no lights front or back and the pitchfork wide across the handlebars. A recipe for disaster when you think back now, but thankfully they all got home safely.

My neighbour and great friend was bizarrely an only child as well, only in this instance an only daughter. As we grew into our teenage years, the crowds of lads coming to play

football got bigger, but I didn't know whether it was the soccer game on the lawn or the opportunity to chat up Mena Lynch that became the main attraction.

I was so nervous for my first trial – for the under-14 Kilmurry Ibrickane football team. The parish priest announced from the altar that it was to be held in Sexton's Castle Field in Coore at the far side of the parish. This was to be my introduction to lads from the far side of the parish. The excitement – among the under-14s anyway – was huge. You'd swear it was an All-Ireland final. This was big time football. This is what I gave up New York for. I remember being really nervous, as I expected Sexton's Castle Field to have real goalposts and perhaps even a stand. It was, to say the least, a bit of a disappointment. You couldn't even call it a pitch. It was the side of a very steep hill at a bend in the road as you headed down from Mullagh to Coore church. There were no goalposts at all, only balled-up coats thrown on the ground. I don't remember doing particularly well, as anything that went near the coats was declared a goal. I was delighted, however, when I was selected in goal for the team.

I'll never forget my first championship experience. News spread around the parish that the under-14 squad was particularly good, and so huge crowds (thirty or more!) followed our progress during the summer of '72. We won the county final, which was played in Kilrush against St Breckan's from Lisdoonvarna. Playing corner forward against me that evening was Eugene Garrihy, dad of Aoibhín, Ailbhe and Doireann, who are all my good friends today.

This was the beginning of my lifelong love affair with Kilmurry Ibrickane GAA. The club means everything to me.

Today we are a powerful force in the Banner County, but back then, we were anything but. Between 1966, when

Kilmurry Ibrickane won their third Clare senior football championship, and 1993 when they won their fourth, we won nothing at senior level except a couple of Aberdeen Arms and McTighue Cups. These were great craic but really they meant nothing. Sadly, that fallow period encompassed my entire playing career. We would begin every year with great enthusiasm but by mid July we would be gone, finished, knocked out of the championship. It is my greatest personal sporting regret that we won so little. More of that a little later.

Inevitably, myself and my friend next door, Michael King, discovered that as well as football, there were girls. We went to our first dances together in the marquee in Kilmihil, where the band The Indians, who were very popular at the time, often played. Many years later, I became great friends with Lorraine Keane (later the well-known broadcaster and businesswoman), whose dad was a member of the band. I never asked him if he

remembered two gobshites from Quilty at the Kilmihil marquee walking around the dancefloor and failing to pull.

I always bowed to Michael's superior knowledge of how to
negotiate these occasions. I clearly remember asking him, as
we entered the packed venue, 'What do we do now, Michael?'

'Marty, put your hands in your pockets and follow me.'

It seems very primitive now, but the reality at that time was
that the girls parked themselves on the far side while the boys
congregated on the side we entered. As per Michael's instructions, off we went around the dancefloor so that we could
have a good look at the girls and they could have an even
better look at us. For those first couple of dances in the marquee, the trick was to ask the only girl you knew for a dance,
as she was more than likely a neighbour up the road and she'd
have to say yes. It gave us a chance to throw a few shapes in
case any of the other girls might be interested. But after three
laps with the hands in the pockets and not a single 'yes' to
boast about – let alone someone asking you to dance – we

adjourned to the only place men like us could be safe: the chip van outside, to talk football and hurling with the lads.

At five minutes to two, however, the slow set would come on and the King and I would re-enter the marquee as the first of the three-song set drew to a close. We used to bring a small bottle of Old Spice; half went over me and the other half over King. He was tall, so he'd be bending down to speak to some girl. I didn't have that particular problem, of course! We got home to Quilty at 5 a.m. Both of us very happy despite the lack of a shift. Ah yes, the King and I were a great team.

I spent much of my teenage years in Michael's house, where I was fed and watered on a daily basis by Michael's mother, Annie, who was a wonderful and a very kind woman. At night, we'd play push-penny with two combs, or table tennis on the kitchen table. There was no net, just a string tied across the middle of the table. We'd batter the ball back and

The King and I, many years later

forth while Michael's parents would be trying to watch TV. I honestly think they were more entertained by us because as sure as God, a row would break out over nothing.

Going to the Hop in Lahinch was a serious challenge. You first had to get permission from parental HQ, and once the green light was given, you had to book your seat in Marty Joe Boland's car, which was a rickety old Ford Zephyr. Marty Joe was the local hackney man. Josie Killeen would eventually take over that role but with Josie, you'd want to start out from Quilty the Tuesday before if you were to have any hope of getting to Lahinch in time for the disco. Let's just say he was a very careful driver.

In my day, however, Marty Joe Boland was the man. He'd easily do two or three runs from Quilty to Lahinch on a Friday night, but by 3 a.m. he would be tired from the wait and would want to call it a night. Whatever you did, you'd have to get to the car before Marty Joe left.

The premier seats were in the back. These were the ones you'd aim for. The girls rolled in next and sat on your lap. If you hit the Lotto, you might get the girl you fancied on top of you. Five below and five on top was the rule in the back seat. It was tight, but it could be done, though it wouldn't be unusual to see Marty Joe rolling by with a couple of pairs of legs stuck out the back windows. Once the back was full, the boot would be flung open and four or five lads would scramble in and lie down, with two or three more sitting on them, their legs hanging over the ledge of the boot. Nobody ever complained. You could get no more than two in the front seat. Marty Joe was adamant about that because he needed room to change gears. In all the nights where we travelled, with anything up to eighteen packed into the car, we were never once stopped by the guards.

3. We Want Morrissey!

It's funny how the mind works. Some memories of home are as clear as if they happened yesterday.

It was while I was in the middle of fourth year in St Flannan's. I was home one Friday night in the depths of winter. The bar was quiet and as the adjoining grocery shop was closed, the lights were all out in there. The grocery shop was very old-fashioned, with a bell over the front door to signal a customer's arrival. The counter was three-sided, with a large ice cream fridge to the customer's immediate left as they entered the shop. That was full of HB and Leadmore ice cream – Leadmore's headquarters was in Kilrush, just down the road. Stacked on shelves behind the server, you'd see detergents like OMO, Drive, Rinso and Ariel. There would be the compulsory bars of Sunlight soap alongside Pledge furniture polish and boxes of Brillo. We sold Curly Wurlys, Fizz Wiz, Cherry Popping Candy, Fig Rolls and Custard Creams, as well as the daily papers: the *Irish Press* and the *Irish Independent*. Sunday mornings after ten o'clock mass were always extremely busy, as people piled in to buy their Sunday papers. The *Sunday World*, which launched in 1973, was particularly popular. The counter adjoined the kitchen on one side and the bar on the other. The bar itself was small, with a large mirror behind the counter and another directly opposite over the fireplace.

Anyway, this particular night was cold and frosty. There were a handful of drinkers at the counter, sipping their pints and talking quietly about the issues of the day. My father and

I sat in the semi-darkness in the grocery shop, talking about school and how things were going. I had done OK in my Inter Cert but I wasn't setting the world on fire. Professor of Mathematical Physics in Harvard University I would never be. Also, I was a bit on the lazy side, and not really all that motivated. The lecture on these failings usually came from Peggy, my mother, so the fact that it was coming from my father prompted me to listen a little more carefully.

'Do you want to be in the pub business all your life?' he asked. 'I get the impression, Marty, that you're not over-excited about running a business. Do you care at all?'

Now, I should come clean at this stage and say that his decision to engage me in this conversation probably stemmed from an incident a few weeks previously. At the time, Geraldine Morrissey from Ballymakea, who was no relation but was like an older sister to me, worked with us in the bar. She was off for the day, and my parents were shopping in Limerick. Bartending duties had fallen to me. What could possibly go wrong? Everything was grand for most of the day, then, in the late afternoon, Michael King arrived in and the craic began. Since the place was so quiet, we decided to have a quick game of football out the back. My grandmother on my mother's side was living with us at the time, so I presumed she'd call me if anyone came in. But what I didn't know was that Nan, as I called her, had decided to go for a quick walk. So there was literally no one home.

The funny thing was that throughout our game of football, I could hear a bus hooting its horn almost continuously. I took no notice. A game had to be won.

Next thing, around the corner at full speed came Michael Pato Callinane. He was out of breath and could barely get the words out.

'Mar ... Mar ... Marty ... Marty ... the pub is packed! The place is full of fucking Americans. They're going mad! Crazy!'

I ran as fast as I could but by the time I got to the bar, the worst had happened. There behind the counter, with faces of iron, were my parents, Martin and Peggy, fresh in the door from Limerick.

'Michael!' my mother bellowed. 'You go home ... and you!' She pointed at me. 'Up to your room now!'

This was the spur for Dad's lecture. I needed to grow up, cop on and think about what I wanted to do in life.

To cut a long story short, I took it all to heart. For a full year and a half afterwards, I worked my ass off, learning things I would never use again. And I rank my greatest achievement not in any of the honours exams I passed, but in the C grade I got in Pass Irish.

I was sixteen years of age when I sat the Leaving Certificate, and to be honest, I hadn't a clue what I wanted to be or do. All my pals were going to University College Galway, or NUIG as it's called now, or to one of the regional colleges in Tralee or Athlone, but I decided I needed to go to Cork, to play hurling and football in UCC. Maybe it was my Cork blood calling, but I decided that I needed to live and breathe Cork, just for a while. I got the points to study medicine, so that's what I chose. Why? Maybe it was the chance to meet nurses, maybe it was because I fancied myself in a white coat and stethoscope. Whatever it was, I forgot one crucial factor. I hated the sight of blood. It wouldn't be long before I was reminded of that ...

It was my first week in UCC and like any good student, I found the science building, the Quarry, the campus kitchen, the canteen and, eventually, the Maltings. The Quarry was essentially a large hole across from the canteen where every year different faculties would play each other in a game of mixed soccer, though these contests would be more accurately described as mud baths. Second science might be drawn against fourth engineering, who were always a cocky crowd, and everyone would come in hope of seeing them beaten. The Maltings was primarily a gym area. Primitive by today's standards, but this was where we played five-a-side, and also where I did quite a few of my exams.

On the Thursday of the first week, there was an introduction for all freshers to the various clubs and societies that dominated student life at the college. This was what I was looking forward to. I found the hurling club quickly enough. You signed a piece of paper stating name, faculty, county and position. Marty Morrissey, medicine, Clare, wing-forward.

No problem.

I moved along the stands and tables set up in the Aula Maxima – UCC's great hall – until I found the long queue for the Gaelic football club. I had watched the All-Ireland minor football final on TV a week earlier and I was pretty sure the guy in front of me was Donal Buckley from St Nicholas's in Cork City. He was wing back on the Cork minor team that had lost the All-Ireland final to Galway. A very good player.

When I reached the top of the queue, I was confronted by one Corkman, Don Good, and one Kerryman, Mortimer Murphy.

'Who are you, boy, and where are you from?' said Mortimer.

'I'm Marty Morrissey and I'm from Clare,' said I.

The response was immediate. Howls of laughter. Howls.

'Do they play football in Clare?' I tried to answer but he went on: 'Have a look there at the list of players that have just signed up. All winners, and all from Cork or Kerry.'

This was the time, I figured, to flash my Cork credentials.

'Lads,' I said, 'I was born in Mallow.'

'Mallow, you say?' said Don. 'Sure that's not in Cork. That's somewhere up near Limerick, isn't it?'

So I only had one thing left in my artillery. 'Lads, I have been Clare minor goalkeeper for the last two years. Surely that means something.'

'It does,' says Murt. 'It means that if we're badly stuck, we'll call you.'

More uncontrollable laughter as I walked away. I knew it was all banter, but I never forgot all the same. I promised myself that I'd show those two. Just you wait.

Despite the slagging, I got on the freshers team that year and played football alongside Robert Bunyan, an All-Ireland winning minor captain from Kerry, and Cork's Jim Nolan, Donal Buckley and Brendan Murphy, son of the then President of the GAA, Con Murphy. I also got on the senior team and had the pleasure of playing with Don Good, who had given me such a great slagging when signing up. There was also the great Sean Walsh of Kerry, father of Kerry and AFL star Tommy. The team included Johnny Mulvihill of Kerry, Christy Kearney, Leo Gould, Sean Murphy, John Meyler (later the Cork senior hurling manager), Wexford's finest Tom Foley and Martin O'Doherty, who had already won several All-Ireland hurling medals with Cork. Limerick's Paddy Barrett and Tipperary's Michael Downes were the two other footballers from the so-called weaker counties. We had a good senior team and a great freshers team. We had great craic together, and while we won absolutely nothing, I made some wonderful friends for life. For the record, we got to the Freshers final but lost by a point to UUJ: 0–11 to 2–4 in a game that was played in Devlin Park in UCD.

I was playing well at the time, in both the Sigerson, which is the inter-university football competition, and the Cork Football Championship, which is why I decided in my final minor year that I'd declare for Cork.

I should say too that I believe that the Clare minor football teams that I played on were among the best in terms of raw talent. The trouble was that our preparation was woefully inadequate.

We never trained. We just got together on the day to take on Cork or Kerry. We got to the final of a Munster league competition but were beaten by East Kerry. In my time, we also lost Munster minor championship matches to Cork and Limerick. The team included Noel Roche, who would go on to play for Ireland in the International Rules series. He also won a Munster championship in 1992 on that famous day when Clare beat Kerry. There was also Paddy O'Shea, the late Georgie Fitzpatrick and John McGrath, whose daughter Siobhán won several All-Ireland medals with Dublin and was named Footballer of the Year in 2019. Tom Bonfil, who marked Jack O'Shea out of it in a Munster football championship match in Ennis, was another team-mate.

When I was in my twenties I used get really angry at how we missed out in terms of coaching and training. We had massive potential but never got a chance to develop.

As it turned out, I was sick on the day of the Cork trial in Macroom and didn't exactly shine. In any case, I was still called to the final trial at the old Nemo Rangers grounds on the South Douglas Road and played OK, despite St Finbarr's and later Cork star Christy Ryan getting a few goals past me.

I didn't make the Cork panel. But at least I tried. The goal-keeping jersey was given to a Nemo Rangers man, Sean Martin, brother of Micheál Martin, who would later become leader of Fianna Fáil and Taoiseach. Sean himself would in time become Lord Mayor of Cork, while his nephew Micheál Óg would follow in his uncle's footsteps and play between the posts for Cork.

Making the UCC team brought me to the attention of the Clare senior football selectors. There's no doubt either that a few welcome words of recognition and praise from Jim O'Sullivan and Michael Ellard in the *Cork Examiner* did me no harm at all at the time.

In fact, there was one Higher Education League game in the Mardyke against UCG which, I think, did me a lot of good. It was a cold Saturday afternoon when the Galway

students came to Leeside. The match was refereed by none other than long-time Cork county board secretary Frank Murphy, who had also been an All-Ireland final referee many times over.

We played particularly well that day and won. These games usually merited a few paragraphs in Monday's *Cork Examiner*, but this Monday was different. I got some shock when I opened the paper to a full-page photographic spread on page 3. There was I dead smack in the middle, sandwiched between Jim Nolan and Wexford's Tom Foley, in a team that contained Sean Walsh, John Meyler, Gene Desmond, Colm Mangan, Donal Buckley and Sean Murphy.

Commandant Noel Walsh, who managed the Clare football team at the time, contacted me the following day and I joined the senior panel. I made a few training sessions, but Cork Senior Football Championship games were coming thick and fast, and next thing I damaged ankle ligaments. That meant that I didn't make the championship panel for the game against Kerry in Miltown Malbay on July 1st, 1979. That turned out to be a blessing in disguise. 'The Miltown Massacre', as it became known, ended in a scoreline of Kerry 9–21 Clare 1–9. I will never forget that game. I sat on the wall watching the match that day with my friends and club-mates, baffled, bamboozled, overawed and humiliated by a Kerry team that were relentless. The silence from the Clare crowd was deafening.

This was of course a legendary team. Men like Charlie Nelligan, John Egan, John O'Keeffe, Tim Kennelly, Ger Power, Paidí Ó Sé, Mikey Sheehy and Pat Spillane. Pat scored 3–3, Ger Power 2–2, Eoin Liston 2–2, Mikey Sheehy 1–4, Vincent O'Connor 1–2, Tommy Doyle 0–5, Jack O'Shea 0–2 and John Egan 0–1. In contrast, Declan Casey from Shannon Gaels got Clare's only goal and Kilrush's Seanie Moloney kicked 4 points. Michael Downes, who later played with Meath, got 0–3, with Noel Normoyle and John McGrath scoring a point each.

And yet it would turn out that Clare actually put up the biggest score against the Kingdom in that entire campaign. Kerry would go on to land their twenty-fifth All-Ireland title in some style; Dublin would only manage 1–8 against them in the final.

The following year I got the call from Noel Walsh to join the county panel and was proud to be sub keeper to Anthony Burke for the Division 2 South final against Wexford. The match was to be played in Croke Park. Croke Park! I couldn't believe I was actually in Croke Park. Once, when we were home on holidays from the States, my parents had brought me to see a Railway Cup final, but actually playing there was of course a very different experience. We had been given these awful yellow tracksuits with our names emblazoned on the back. You wouldn't wear them for a dare. I still have mine at the back of the wardrobe at home, not that I'd fit into it any more, sadly.

At half-time, myself and the other subs headed down to the Hill 16 end and kicked balls to each other, as you do. I took about five kick-outs to convince myself I could kick long and accurately if I was needed. I always admired Noel Walsh for what he was trying to do for Clare football, but there were of course times when I was annoyed that he didn't pick me. My team-mate and corner back in UCC, now Dr Tom Foley, played corner back for Wexford against us, as did the legendary George O'Connor. And we lost. 1–14 to 0–7.

Clare footballers don't get to GAA HQ often. As we took the long road home that evening, I genuinely thought I'd never step on to the Croke Park turf ever again. Little did I know that it would become, many years later, almost like a second home to me. Life is strange that way.

With the league out of the way, the Munster football championship beckoned. I've always loved the Munster football championship, and have some great memories of the games we played.

On May 11th, 1980, Clare met Limerick at Shanahan McNamara Memorial Park in Doonbeg for the opening round. We had a squad of twenty-nine named on the day, but between injury, illness and unavailability, no fewer than twelve of those named had to cry off. When we did a quick head-count in the Doonbeg dressing-room, there was a general feeling of dismay when we realized that there were only seventeen of us. One of the selectors was sent out to where the supporters had gathered on the embankment to see if there were any candidates ripe for elevation to inter-county level. As it turned out, Jimmy Murray, a fine footballer from Kilkee, had just paid his £1 admission fee and was standing chatting to his pals when he was spotted by the eagle-eyed selector.

And so the immortal words were bellowed across the car park: 'Hey, Jimmy! Do you have your gear with you?'

He did. We now had three subs: Jimmy Murray, Tom Bonfil and myself.

We struggled to find our rhythm in the early stages of the game. This was hardly a surprise, since the majority of those who had done any training together simply weren't there. Limerick were getting the better of us when first Tom Bonfil and then Jimmy Murray were introduced. That left Clare with a single substitute.

Me.

'Please God,' says I to myself, 'let nobody else get injured.'

An Clar

Dathanna: Gorm is Oir
Saffron & Blue

(1) A. de Burca
Anthony Burke
(Kilrush)

(2) G. Mac Eocaidh
Gerry Keogh
(Kilrush)

(3) G. Mac Concra
Gerry Crowe
(Civil Service)

(4) M. Mac Eocaidh
Martin Keogh
(Shannon Gaels)

(5) P. Mac Garra
Pat Garry
(Kilmihill)

(6) D. O Docartaigh
David O'Doherty
(Kilrush)

(7) B. O Ragallaigh
Brian O'Reilly
(Kilrush)

(8)

(8) N. O Normaile
Noel Normoyle
(Kilmihill)

(9) S. Mac Graith
John McGrath
(Shannon Gaels)

(10) M. O Muiri
Michael Murray
(St. Josephs)

(11) T. O Tubraide
Tommy Tubridy
(Doonbeg)

(12) N. de Roiste
Noel Roche
(Kilkee)

(13) T. O Curcain
Tommy Curtin
(St. Brecans)

(14) S. O Maoldomnaigh
Sean Moloney
(Kilrush

(15) M. O Deabain
Michael Downes
(Navan O'Mahonys

Fir Ionaid: (16) M. Morrissey (Kilmurray Ibrickane) (17) S. O'Doherty(
               (18) T. Bonfield (Naomh Eoin) (19) J. Kelly (Kilrush)
               (20) E. Kileen (Kilkee) (21) J. Murray (Kilmurray Ibricka
               (22) M. Keating (Kilmihill) (23) P. Coakley (St. Josephs)
               (24) P. Davenport (Ml. Cusack) (25) P. O'Shea (Kilkee)
               (26) O. Casey (Shannon Gaels) (27) T. Power (Kilmurray I
               (28) M. O'Sullivan (Shannon Gaels)

Clare	Cúil	CÚilíní	Seachai	70 Sl.	Saor-P
1adh Leath					
2adh Leath					
Iomlán					

Team sheet from the programme for Clare's Munster Football Championship match against Limerick on 11 May 1980, with one M. Morrissey listed as sub keeper

But then Noel Normoyle went down. And stayed down. As he was being attended to on the pitch, I couldn't help but hear the conversation among the Clare selectors.

'What will we do if Normoyle can't continue?'

55

They looked over to where I sat.

'Jesus . . . we only have fucking Morrissey left!' said one.

'Will we put him in corner forward?' said another.

'No, no no.' A third shook his head vehemently.

I glanced over to where my own Kilmurry Ibrickane club-mates stood watching the game just inside the wire, and felt the blood drain from my cheeks when I realized that they had heard the exchange as well. They grinned and nudged each other. Next thing the chant began.

'We want Morrissey! We want Morrissey!'

To my horror, this began to spread slowly through the ground as everyone realized what was going on. Within about half a minute, half the place had taken up the cry.

'WE WANT MORRISSEY!' *Clap Clap Clap.* 'WE WANT MORRISSEY!'

I genuinely think that if it wasn't for the fact that I was having the piss taken out of me by about a thousand Clare people, they would have brought me on.

Eventually the first selector said, 'He's only a fucking goal-keeper, we can't put him in.'

By some miracle, Noel Normoyle recovered, play resumed and we managed to salvage a draw. Clare 0–11 Limerick 0–11.

Two weeks later we travelled to the Gaelic Grounds in Limerick for the replay. This time we had a much stronger team – which now officially included Jimmy Murray.

Our supporters were few and far between, however. No one had forgotten the Miltown Massacre the previous year, nor indeed our lacklustre display in Doonbeg a fortnight earlier.

The dressing-rooms in the old Gaelic Grounds were small, low-ceilinged and shabby, and illuminated by a single bulb.

With the entire squad squeezed in, the place was hot and smelly, with barely enough air to breathe. I sat wedged in beside my two Kilmurry Ibrickane team-mates, Eugene Killeen and Tony Power, and looked around the room. We might all have been wearing the same jersey, but there was no mixing going on. The Miltown lads sat together, the Kilkee and Kilrush contingent sat together. The intense bond within clubs had not been broken down enough for us to gel as a team. And as I looked around, I remembered waiting at the dry wall in Quilty with a handful of my club-mates for a lift down to county trials in Lahinch many years earlier. This was the advice we were given by our own club official: 'Pass the ball to each other and don't give a single ball to those fuckers in Doonbeg because they won't pass it to you.'

With that attitude, it didn't seem likely that we would ever come together as a unified county team.

That day in the Gaelic Grounds, Dave Weldrick, who had guided Thomond College to Limerick, Munster and All-Ireland club titles in 1978, was in charge of us. He gave a rousing speech, and this was followed by one from our captain, Seanie Moloney. Seanie's speech ran along traditional lines: 'We are not here for the craic, lads. We are here to win. I want ye to die for each other, to step up to the plate and do it for yer county . . .'

At this, the tall lads – Georgie Fitzpatrick, David Doherty, Pat Garry and Noel Normoyle – began thumping the ceiling. That'll tell you how low it was. By now the sweat was pouring off us, so when Seanie says, 'Right lads, let's warm up,' there was a unanimous and beautifully timed response: 'Ah Jaysus, Seanie.'

But Seanie took being captain seriously, and roared, 'Come on to fuck lads. We need to warm up!'

We were all sweating like pigs and now that we were standing, we could barely move. Seanie started shadow-boxing. Then came the Clare set, where we would batter the floor on the spot and count one to ten as loudly and as quickly as we could. It was deafening. We could be heard in Quilty. There was a final roar of 'UP THE BANNER!' and the dressing-room door was almost pulled off its hinges as we burst out, turned down the long dark corridor and ran towards the pitch. Within seconds, however, I crashed into the guy in front of me who had crashed into the guy in front of him.

'What's wrong?' we asked.

Seanie roared, 'We have no fucking ball!'

So back we ran to the dressing room. A Munster championship game and no one had thought to bring a ball. There was war. Was it any wonder Clare football was in the mess it was in?

So we hatched a plan.

We danced the Clare set once again, battering the floor like no Clare team ever did before or since, the tall lads banging their fists off the ceiling with such force that the bulb broke and we were plunged into complete darkness. Seanie tore open the door and we sprinted down the dark corridor and out on the pitch again. This time, the first three lads out ran down to the Caherdavin Road end where Limerick were warming up and stole as many of their balls as we could get our hands on, kicking with great precision down to the city end where we were to do our warm-up. We laughed and Limerick protested, but they had the last laugh, and beat us by 0–11 to 0–10.

The following year we beat Tipperary to qualify for a Munster semi-final against Kerry. The match was played in Listowel and we got another hammering: 4–17 to 0–6. It just seemed hopeless, and yet despite the heartbreak, there were those who kept going. Players like my great friend Noel Roche persisted through loss after loss until finally he fulfilled his ambition and saw his dream come true in 1992, when Clare won the Munster championship for the first time since 1917, a gap of seventy-five years. Beating Kerry in the final made it extra special – more than making up for the Miltown Massacre thirteen years earlier. By then of course I was long gone from the Clare panel.

I have to say, I get a bit of a laugh these days at players announcing their retirement from inter-county football or hurling. This has become very trendy, but unless you've won five or six All-Irelands, or are a very special talent in an unsuccessful county, then please forgive me if I don't react. Most of us were 'retired' by somebody else who either thought we weren't good enough any more, or just didn't value us. We were dropped, in other words.

You only have the jersey for a little while. Wear it with pride. Love it. Honour it. Enjoy it while you have the loan of it, then hand it back and say, 'Thank you.' End of story.

When I finished playing with UCC, I transferred from Kilmurry Ibrickane to St Michael's in Cork through the intervention of Ned Lenihan, whose daughter Paula I would later become friends with when we worked together in Cork Multi Channel. Part of the reason I transferred was this. When I played in the Clare minor final in 1976, I felt my chances of playing senior football for the club, or indeed playing for Clare, were limited because my great friend and hero in the parish was Anthony Burke, who was both the club's and the county's senior goalkeeper.

Anyway, I played several games for St Michael's, a club which welcomed me with open arms, and made great friends with Cork stars like Eamon O'Donoghue, Tom Cashman and Dermot McCurtain. Maybe I should have given greater commitment to the club, but the truth was that my heart was in West Clare. I had learned so much from the UCC and St Michael's experiences, and had all these coaching ideas swirling around in my head. What I really wanted to do now was go home and do something with them.

The opportunity to do that came in a rather unexpected way.

Paddy Keane, a native of Kilfenora, was heavily involved in Kilmurry Ibrickane at the time. He asked me would I take charge of the under-16 and minor teams for the summer. I was home from UCC, and had damaged ankle ligaments and so couldn't play myself.

'I will, but is it alright Paddy if I do it my way?'

'Do it any way you want, Marty.'

It was 1979. We hadn't won an under-16 title in ten years, and nothing at under-age since my team won the under-14 championship seven years before that. I called training by putting a message into the parish newsletter and asking the priest to announce it from the altar at masses in Quilty, Mullagh and Coore. In response, lads cycled from the four corners of the parish to the meadow over at the old Quilty road, between Quilty and the Crosses of Annagh. It had a set of lopsided goalposts but was the closest thing we had in the parish to a pitch. We togged out in the ditches, we trained on the front and back beaches in Seafield and we laughed an awful lot.

At the time, myself and many of the other senior players in the club complained that our game plan didn't suit the talent we had. Physically, we were a small team, and that meant that the big long rooter of a kick to a small full forward line was useless. The ball would come back quicker than it went in. It was very frustrating, but at the time, there was no great appetite to change.

Because I was given free rein with the under-16s, I could try something different. The strategy I employed was based on the Kerry model of the seventies, and it was all about goalkeepers finding a man in space, and then keeping possession. So we started with all the drills I had learned in UCC. These young lads had no agendas or preconceived notions. They just wanted to play football, which they did with great style and purpose. I hadn't a clue whether we had a good team or not at this point, but we got through to the under-16 semi-final against Kilrush on a Friday night in mid-August.

Then on the Thursday, my mother got a call from North Cork telling her that Lena Roche, a cousin from Main Street in Doneraile, had died. The funeral was on the following evening, the exact time that we were to play Kilrush in the under-16 football championship semi-final. I had to go to the funeral or I would have been murdered at home, so I tried to get somebody to take charge of the team.

All the lads I asked said that I needed to be there, that the young lads were now used to me and trusted what we were doing. One individual said he'd do it and that we should play a particular player – but he was over-age! That culture was commonplace across the country, but I didn't subscribe to it. If the lads were good enough to win the championship, we'd do it absolutely honestly and on merit. So I called up Kilrush and told them that a relation of a player involved in the match had died – which was, by the way, the only excuse acceptable for a postponement – and could we change it to the following Monday evening in Doonbeg.

There was war when it was discovered that it was a relation of mine who had died, but the match was rescheduled.

Thankfully, the lads gave a brilliant display and eventually won through to a county final, against a team that had hammered us to the point of embarrassment only five months previously. On the evening of the 1979 All-Ireland hurling final in which Kilkenny beat Galway, we travelled up the road to Miltown Malbay and against all the odds won the county title on an unforgettable scoreline of Kilmurry Ibrickane 1–2 Éire Óg Ennis 1–1. It was a miserable evening. All the fancy moves we had imagined, all the drills we had introduced, went out the window, and victory came down to sheer spirit.

The following year we met Éire Óg Ennis in the first round of the minor championship on Easter Sunday in Miltown Malbay, and lo and behold they hammered us again. More significantly, we also lost Kieran 'Pudsy' Ryan who broke his leg near the town goal that day. His injury was a

massive blow to him personally but also to the team that year, as like any rural club we had limited resources.

These blows hit the confidence of the squad really hard, which is why I hatched a devious plan. First, I organized a challenge game against Shannon Gaels. We beat them easily enough, and when that was done, I called up Seamus Hayes, sports editor of the *Clare Champion*, and asked him if he'd put in a few words about the challenge match if I gave him the details. Of course he would. So I did up a match report, making sure to emphasize the contribution of certain individuals who I felt needed a psychological boost. This was in the days before local radio, let alone the internet. Seeing your name in the *Clare Champion* was a big deal. That little trick helped to re-ignite our campaign and we made it through to the county minor final and once again, we beat Éire Óg by a single point.

I quit management after that. At the club AGM a few months after we won, there seemed to be more emphasis on the fact that we lost the under-16 championship than on our victory in the minor championship. The lads very kindly asked me to stay on but I'd had enough. I wanted to concentrate on playing for a while. Training and managing Kilmurry was very time-consuming for a full-time student. Don't get me wrong, I loved it, but I felt I had more to give on the pitch, plus I wanted to throw myself into socializing. Because of my management duties, I'd had to give up meeting girls for, well, a month at least!

The other interesting development was goalkeeper Anthony Burke's transfer from Kilmurry to Kilrush, with whom he would go on to win several county championships. His decision meant that I now had a chance of playing senior football with the club. This will tell you the kind of character Anthony was: when I came back home to Kilmurry Ibrickane, he would come down to my house and we'd hop over the wall into Joe Flynn's meadow. There, he would coach me on my kick-outs. We would keep at it and at it until darkness descended beyond Mutton Island on the Atlantic horizon. That work paid off, and with his help I managed to get both distance and height in my kick-outs. Back then, all kick-outs were taken off the ground. You have no idea how much I would have liked to have one of those fancy tees that Roscommon's Shane 'Cake' Curran developed.

I played senior football all through the 1980s until 1992, most of it as player/manager. Eventually, however, I had to concentrate on my job with RTÉ Sport. In 1990, I was doing a TV commentary in Clones on an Ulster championship match on a Sunday afternoon, and drove like a lunatic to be in Cusack Park in Ennis for a Clare senior football championship match against St Fachtna's. It was total madness. I came through the tunnel as the ball was being thrown in.

It is one of my sporting regrets that we lost that quarter-final tie. I think that maybe we were already eyeing up a semi-final clash with our great rivals Miltown Malbay. I believe too that we really could have won the championship that year.

At the time our club was starved for success. We had the passion, we had the love, we had the talent, but we simply didn't have the self-belief or the organization.

That would change. The site for the new football field was purchased in 1987 by J. J. Darcy and Tony Power. When Michael Talty came in as chairman in 1989, his leadership made a huge difference, and led, among other things, to the development of new grounds. Instead of the meadow with the lopsided goal-posts, we got Páirc Naomh Mhuire, with our own stand and floodlights. We were way ahead of our time back then, as we raffled a house and cars to try to raise £60,000 to buy fourteen acres and the house. A host of wonderful people stepped up and did incredible work in driving the club forward. Patrick O'Dwyer took over the senior team from me in 1993 and guided them to the Clare senior football championship title for the first time since 1966. He went one better in 2004 when he guided us to a Munster club title for the very first time in our history. We travelled to Pearse Stadium in Galway the following February for the All-Ireland club semi-final, but Ballina Stephenites from Mayo had the edge on us that day.

Six years later we won our second Munster club title when Evan Talty scored an incredible winner against Kerins O'Rahilly's of Tralee in the dying moments of the match. We then had to travel to London to take on Ruislip in the All-Ireland quarter-final.

That, for me, was one of the greatest days in our club.

It wasn't just that we won the match. This was the GAA at its best: the people of Mullagh, Quilty and Coore travelling in huge numbers in cars, planes and trains to see their team play. Some had never crossed the Irish Sea before.

We went on to beat Portlaoise in the All-Ireland semi-final and so became the first and only Clare club so far to reach an All-Ireland club football final in Croke Park on St Patrick's Day. Micheál McDermott was the manager, and he did a great job to get us there. Doubling up as the Kilmurry and Clare football manager over those months must have been very difficult for him.

I still maintain that Odran O'Dwyer, one of Clare's greatest ever footballers, and a man that played for Ireland in Australia in the International Rules series, should have started in Croke Park. The fact that he didn't still annoys me. That said, we lost to a better team: St Gall's from the Falls Road in Belfast.

The transition of our club from mere participants to a winning side isn't down to any one person. It's been a collective effort, inspired by a love of football and a tremendous sense of pride in who we are and where we come from. Since 1993, Kilmurry Ibrickane have won ten Clare senior football championships, ten Cusack Cup (senior league), thirteen under-21 championships and two Munster senior club titles, not to mention qualifying for that All-Ireland club final. That doesn't happen by fluke. It's thanks to huge numbers of volunteers giving their time to coaching kids, raising money, training teams and driving players around. That wonderful collective effort instils the true meaning of one parish, one club. That's us. Kilmurry Ibrickane. It took us a while to get there, but by God we got there.

4. The Junior C Years

Once we were beaten in the Clare county football championship, a few of us would pick up the hurleys and go play with the local junior team, Clonbony. They were based in Miltown Malbay and drew their hurlers from Miltown and Kilmurry Ibrickane – two clubs that were arch-rivals in football. Before this, I had played minor hurling with Ballyea, since there was no other club that played minor near me.

One year, I remember getting a call from Tom Malone of Clonbony, inviting me to play a junior league game the following Saturday evening against O'Callaghan's Mills in Newmarket on Fergus. I was doing nothing else, so off I went.

Tom was born in 1915 and lived all his life in Miltown Malbay. He was a visionary in many ways. His business interests ranged from pubs to dance halls to cinemas. He was also a man of the people, deeply involved in every aspect of local life. He loved to see people involved in the community, be it playing in the Clonbony Pipe Band, which he formed in 1936, or wearing the green, white and gold of his beloved Clonbony, in either football or hurling. A nationalist and a republican, he loved his country. I knew Tom all my life, but not once did he bring up his political beliefs, and he never tried to persuade me of anything except to continue playing with his team.

I always had an absolute ball with Clonbony. There was little or no training, and if we did train, lads would be pulling

fags within half an hour of finishing. It was social hurling at its best.

We did the double one year by winning the Junior league *and* championship. The excitement! It was like we had won the All-Ireland. Tom cried, Tom laughed, Tom tried to sing and Tom cried again. The county final must have attracted one of the biggest crowds in junior championship history to Roslevan, where we faced Ennistymon.

I should point out at this stage that this wasn't the Junior A, or indeed the Junior B. It was Junior C, so it wouldn't take a lot to break attendance records. Truthfully, however, the terraces were full and there was no space available along either sideline. It was rare that people from the two neighbouring clubs stood shoulder to shoulder in common cause. God love them, Ennistymon had no chance really.

We had some really good hurlers on the team. Joe Cullen was a big, tall, courageous man who usually played with his teeth out. He was a great footballer for Miltown and a great warrior for Clonbony. He used to play centrefield or centre forward, with myself out on the wing at right half forward. I wasn't exactly great at mixing it, to be honest. These were the days of no helmets or mouth guards. Joe would leap high into the sky for the sliotar and come down with it 99 per cent of the time. He would then bulldoze his way through a crowd of opponents with sticks whirling around him. He'd nearly always look for Sean Malone, but if Sean was unavailable, he'd pick me out. Every time he hand-passed, there was always a bit of advice. 'For fuck sake Marty, put it over the bar . . . I'm dead.'

I tried to oblige as many times as I could.

I was also the free-taker, so often got a few headlines in the local paper that I probably didn't deserve.

Bonfires blazed and cars blew their horns as we travelled back from Roslevan to lovely old Miltown. The pipe band was waiting for us and we were heroes for a little while. Hurling had finally found a home in West Clare.

There are great stories told about Tom Malone. One time an ex-player who had left these shores returned home for a holiday and ran into Tom on the main street. The ex-player complained that he had never received his championship medal.

'That's desperate,' said Tom, who immediately began rummaging in the pockets of his overcoat. He drew out something small and silver, pressed it into the man's palm and closed his fist around it.

'There you go now,' said Tom, 'there's a medal for you and thanks for all the years you gave us.'

Tom continued on down the street, leaving the disconsolate former player staring at the medal Tom had given him. It was a Miraculous Medal.

The man never complained again.

I got a call from Tom one day asking if I would play a hurling match against Naomh Eoin in a tournament in Kilbaha, that well-known home of hurling. I said I would, but that I had no transport. Tom assured me that he would pick me up himself.

I waited at the gate at the appointed hour but no car pulled up, only a massive blue lorry – the local potato lorry, owned by Eamon Walsh, who had a stall on the main street at the time.

Tom leaned out the window: 'Quick! Hop in the back. We're a bit behind. This feckin lorry is very slow.'

In the back, among the spuds, was the most talented group of men I ever played hurling with. Legends like Martin Lafferty, Liam Ryan, Jim Green, Paddy Keane, Joe Cullen and the Griffin brothers. We sang our way down the west coast of Clare and right out to its furthest tip at Loop Head.

The 'pitch', if you can call it that, was no more than a meadow that had just been cut. Every time there was a pull on the sliotar, dust and hay flew in all directions! Nor was it a place for the faint-hearted. Tom was awfully excitable on the sideline. He was a traditionalist and hated fellas trying to pick up the ball.

'Jesus Christ, lads . . . will ye pull on it!'

Paddy Bonfil was playing full back for Naomh Eoin. He was a big man with a powerful physique. At one stage Tom told me to go in full forward but for health and safety reasons I declined.

It was 3 a.m. before we got home in the blue potato lorry, having drunk and sung the whole way back from Loop Head.

On another occasion, I remember playing a junior league game on Tom's own pitch, at the back of Main Street in Miltown. Tom had put up dressing-rooms and all, at a time when senior clubs in the county still hadn't their own field. Now you see why I called him a visionary.

We started the match with a man short, so at half-time, Tom pulled on the Clonbony jersey, pulled the socks over the trousers, laced up his boots and took his place at top of the left. He was seventy years of age!

It was in that same field that I got my teeth knocked out on the Saturday night of an August bank holiday weekend. I was soloing through and had only the goalkeeper to beat when someone pulled right across my face. I knew immediately I was in trouble. Two teeth gone and a third hanging on for dear life.

I was lucky that I had a cousin a dentist. The late Frank O'Sullivan was a Tramore man, born and bred. His Clare mother, May, was my father's first cousin and had been a nurse in Ardkeen Hospital in Waterford for years. Frank took me into his surgery on the Monday and for several days that week took X-rays and impressions so he could patch me up and restore me to my former beauty. I never had great teeth, so Frank not alone had to replace all my front teeth but also to colour match them with what remained.

On holidays in Miami several years later, I called in to see an old friend of mine, who was also a dentist.

He took one look at my mouth and said, 'They've got to go, Marty.'

And so the Marty smile was born! I told nobody what I was doing but most holidays over those years I would get more and more of my teeth either pulled or crowned. In the end I had no choice because the blow from the hurley had damaged nerves as well.

At the end of January, the year after we won the Junior C league and championship double, my name was listed in the *Clare Champion* among those who would play with the Clare hurlers in a pre-season challenge match against Galway in Kinvara. West Clare was always considered exclusively football territory, which is probably why we seldom had the chance to play hurling for Clare, so I was thrilled. Clearly this would be a huge step up for me but I relished the challenge.

When we arrived in Kinvara, the selectors asked me where I played. Not a great sign, I thought, but I told them that I played wing forward.

When the team was announced I couldn't believe I was starting, but the delight turned to dismay when I saw I was picked at corner forward. One of my greatest attributes at the time was that I could run, and run fast, so out on the wing I had some chance of making an impression. At top of the right I would struggle. But I said nothing and decided I would make the best of it. Out we ran on to the field. There were no fancy warm-ups in those days. You'd just try to get a touch of the ball and lash it over the bar for a bit of confidence.

Galway won the toss, and elected to play into the goal at which we were warming up, so I had to turn and make my way down to the far end of the pitch. As I jogged down, I kept my eyes on the corner back against whom I'd be playing. He was swinging his hurley back and forth in preparation for my arrival. The closer I got to him, the greater the sense of foreboding. Oh God. My worst fears were realized.

It was Sylvie Linnane.

The meanest, toughest corner back in the game. He shook my hand, but said nothing. Then, just as the ball was thrown in, he moved in close to me and whispered into my ear, 'Don't even think about moving from there or you are dead.'

I tried to move away from him. He stayed right in my face. I swivelled to the left. He glided to the left. I pivoted to the right. He jived to the right. He hooked, he blocked, he gave no quarter. I rambled out the field only for a Clare selector to shout at me, 'Morrissey! Get back into the corner!'

I felt like shouting back, 'Can you not see the problem I have here?'

There was one ball that came my way. It was hit beautifully into space out towards the sideline. It was mine all the way. I ran, Sylvie ran. I could hear him coming like a bull behind me. The *thump thump* of his boots and the heavy breathing that I could nearly feel on the back on my neck. I lifted the ball on the hurley and next thing me and the ball went flying into the biggest pool of water in all of Galway.

The Galway crowd roared. 'Good man, Sylvie! That's the way to hit 'em!'

When I got up, I was drenched from head to toe. I'll never forget Sylvie's ear-to-ear grin. He knew he had done his job.

'I told you to stay in the corner,' he said.

I never heard from the Clare hurling selectors again.

Tom Malone was ninety-two, and president of Clare GAA, when he died in 2008. It was a sad day as the Banner County lost one of its legendary figures.

Tom's son Sean was a member of that great junior league and championship-winning side. During his oration, he spoke about his childhood and about days when he would come home and enter the kitchen not knowing who would be there.

'Sometimes there were poets, other times Gaelic footballers, many times musicians and often a patriot on the run.'

Led by a lone piper, Tom Malone was carried down Church Street and up the Ballard Road to his final resting place. I was

proud and honoured to be asked to be part of the guard of honour outside the church, and to lift his coffin with so many other friends and former playing colleagues up the hill to the cemetery. A true legend. For all of us who were fortunate enough to know him, he will never die.

5. Mr Morrissey, Sir

It started with a knock on the front door. Little did I realize as I went to answer it that my life was about to take a completely unexpected turn.

I glanced out the window and saw a dilapidated blue Fiat, a car that I would become quite familiar with over the next few years. The silencer had gone, which meant that you could hear it coming a mile and a half away.

I opened the door to a fresh-faced woman with bright eyes and a glowing smile. She asked me if this was Martin Morrissey's house. I said it was and invited her in. She wore no veil but I guessed from the cross on her lapel she was a nun. She introduced herself as Sr Cecelia Houlihan, the principal of St Joseph's Spanish Point, which, for those of you who don't know, is just outside Miltown Malbay. She told me that she wanted to speak to Martin. Dad wasn't home, but I made her tea and in the course of the conversation, she told me that Fr Jack O'Keeffe, a curate in Miltown, and formerly of my own parish, had recommended she have a word with a Martin Morrissey about coaching the school football team, as boys were now enrolling in the school for the first time.

Dad was my hero; a gentleman and a wonderful father, but he hadn't a clue about football. Not a notion. So I realized it wasn't him she was after at all, but yours truly. I had managed Kilmurry Ibrickane to win the under-16 and minor championships at this point, and everybody knew I was sport mad.

By now, I'd gotten over my desire to wear white coats and

stethoscopes but hadn't gotten over my dislike of blood, so I'd transferred from medicine to science, with the intention of returning to medicine later, and was now studying for my H. Dip in Education in UCC. Lectures were held in the evenings on campus, which allowed students to go on teaching practice during the day wherever we got the hours. My school was the Presentation Secondary School on Joe Murphy Road in Ballyphehane, in the general vicinity of Turners Cross and Musgrave Park. I absolutely loved my year in Ballyphehane. Sr Cecelia knew I was a student, but asked if I would coach the boys at the weekends, if and when I was home. I found the request a little odd, but I readily agreed. I had coached many of the young footballers in Spanish Point when they played under-16 with Kilmurry, and thoroughly enjoyed working with them now at the school. When the following summer came to an end and I was due to return to college, Sr Cecelia, to her eternal credit, came to me with another proposition. Would I stay on to teach PE for the month of September? To make it a little more worth my while, she gave me an extra few hours: teaching science, history, commerce and even religion! Considering I was returning to college a month later, I thought this was a great opportunity. I would get some valuable experience, as well as an extra few bob.

I had no car but Sr Cecelia had the answer to that problem. She arranged that the main man in the physics and mathematics department – John McGeorge – would pick me up, as he lived just outside Doonbeg and would be passing my house on the way to school.

My home place is located about a mile and a half on the Doonbeg side of Quilty. Sr Cecelia gave me John's number, so I called him up to arrange the lift. He asked, in a broad

Scottish accent, if my house was on top of the hill or the bottom.

I told him that it was at the top of the hill at Lynch's Cross.

'That is good,' says he.

'Why?'

'Because, if you know your science, Mr Morrissey, $v = u+at$. In other words, final velocity equals initial velocity plus acceleration multiplied by time. I will lose energy in the van if I have to stop at the bottom of the hill, but since you are on top of the hill, I will lose less energy.'

I looked at the phone. *Jesus, I just want a lift to school.* When I put the phone back to my ear, he was concluding the science lesson.

'. . . and on that basis, I will pick you up at 8.45 a.m. Be ready. Goodnight.'

Click.

Over time, I got to know John McGeorge really well, and I came to like him enormously. A genius, but a bit eccentric. He was a fountain of knowledge and could be fascinating company if you were in the mood.

I was hardly a week in the place when the legendary Sr Baptist got sick and I was drafted in to take her classes. This was a serious challenge. I had no fewer than forty-eight students in honours biology, and though I was only required to take those classes for a few weeks, it was still a huge responsibility. Now my plans changed. I would cover for Sr Baptist for a few weeks and then head back to college in Cork when she got better. Days before I was due to leave, Sr Cecelia asked me to stay for an extra two weeks, until the end of October. I did, but when that time was up, she pleaded with me to stay for the rest of the academic year. The Leaving Cert maths and biology classes were going well, Sr Baptist was still very unwell, and finding a replacement for me would be really difficult. Long story short, I agreed to stay. Instead of teaching for four weeks, I taught at Spanish Point for almost four years, and I loved every minute.

Two of the students I had in that original Leaving Certificate biology class – Deirdre Vaughan and Caitriona Cleary – are now teachers themselves in the school, which is something that I am proud of and like to boast about. Also in that biology class was a young lad from Cree called Paul Mescal. Many years later we would be re-united in the most bizarre and unexpected way.

In 2020, RTÉ Radio 1 assigned me a two-hour show on Bank Holiday Monday mornings from 9 to 11 a.m.

Let me be honest with you. I've been trying to get a gig on Radio 1 for years. I love the chat and the craic you can have on the wireless. So getting the bank holiday slot was a huge opportunity. I really wanted to make the most of it and get the best possible guests.

The first Covid-19 lockdown was made a little more tolerable for hundreds of thousands of people by the hit series *Normal People*, starring Daisy Edgar Jones and Paul Mescal, and directed by the brilliant Lenny Abrahamson.

My producer Ana Leddy discussed the content and format of the show and we both agreed that we needed a bit of stardust. I suggested we try to get either of the two co-stars, so Ana wrote lovely emails to their agents in London, but without success. Paul Mescal was from Kildare, but that name – Mescal – was uniquely Clare; I hadn't heard it anywhere else. That's when I remembered the Paul Mescal that I had taught all the way back in 1981. He had been a brilliant actor, and had taken the lead role in the 1983 school operetta *HMS Pinafore*. He'd been outstanding as Captain Corcoran.

So I rang Paul Mescal, my former student, thirty-six years after he left the school.

'Hi Paul, how are you?'

'Great, Marty. Wonderful to hear from you.'

'What are you doing these days?'

'Ah sure, after I finished in Spanish Point, I did primary teaching. That's what I've been doing ever since.'

'Fair play to you,' says I, then I got down to business. 'C'mere Paul. Have you been watching this programme on TV, *Normal People*? By any chance do you know your man who has the same name as yourself? I figure he must have Clare connections.'

The laughter at the other end of the phone was loud and infectious.

'Do I know him? I certainly should . . . he's my feckin son.'

And that was how we got Paul Mescal the actor on RTÉ Radio 1 the following week on Bank Holiday Monday.

The science laboratory was my favourite room in the school. It was Sr Baptist's pride and joy. Skeletons, charts, cylinders, Bunsen burners everywhere, with spectacular views of Mutton Island and the Aran Islands on the Atlantic horizon. It was a bright, airy room, full of curiosity and experimentation, and yet tranquillity too – possibly as a result of the building's wonderful location.

It's never easy to enter the staff room for the first time as a young teacher, but I have to say I was made to feel welcome immediately. I treasure the memories I have of the eleven o'clock break, and the sometimes serious, sometimes hilarious staff meetings, the details of which I couldn't possibly divulge here.

Billy Moroney and Pat O'Loughlin, known affectionately as 'Pat O', did outstanding work with the basketball teams,

Aidan Donnelly was a superb English teacher and was wonderful with the footballers. Bláithín Brick was a great woman from Dingle who spoke beautiful Irish. She was the career-guidance person in the school. I loved the storytelling of Harry Hughes and the Kerry pragmatism of Muiris Ó'Rócháin: two of those who started the Willie Clancy Summer School way back in 1973. I loved the way Maire Lynch always told it as it was, the warmth and beautiful cakes of Sr Agnes Marie, the hearty laugh of the late Joe Heinrichs and the smell of Joe O'Connor's pipe wafting through the air. Add in Sr Goretti's musicals, you had a school that was bursting with life.

I took charge of the Spanish Point football team at a time when relations between my own club Kilmurry Ibrickane and Miltown Malbay were at an all-time low. All matches between these neighbouring clubs were fractious affairs, always threatening to boil over. Sometimes they did. A minor championship match between the two in Doonbeg the previous summer had been abandoned, with supporters running on to the pitch, fists and umbrellas flying. Now here was I, a dyed-in-the-wool Kilmurry Ibrickane man, working in the parish of Miltown. But was it a problem? Not a bit. These young lads were simply brilliant and we bonded very quickly. We were St Joseph's Spanish Point, and we were the new kids on the block. We entered the Clare and Munster colleges competitions and got off to a flying start, defeating strongholds like the Christian Brothers Schools in Kilrush and Ennistymon. We qualified for the Clare colleges final and had to take on the might of St Flannan's, who were competing two divisions above us in Munster Colleges A, while we were down in Munster Colleges C.

Sr Cecelia passionately believed that football would be crucial to the school's reputation, which is why she allowed the fourth and fifth years to travel to the Clare colleges final in Lahinch. Being a St Flannan's boy myself, I knew that the Ennis college would see us as a soft touch. *A girls' school from West Clare.* I made sure to emphasize this point to the lads at every opportunity.

It was a historic day, not least because Miltown and Kilmurry Ibrickane people travelled in their droves to *shout for the same team!* The bad feeling of the abandoned minor match was forgotten and the whole community united behind St Joseph's. And we did not let them down. The team performed heroically and produced a scintillating performance to win by the minimum of margins. We were now Clare colleges champions. We were heading into Munster and anything was possible!

In the Munster colleges semi-final we were drawn against Caherciveen CBS – better known today as Colaiste na Sceilige. I need hardly say that the record of Clare teams against Kerry teams was not very impressive, so I approached the fixture with a certain sense of foreboding. But everyone was so positive about the team that we all travelled with a great sense of optimism. A cavalcade of buses trekked down to Austin Stack Park in Tralee for the match, where we produced an awesome performance and defeated the Kerry champions.

The Munster final was played in Cloughjordan against surprise packets Cashel CBS, who had knocked out the favourites Carraig na bhFear of Cork after a replay. The build-up to the school's very first Munster final was tense. Sr Cecelia asked Sr Agnes Marie to give the boys carrageen moss – a seaweed rich in nutrients and antioxidants – as she had heard of its health benefits. The girls on the various schools teams didn't appreciate the lads getting preferential treatment, but the truth was the boys hated the stuff. I had to figure out a way of dumping the carrageen without anybody knowing it.

I will never forget Munster final day. It was a dull, wet, miserable morning as the students donned their maroon and blue and climbed into the buses before heading for Tipperary. Conditions were every bit as difficult in Cloughjordan, and consequently, the match itself was tough. Like so many finals, it was all about the winning. Though it wasn't our most swashbuckling performance by any means, we did enough. St Joseph's Spanish Point won their first Munster senior colleges football title.

Sean Burke, a great footballer, and more importantly a

fantastic warrior for the team, got the goal that swung the battle our way. When the final whistle blew, Miltown men hugged Quilty women, Cooraclare women kissed Doonbeg lads, while the nuns thanked God and embraced everyone!

It's hard to explain the impact of that victory. Yes, it brought pride and honour to West Clare, but more importantly, I think it gave us all a different perspective on ourselves. Communities that had been intense rivals came together for one purpose. The journey home was unforgettable. Bonfires blazed as we approached Miltown Malbay. The town was packed with thousands of well-wishers. Tom Malone's Clonbony Pipe Band met us on the Ennis Road and paraded us through the main streets of lovely old Miltown. A stage was erected in the square and people danced and sang the night away. St Joseph's Spanish Point hadn't just won a football match, they hadn't just won a Munster title. The school had united the entire community. It was historic. It was emotional. It was unforgettable.

At the end of the academic year, as Leaving Cert exams approached, we decided to organize a big night out for the team, their families and the local community. Some suggested we go to Johnny Burke's pub (the Armada Hotel today) across the road, or go down the road to the Quilty Tavern. But I was having none of it. I insisted we have our night in the school hall, and the footballers totally agreed with me.

Given the importance of the night, I decided to be a bit adventurous. This involved going to visit the school's next-door neighbour the next time he was home. I kept an eye on the house for a few weeks, until eventually, I saw the Gardaí sitting outside the gate and knew that now was my chance.

At the eleven o'clock break, I walked down the school

avenue and turned left to the neighbour's house. There, I told the Gardaí in the squad car outside that I wanted to meet the President of Ireland, Dr Patrick Hillery. They laughed at me, but I persisted and eventually they agreed to telephone the house. Within minutes, I was summoned to the front door. I knocked, the door slowly creaked open and there stood the President in his cardigan, smiling broadly at me. I told him who I was – he knew my father – and I asked him if he would present the Clare and Munster Colleges medals to the lads. He brought me into the hallway and then down into his sitting-room, where he began leafing through his diary. We agreed a date and he promised me he would be there. I walked out of his house in a daze.

When the night came around, we celebrated in style. I doubt there's ever been a night like it in Spanish Point since. How could there be? Look at the line-up we had! The Bannermen were huge at the time, with local legend singer/songwriter P. J. Murrihy, the late Mícheál Sexton and Dave Culligan playing music that had the people waltzing, jiving and set dancing the night away. As I write this, I am transported back in time. I can hear that wonderful music, my foot wants to tap and my body wants to move. The dance floor was heaving, yet there was no alcohol whatsoever; the mineral bar did a roaring trade. We were Munster champions and the President of Ireland, Dr Paddy Hillery, was among us. He insisted on leaving his security detail at home and strolled in next door under his own steam at the end of the night.

The next time we would meet would be five years later. I had by this time left teaching and was working as a TV presenter/editor on a programme called *Cork This Week* for Cork Multi Channel TV, or 'De Multi' as it was universally known.

The President was in the southern capital to officially open a SHARE building. I was there to cover it, and hoped I might get a few words with the man, but Áras an Uachtaráin officials told me that the President of Ireland would NOT be doing any interviews, least of all with somebody from De Multi.

But when I caught President Hillery's eye that morning, he immediately smiled and so I approached for the second time and asked for another favour. Once again my fellow West Clare man delivered. He re-organized his schedule to give me fifteen minutes all to myself!

I can honestly say that as long as I live I will never forget the friendships forged at St Joseph's, and nor will I forget the wonderful journey I took with the finest group of young men that I've ever had the pleasure to work with. These immensely talented footballers were boys of integrity who grew into men of honour. It was just my good fortune to be their manager. I am very proud that my first job was in the parish of Miltown Malbay, and that unique connection will be part of me as long as I live.

And thanks to my involvement in St Joseph's Spanish Point, and knowing both parishes so well, another surprise twist came to my life less than a year later.

6. Tractors, Trailers and McNamee Awards

In October 1984 my club, Kilmurry Ibrickane, qualified for the county under-21 final against Miltown Malbay. The local postmaster, Patrick Galvin, phoned me early Saturday morning, the day before the match, to ask if I would commentate on a video of the final.

I laughed at the idea. 'Absolutely not!'

On my recommendation he tried a few other lads, but by that night he still had no one, so he came back to me. Many of those on the squad had been on the Spanish Point team that had won the Munster colleges title, so I knew them all very well, and I suppose it was because of this that I reluctantly agreed, and travelled to Doonbeg the following day to meet the cameraman, Paschal Brooks from Ennis.

A Kilmurry contingent sourced a tractor and trailer and brought them down to Doonbeg, parked on the embankment and nailed some plastic sheets to the side. This was my very first commentary box.

It was my first time meeting the two Paschal Brooks, father and son, the senior and junior edition, and we clicked immediately.

I remember the date – October 28th – only because it was my birthday and being Hallowe'en time in West Clare, it was cold, wet, windy and miserable. The winds coming in over Loop Head meant the thick plastic sheeting the lads had fixed to the trailer kept blowing ferociously and had to be re-tied several times.

Paschal handed me the microphone and said, 'Talk,' and talk I did.

I was never one of these lads that fooled around with tape recorders, so I had never heard myself speaking properly until later that night when I went to Brooks's in Ennis to see the results of what we had done. I had a mop of dark curly hair and a black raincoat which I thought made me look trendy, but when I see clips of that first video now on You-Tube, I cringe with embarrassment.

You've got to remember, this video lark was new and exciting and to see how I looked and sounded was a bit of a shock. The view of oneself is totally different to the reality, but I believe that whatever talent God has given each one of us, we are all unique and different, and we should try to make the most of it.

To be honest, my first commentary sounded awful to me. I felt I had a thick Clare accent and I didn't know whether I wanted to be Michael O'Hehir or Mícheál Ó Muircheartaigh or a cocktail of both. At that time, that's all we knew, the two Mícheáls.

We showed the video on the Monday night in the Quilty Tavern and a huge crowd turned up to see it. Admission was 50 pence. I thought they'd all laugh but they didn't.

I met the postmistress, Mary Kate Galvin, the following day and she was so positive and so excited.

'You need to apply to RTÉ, Marty,' she said.

'Like hello . . . Mary Kate?' said I. 'It's my first ever video and I can't just start applying to RTÉ, for God's sake.'

Two weeks later, we got our second booking. The Munster club hurling final between Sixmilebridge and Patrickswell in Semple Stadium. I went from the back of a tractor and trailer in West Clare to a real commentary box in a real stand in Thurles. And that was it. I was hooked. I wanted to make a career out of this.

This probably sounds silly, but in the mid 1980s, RTÉ seemed to me to be in a different galaxy. I had been to Dublin many times but I didn't really know anyone there, and on

graduation from UCC, I went straight into teaching in Spanish Point.

I loved Gay Byrne and Mike Murphy, almost to the point of adulation. At the time, Teresa Lowe was presenting *Where in the World*, George Hamilton and Jimmy Magee were the anchors on *Know Your Sport*, Ronan Collins hosted *Play the Game*, and *The Den* was up there at the top of the charts with Ray D'Arcy at the helm, just as he is now. I sat in my room in West Clare and wondered how on earth you got any of these gigs. What would they want with a lad from Clare? I figured that RTÉ must only be for Dublin people. I knew no one who worked there, no one in the media. So how the hell did you get in? Would I call them? Actually call RTÉ? I debated this endlessly in my head. Once or twice I came close to actually picking up the phone, but simple things would put me off. My grandmother, or one of my parents, might be home when I got back from school. I couldn't tell anyone what was going on in my head, not even my closest buddies. I thought I'd be laughed at, I thought I'd be told to cop on.

My parents – especially my mother – would have gone ballistic. I could hear her voice in my head. *What is wrong with you? You have a permanent, pensionable teaching job, a few miles from home and you want to go off on some hare-brained notion of working for RTÉ?*

But eventually, I got the courage to pick up the phone, dial the number and ask to speak to the sports department. Sandra Barnes and Mary Banks were the first two people I spoke to, and I couldn't have been luckier in terms of the welcome I got and the good advice I received. Mary told me to send my videotape to Fred Cogley, who was head of sport at the time, and she would get him to have a look at it. So that's exactly what I did.

The days and the weeks went by and eventually I got a response from Fred, cc'd by Mary Banks. It was a rejection letter, though the nicest one you could imagine – which, as I would find out eventually – was pure Fred. He encouraged me to keep at it and suggested I try radio, as they might have more opportunities than TV. This turned out to be excellent advice, and so, enthusiastic as ever, I rang RTÉ again, this time asking for the radio sports department. I was told that Ian Corr was the head of radio sport, but that he wasn't there, and that I should call back later. So I called again. And again. And again. I knew in my heart there was a thin line between being persistent and being a pain in the arse, so what do you do? Stop or keep going? They never advertised vacancies, so I figured that the only thing I could do was keep calling.

One day, I got the late Vere Wynne-Jones on the line. He advised me to change tack, and instead of Ian Corr, I should ask for Maurice Quinn, who would be in the following morning for a meeting. I was in school the following morning, of course, but at the eleven o'clock break, I drove over to the telephone box outside Lahiff's post office in Spanish Point and rang RTÉ. It was May 1985.

Maurice Quinn answered the phone himself and told me to send my videotape to him in Donnybrook and that he would also show it to Tim O'Connor, the head of sport. I was confused. Wasn't Fred Cogley the head of sport? Maurice told me that Tim O'Connor was the *group* head of sport. In other words, he was the Real Boss. *He* was the one who would decide whether you got a chance or not. That was serious power.

So I posted my VHS to Maurice and waited for a response. The reply, when it came several months later, shattered my dreams. Here's the letter, hammered out on a good old-fashioned typewriter.

Dear Mr Morrissey

As promised, I got Tim O'Connor to listen to your commentary tapes. His reaction, I'm afraid, is negative. He thinks your voice is too thin, too high pitched to be successful in television.

So that, as they say, is that. As I explained to you, the Radio Sports Department already has a number of GAA commentators and I do not see much possibility of our using you in the foreseeable future. I think your best hope of getting a toe in the door would be Local Radio, whenever that comes on stream.

In the meantime, I wish you the best of luck in your endeavours. I'm sending you back your tapes with this note.

Yours sincerely,
Maurice Quinn

Game over. It was the end of the road.

It was late August and the school was about to open for a new academic year. Within a week of receiving the letter, my mind had switched to preparing my classes and staff meetings with my colleagues. I was lucky that I had my teaching job. I use the word 'job', but hand on heart it never felt like a job. I simply loved it.

I decided to buy a car and of course, despite everyone telling me I needed to get a second-hand banger, I had to get a new one. I went into the Bank of Ireland branch in Miltown Malbay, where Christy Moore once worked, and took out a car loan. The bank manager was Gerry Fitzgerald, a great Kerryman from Fossa, who guided Milton Malbay to a senior championship title a few years later. Gerry and his beautiful

Radio Telefís Éireann

RTE

Baile Átha Cliath 4, Éire telefón 01-693111, teleics 25268
Dublin 4, Ireland telephone 01-693111, telex 25268

27th August 1985

Mr. Marty Morrissey,
Hillcrest,
Mullagh,
Ennis,
Co. Clare.

Dear Mr. Morrissey,

As promised, I got Tim O'Connor to listen to your commentary
tapes. His reaction, I'm afraid, is negative. He thinks
your voice is too thin, too high pitched to be successful on
television.

So that, as they say, is that. As I explained to you the
Radio Sports Department already has a number of GAA commentators
and I do not see much possibility of our using you in the
foreseeable future. I think your best hope of getting a toe
in the door would be Local Radio, whenever that comes on stream.

In the meantime, I wish you the best of luck in your endeavours.
I'm sending you back your tapes with this note.

Yours sincerely,

Maurice Quinn
Head of Radio Sports Programming

wife Paschaline have been my friends since that time and
now own a bookshop in Bandon, Co. Cork.

With the loan in my hand, I went to Tom Hogan Motors
on the Galway Road in Ennis and bought myself a brand
new sparkling silver Toyota Corolla. The registration number

was 88 RIE and so very quickly the local bingo fans chris-
tened it 'Two Fat Ladies RIE'.

I loved driving up the West Clare coastline every morning,
leaving my home townland of Shandrum, passing through
the village of Quilty and on past Emlagh and Caherush
before crossing the Ballaclugha bridge which separates the
parishes of Kilmurry Ibrickane and Miltown Malbay. Then
it's a left turn at what was once O'Malley's caravan park and
shop, but today is the Bellbridge Hotel. That wonderful view
of the sea envelops you as you take the sharp bend to the
right. Next comes Spanish Point beach with its beautiful,
bright colours and the Armada Hotel standing proudly on
the cliff in the distance. Finally, you pass Mary Cleary's shop
on the right before arriving at the school gate.

At the weekends, it was back to playing hurling and football, and of course doing the videos with Paschal whenever
we had a booking. Although the GAA were our primary clients, we decided we needed to diversify and show we were
more than one-trick ponies.

When I was fourteen years of age, I got golf lessons from
Bob McCavery, the professional at Lahinch golf club. Within
a year, I got my handicap down to 15. Though I could always
drive reasonably well, my chipping and putting was a bit of a
disaster. That old adage is true: *Drive for show, putt for dough.*

The South of Ireland is a prestigious competition held at
Lahinch golf club every July. I was a member of the club at
the time and so was Paschal's father, so we had enough contacts to get permission to film the final for the very first time
in 1986. This was played out between John McHenry from
Douglas in Cork and Liam McNamara from Woodbrook in
Dublin. We had a single camera, which meant that trying to
cover all eighteen holes around Lahinch, and to tell the story

of the final, was one of the most difficult assignments we had ever undertaken.

It was, however, a beautiful day; sunny and warm, with a strong breeze blowing in from Liscannor.

I carried the tripod over hills and sand dunes while Paschal went off the shoulder with the camera. Trying to keep track of every shot, wading through crowds to commentate live on the play coming down the fairway and around the greens, was next to impossible.

Paschal would stand wide-legged on the verge of every green with his camera perched on his shoulder. Why wide-legged? Because, well, I was on my knees between his legs, holding on to the microphone, which was connected by a much-too-short lead straight into the camera.

I was in that compromising position on the eighth green when, typical of my luck, who should come along only one of my first-year students.

'Hello, Sir!' he shouted, 'what are you doing there?'

I decided to pretend that I didn't hear him.

'HELLO, MR MORRISSEY! WHAT ARE YOU DOING DOWN THERE?'

Of course this made every single person in the crowd turn and look in my direction. The mortification!

'Just doing a little bit of filming, Johnny,' I said, with as much dignity as I could muster.

Worse was to follow. The plan, as I say, was that I would commentate live at every hole, but on the sixteenth green, an eerie silence descended on the place as John McHenry stepped up. You could hear a pin drop.

What could I do? 'Here's John McHenry on the sixteenth green, putting now for a birdie . . .'

All heads swivelled to where I crouched between Pascal's

94

legs and there was a chorus of shushing and *shut ups!* thrown in my direction.

But Brooksie had a plan. He took off his boot, whipped off his sock and put it over my microphone.

'Talk into that,' he said, 'and keep it close to your mouth.'

The idea of that sock was to stop the wind howling through the microphone. I looked at him in disgust. 'Absolutely not! The smell is awful!' And it was. But I hadn't much choice, and we didn't disturb anyone else for the rest of the final.

John McHenry won the title three and two, turned professional for a while, and is today the general manager of Douglas golf club. I think he's the only one who has a copy of that video.

We also covered cycling events like the Clare 250-mile cycle. This began in 1980 and continues to this day. Every year, hundreds of wonderful people volunteer to cycle around the county over a weekend to raise money for a cancer centre, which was built eventually in the woods of Ballygriffey on the outskirts of Ennis.

Somebody had the idea that if we filmed the race from start to finish, the footage could be shown around the county and might inspire others to participate the following year.

So off we went.

Pascal's van had a door at the back that opened upwards, and this made it ideal for filming a race because he could set the camera up on the tripod at the back of the van while I sat on the floor with my legs dangling over the edge. Sure, what could possibly go wrong? I had visions of us staying in front of the pack, then occasionally driving past them just like the Tour de France.

So the horn blared and the race began. The van, driven by a friend of Brooksie's, jolted to life and took off in a burst of speed and enthusiasm . . . which sent camera, cameraman and commentator flying out the back door and crashing on to the road. Thankfully, unless you counted badly bruised egos, there were no serious injuries. If the crash didn't kill us, however, the fumes coming out the back of the van nearly did. I never get headaches, but I got a massive one that weekend and I have no doubt that it was caused by the diesel fumes that we inhaled almost constantly over those three days.

We decided we'd be better off sticking with the GAA.

One of the most memorable games we covered was the Galway county hurling final in Caltra. Yes, that's what I said. Caltra. The heart of Galway football country. When we got the message, I thought that someone had made a mistake about the venue. It should be Athenry or Ballinasloe or Pearse Stadium. Caltra? Never. I argued with Paschal all the way to Caltra but when we arrived we realized it was the Galway county hurling final all right, the Galway *Travellers'* county hurling final. I can't remember where the teams were from, but I remember the team selections quite clearly. Of the thirty players on the field, twenty-eight had the same surname. Ward.

It was: 'Johnny Ward to Mickey Ward, hooked beautifully there by Tommy Ward, who is the son of Johnny Ward who is playing on the opposing team . . .'

I have to say that the travelling community involved in that game were the most welcoming and decent people that we ever came across in our travels. Afterwards, we had a few drinks with them in the local pub. They sang songs in celebration and thanked us profusely for travelling from Clare to Galway to cover the match.

All my attempts to break into RTÉ might have come to nothing, but despite the disappointment of Maurice Quinn's letter, I continued to apply anyway. And continued to get nowhere. More letters of rejection came, but crucially, none actually said, 'Leave us alone.' No one said 'Stop!' Or at least I didn't see the word 'Stop' on any of the letters. I took this to mean that while they didn't want me, I could keep applying if I wanted.

So I did.

Gerard Kelly, the principal of the national school in Cooraclare, who was always very supportive of myself and Paschal, suggested we do a documentary on Cooraclare getting to the Clare football final in 1986. Cooraclare is one of our neighbouring parishes and is located between my own place and Kilrush. Because my grandfather was from there, I always had a grá for the people.

Now, any decent documentary has certain crucial ingredients like research, idea development, editing and the like, but we didn't go in for all that fancy stuff. We just went down to Cooraclare and filmed various sequences, then filmed the county final itself in Cusack Park between Cooraclare and Éire Óg. Cooraclare won, as we'd prayed they would.

Despite the lack of preparation, the final product turned out reasonably well, which is why we entered it for the GAA's McNamee Awards, which by chance I happened to see advertised not long after we had finished filming. Named after former president of the GAA Paddy McNamee, they are held annually to honour excellence in the area of communications, public relations and journalism.

We reckoned we had no chance, but one day the call came from Croke Park. Our documentary had won. We couldn't believe it. We travelled to Dublin early on the Saturday night of the presentation, hitting a few well-known pubs before heading to the old Berkeley Court Hotel in Ballsbridge for

At the 1987 McNamee Awards with Paschal Brooks Sr, Mary Brooks, Paschal Brooks Jr and my father

the awards themselves. We changed our clothes in the van, drowned ourselves in Old Spice and in we went.

It was my first time meeting the legendary Michael O'Carroll, a brilliant TV executive producer/director who was as innovative and imaginative as producer/directors should be. From Moneygall in Co. Tipperary, Michael was one of the judges, so I thought that this might help my attempts to break into RTÉ. After the presentation, it was on to Legs's nightclub on Leeson Street, where a great time was had by all.

When I was on the Clare minor football team, I made great friends with Denny Cullinane from Ennistymon. We might have only got a year or two playing together with the Banner, but for years after, we played against each other in the club championship, and in every game, Dinny had a shot at goal. He would never take his point; it was a personal duel between us. Eventually, he gave up.

I have great time for Dinny and his wife, Angela, who have built a fine business together in the town. Davy Fitzgerald also discovered Dinny's many talents years later. He was an integral part of Davy's backroom team when Clare won the All-Ireland in 2013. Anyway, Dinny asked me if we would film a documentary on Ennistymon GAA club, as they were celebrating a special anniversary. We entered that documentary, *Memories of Ennistymon*, for the following year's McNamee Awards, thinking they'd never give it to us two years in a row, but they did.

In 1988, Mícheál Ó Muircheartaigh was a judge for video of the year, and was himself a hall of fame recipient. It was a very special night, as not only did I win an award, I also got to meet my broadcasting hero. Ever since, Mícheál has claimed that he discovered me.

Those two McNamee awards gave me itchy feet. I think if I had spent a few years in Dublin, Cork or Galway having a wild time, I might have settled more easily in the west. I loved home, but maybe I got my teaching job in West Clare too early in my life.

It was a strange time. I figured I'd never get a break in broadcasting so I started a Master's in Education at UCG – NUIG as it is now. There, I came across the great Professor Kieran Woodman from Hollywood in Co. Down. He gave me an insight into editorial judgement, the laws of libel and how reports are put together. My thesis was on *The History of Education Broadcasting in RTÉ*, which I completed many years later under the brilliant guidance of Professor Maureen Egan, and with help from my late father Martin.

The truth was that going to Galway every Friday evening for lectures after a week of teaching was primarily a distraction. I wasn't too sure what I was going to do with a master's degree, even if I managed to graduate (there were times when this looked a little unlikely). I could never see myself pursuing an academic career, I just wasn't disciplined enough, and yet I was sufficiently motivated to pursue the master's in the first place . . .

I couldn't see myself teaching for the rest of my life. I was restless again and, truthfully, I was a little lost at the time. Living at home with my parents was grand, but only grand. I was mad for road and new adventures. Life was short. Life was for living. I needed to go.

7. De Multi

In January 1988 my father spotted a job advertised in the *Sunday Independent*. Cork Multi Channel TV was looking for a presenter/reporter. I had never heard of Cork Multi Channel.

I had a large number of exam classes that year. Teaching, by its nature, is mentally exhausting. Add in training the football team on bitterly cold evenings and I can honestly say that by the time I got home, I had little energy left for anything else. Dad kept asking: 'Did you apply for that job in Cork yet?' Eventually, I did.

Cork Multi Channel was a cable TV provider which brought TV channels from Britain and Europe to Cork City and its surrounding areas. What was unique about their offering, however, was what they called the Show Channel, which was strategically placed between the RTÉ channels and the BBC channels on the little black set-top box. So, on your way up through the stations, you couldn't help but hit the Show Channel on the way. It was full of locally grown content. Most of this consisted of magazine shows which had a specific theme, ranging from local news to cooking and fashion. It was all low-budget and a bit ramshackle; production values couldn't really compare to any of the terrestrial or satellite channels, but it was still popular with the public.

The job was for programme editor and presenter of *Cork This Week*. This was a news and current affairs programme, but with a light touch, encompassing all aspects of life on

Leeside – special events, celebrities visiting Cork and things like that. It aired twice a week, on Tuesday and Thursday evenings.

Based on the job spec outlined in the ad, I feared that I didn't have the necessary experience for such a prestigious position. I also figured that there was plenty of talent in Cork, and that it was unlikely they would go for an outsider. I could of course mention that I was born in Mallow, though the last time I'd played that card, it hadn't done me any good.

Plus I didn't really know anyone in Cork. I'd gone to college there, of course, but I only knew GAA and rugby lads. I did have four grand-uncles on my mother's side. Tim Twomey worked in the beet factory in Mallow, while his brother Dave was a butler in the Parknasilla Hotel in Kerry. Paddy was a trained horticulturalist, who lived in a cottage at the entrance to a huge estate outside Mallow. Another brother, Michael Twomey, was locally famous in his day. He emigrated from Cork in 1946 and worked as the lift attendant in the Ritz Hotel in London before graduating to become head waiter, where he served prime ministers, presidents and TV and movie stars. Great, but no media contacts – no one who could offer any advice to an aspiring TV presenter.

My father had a friend, Finbarr O'Connell from Bishopstown, who had a buddy, Robin O'Sullivan, who I would learn in time was one of the best and most decent PR people you could hope to meet. By chance, Cork Multi Channel was a client of Robin's, and he was kind enough to offer to have a chat with me over the phone about the job. He told me that there was nobody earmarked for the job and that I had as good a chance as anybody else. That gave me the confidence to apply.

I got a letter back to say I'd been shortlisted for an interview and screen test, and so I travelled, in hope, to Cork.

The front office was a wall of TV screens, with long

queues of people lining up to pay their subscriptions. I was led past these into the office, where I met Jim O'Shea, MD of Cork Multi Channel. Mr O'Shea to me. He made me feel like I was back in school again. Robin had warned me that Jim was 'a bit different'. He always wore a shirt and tie; no jacket, and with the shirt sleeves rolled neatly to the elbows. He had a very tight haircut and piercing brown eyes. I kind of knew by looking at him that this guy had a bit of a temper. Through the interview, he did most of the talking, which was fine by me. Then I was brought down for my audition, which was a simple ad-lib, as if you were presenting an item on the show. There was no such thing as an autocue or teleprompter. I thought I did OK but wasn't too sure.

Mr O'Shea met me on the way out, shook my hand, thanked me for applying and said that they'd be in touch. I went back to Clare convinced I'd never hear from them again, but two weeks later I got another letter saying I had been shortlisted for a second interview and a further screen test.

Now I was excited. The prospect of actually landing a job in broadcasting suddenly seemed real. The second interview was another one-on-one with Jim O'Shea, but the screen test involved using an autocue *and* ad-libbing on a random topic before turning from one camera to another. When it was over, I was shown out the back door, to where all the vans were parked. I did not take this to be a good sign.

When a third letter arrived with the Cork Multi Channel logo on the front, I was convinced it was going to be 'Thank you for your application but no thanks . . .', so you can imagine my surprise – shock even – when I opened the envelope to find a letter signed by Jim O'Shea offering me the position of presenter/reporter/editor of *Cork This Week*, starting as soon as possible.

My salary was £10,000 per annum. I wasn't going to get rich out of this gig, but it was a start. By this time, Sr Marie McNamara had taken over as principal of St Joseph's from Sr Cecelia, who had moved on to another branch of the order. (I would meet Sr Cecelia many years later, and in peculiar circumstances. More about that anon.) Like myself, Sr Marie had never heard of Cork Multi Channel. She was very supportive of my plans, however, and agreed that I should apply for a career break.

For the next six weeks, as I waited for the career break to come through, I tortured myself over whether or not I was doing the right thing. Was this madness? I had a permanent pensionable job – which I loved. I had three months of the summer off – free to play hurling and football and travel the world if I wanted to. I could easily live out the rest of my days in West Clare, teaching and being part of this great community.

But I had to try this. I just had to. And I knew in my heart, even though I kept my options open, that I would probably never go back to Spanish Point. I would never return to teaching. I was determined enough, and stubborn enough, to keep trying, to never give up. This would be the start of a new adventure.

On Tuesday May 11th, 1988, I started in Cork Multi Channel. On my arrival in George's Quay, I was brought down to my new boss's office, where Jim O'Shea greeted me warmly.

I was nervous, excited and *so* looking forward to working in television for the very first time. The programme *Cork This Week* already was well-established, but it needed to be upgraded and rejuvenated, and I wasn't quite sure how to go about it. All I knew was that the team of camera people, lighting engineers, sound operators and VT editors would be crucial. I couldn't wait to meet them.

Jim was about the same size as myself. He was full of good

humour, a bit loud at times, and he nearly always had a Parker pen in his right hand. When listening to you, he always held his head slightly sideways. He was full of confidence, and he wasn't just a good talker, he was also a doer. The Show Channel had been Jim's brainchild following the massive response he'd gotten to broadcasting the Cork St Patrick's Day Parade in 1985.

He led me down the corridor to the senior sound engineer's office. 'Mark O'Shea' was the name on the door. Loads of O'Sheas in the Rebel County, I thought. He's hardly a relation.

Jim knocked.

'Enter.'

There, slouched in his chair, with his feet crossed on the desk, was the senior sound engineer.

'This is my son, Mark,' Jim proudly declared.

Mark had short blond hair, a leather jacket and the baggiest trousers you ever saw. I couldn't resist. I had to know.

'How old are you, Mark?'

'Seventeen,' said Mark.

I tried to hide my shock, but I'm sure my face said it all.

A minute later we were outside the senior cameraman's office. Loud rock music blared from the other side of a door with the name 'Daniel O'Shea' printed on the nameplate. Surely not, I thought.

Jim knocked.

'Yeah?'

Inside, Daniel O'Shea was hitting a ball up against the wall, and the music was so loud that you couldn't hear yourself speak or think.

'Turn that thing off!' Jim roared. Daniel duly obliged. Again, I had to know.

'How old are you, Daniel?'

'Fifteen.'

Sweet Jesus, I thought to myself, what have I done? I had left the safety of a permanent, pensionable job in the teaching profession to embark on a broadcasting career with a teenage TV crew. If they were in West Clare they would have been my students.

But when I was brought out to the pre-fab office at the back, my worries began to dissipate. There, behind a desk, was a small man wearing a dark anorak and a roguish smile. This was John Murray, and to my very great relief, he wasn't a teenager. From Grange in Cork City, we would become great friends in the months that followed. He welcomed me warmly; I noted how he relaxed immediately the minute Jim O'Shea left the room.

I shared my apprehensions about my new crew with John and he roared with laughter. It turned out that *he* was the primary cameraman for Multi Channel, and the major supplier of content for the *Cork This Week* programme. He would be working with me for most of the time.

'The two boys are grand, but that's what they are. Boys. We'll work with them and around them.'

He told me to go home and go to bed at a decent hour as we were due at a very early morning 'shoot' the next day. John didn't drive, so we arranged that I would pick him up at his house in Grange at 4 a.m.

This was in the days before sat-navs or Google Maps. The only way to know where to pick John up was to drive him home that evening. Over the years, I would spend many a day and night with John and Kay Murray, discussing everything from religion and sex to politics and work.

I drove across Cork city that evening, from Grange on the south side to Montenotte on the north side, where I had rented a room from Mrs O'Herlihy. Hers was a magnificent

old rookery of a house, just past the Country Club Hotel –
now the Montenotte Hotel. There was a short driveway
down to the house, which was surrounded by tall trees that
provided shade twelve months of the year. They rustled continuously. Even on a calm day, it was never completely silent.
But it was the view from the house that I fell in love with.

From my window, I looked down on Páirc Uí Chaoimh,
with panoramic views of Cork Harbour beyond. It was truly
breathtaking.

It rained on my first night, and there was a leak near where
I slept so I had to get up and move the bed out from the wall.
But I could hardly sleep with the excitement. I was afraid too
that if I did nod off, I wouldn't wake up. I had an old-
fashioned alarm clock where you twirled the yoke at the back
until you could twirl it no more. Eventually, I fell asleep with
the light on, but jerked awake when the alarm erupted and
rattled my head with noise.

It was 3.30 a.m. on May 12th, 1988. The day the magnificent *QE2* was coming to Cobh, the first ocean liner to enter
Cork Harbour in seventeen years. Passengers had paid anything from £800 to over £2,000 for the pleasure of travelling
across the Atlantic Ocean on the *QE2* to New York. A flo-
tilla of boats left Cobh to greet the liner where she docked at
the mouth of Cork Harbour, and on board one such vessel
was cameraman John Murray, VT editor and sound engineer
Mark Bowes, and myself. I did my very first PTC – that's
piece to camera – way out to sea with the *QE2* in the background as we bobbed around in the morning swell.

It was at this moment that my concerns were washed away
and all was right with the world again. This adventure might
work out after all.

*

With cameraman John Murray and sound engineer Mark Bowes

Cork Multi Channel TV would turn out to be a breeding ground for a long list of broadcasting people. Tony O'Donoghue, who later became RTÉ's soccer correspondent, started there, as did Michael Corcoran, RTÉ's radio rugby commentator. Des Curran, who commentates on a number of sports, and Paul Byrne, who became Virgin Media's southern correspondent, are both veterans of 'De Multi'. Behind the scenes was another excellent cameraman, Chris Keating. From Togher on the south side of Cork City, he went on to become an award-winning director and video designer for artists like Mariah Carey, Beyoncé, Def Leppard, Maroon 5, Usher, Prince and many more. On Monday and Friday nights, *Sport This Week* was presented by Trevor Welch, who was a huge Manchester United fan and had a sweet left peg, as I later discovered when we played in the Night Owls league.

This was one of the great joys in my life while I was in

Cork. I played with Cork Media and we won the cup the winter before I left. The late Pat McAuliffe was manager/organizer, along with Noel Spillane, who was soccer correspondent with the *Cork Examiner*. I was in goals and Pat Mc played centre half. The team also included the swashbuckling photographer Eddie O'Hare, whiz kids Declan Kelly (later CEO of Teneo), Tony Leen (now sports editor of the *Irish Examiner*), Tony O'Donoghue, and of course Trevor Welch.

Funnily enough, I never contributed to Trevor's programme at all. It proved very popular, as the Rebel County was a formidable force in many sports at the time. Cork City were highly competitive in the League of Ireland, and took their first steps in European football in 1989. Blue Demons were dominating the basketball scene, the Cork rugby clubs were thriving and of course, in 1990 Cork GAA did the double, winning both hurling and the football All-Ireland titles.

Tony O'Donoghue presented *Music This Week* on Wednesday nights. This was essentially Cork's answer to MTV, though all the videos were pirated. Copyright wasn't a word you heard too often around De Multi. Tony recalls being paid so little that he was still able to claim the dole. What made that even more amusing was the fact that Cork Multi Channel was only two doors up from the dole office. He'd be standing in the queue to sign on and someone would roar at him in a broad Cork accent: 'Hey Tony boy, are you the lad from the TV? Will you play a request for my girlfriend? She loves you but I can't see what she sees in you.'

One particular Friday night, Trevor Welch had two guests on *Sport This Week*. Jimmy Magee, who was in town for the athletics in the Mardyke, and the Scottish comedian Billy Connolly, who was doing a gig in the Opera House. Billy was a big star at the time, and Jim O'Shea was a massive fan and was really looking forward to meeting him. Disaster struck, however, when the seat of Jim's trousers ripped shortly before Billy was due to come through the door. Did that stop him? Not a bit of it. Billy was wearing a bright orange suit, if I remember correctly. As we were welcoming him to the studio, in walks Jim, dressed immaculately in his carefully ironed white shirt and tie with trademark rolled sleeves. From the waist up, it was perfection, from the waist down it went a bit pear-shaped: multi-coloured boxer shorts and bare white legs. To be fair to him, the neat black socks and shiny black shoes finished the ensemble off nicely. Billy Connolly was as shocked as anyone else, especially when he found out that Jim was the boss. He leaped out of his seat and roared in that gorgeous Glasgow accent: 'You? You're the fuckin' MD? What in the name of Christ are you doing in the studio in your boxer shorts? Are ye all mad in Cork?'

Afterwards, Billy often told the story of the TV station chief executive in Ireland who came down to meet him in his boxer shorts. You just couldn't make it up!

Multi Channel broadcast every Cork City game, which made us very popular among the fans, but RTÉ would also show up occasionally to cover a match. Cork City supporters used to hang out in the Shed, which was behind the goals, near the entrance to the Horseshoe Inn on Curragh Road. On one particular evening, someone spotted an RTÉ van and it went around that the national broadcaster would be in the ground that night. Next thing, the chant began: 'Who the fuck are RTÉ? Who the fuck are RTÉ?' Followed by 'Multi Channel! Multi Channel! We love you!'

Sometimes, when Trevor was in the middle of his commentary, they would sing out: 'Trevor, Trevor, give us a wave, boy!' Being a man of the people, Trevor would always oblige.

A few years after I left Multi Channel, I was back at Turner's Cross for a game. I had to leave early for some reason, and a gang of Cork City fans spotted me as I exited the grounds and launched into a new song, one inspired by *The Sound of Music*.

'So long! Farewell! Marty, Marty, Marteeee! So long! Farewell! Marty, Marty, Marteeee!' Finishing with that two-handed clap over the head. I felt I had finally made it.

Cork Multi did some amazing things. In 1989, Trevor persuaded Jim O'Shea that De Multi should cover Cork City's first European game against Torpedo Moscow *in* Moscow. Jim eventually agreed, on one condition. Well, two conditions really. The crew had to consist of sons Daniel and Mark. Trevor didn't care. He got a five-day trip to Moscow and saw the game. Everybody was happy.

But the subscribers weren't always happy. In fact, they were sometimes very angry, and it was hard to blame them. The channels would go down from time to time, and when you switched on your TV, all you would see was a message in big, bold 1980s graphics: 'Apologies over the lack of service. This is due to atmospheric conditions over Knocknaheeny.'

The laughable idea that atmospheric conditions over Knocknaheeny could interfere with the TV reception got widespread coverage – to the point that they stopped showing the message.

The experience I gained in Cork Multi Channel was invaluable. It was quite a challenge to produce and present two thirty-minute magazine programmes that incorporated news, current affairs and entertainment every single week. In addition, I also learned the basics of putting a report or a VT package together by working every day with VT editor Mark Bowes, a Welsh lad who certainly knew his stuff.

A general election was called in May 1989, and since we fancied ourselves as every bit as good as RTÉ, we decided to hold live debates on *Cork This Week*.

My first one featured Bernard Allen from Fine Gael, Kathleen Lynch from the Workers Party and a young fella called Micheál Martin from Fianna Fáil. Bernard was then Lord Mayor of Cork and Micheál had failed to get elected two years earlier in the South Central constituency. At this stage, I knew all three fairly well, so while I was a bit nervous chairing my first political debate, I was confident enough I could pull it off.

Camera, lights, action! The signature tune played, the lights went up and we were live on air. I threw in the first question and off they went. Allen pulled hard, Martin responded with the hands outstretched, as he does today, while Lynch was witty and incisive. The half-hour debate just flew by. I enjoyed it and I thought I did OK, but I worried about the post-debate situation. These three had torn strips off each other. Would they ever talk to each other again after so bruising a battle? The signature tune played, the lights went off, we were off air.

Bernard Allen told Micheál Martin he had made a few good points, and that he had hit him – Bernard – hard a few times, while Micheál acknowledged that Bernard had stumped him once or twice. Kathleen Lynch told them they had both lost the debate and that they were two of the greatest bullshitters in Irish politics. They all laughed.

I assumed that they would head home or get back on the election campaign. Instead, all four of us headed to the Anchor Bar – a place I loved – a few doors down on George's Quay where we drank till the early hours of the morning, and shared toasted ham sandwiches and chips kindly provided by the proprietors, the O'Leary family.

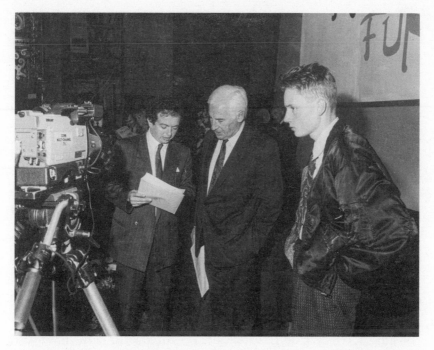

Interviewing Peter Barry TD during the 1989 General Election, with senior sound engineer Mark O'Shea, who by that time was eighteen years old

When I meet any of the three today, I'm always quick to remind them that it all started for them on that live debate on Cork Multi Channel TV, and that when all is said and done, they owe their careers in politics to me. Strangely, none of them agree.

We had our controversies too – most of which centred on the workings of the local authority.

There was a lot of outrage in 1988 when Irish film censor Sheamus Smith allowed *The Last Temptation of Christ* to be shown in cinemas. This was Martin Scorsese's controversial religious drama starring Willem Dafoe as Jesus. A small but vocal group, armed with placards and banners, assembled outside the opera house to protest against the movie. They were boisterous, and very hostile when we showed up, until we explained that we were there to get their reaction rather than to promote the film. After that, they calmed down a little, but in the end they achieved nothing except a brief appearance on *Cork This Week*.

Many international celebrities came to town while I was based in Cork, but none bigger than Michael Jackson, who played two concerts in Páirc Uí Chaoimh in July 1988 on the Bad tour. The place went mad. Crazy. Looking back now, it's hard to comprehend just how big an impact his impending arrival had on the city. Of course, there was no hope whatsoever of getting an interview – although we did ask – so we were reduced to filming . . . wait for it . . . his bedroom. The Dunboyne Suite in Jury's Hotel on the Western Road had to be adapted to Jackson's personal requirements. Dick Burke, a proud Tipperary man and one of the top hotel managers in the country gave us exclusive advance access to his room.

Jackson and his entourage arrived into Cork Airport on a private jet, where he was met by a few hundred fans who watched him descend the steps of the plane and climb into a waiting limousine. That entourage included his 'best friend' Jimmy Safechuck, who was ten years of age – twenty years younger than the King of Pop. It would be many years before all the terrible allegations about Jackson emerged.

We may not have got an interview with the star, but we did manage to get Kim Wilde, who was the warm-up act on the Bad tour. Kim had come to prominence seven years previously when she had her first huge hit, 'Kids in America'. We interviewed her upstairs in the Imperial Hotel on the South Mall. I had only been working in TV for three months and had little or no experience interviewing stars, but I liked Kim immediately. She was incredibly beautiful, and very pleasant, if a little distant. I'm sure she was wondering who was this gobshite from a local cable TV station sitting across from her. She was used to being interviewed by the likes of Tony Blackburn, Peter Powell, Kenny Everett and Co. As it turned out, however, the interview was over before we even got going. I'd only asked two questions when her manager, or agent, or whoever it was, cut in.

'Right, that's it. Your time's up, mate.'

'What? You can't be serious.'

'That's it. Bye bye.'

Soon I grasped that there's a huge difference between Irish and British stars. Or perhaps the trouble comes down to obsessive and/or egotistical managers. If you can bypass them, you'll usually find that the star they're trying to herd is a decent human being. I learned very quickly to engage with my guest, make small talk, have a laugh and make a connection *before* the camera rolls, so that they're relaxed, and maybe even interested in what I might have to ask.

The Michael Jackson show was long sold out before I landed the job in Cork Multi Channel, but I still got to hear every song, sitting on the window of my rented room in Mrs O'Herlihy's two-storey house in Montenotte. I could see the packed arena, and though the sound might have been a little distorted crossing the River Lee, it was still a memorable experience.

Kim wasn't the only star I met during my time in De Multi. Johnny Cash – dressed in trademark black – was a lot taller than I expected, and a lot quieter too. Glen Campbell was a far more open character, and consequently more likeable. One of the warmest and most interesting men I met was Donald Woods, the South African journalist, anti-apartheid campaigner and friend of Steve Biko. His opposition to the racist regime led to his persecution by the South African government. He was forced to flee to London, and subsequently had a major role in promoting the economic sanctions that helped end apartheid.

My personal highlight, however, was meeting the legendary actress Audrey Hepburn, who came to Ireland as a UNICEF ambassador. I always loved Audrey as a child, before later transferring my affections to Jennifer Aniston! I remember getting a letter from UNICEF enquiring whether I wished to interview Audrey when she came to Dublin to promote an upcoming event. I immediately said 'yes', although going to Dublin for an interview was unheard of. Because it was Audrey, however, Jim O'Shea said, 'Go for it.'

And so we travelled to the Westbury Hotel in Dublin to meet one of the biggest stars Hollywood had ever produced. I'll never forget seeing her open the door and walk elegantly into the room in a beautiful white dress. She smiled warmly. I was awestruck.

'Hello,' I said. 'How are you?'

She replied in that gentle voice, 'I'm very well, Marty.'

She knew my name! Nobody has called my name like that before or since. I was in love.

She answered all my stupid questions, questions that she had answered thousands of times before: 'How did she end up in Hollywood?' 'What was Cary Grant like?'

She was graceful, dignified and tremendously patient. Funny enough, I left with the distinct feeling that despite all her success and fame, she was a lonely woman. Five years later, she died of abdominal cancer at the very young age of sixty-three.

Back in Cork I was asked to be master of ceremonies for various local events like the Belle of Ballincollig, the Rose of

Tralee Cork final and the Miss Cork final, where I became great friends with the 1988 Miss Cork, Orla Long, who subsequently ended up working with us on Multi Channel. I loved each and every one of these events and met the most beautiful women. In particular, I met and interviewed the stunning Collette Jackson, who was Miss Ireland at the time, and I got to know and become friends with the beautiful Barbara Curran, who was Miss Ireland in 1989. She came to West Clare with me on a few occasions.

Throughout this time, I was still calling RTÉ Sport every few weeks, hoping to get some white smoke but it was always black. I sent tape after tape to Donnybrook, and year after year I was passed from one person to the next. One year, Jim Sherwin gave me some feedback. To use a medical analogy, he didn't think the patient would make it.

Just before Christmas 1988, I decided to call again and this time I got Frank Whelan, who was then contracts manager in TV Sport. In time, he would turn out to be a great friend to me. He said that if I was going to be in Dublin any time, to give him a call and we would meet for lunch or coffee. I had no plans to go to Dublin, but I told him that I was due up the following week. And so we met in Madigan's Pub in Donnybrook just a few days before Christmas. I explained, once again, that my heart's desire was to become a commentator for RTÉ. I didn't realize it, but in his own inimitable way, Frank was actually interviewing me. He told me bluntly that at this stage, after my years of sending tapes and calling up, RTÉ should either hire me or tell me to fuck off. He said he would talk to the big boss, Tim O'Connor, after Christmas and let me know where I stood. And so I waited. And prayed. And waited some more.

When January came and went without any contact, I feared the worst. Then, one day in early February, the phone rang. It was Frank Whelan. For those few moments as we went through the initial pleasantries, my brain was running at about a 1,000 m.p.h. I convinced myself that it was yet another negative response. I was thinking that maybe now was the time to concede defeat. I had given it my best shot.

'I spoke to Tim after our usual Wednesday meeting today,' said Frank, 'and we want you to do the national football league game this Sunday in Croke Park between Dublin and Armagh. Are you available?'

Right, I thought, another audition.

'And when will I get the result of this audition?'

'The result? You will get the reaction on Sunday night,' said Frank.

I laughed. 'Jesus, Frank, you must be God in the sports department because that will be the quickest response I'll ever have got from an audition.'

Then Frank floored me. 'You'll get the result on Sunday night because we're going to put it out on *Sunday Sport*, so get your act together and don't fuck it up.'

I couldn't believe it. It wasn't an audition. It was an actual gig, an actual commentary gig with RTÉ. I was shaking with both delight and nervousness. *Sunday Sport* broadcast GAA national league highlights, and it had great viewing figures because it was the only shop window available to GAA audiences at that time of year. I had been trying to get a gig in RTÉ since 1985, and finally, after four years of continuous rejection, the door had opened a crack. I thanked Frank profusely for flying my flag and persuading Tim to give me a chance. I will never forget how he helped me. I hung up and rang home straight away. Dad was delighted. But then he gave a dose of reality.

'Prepare well now and don't get distracted.'

I told him not to worry, I could give the nightclubs of Cork a miss for one night.

Later that afternoon, I knocked on Jim O'Shea's door to let him know what I would be doing on Sunday afternoon. I wasn't quite sure how he would take it, but he was genuinely delighted, and immediately started planning how he could maximize this to the benefit of Cork Multi Channel. I realized as I stood in his office that Jim was even more carried away than me, so I tried to calm matters down.

'It's only the highlights, Jim. I might only be on air for six or seven minutes.' That was what my head was saying, but my heart was thumping like mad.

Considering Jim was not a GAA man at all, it says a lot about his character that he was so positive. He understood the opportunity that I was being given.

Months earlier, I had persuaded him that we should broadcast the Cork county hurling final in Páirc Uí Chaoimh between Glen Rovers and Sarsfields. When Jim realized that broadcasting the match would do wonders for the sale of black boxes, he declared I was a genius.

It was the only match that I commentated on for Cork Multi Channel, and for the record, Glen Rovers won 4–15 to 3–13. Tomás Mulcahy was the winning captain and Donie O'Donovan was the Glen manager. Tomás became Cork captain the following year, which was the year of the historic double.

Anyway, the following Sunday I was in Croke Park on an overcast and bitterly cold Sunday afternoon in February 1989. The place was desolate and more or less empty, with just a few supporters scattered on Hill 16 and a few more huddled together in the Hogan and Cusack stands. Frank Whelan had called on the Friday to explain that Max Mulvihill was going to be my producer on the day, and to tell me that I'd be working with a camera crew rather than the outside broadcast unit. Single camera coverage is fairly basic. Because it's only one camera following the action, the quality of the camerawork will be another factor in determining how long the package will get on TV. They film it on location, bring back the tapes to RTÉ and edit in one of the many edit suites. A good cameraman, a good programme editor and a good VT editor back at base can make single camera coverage look brilliant, but it takes skill and talent to make it happen.

Obviously I was being given a chance, and sure what could go wrong? Once edited, it would be a very short package, and with Max Mulvihill there to 'produce' me, or more precisely, to mind me, I guessed that I was in safe hands.

Max always put me in mind of Charles Bronson. He was the strong and silent type, with that rugged, moustachioed look. He knew more about broadcasting than most of the sports department put together. My crew for the day were the Emerson brothers, Declan and Paul. Declan was the cameraman and Paul was on sound.

This was the old Croke Park. Up on the upper level of the Hogan stand, you pushed through a creaky wire gate which brought you out on to a narrow pathway which was hanging from the roof over the heads of the crowd on the lower deck. I'm not exactly tall, but even I found myself stooping to get through the door. You then arrived into this very small space, like a confession box, with a narrow, sloped window.

It was only when you sat down that you got the full panoramic view of Croke Park. I remember asking Max if this was where Michael O'Hehir and Mícheál Ó Muircheartaigh sat for All-Ireland finals.

'It is,' he said nonchalantly.

I was mesmerized. In that moment, I felt overcome by history and completely unworthy of being there. Not good when you're about to do your first commentary and you need to impress.

'Are you nervous, Marty?' This was Declan Emerson.

'To be honest I am.'

His brother Paul chimed in. 'Ah Jaysus, don't be worried at all at all, sure there's only going to be a million and a half people listening to you tonight.'

I laughed. The Emerson brothers laughed. Max Mulvihill laughed, and that laughter helped to calm me down. In time, of course, I learned that not once in the history of RTÉ had *Sunday Sport* ever come remotely near to having a million and a half viewers.

At half time, I asked Declan what he thought of my performance?

'Fucking brilliant,' he said before admitting he hadn't heard a word I had said as he was next door on the open platform where the cameras were stationed.

But Paul kindly reassured me I was doing fine 'for a Culchie'.

I will never forget Max Mulvihill or the Emersons, Declan and Paul, for their kindness, encouragement and great wit on my first day working for RTÉ Sport. Paul Emerson passed away suddenly in July 2013 but I want to salute him here.

The following Wednesday night at 10.30 p.m., the phone at home in Clare rang. I answered and it was Tim O'Connor. Tim, if you remember, was THE Boss. Even over the phone, I could sense that this was a man of stature. We spoke for over an hour and a half that night. We got to know each other a little. I told him my dreams and aspirations, we shared a few laughs and bonded a little.

He just wanted to make sure I wasn't an asshole. I'm not making this up. That's what he said.

He thought I had done OK in the match between Dublin and Armagh the previous Sunday. He told me that despite myself, I might actually make it. But he also told me categorically that I would never be No. 1, or No. 2, or No. 3. He said I had a good chance of coming in at No. 4, if and only if they ever needed four GAA commentators, and that was highly unlikely. He was laughing as he said this, so I wasn't sure whether or not he actually meant it. I got off the phone not knowing whether to laugh or cry. Tim said that he wanted to hear more of me. He thought that I had something, but he wasn't sure what. He was willing to give me a chance, but he wanted me to do three things for him, starting immediately.

1. Work hard and learn.
2. Prepare well.
3. Sometimes during matches 'just shut the fuck up' and let the pictures tell the story.

That was Tim O'Connor, the man who gave me a chance, who believed in me and to whom I ultimately owe my career. We had some major differences over the years but we also had many great chats. I never met anyone that knew more about RTÉ television sport, and what it should be about. It was Tim that brought Bill O'Herlihy from current affairs to sport and allowed him to be a brilliant anchor, despite the fact that Bill knew little or nothing of the sport he was broadcasting. It was Tim who teamed him up with John Giles, Liam Brady and Eamon Dunphy to become that fabulous punditry foursome. It was Tim who decided that a fine young broadcaster from Cork, Ger Canning, would replace Michael O'Hehir and it was Tim who poached George Hamilton from the BBC in

Belfast. And it was Tim that gave a West Clare lad who started his career on the back of a tractor trailer in Doonbeg a permanent job five years after that first February league game.

Back in Cork Multi Channel, I had the pleasure of working with some very talented people. My two best friends in the job were Paula Lenihan and the aforementioned John Murray. Paula was simply brilliant at her job and would go on to build a huge reputation in print media with the *Irish Mirror* and *RSVP* magazine. John's departure from the station to become communications director with the Diocese of Cork and Ross was a turning point for me. With first John and then Paula leaving, I began to think about moving on. I had

Interviewing Des O'Malley

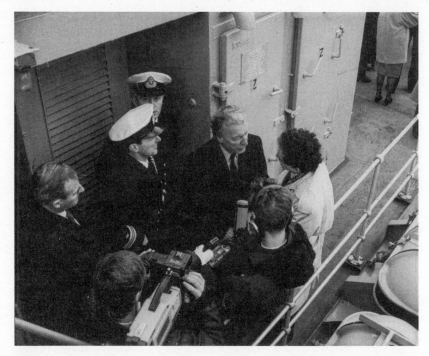

Interviewing An Taoiseach Charles J. Haughey aboard *LE Orla*

packed an awful lot into *Cork This Week*, and would like to think that I raised the standard editorially. I was now getting regular freelance work from RTÉ Sport, but at the same time I began to wonder what else might be out there.

After the General Election in 1989, I had planned a week of filming in London, highlighting the work of Cork people in that city. The O'Shea brothers travelled with me, but most of the work was done by Chris Keating, Mark Bowes and myself. When that week was finished, I had decided to stay for an extra week to see if I could get work in a radio or TV station. I started off each morning at eight, armed with a bag full of demo tapes of the work I had done over the previous twelve months in Cork. At night, I'd try and find out who were the people in charge in the BBC, Channel 4, London Weekend TV and ITV. Amazingly, on the Friday morning I got a call back from WH Smith's Lifestyle TV, a cable station which was the precursor to Sky and UK Living, and was carried on every cable network in the UK. After a short discussion, I was offered a three-month contract, starting in ten days' time.

I asked them to give me the weekend to think about it, and as I boarded the plane at Heathrow Airport, there was so much going through my mind. Was moving to London the right thing to do? Should I stay in Cork Multi Channel for another while? After all, I had only been there for a year. We were coming into the busiest time of the GAA championships. How in the name of God could I manage if RTÉ offered me more weekend work? And what the hell would I do once the three-month contract was up? And what would my parents think of me giving up a permanent pensionable job in West Clare to go to Cork only to give *that* up after a year to go to London . . . and then probably end up unemployed for the first time in my life? Why the hell didn't I go home with the lads and forget about slogging around London with my bag of demo tapes?

But in my heart I knew. It was time to leave Cork Multi Channel.

So, on Monday morning, I knocked on Jim O'Shea's office door.

'Yessss?'

He was sitting behind his large desk, wearing the standard bright white, impeccably ironed shirt, sleeves rolled up and a tie loose about his neck.

'What's up?' he barked.

I could tell straight away that the mood was not good. The brown eyes were razor sharp and the face was already a bit flushed. But there was no backing down now.

I explained that I'd had a job offer from Lifestyle Television in London, that it was a three-month contract and that this was an opportunity to develop myself, to gain more experience and learn something new.

'So you're leaving?'

'Well, yes . . . but I thought we might talk about it and see if I could take . . . a short sabbatical? For three months?'

Basically I wanted my bread buttered on both sides.

'Absolutely not!' he said, his cheeks turning an explosive red.

'Well then, in that case, Mr O'Shea,' I said, 'I am sorry but I have no option but to quit. I want to try this.'

'You can't quit!' he roared. 'You're fired!'

I looked at him incredulously. 'But you can't fire me, I just resigned . . . I'm happy to serve my notice . . . and I have plenty of programmes pre-recorded.'

'You will not serve your notice . . . I want you to gather your things now and be gone in an hour.'

I was devastated. Had this really happened? I went back to my desk and started gathering up my things. I could barely get it together to tell the lads what had transpired.

Before the hour had elapsed, as I was still numbly putting my bits and pieces into Dunnes Stores bags, the phone rang and I was summoned back to Jim's office. He had calmed down a little, and admitted that he had over-reacted earlier. He said that he didn't want to lose me, but at the same time, he could see things from my perspective, and understood why I might want to take my chances in London. He asked if I wanted a reference, thanked me for what I had done with *Cork This Week*, wished me the best of luck and shook my hand.

I walked out the back door, got into my car and drove away down George's Quay. I never went back.

Jim O'Shea had given me an incredible opportunity to broadcast, to learn, to experience and to experiment at a time when there was only one other broadcaster in the entire country: RTÉ. Jim was unique. A special individual both professionally and personally, but regrettably, from the day I quit to the day Jim died, we never met or spoke again.

8. London TV and Clare Radio

I had mixed feelings travelling back to London. I was nervous but excited by the adventure ahead, and at the same time a little unsure about how I'd pull it off. The plan was to work in London Monday to Friday, then fly home to commentate on a game if I was assigned one. RTÉ would call my home in Clare on a Wednesday afternoon or a Thursday morning, I would call them back from a telephone box in London and they'd tell me I was needed in Clones, or the Hyde in Roscommon or Semple Stadium in Thurles on Sunday. RTÉ assumed, I think, that I was in Clare or Cork. I kept the fact that I was in London to myself, purely because I was afraid that they'd stop calling me if they found out. And I never charged the organization a single penny for flights home, mainly because I knew they wouldn't pay for them!

I rented a room in Hammersmith and travelled on the Piccadilly Line every morning to Piccadilly Circus in the heart of London, where Lifestyle TV was based. The summer of '89 was hot and humid in London, and most evenings I couldn't wait to get home to have a shower and put on the tracksuit. I used to love going for a walk on those long summer evenings. Later, I bought a bike and got to know London reasonably well.

I worked in a small office with a handful of producers, and right from the beginning, I felt that I was learning something new every day, particularly about developing contacts and dealing with agents. Nothing was ever a problem once the guest was booked. Almost all of them were great, decent people. Getting past the agent in the first place, however, that was always the mega problem. And guess what? It's exactly the same today. Nothing has changed, though I should say that the Irish abroad are absolutely fabulous. Once they hear you're one of their own, they can't do enough for you.

Pam Rhodes was the main presenter on Lifestyle. She later joined the BBC and became well known for presenting the long-running religious series, *Songs of Praise*. She's also had a successful career as a novelist.

The continuity announcer who linked the various pro-grammes on the channel was David Hamilton, better known as Diddy David Hamilton, a man familiar to us all in Ireland as a presenter on BBC Radio between 2 p.m. and 5 p.m. He's hosted a plethora of shows, including *Top of the Pops*, and was a regular presenter on Thames TV, ITV and a number of other networks.

At home, the station was carried on Cablelink, and, ironi-cally, on Cork Multi Channel. In addition to Lifestyle, WH Smith also operated Screensport, which, as the name sug-gests, was an all-sport channel. When I got my job in Lifestyle, it was implied that I might get work on Screensport as well if I was interested, but it never really appealed to me. I was offered a day's work on one particular Saturday but I was returning home to do a match for RTÉ so I declined.

The first project I was involved in was a programme on Ireland, to be broadcast in November. We spent May and June researching. This bored me to tears. It was the filming that I enjoyed the most: getting out and meeting people. With a viewership of 10 million across twelve European countries, this was probably the biggest satellite TV promotion the country had ever had. At the beginning, our interviews with

Irish personalities took place in London. I interviewed Terry Wogan, and the playwright, novelist and journalist Hugh Leonard. Then I suggested that it made more sense to interview Irish people in Ireland. I had imagined locations like Killiney or Howth in Dublin, the Wicklow Mountains, the beautiful pier area in Wexford town, the Killarney Lakes – wonderful locations that would show off our country to a worldwide audience. You can imagine my shock when I was told we would be filming in the Blackrock Shopping Centre in Dublin. I would host Daniel O'Donnell, Olivia Treacy, Leslie Dowdall of In Tua Nua fame, Paddy Moloney of the Chieftains and journalist Terry Keane in a shopping mall. When businessman Feargal Quinn was added to the list, I realized what was going on. A sponsorship deal had been struck.

I objected strongly to the plan, and tried to point out that you didn't have to be in the shopping centre to get the sponsor's message across. The station was a bit black and white when it came to decision-making however. They were not for budging.

On the way home from a walk one sweltering June evening, I rang home from the telephone box on my street and was told that somebody called Caimin Jones had rung looking for me. I knew two Caimin Joneses. One was a broadcaster from Scariff who worked with RTÉ Cork local radio and the other was heavily involved with handball. I presumed it was the former.

The following day was a mad crazy day so I didn't get to talk to Caimin until that evening.

'Are you still in that Multi place in Cork?' he asked, with no little sarcasm in his voice.

'No,' says I, 'I left a month ago. I'm actually calling you

from London.' I explained that I was now working with Life-style TV.

'Look, I'll give it to you straight,' he said. 'Would you like to come home to Clare?'

'What?'

'We're opening a new radio station. We're going to call it Clare FM. Very original, I know. I'd like you to be the news editor.'

I was shocked at the offer. I had no experience at all in radio, and my initial response was negative. I had just started a new adventure in London, and I didn't want to come home so soon. I didn't say any of this to Caimin, however. I thanked him for thinking of me and said that I'd mull it over.

Caimin asked if we could have a chat when I was home next, adding that no matter what my decision, he would like to get to know me. He also added that if I was interested in the job, 'I suppose I'd have to interview you.'

I told him I'd be home on Friday night, so we agreed we'd meet on Saturday.

'Call me on Saturday morning and I'll tell you where I'll be,' was the instruction.

So I called Caimin on Saturday morning and we agreed to have 'coffee' in Bofey Quinn's, a well-known pub on Main Street, Laghtagoona, Corofin, at twelve noon.

It would turn out to be one of the most memorable days I have ever spent, as Caimin regaled me with story after story about his days in RTÉ Cork local radio, and the shenanigans involved in setting up the new station in the Banner county. The licence to broadcast was awarded to the Clare Community Radio Ltd consortium. The principal shareholders were the Galvin family, who owned the *Clare Champion* as well as a number of other enterprises.

Caimin was an intelligent, witty and engaging conversationalist. He persuaded me that this would be an exciting time to be in Clare and that the team I would be in charge of would be young, exciting and different. Joining me in the Clare FM newsroom would be a young journalist from Shannon who Caimin thought had huge potential: Rachael English. There was also a bright young woman who was leaving teaching to join us: Davnet McDonald. The fourth member of the news team was Anthony Galvin.

We left the pub some time after eleven o'clock that night. I remember that after the music started that evening, I was on the dance floor jiving with some mad women from Tuamgraney who were mighty craic.

Caimin kept asking me, 'Will you take the job?' I think it

was around eight o'clock that night, shortly after the sing-song began, that I finally gave in. I got the ultimate compliment at the end of the evening, when a bleary-eyed Caimin looked at me and said, 'For a fucker who doesn't drink, you are sound.'

I drove Caimin home in the early hours and as he got out of the car I asked him when we'd have the interview.

'You just fucking did it,' said Caimin. 'You're hired! Good night!'

I finished up in London in mid-August, only two weeks earlier than planned, and with Lifestyle TV's blessing and approval. The Irish programmes had been filmed and would be edited and ready for broadcast in November. Being released a little early from my contract meant I could accede to Caimin's request that I be in Ennis a few weeks before we began broadcasting, so within a few days of coming home, I was in the Clare FM studios on Francis Street in the shadow of Cusack Park, getting to know Rachael, Davnet and Anthony.

One of the first jobs was setting up stringers – freelance journalists to cover news and sports events. Clare people have many passions, but music and sport are the two big ones. It was part of my responsibility to get sports coverage in the county up to scratch right from the throw-in (excuse the mixed metaphors). There was one major problem. We had no money to give anyone, which meant that everything we asked of people had to be done on friendship, goodwill and passion for their sport. I was lucky I had so many friends in the county. Matthew McMahon was an auctioneer in Clare Marts. He had been a year ahead of me in St Flannan's, and would go on to cover GAA matches from junior B to senior championship across the county at the weekends. So too did Des Crowe, and the late Michael Gallagher. From September

1st, the airwaves around Clare were buzzing as the new radio station began broadcasting from Francis Street on an experimental basis, road testing its signal and its equipment before officially opening nine days later. On the Saturday night before that official opening, Johnny Hill, a salesman with Shiels Ford Garage in Ennis, went to the ladies All-Ireland under-16 football final in Duggan Park, Ballinasloe between Clare and Mayo. This meant that his was the first live match report on Clare FM. As soon as the game was over, he went across to Hayden's Hotel in the town, found a telephone in the hallway and with a fistful of coins for the phone in his pocket and his notebook open before him, he spoke live to me in the studio. For the record, Clare won.

Jim Madden and Brendan Wall were outstanding on the soccer front, while Michael Maher from Kilmaley kept an eye on the camogie world. James Sexton's love of athletics was infectious. He and Tommy McCarthy were brilliant in their coverage of that discipline.

On September 10th, 1989, Clare FM was officially launched by my old pal, President of Ireland Dr Paddy Hillery. The new station was following in the footsteps of the pirate station Radio Corofin, which was started by local man James Tierney in the 1970s, and of course West Coast Radio, another pirate which operated in the early 1980s, and where I had my first taste of radio work.

During my time doing videos with Paschal, several people had said to me that the best way into full-time broadcasting was to try and get a gig in radio. Some of my Ennis pals told me about this pirate radio station that was broadcasting out of some dingy room in the market. It was being run by a guy called Ollie Byrnes. I got in touch with Ollie, he welcomed me with open arms, gave me a few lessons on how to operate the desk and before I knew it, I found myself broadcasting live on West Coast Radio on Saturday afternoons. This experience gave me the fundamentals and taught me that good radio takes preparation, research and teamwork. It also taught me that I didn't want to be a DJ. Chat radio, that was more my style. Ollie would later leave broadcasting to become an author and has published six books on Clare hurling and local history.

As it turned out I wasn't at the official launch of Clare FM as it coincided with my first assignment for the station, which was the Clare football final replay between Doonbeg and Kilkee in Cooraclare. I remember double-jobbing that day because in addition to reporting for Clare FM, I was back on the trailer with Paschal Brooks to film and commentate on the game.

Phoning in my reports to the station was a source of great, well, embarrassment or craic, depending on how you looked at it.

Back in 1989, mobile phones were not the sleek little computers they are today. I had been given this monster of a yoke with a long, solid antenna, making it look more like a machine gun than a mobile phone.

'Who are you shooting today, Marty?' one wit in the crowd called out.

'That mobile phone is nearly taller than yourself!' added another.

Dialling in was even worse, because every time you pressed a button, it beeped loud enough for the goalkeeper at the far end of the pitch to hear. And of course the signal was diabolical. Which meant I had to shout.

'Hello Ita, Marty here.'

Someone in the crowd called out, 'What are you doing later on tonight, Ita?'

Gales of laughter.

'Can you put me through to studio please, Ita?'

Another wit: 'Don't bother, Ita, we know what's happening, sure aren't we here?'

More howls of laughter.

Caimin Jones was the reason Clare FM was so good. He knew his broadcasting, and knew it well. He slowly put the jigsaw together, basing our days loosely on the RTÉ 1 schedule. The day started with *Wakey Wakey*, hosted by Ger Sweeney, who would often speak to his biggest fan, Mary from Ballyalla. In time, it would emerge that Mary was in fact Ger's father Tom, putting on a funny voice. Caimin himself was next. He presented *On a Clare Day*, which was produced by his brilliant sister, Anne. Austin Durack, who was a fine songwriter, did what I call the Ronan Collins slot. After the news, Alan Cantwell, later of 98FM and TV3, and adviser to a variety of government ministers, took over. Between 2.30 and 5.45, his show rocked. So too did Áine Hensey's show, which came on air at 6.15 p.m. after news and sport, and specialized in traditional music.

Tommy Kelly finished the evening with *Clare Rocks*, and his knowledge of his subject was simply superb. He was Clare's Dave Fanning (although he was from Galway). Thirty plus years later, Mike Gardiner, who started on that very first day in September 1989, is still presenting country, oldies and Irish on Saturdays and Sundays. Mike had his own band, and would usually have a gig on Friday and Saturday nights. He's always had a great voice: 'Now Mary O'Brien from Kilkishen is sixty today. Well done, Mary. She loves a bit of Daniel O'Donnell. Well, Daniel is going to sing here for you now, Mary. This comes from all your family.'

The record would play and Mike would turn to me as I

was getting ready to read the news. 'Jaysus, Marty, will you ever go outside and get me a cup of coffee quick. I'm dying!'

John Carey was excellent on the radio, but I would say that, since he's a past pupil of mine. Jerome Forde, from Limerick, was a fine broadcaster, whose company I loved. In addition to a job, he found love in Clare FM, marrying the beautiful Jacinta Eade who was the weekend receptionist at the time. Add in Fr Gerry Kenny, Fr Cletus and Fr Brendan Quinlivan and you had love, spirituality and the Catholic Church well covered. Colette Dinan, Clare's answer to Rachel Allen, gave cookery lessons on air. Dympna Moroney also got her love of broadcasting on the pirate station West Coast Radio some years earlier. She's enjoying a wonderful career, and is a great friend and colleague. Today, she holds a senior management position in the RTÉ newsroom.

But of course it's not all about on-air talent. Every broadcasting network relies on a massive team effort from those who work behind the scenes.

We had two of the greatest sound engineers in Clare FM. Cathal McLysaght was the man Monday to Friday, and on weekends, Matt Purcell from Feakle would take over. In time, Cathal moved to Today FM where he worked with Ray D'Arcy and Matt Cooper and Co. Matt Purcell remains one of my closest buddies, and still works with me on all my own gigs (though I always tell him that it's only because everybody else is booked out).

John O'Connell was the first sales and marketing manager in Clare FM and he was a bit of a wizard. He would come up with crazy ways to make money for the station. He appointed a great friend of mine, Fiona Buckley Kitt, as 'traffic controller'. This was the term we used for the person who oversaw the flow of advertisements booked to go on air. Fiona's appointment was announced on Clare FM and there was a bit of a write-up in the *Clare Champion*. Within an hour, she was bombarded with calls.

'Is it that bad on Francis Street?' queried one caller.

'What do you mean?' says Fiona.

'Well, it must be fierce busy down there if you're in control of the traffic. Would you not call the Gardaí?'

Dominic Considine was the next head of sales and marketing and was a very focused and determined individual. He drove the sales team with great passion and gusto, and followed a hugely successful career path afterwards. John O'Flaherty was the station administrator and is one of life's great gentlemen.

My salary in Clare FM was £12,000 per annum. The other three journalists in the newsroom were on considerably less. They were unhappy about the poor pay and long hours, and tried many times to negotiate a better deal, but without success. I intervened with Caimin on their behalf several times, but again, no compromise could be found. Ultimately, they felt they had no option but to make a stand. They decided to boycott the two o'clock news bulletin, and I decided to support them. So, instead of reading the news, we decamped across the road to the Sherwood Inn for extended dinner and dessert.

When we returned to work just after two, Caimin was apoplectic with rage. He said it was unprofessional and I, in particular, should have known better and had more cop on. He was absolutely right, but at least he was left in no doubt as to the frustration of this highly talented group of people. I still think the protest was worth it, if only to convey that we, as a group, were united and determined.

I enjoyed a very special time in the newsroom. The four

of us – Rachael, Davnet, Anthony and myself – started with a blank sheet of paper. No contacts, no infrastructure, nothing. Every day we had to fill the hourly bulletins, with more extensive bulletins at one o'clock and six o'clock. Some days they would fill themselves, but many times it was very quiet and by twelve noon, we'd have nothing, absolutely nothing to report on. This emergency situation had only one solution. One of us would pick up the phone and call Councillor James Breen.

When we called him, the Kilnamona man was usually either saving hay, cutting turf or milking cows. This meant that he mightn't be up to speed with the burning issue of the day (which could be something as serious as Clare County Council deciding that it would no longer cut the grass on the Fairgreen). Nonetheless, with a little prompting, he always had something to say. Now, some might say we were just making up the news. You're probably right but when the clock is ticking towards one o'clock and there's absolutely zero news, you'll take extreme measures. James often saved the day.

We had to give the mart prices at the end of every six o'clock bulletin. Rachael English absolutely loved reading these, relishing the challenge of saying 'heifers, Friesians and bullocks' on the radio. Occasionally you'd hear her giggle when she stumbled over the pronunciation of some animal breed. She was then and is now a brilliant broadcaster and a hugely successful author. I have no hesitation in saying she was the real news editor in Clare FM, and saved my ass several times.

We were the first local station to announce the death notices. That was Caimin's idea. When he told me, I laughed. But he explained that there was a generation that looked up the papers every day to see who had died. I remembered that my father did that, and realized that maybe he had something.

It was, however, difficult to get the tone right, especially if we had just come out of something upbeat. The potential for an embarrassing moment was always massive. But I think we got it right by always sticking to the same phraseology: 'Clare FM regret to announce the following deaths . . .'

One of the most talented lads that I met in my career is a young fella from the village of Annacarty, Co. Tipperary. Paul Collins spent over two decades on the national airwaves with Today FM, and despite being from the Premier county he wasn't bad at all. Paul tells a great story about himself.

When he was starting out, he was once interviewed for a radio gig in Clonmel. It did not go well, at least not according to the radio executive who interviewed him. The man told Paul in no uncertain terms that he was 'cat' and that he should consider an alternative career. In the car on the way home, a dejected Paul turned on the station for which he had interviewed, just as the social announcements came on. They included this gem: 'Greyhound bitch wanted as foster mother for a litter of pups, and a set of false teeth found outside the church gate in Tipperary Town.'

Next thing the radio exec who had interviewed Paul began his show, which opened with the obituaries: 'We regret to inform you of the following deaths: Mary Guilfoyle, Hollyford, Paddy Coughlan, Skeeheenarinky and Larry Dwyer, Cappawhite.'

Then there was silence. Then more silence.

After what seemed like an eternity, there was a shuffling of papers, the presenter coughed and said, 'Apologies but these people are in fact today's Bingo winners. So congratulations to you Mary, Paddy and Larry. Ye are not dead at all, thank God, but you all share in today's jackpot of £170.'

As the young Mr Collins drove back to Annacarty, he

thought this career setback may not have been the worst thing in the world.

I was at home in Quilty one night when I got a call from Tim O'Connor to tell me there had been 'rumblings upstairs'. 'Upstairs' in RTÉ parlance means upper management, which is variously spoken of with trepidation, respect or total irreverence, depending on the circumstances. My own circumstances, it turned out, had become a little precarious. The trouble was that I was working as a commentator/reporter in RTÉ Sport at weekends while Monday to Friday I was working in local radio, which meant I was part of the growing competition to the national broadcaster. Tim was a little concerned about my present and future status. I wasn't sure what to do about this, but within a week he was back on to me, to say that a job had opened up in RTÉ Cork local radio. Would I consider it? I said I would gladly return to Cork but the thing was I mightn't get the job.

It was easily four weeks before the position in Cork was advertised, but as soon as it was, I got my CV together again and sent it in. It would turn out that the vacancy arose as a result of Mary Wilson's elevation to the newsroom in Dublin, where in time she would become RTÉ's legal affairs correspondent before later becoming the presenter of *Drivetime*, then *Morning Ireland*. So these were seriously big shoes to fill.

Around the same time, I saw a job advertised with the BBC in Manchester. They were looking for a reporter/researcher for an investigative news/sports TV programme called *On the Line*. This really appealed to me. Going back to the UK while trying to hold on to the gig in RTÉ would be challenging to say the least, but the lure of a BBC job was really tempting. I had also learned enough about the way RTÉ management thought to know that they would be highly impressed with me working with the Beeb. So I applied.

When I got the letter back saying I had been called for an interview in Manchester, I took two days off to make the journey. It was a miserable day at the end of February when I flew from Shannon to Manchester. Despite the fact that I'd never been there before, for some reason I felt more comfortable in these strange environs than I had in London.

In the interview, the three-man panel asked me more about Irish sport than events in the UK. That, I felt, worked to my advantage. In fact I would say that this interview was probably the best one I had ever done, and I think that was because I was so relaxed. If I got the job, fantastic, but if I didn't, so be it.

By the time I got downstairs, however, I found I now really wanted the job, and so the nerves began to kick in. The studios were far bigger than those of Cork Multi Channel and there were far more people and things on set: a make-up department, auto-cues, flying jib cameras and a massive set with backdrops and everything.

The screen test was a real screen test. I had to sit in the presenter's desk and interview someone – someone who they assumed I wouldn't know. This would turn out to be Adrian Chiles, who was also starting out on his career, and who would later present *Match of the Day 2* and also *Daybreak* with Christine Bleakley. Adrian played the part of someone who wasn't easy to interview, but I soldiered through it and after about ten minutes, a voice in the earpiece I wore told me to end the interview, thank Adrian, turn to Camera 1 and say 'Goodbye'.

I thought that it was 'Goodbye BBC' too.

The following week, I was in the RTÉ Cork studios, being interviewed by Máire Ní Mhurchú, head of RTÉ Cork local radio. She gave me a fair but robust grilling. Local knowledge was crucial in this gig, and my days in Cork Multi Channel stood to me.

And so I waited.

A week later, two envelopes were waiting for me at home. One had the BBC logo on the outside, the other one had the St Brigid Cross, which was the RTÉ emblem at the time. In an extraordinary twist of fate, I was offered both jobs. The two offers had arrived in the same post on the same day.

The salary for the BBC gig was quite low, and between rent and flights home it just wouldn't have made sense. And in any case, I found that once I was offered the Cork job, my mind was made up. I was heading back to Leeside.

I went in to Caimin the following day and we had an honest and frank discussion. He was positive, understanding and knew that the move to Cork was the next logical step for me. We went to the Old Ground Hotel and Caimin treated me to lunch.

My Clare FM adventure, which ran from August 1989 to March 1990, was littered with firsts. To be the first news editor at the station was, and is, very special to me, as was filling in for Caimin's *On a Clare Day* for the whole month of January.

So I resigned and had a wild party in the Queen's that went on for two nights.

Then I moved back to Cork.

9. Back on Leeside

It was March 1990 when I arrived back in Cork. Not to George's Quay this time, but within shouting distance, a little further along the south channel of the River Lee on Union Quay. The RTÉ studios were part of an old building that also housed the School of Music, and even back then the place looked and felt ancient. It had a musty odour with a hint of disinfectant, telling you that the place had history, gravitas and cleanliness. The hallway was paved with these green ceramic tiles, so that whether you wore high heels (which, for the record, I didn't) or even ordinary shoes, your footsteps reverberated around the hallways and high ceilings above. You went up the stairs to the first floor, where you were faced with a big set of double doors, with the recently rebranded RTÉ 89FM logo emblazoned above. On my first day, I was warmly greeted by Tom Creedon, who was the receptionist and the smiling face of Cork local radio for many years.

'How are you, Marty boy? Welcome to the madness on Union Quay!'

Madness. How right he was.

Pat O'Donovan, the producer, came out to welcome me to the RTÉ team. He led me into the newsroom. There, sitting in the corner, was the silver fox gaeilgeoir, Barraí Mescal, shrouded in a thick fog of smoke which he had created all by himself. Barraí had long, curly grey hair, and wore tight jeans and cowboy boots.

'Dia dhuit a Mháirtín,' says Barraí, starting a friendship

that has continued for over thirty years. There's nothing quite like a good bitching session about RTÉ with Barraí. He intersperses his conversation and indeed his many rants with the Irish language, making them all the more colourful and interesting. There's a great story told about Barraí, who was in studio one day when Alf McCarthy was presenting *Cork-about*. Barraí was there to interview businessman Denis Murphy on issues related to the harbour.

'So Mr Murphy,' said Barraí, 'do you believe the Cork Harbour commissioners have missed the boat on this issue?'

Everybody laughed, but Barraí couldn't see the funny side. So he asked the question a second time, this time far more assertively.

'MR MURPHY...DO YOU BELIEVE THE CORK HARBOUR COMMISSIONERS HAVE MISSED THE BOAT ON THIS ISSUE?'

The laughter in studio only intensified, and a commercial break had to be called.

As I turned the corner in the tiny, L-shaped newsroom on that first morning, I met Eileen Whelan from Wicklow, a fabulous newsreader and journalist, currently assigned to reading the one o'clock news on RTÉ 1. Juliette Coughlan, Siobhan Looney and Shirley Murphy, who today works on *Nationwide*, rotated on switchboard duties.

I was brought down to the studios and introduced to the rest of the gang, Eamon Galvin, Antoin O'Callaghan, Olan O'Brien, Ken O'Callaghan, Niall O'Sullivan and the late Mick Fitzgibbon. Kathleen Corcoran was the mother of the RTÉ Cork family. This great Cork woman had a heart of gold, and kept us all well grounded. She also kept the place spotless, and any new babies born to any members of staff had to be brought in to be seen by Kathleen.

She asked one colleague, 'Is it a boy or a girl?'

'It's a boy,' came the response, to which Kathleen replied, 'Hello, boy!'

She would often sing out from the canteen: 'Marty boy, do you want a hang sangwich?'

To be honest, I couldn't imagine that scene happening in RTÉ today. Things have become a lot less personal.

Máire Ní Mhurchú, the head of RTÉ Cork 89FM, was an elegant lady who always dressed beautifully. She wore fitted coats, usually green, cream or black, with a matching scarf and high heels every day of her working life. She always reminded me of the school principal, and I think we felt more like her students than her staff. She invited me into her office halfway down the long corridor. I was expecting to be issued with instructions, but that's not what she had in mind. Máire urged me to listen and learn from the talented people around me, but at the same time to be my own man, to try things out and not be boxed in. She advised me to be adventurous.

'I think you'd get away with it,' she said with a roguish smile.

This was a complete shock to me, as Máire was reputed to be very conservative. Indeed, I would find out over time she did everything by the book. She once told Tony O'Donoghue, who, like myself, was now ex-Cork Multi Channel, to go home and shave. Tony pleaded he was only going on the radio and nobody would see him, but his plea fell on deaf ears. Home he went.

I took Máire's advice and determined never to be tied to one job for too long, nor labelled a one-trick pony. I always wanted to diversify; I always wanted to try different areas of broadcasting. It's an attitude that has stayed with me through-out my career.

Corkabout was the flagship programme on the station. This was presented by Alf McCarthy between 11 a.m. and 1 p.m. Next, *Liveline* was broadcast from Dublin, and then, from 2.45 p.m. until 6 p.m., Stevie Bolger – better known as Stevie B – and Gerri McLoughlin presented music-driven programmes. Music and drama played a huge role at the station. Producer Aidan Stanley deserves due credit for bringing live music into the studios, while the drama *Under the Goldie Fish*, written by Conal Creedon and starring Alan Short, was hugely popular for a while. *Lark by the Lee, Telethon* and *Cork Rocks* were wonderful music events that took place during my time at the station, all well supported by RTÉ. Bands like The Divine Comedy, Into Paradise, A House and In Motion found themselves lugging gear up several flights of stairs so they could perform live. Colm O'Callaghan was brilliant. His knowledge of the music scene was top class. Many of the bands that came to the Cork studios were there because of Colm's persuasive skills. The music show *No Disco*, which was a massive hit with Irish audiences, was Colm's brainwave.

Tony O'Donoghue did a weekly gig guide which was always brilliantly scripted, and gave the impression that the HiLand nightclub in Newmarket was the mecca for all music fans. I went once with Tony but didn't get the shift, so I never went there again.

Some of the country's finest broadcasters came through the RTÉ Cork studios: Alf McCarthy, Donna O'Sullivan, Caimin Jones, Vincent Hanley, Gillian Smith, Stevie Bolger, Michael Corcoran, Ger Canning, Mary Wilson, Eileen Whelan, Paul Scanlon and Tony O'Donoghue, to name a few.

As somebody once wrote in the *Blackpool Sentinel*, Cork local radio was exactly what the people of Cork wanted when it opened in the mid 1970s: a radio station telling them how wonderful they were.

I attended quite a few Cork Corporation meetings in City Hall, and to say the least, these meetings could be mind-numbingly boring. Occasionally, however, the local councillors would come out with something that made it worthwhile.

Local Councillor Bernie Murphy came into studio one day as a guest on *Corkabout*. When asked what he thought of the Contraceptive Bill that was before the Oireachtas, he replied, 'To be honest, I think it should be paid.'

Alf McCarthy was one of the most talented broadcasters I know. I simply love the man's company. He was presenting *Corkabout* one morning – back when Caimin Jones was still working at the station – and was introducing a segment in which Caimin was interviewing a pastor from the USA who had come to Cork on an ecumenical crusade.

So Alf opened the show brightly: 'Good morning and welcome to *Corkabout* with me, Alf McCarthy. To start us off, let me welcome Pastor Alan Jones from Pennsylvania who is in Cork this week to talk about emukenism ... emukin ... ecumim ...'

No matter what he said or tried to say, he could not pronounce the word.

So Caimin interjected. 'Sometimes, Alf, it's difficult to say "ecumenism" on a Monday morning.'

All through the interview between Caimin and the American pastor, Alf was practising quietly to himself. 'Ecumenism, ecumenism, ecumenism.'

He had it.

So, to prove a point, Alf decided to back reference the conversation in studio when it was finished.

'And that was our reporter Caimin Jones, speaking to Pastor Alan Jones from the United States of America on a very interesting topic. Emuken ... Ecunem ... Emukin ... Ecumim ...'

It just wouldn't come out. So, much to Alf's embarrassment, they cued a commercial break.

My other favourite true story involves Stevie B. Stevie was originally from Dublin and his reddish hair, his rings and dangling bracelets suggested an Irish version of Elton John. A very good broadcaster, he also loved giveaways and was always handing out prizes on air. This particular day, he had two tickets to some upcoming show in the Everyman Palace to give away, so he scheduled a quiz and when the callers started to dial in, he picked one and said, in a deep, sexy voice, 'Hello, Caller 2. What is your name?'

Caller 2, who was nearly always female, said breathlessly, 'I'm Stephanie from Ballyvolane. I can't believe I'm finally talking to you. I saw you the other day walking down Patrick Street and in fairness you're in good shape, boy.'

This was followed by a shriek of laughter. Stevie B absolutely loved the flattery, but he stayed professional and moved swiftly to the quiz.

'Thank you, Stephanie from Ballyvolane, now here is your question. Hamlet was the prince of what Scandinavian country? Your ten seconds start . . . now!'

Stevie had picked what he had hoped was a fairly easy question, but it was clear that Stephanie was struggling.

'Give us a hint,' she said.

'The hint is in the question. Which *Scandinavian* country . . .'

Stevie really wanted Stephanie to win, so he discreetly stopped the clock and reset it, then reset it again, then again, to make it the longest ten-second quiz in broadcasting history.

Eventually Stephanie blurted out, 'Is it Sweden?'

'That's close enough,' said Stevie B. 'You are going to the Everyman Palace!' He then added, in a burst of generosity, 'And we'll throw in dinner as well.'

Alf McCarthy, who was producing Stevie's show, went apoplectic and shouted down the talkback, which is what we call the communication line between the presenter and the producer on the other side of the glass. 'Why did you say that, Stevie? It's the wrong answer and we don't have any dinners to give away!'

'Don't worry, Alf, she'll love the show so much, she'll forget about the dinner. And who cares if it's the wrong answer? Did you not hear her? She loves me, baby!'

Cue laughter, cue end of quiz.

On another occasion I met this beautiful blonde girl and we went for a long lunch together. I got the shock of my life when I realized that it was 2.45, because I was reading the news headlines at 3 p.m. Even if there was no traffic whatsoever, it was still fifteen minutes to the studios on Union Quay. I ran for the car, dived in and drove like I never drove before, praying the whole way for green lights and no traffic. It was 2.59 when I screeched to a halt outside the RTÉ studios. There was no time to go round to the car park next door because you had to get out, lift up the bar, park the car, then go back and bring the bar down again. I didn't even turn off the engine but abandoned the car, burst out one door, in the other and sprang up the stairs, taking about four steps at a time. Tom Creedon was beaming at me as I flew through the double doors.

'I'd say you've about ten seconds, Marty.'

I ran into the newsroom but couldn't find the script I

had written earlier, so in desperation, I grabbed the *Evening Echo* and sprinted down the corridor. Stevie B waved at me frantically through the glass. The jingle was going as he announced that it was just after three o'clock here on RTÉ Cork 89FM.

'Let's go to the newsroom now and join Marty Morrissey.'

'Thank you, Stevie,' I said, trying to slow my breathing down, and proceeded to read the headlines from the paper, following them up with a little extra detail from the articles themselves. Then, turning the page slowly and quietly, I supplemented all this with material from pages 2 and 3.

'That's the news for now, Stevie,' said I, and Stevie cued an ad so we could both relax for a moment. Alf McCarthy, who was producer that day, came thundering down the corridor and told me in no uncertain terms what he thought of me being so late, and then reading the news from the *Echo*.

'And just so you know, Marty, that paper you used in the bulletin?' He pointed to the *Evening Echo*, which I still held.

'Yes, Alf?' I replied sheepishly. By now, everyone in the building had appeared to see what the commotion was about.

Alf, being a brilliant actor, paused and waited just like they do in *X Factor* before they announce the result.

'It was fucking yesterday's *Evening Echo*. You could at least have used today's.'

The place erupted into laughter. But even after it calmed down, I remained on edge, waiting for the complaints to start coming in. Surely someone would have noticed what I had done. But there wasn't a single call. My guess is no one was listening.

I never missed a bulletin again, although truthfully, I had a couple of close calls.

*

It was a Friday in May 1993. I had the afternoon off and had planned to play a game of tennis with a friend of mine at the tennis village on Model Farm Road. I had been in the city that morning recording a piece for *Nationwide*, and because it was for the TV, I was all dolled up: white shirt, dark pink jacket, navy trousers. Not to be boastful in any shape or form, but I would describe myself as dapper! I went into the jacks to tog out for the tennis: white runners, navy togs and a navy and blue T-shirt. It was a pretty dire T-shirt, to be honest, and to my dismay, I realized I had forgotten my navy hoodie.

Anyway, I slunk out of the building hoping nobody would see me in my shorts and unsexy top, but as I was about to climb into my car, I heard a window open overhead and Tom Creedon leaned out.

'Marty, Marty. I have a call for you.'

'Who is it, Tom?' I asked.

'She won't tell me her name. She said you'd know. She works in the Silver Springs Hotel.'

I knew immediately who it was. An ex-girlfriend from my days in De Multi.

'Tell her I'll call her back, Tom.'

But Tom said, 'Marty, come here to me for a sec.'

So I walked from my car over to the wall until I stood just below the window.

Glancing around to make sure there was no one in the vicinity, Tom whispered down, 'It's to do with Paul McGrath!'

A little earlier that year, the Aston Villa and Ireland defender had scooped the PFA Players' Player of the Year award – one of only six defenders ever to have won. After the ceremony he dropped out of circulation, and in the run up to the Republic of Ireland's crucial qualifier with Albania in Tirana on May 26th, there was no sign of him. This was the big story at the time. Where had Paul gone? And who would find him first?

Anyway, I wish I could say I jumped into the nearest telephone box and changed into my Superman outfit. The best I could do, however, was to put on the pink jacket over the navy and blue T-shirt and pull on the jeans over the shorts. I rang my friend in the Silver Springs and she told me that there was no point coming there any more. Paul was headed for the airport. I rang the RTÉ cameraman Tony Cournane and soundman Brian O'Mahony, told them that we might have a story and asked them to meet me there.

Cork Airport in 1993 was totally different to how it is today. It was quite small and compact and everybody knew everybody else. When we arrived, I went straight to the long line of taxis queuing up at the entrance to the terminal. I had covered a number of taxi disputes in my days presenting *Cork This Week* at Cork Multi Channel, and so I knew most of the taxi drivers. The first taxi man I asked pointed down the line towards – let's call it Paddy's Taxi. I sprinted down, looked in the window of the cab, but could see no one inside. So I asked another taxi man: Have you seen Paul? With a nod and a wink, he said the same thing.

'Try Paddy's Taxi.'

So I went back again, and this time the back door opened and Paul McGrath, who had been lying beneath a blanket on the floor of the cab, burst out and sprinted for the front door. In half a minute, he was safely ensconced in the VIP room just inside the doors of the airport.

Now the fun started as we, along with several other journalists who'd picked up the trail, camped outside the door waiting for Paul to emerge. Finally we were rewarded when

Paul's girlfriend (later his wife) Caroline made a dash from the VIP room, closely followed by Paul, closely followed by myself, Brian and Tony, closely followed by the rest of the media scrum. We trailed them up the escalator, and as we approached security and passport control, I started to pull on the brakes. These were different times, however. One of the guys on passport control beckoned me on. 'Come on, Marty! You'll get him!'

In through the departure lounge, past bewildered passengers to gate number two, where a group of smiling flight attendants started to chant, 'Ooh ah Paul McGrath,' then, when they saw me and the rest of the media in hot pursuit, they changed it to 'Ooh ah . . . Marty Morrissey!'

You couldn't make it up!

On we ran, downstairs to the tarmac where three planes were parked parallel to the terminal building, one behind the other.

Paul's girlfriend Caroline was halfway up the steps of the nearest plane when we heard Paul call up to her, 'Caroline! That's the wrong bloody plane. It's the next one!'

This was the delay we needed. Myself and Tony Leen from the *Examiner* fell into step with Paul as he made his way towards the right plane.

Marty: Have you been in contact with Jack Charlton?

Paul: No.

Marty: Do you think this will ruin your future international prospects?

Paul: I hope not.

Marty: How are you feeling?

Paul: A little bit sore around the knees but that's about it.

Tony Leen: Do you think you will be back for the next two games?

Paul: Who knows?

Marty: Do you think Jack Charlton is very angry with you over the fact
that you didn't contact him personally?

Paul: I did actually leave a message for him a few days ago.

By now Paul was at the aircraft that would bring himself and
Caroline to Birmingham. He dashed up the steps and was gone.
Meanwhile, I rushed back to the studios and began editing the
piece for inclusion in the *Six One News* later that evening.

Let me say at this point that I was (and remain) a huge fan
of the man, but my job was to find out where he was and to

try to get a word with him. He was *the* story. Truthfully, however, this was not a part of the job that I enjoyed. A few weeks later, I got a handwritten note from another hero of mine, Christy Moore. I'd never met him. In the letter, he asked if we had nothing better to be doing than chasing one of our country's greatest heroes.

I met Paul years later and told him that while some people congratulated us on the scoop, I never considered it one of my finest hours. To his great credit, he said that he understood that I was just doing my job and said that he had no hard feelings. What a gentleman.

The Republic of Ireland won that match in Tirana 2–1 with a late Tony Cascarino header. Two weeks later Paul McGrath played against Latvia in Riga and scored the second goal in a 2–0 win.

Máire Ní Mhurchú retired in 1993 and there was great debate, gossip and discussion about who would get the job as the new head of RTÉ Cork. That person would be Gerry Reynolds, who had been the first midlands correspondent for RTÉ in 1988, and later spent some time in a similar role in Limerick and the Mid West region. His brother Kevin is an excellent producer in RTÉ Radio, and has made some wonderful dramas and documentaries. Their other brother, Paul, is an exceptional talent and a top-notch crime correspondent for the station. I consider the Reynolds brothers among my best friends – and confidants too, at times when I doubted myself or got fed up when RTÉ management wouldn't give me a gig or wouldn't listen to my complaints. That friendship started when Gerry came to Cork in 1993.

He was a bit of a whiz kid: baby-face looks, reddish hair, sexy glasses and a swagger in his walk.

There was a great hurler from the Na Piarsaigh club play-ing with Cork at the time, called Tony O'Sullivan. He was an exceptional stickman and was magical on his day in the blood and bandages of Cork or the black and amber of his club. The Cork crowd love a good nickname, and Tony O'Sullivan was so brilliant that everybody called him 'Baby Jesus'.

Pretty soon, because he was so good, Gerry Reynolds acquired the same nickname in RTÉ Cork. If he heard good news, Gerry would shout out that Al Pacino exclamation in *Scent of a Woman*: 'Hoo-ah!'

RTÉ Cork now became a major broadcast centre. Gerry succeeded in having *Nationwide* based in Cork, and estab-lished a strong TV production centre where stars like Derek Davis and Michael Ryan worked. He hired some great peo-ple, many of whom were subsequently promoted to some of the most senior posts in RTÉ.

Mileage, overnights and taxi vouchers have always been crucial elements of the RTÉ financial payment infrastruc-ture. On one occasion, an auditor was sent down to Cork to take a look at the books and ensure everything was being run correctly. As he worked through the taxi expenses, there was one guest whose name kept cropping up.

Finbarr.

Despite often taking taxis to and from the studio, his name did not appear on payment lists. This meant that Finbarr wasn't signing the legal forms to allow his contribution to be broadcast, and nor was he getting the admittedly very small fee for that contribution.

The production team of the station's successful drama, *Under the Goldie Fish*, which was written by Conal Creedon, were summoned before the auditor and asked to explain. They told him that Finbarr was a regular contributor, but that he had agreed to forgo his fee in recognition of the wonderful creative opportunity he was being given. On this basis, Finbarr was allowed to continue to get his taxi on recording days. After the auditor had gone home, however, Gerry discovered that Finbarr was in fact a dog. Conal Creedon's dog. The dog was a vital part of the production, and to ensure he looked good, he always got a wash and blow-dry on the day of filming, and so arrived in studio spotlessly clean. But Gerry was having no more of it, and from that day on Finbarr had to walk to the RTÉ studios.

1990 was a fantastic year to be in Cork, not least because of the historic double. There is a great story – and a true story – told of what happened in the Cork dressing-room at half-time in the 1990 All-Ireland final.

Galway were five points up, had played really well and looked to be in control in so many key areas of the field. From their perspective, the job was half done. Joe Cooney was awesome at centre forward, the late, great Tony Keady had scored an inspirational point after a great solo run from centre back. Pete Finnerty, Martin Naughton, Noel Lane, Michael 'Hopper' McGrath, Pat Malone, Anthony Cunningham and Brendan Lynskey were all winning their individual battles. Another half an hour of the same level of endeavour and performance and there was little doubt but that Liam MacCarthy would be heading west of the Shannon.

The atmosphere in the Cork dressing-room was tense, to say the least, when the manager, Canon Michael O'Brien, herded several of the players into the shower area and told them to take off their jerseys. Next thing he threw a bucket of freezing cold water over Mark Foley, John Fitzgibbon and Jim Cashman, bellowing, 'Will ye wake up out there?'

Meanwhile Tomás Mulcahy and Tony O'Sullivan were

going around to each player, offering individual words of encouragement. Jim Cashman, who was charged with the impossible job of marking Joe Cooney, dried himself off, then approached the great Dr Con Murphy.

'Jesus Christ,' said Jim, 'Cooney is on fire. What will I do with him?'

Dr Con, who is one of my favourite people in the world, could only say, 'He can't keep it up, he's bound to get tired soon.'

When they came back into the main dressing-room again, Canon O'Brien was roaring at his players. 'I only have three forwards working for me today!'

Immediately Kevin Hennessy put up his hand and asked, 'Excuse me, Canon, but apart from myself, who are the other two?'

The dressing-room broke into wild laughter.

This shattered the tension, and many of that Cork team of 1990 will tell you that Kevin Hennessy's intervention when the Canon was in full flow was a vital moment, that it released something, and that from then on they were relaxed and focused. The Canon, with a Cork jersey in his hands, fell to his knees and pleaded with his players to give everything for the next half an hour. For themselves, their families, their clubs, their community and above all else, for Cork.

For a team that could only score 1–8 in the first half, Cork were unstoppable in the second half, racking up a total of 4–7 to register a final score of 5–15 to Galway's 2–21. It was a remarkable recovery.

Kevin Hennessy is one of my favourite people. A great hurler by any standards of course, but also great company. He has a wonderful sense of humour. He's had a tough time with health problems in recent years, but his courage and the love of his family have seen him overcome tremendous challenges. On that day – September 2nd, 1990 – he scored the fastest goal that was ever scored in an All-Ireland hurling final, after just forty-eight seconds. Every year since then, he has eagerly awaited the throw-in on All-Ireland day, nervously fiddling with his watch as he sits at home on his couch in Midleton. Once the forty-eight-second mark has passed, he's back smiling, cracking jokes and shouting at the TV. His record is intact for another year.

I was lucky enough to be with the victorious team on the open-topped bus for the homecoming the day after the match. I had my Marantz, which is a little radio recorder, and was trying to get interviews, when some of the Cork hurlers started slagging me about being from Clare. What did I know about hurling? And more to the point, what was I doing on the bus?

It was then that Kevin Hennessy came to my rescue. He threw his long arms around me. 'You leave my Marty alone! You'll have to throw me over first!'

He was immediately surrounded by Tomás Mulcahy, Teddy McCarthy and Ger Cunningham. They grabbed Hennessy by the legs and pretended to throw him overboard as we turned the corner on to the Grand Parade.

This was the first of many homecomings I would cover for RTÉ Sport and TV news, and like every single one since, all plans went out the window and the arrival of the team ran hours behind schedule.

Two weeks later, at about five o'clock on September 16th, 1990, the people of Cork entered seventh heaven as their footballers emulated their colleagues on the hurling team and won the All-Ireland football final. I was at the winners' hotel in Dublin that Sunday night, and what a night it was. It was just story after story; I laughed so much I had a sore throat the next day. On the Monday, I travelled to Cork as we were broadcasting the homecoming live on RTÉ Cork 89FM. I will never forget the scenes at Kent railway station when the team arrived home. The bus edged slowly through the welcoming multitudes on Patrick Street, continued down the Grand Parade and then turned left on to the South Mall before stopping outside the Imperial Hotel. There, the honeymoon suite had been reserved for RTÉ and the victorious team.

It was a luxurious room, dominated by a king-size bed, with beautiful arrangements of flowers placed strategically on various tables. There was even a bottle of champagne and a handwritten note from the manager welcoming us to the hotel and congratulating us on our recent wedding!

Within minutes of our arrival, a radio studio was hastily assembled by a team of sound engineers. Microphone stands and sound gear were set up, with wires strewn across the floor as we prepared for our broadcast later that night. Outside, on the stage on the South Mall, hurling captain Tomás Mulcahy and football captain Larry Tompkins swapped the Liam MacCarthy and Sam Maguire Cups before scrambling through the massive crowd, which burst spontaneously into 'The Banks of My Own Lovely Lee'.

Alf McCarthy, the Gay Byrne of RTÉ Cork, presented the special homecoming programme from the honeymoon suite, while I operated as reporter and runner, cajoling guests to come upstairs to the suite to be interviewed. Alf did all the social and cultural interviews, while I concentrated on the hurlers and footballers.

That night solidified my friendships with some of the greats of Cork hurling: Ger Cunningham, Jim Cashman,

Seanie O'Gorman, Denis Walsh, Tony O'Sullivan and Seanie McCarthy, who today owns Soho, a great pub and nightclub on the Grand Parade. Teddy McCarthy was there too, a true legend of the games we love. He was on both Cork teams in that remarkable month of September 1990.

Some years later, after Clare had won All-Irelands in 1995 and 1997, several Cork people came up to me and made this point: 'What are ye getting so excited about in Clare after winning two All-Irelands in a hundred years? Sure didn't Teddy McCarthy win two All-Irelands in two weeks?'

I suppose it's all about perspective.

Ger Fitzgerald was a great hurler and gentleman, while Mark Foley from Argideen Rangers will always be remembered for the 2–7 he scored in the Munster final that summer. He's now a dentist in Bantry. I remember with great fondness the late John Kerins, a member of An Garda Síochána and a superb goalkeeper from St Finbarr's, whose lovely wife Ann I am still in contact with today. There was also the great Nemo Rangers man Stephen O'Brien, and Barry Coffey, whom I often meet in Clare these days. Conor Counihan, Dave Barry and Tony Nation were all players I greatly admired and got to know quite well. Niall Cahalane could be a devil on the field, but he is a loyal friend. One of the best nights I had was when Niall invited me to present the Cork county championship medals to the Castlehaven footballers in West Cork when they won the county championship in 2013.

It was a cold night in January 2014 and there was a young guy there – let's call him Barry – who, according to those who spoke before me, fancied himself as the local sex symbol. When it was my turn to speak, I felt I needed to set the record straight: 'Thank you very much, ladies and gentlemen, for the very warm welcome. Now, I am very sorry to disappoint Barry, but you need to know this. I am the sex symbol of Cork . . .' The audience burst into laughter. I added: 'Know your place, Barry. Get in the queue for that title.'

Just over a year later, the mood had changed in Cork. The Cork footballers had failed in their bid for three Munster titles in a row. Worse still, they'd lost to Kerry.

There were moves afoot to oust manager Billy Morgan. A diary of his activities had been kept secretly over the preceding couple of years. It was full of petty indiscretions: he had been seen out with players; when the chairman of the Cork county board refused to come up with £25 a session for weight training, Billy hadn't been shy about telling him what he thought of him. There was something about a player breaking a wash-hand basin as he climbed through the window of a guesthouse in Offaly in the wee small hours after a challenge match.

Billy Morgan had delivered an All-Ireland title the year before, and had captained Cork to All-Ireland victory in 1973, so this sudden attack did not go over well. There was outrage. The Cork public, who normally only get incensed about hurling matters, were deeply unhappy. Billy Morgan was the heartbeat of Cork football.

At the time I was renting a room from a great landlady and friend, Teresa Lenihan in Douglas, just around the corner from where the Morgans lived. I should come clean here and say that I had always been a Billy Morgan fan. I don't remember what age I was but probably no more than twelve or thirteen when I wrote him a letter saying I wanted to be a top-class goalkeeper like him when I grew up. I was so obsessed with the Nemo Rangers man that I remember when I was practising my kick-outs, I used to walk back after placing the ball on the ground, just like Billy. I wore a green jersey just like Billy. I wore red socks up to my knees just like Billy. I even wore a black cap just like Billy's. I was so obsessed that my father decided that I should meet my hero and so we drove to Bishopstown and knocked on Billy's front door. I honestly don't know if we doorstepped him (which would have been very rude) or if my father arranged it beforehand. Billy must have thought I was a mad young fella, but what I remember now is how quiet and shy he was with me at the time.

Years later, when I was manager of Kilmurry Ibrickane and we were trying to build a team and think outside the box, I arranged a challenge match between ourselves and Nemo Rangers in Cork. Billy Morgan was in goal for Nemo. I was in goal for Kilmurry Ibrickane. To this day I can remember how much that meant to me. Silly I know, but I got a great kick out of it.

I was asked to go over to Páirc Uí Chaoimh by RTÉ radio sport producer Pat O'Donovan, a proud Mallow man, to cover the Cork county board meeting at which Billy's future would be discussed, and to report live on the late sports bulletin on Radio 1 that night, and again the following morning on *Morning Ireland*.

The long tunnel underneath the stands in the old Páirc Uí Chaoimh was a cold, bleak spot, even on a hot summer's day. On a bad winter's night, it was absolutely freezing. The wind whistled through the tunnel, and through the knot of journalists waiting for the meeting to break up.

But as the county officials filed out, nobody would talk. The following morning, Billy Morgan spoke to me live on *Morning Ireland*. This was one of the first little exclusives I got in my career. Billy Morgan had the reputation of being grumpy and didn't suffer fools too easily, but he always treated me with great kindness and we never had a cross word. Any time I asked him for an interview over the years, he gave it, even on days when Cork lost and the mood wasn't the best. Maybe that letter I wrote as a child helped me, but to me he will always be a great player, a brilliant coach and manager and just simply a legend in the GAA world I love.

Eventually, commonsense prevailed and Billy was reinstated. It helped that the players wouldn't hear of his departure. Billy subsequently won three more Munster football championships over the next five years.

I have so many outstanding memories of my days on Leeside. Going to the final practice run of the Eurovision Song Contest in Millstreet was just awesome. The way RTÉ produced that incredible extravaganza and beamed it around Europe – all from a show-jumping arena – just filled me with pride. I always loved Niamh Kavanagh's song 'In Your Eyes', and was thrilled when she won the competition.

I remember my trip to Derry's Guildhall with Councillor Denis Cregan when he was the Lord Mayor of Cork between 1991 and 1992. 'Dino', as he was affectionately known, served almost twenty years in the Seanad, and sat on Cork City Council from 1979 to 2009. We became great friends. Today, he and his family own a chain of fish and chip shops – called 'Dino's' – in Cork city and county, and I hear too that they're expanding to Dungarvan in Co. Waterford.

During the Troubles, the Guildhall in Derry was the focus of multiple terror attacks. The building was badly damaged by two bombs in 1972 but was restored and reopened in 1977. The square in front of the building regularly plays host

With the Lord Mayors of Cork and Derry in Derry's Guildhall

to important events, not least of which was Bill Clinton's address when he visited the city in November 1995.

It was to this hallowed hall that Dino arrived with his Cork entourage and was warmly welcomed by the council officials in Derry before walking down the long dark corridor towards

the mayor's office. The mayor of Derry at the time was David
Davis, an Independent Unionist, who was calmly waiting at
his large desk to welcome the Lord Mayor of Cork, Cllr Denis
Cregan, to Derry. But Dino was so enthusiastic about being
there that when he saw the Derry mayor, instead of shaking
his hand, he immediately embraced him passionately and
said, 'Listen here boy, ye have to stop shooting yerselves up
here. Honestly, it's not good for ye.'

This was seven years before the Good Friday Agreement.

Away from radio, I occasionally got the chance to fill in
for Tom McSweeney on TV news. He was RTÉ's southern
correspondent before Paschal Sheehy. I remember going to
Cobh to meet and interview Sonia O'Sullivan when she won
her European championship gold medal in the 3,000 metres
in Helsinki, and again when she finished fourth in the same
event in the 1992 Olympics.

The O'Sullivans are proud Cobh people. Sonia's dad, John,
was a Cobh Ramblers' goalkeeper and served in the Irish
Navy. The square and the narrow winding streets leading up
to Cobh Cathedral were packed for Sonia's homecoming.
She would of course go on to win silver at the Sydney Olympics in 2000.

I joined RTÉ 89FM in March 1990. Throughout my time
there, I worked freelance at the weekends, commentating on
matches and occasionally filming championship previews for
either *Sunday Sport* or the *Sunday Game*. Although I was very
happy in Cork, my ambitions hadn't changed. I always wanted
to work for RTÉ nationally and operate out of Dublin.

July 19th, 1992 is one of the most important dates in my life.
Understanding that fully requires a little perspective. Like all
young boys, I dreamt of playing with Clare in an All-Ireland

final, but despite playing minor and under-21 for Clare, I realized that:

a) I wasn't probably good enough
b) I didn't train hard enough
c) I discovered that girls, socializing and fast cars (i.e. my mother's Volkswagen) were more attainable, and
d) Clare were going nowhere anyway.

I mentioned before that I had sat on the wall and watched the Miltown Malbay Massacre unfold in 1979, when Kerry scored 9–21 to Clare's 1–9. Pat Spillane played a big role in Clare's destruction. Neither he, nor any of the other Kerry greats, took their foot off the accelerator that day. But I'm a Scorpio, and we never forget! Thirteen years later Clare faced Kerry once again, this time on Munster football final day. When I arrived at the RTÉ OB unit parked in the front car park of the Gaelic Grounds in Limerick, I was greeted by howls of laughter and slagging, most of it from Pat Spillane, who was my commentating partner on the day. The reason for his mirth? I had written a piece for the *Sunday Independent* about my memories of being a sub goalkeeper with the Clare footballers when we faced Limerick in the Munster championship. Adhamhnán O'Sullivan was the *Sunday Independent*'s sports editor from 1988 to 2006. It was he who asked me to write about Clare, our love of football and my own exploits. That first call began a relationship with the *Sunday Independent* that lasted four years, until I was so busy in my job for RTÉ that I just didn't have the time to do justice to my column. But I really appreciated Adhamhnán's trust in me and I'm very proud to have written that column.

In 1992 I was still freelancing with the sports department but working full-time with RTÉ in Cork. I was also deeply involved with my own club at the time, travelling up and

down to training, and obviously too, I had close friendships
with so many of the Clare players; the likes of Aidan 'Horse'
Moloney, Dermot Coughlan and Michael Roughan. I knew
the entire squad really well, including my distant cousin Tom
Morrissey, and Noel Roche, with whom I'd played minor and
under-21 for Clare.

The Kerry team on July 19th included several big names.
Jack O'Shea was playing his last championship match. Seamus Moynihan was playing his first, and of course the great
Maurice Fitzgerald was there too. Despite this, I still felt sur-
prisingly confident that Clare could pull it off, *if* everything
went right for us on the day. John Maughan, the Clare manager, had come from Mayo and brought a new attitude, a
new philosophy. Under his guidance, we had already won the
All-Ireland B championship, beating Longford in Ballinasloe. But this wasn't Longford. This was Kerry.

As events unfolded, I began to believe that the impossible
dream was truly possible. James Hanrahan made a great save.
My great friend and neighbour Aidan Moloney, who I had
coached to those under-16 and minor championship successes, was playing well at centrefield, while the Clancy
brothers from Corofin, Seamus and Colm, were outstanding.
Noel Roche and Gerry Killeen scored great points; Martin
Daly's flicked goal and Francis McInerney's leadership would
deliver an amazing day for Clare football.

When Tom Morrissey caught a great ball in the middle of
the field, I said 'Good man, Tom!' as any decent cousin
would, except of course that I was doing the TV commentary and was supposed to be neutral!

Every chance I got, I rubbed it into Pat Spillane, my co-
commentator. At one stage Pat said that unless I calmed
down I would fall out of the commentary box. I'm not sure

to this day did he mean by accident or that he would lend a helping hand.

The full-time whistle blew. What a moment! Clare 2–10 Kerry 0–12. The shock of the year had just happened. Clare were heading to Croke Park. The Banner had just beaten the Kingdom in a Munster final.

I knew what this meant to my own crowd. And so I said, at the end of the game, 'There won't be a cow milked in County Clare for at least a week!'

Nothing original in it, I'm afraid, as it was something my neighbours would often say if we won a match at home. But as they say these days, it went viral!

Decades later I still get slagged about it. I can be in Ballybofey or Rosslare and some wise wag will always say, 'There won't be a cow milked in Donegal,' or 'There won't be a cow milked in Wexford tonight, Marty.'

The Sunday Game at the time was a highlights programme. Only All-Ireland semi-finals and finals were shown live. That night, Michael Lyster introduced the Munster football final highlights to one of the biggest audiences ever. People around the country simply could not believe that Kerry had been beaten, and by Clare?

But there was one more little twist in the tale. For some inexplicable reason, the highlights of the match were shown not once but twice on *The Sunday Game* that night.

Some say it was because of a power failure in parts of the country, and that the switchboard in RTÉ lit up with people begging to see Clare winning and Kerry being beaten. To the best of my knowledge, it was the only time in the history of *The Sunday Game* that the same match highlights were shown twice on the same night. The county went mad for weeks. It was a great warm-up for what was to come three years later, and the hurlers would openly admit that the success of the footballers in '92 inspired them.

I remember the Monday night when the Clare team brought the Munster trophy to Miltown Malbay, Quilty and Doonbeg. I was MC in Quilty for the evening, on the back of a lorry in front of the dry wall, and the welcome each player got still rings in my ears.

I will be forever grateful for Ger Canning's kindness in swapping semi-finals with me so I could do the commentary on the All-Ireland football semi-final between Clare and Dublin. It was so emotional to see the Clare footballers run out on to Croke Park before a packed arena. I can still hear the roar of the crowd, I can still see the massive welcome the Banner got from the Dubs on Hill 16. It was a special day and do you know what? I think if Padraig Conway's goal had been allowed (and I still think it was perfectly legitimate!), we just might have beaten the Dubs as well.

The Clare football team of 1992 and the management team of John Maughan, Noel Walsh and Pat Hanrahan did wonders for our county. They brought us to an All-Ireland semi-final against Dublin. But they gave us more than that, they gave us a sense of pride and a belief that anything was possible.

So I had made progress, and was now in almost daily contact with people in the sports department. At the same time, I only ever met group head of sport Tim O'Connor once a year in December for my annual review. I was never shy about telling him where I wanted to be. We would go through my performances and, thankfully, he always said he was happy enough.

So it was a bit of a surprise when Tim rang in early March to know if I could meet him in Killarney.

We met in Hotel Europe, near Fossa on the Killorglin

Road. It was there, over lunch in the restaurant, with the magnificent Lakes of Killarney glistening in the spring sunshine, that Tim told me he was calling me ashore, as he put it. He was bringing the culchie from the Wild West to the metropolis of Dublin. After all my efforts, I was finally getting a full-time job in the sports department. The pay was crap, but I didn't care. After the best part of ten years, I was finally getting what I had worked so hard for. It was an emotional moment.

By design or accident, Cork has played a huge role in my life, and the people of this great city and county have been very good to me. Leaving Cork was not easy. There was history. There was a connection. And one of the things I loved most about Cork was the social life it gave me. I loved Halpins, Counihan's, the Old Oak, An Bodhrán, the Long Valley, the Joshua Tree, Clancy's, Barry's in Douglas and, in later times, Rearden's. The night was never complete without trying for the shift in nightclubs like Shandra's, Sir Henry's, Sidetracks, Tropics and Surfers.

When I look back now at photos of myself in the 1990s, I'm slightly appalled at the get-ups. It was always jeans, shirt and jacket. How I pulled any babe would baffle Einstein himself. The only thing that I can say in my defence was that we always had a great laugh. I reckon I am a pretty good example of the fact that laughter is a wonderful aphrodisiac. I might have told the mirror I was a ride before I went out, but the truth was that between the bushy hair, not great teeth at the time, and not much taller that 5 ft 7, I hadn't much to offer.

Sidetracks was always a little posher than Sir Henry's. In the former, the jeans, shirt and jacket combo was the only way to go. In the latter, you would sweat more than in three nights' hard training in Páirc Uí Chaoimh or the Mardyke. I

literally kept fit by going to Sir Henry's nightclub. By the time
I got home, the jacket would be missing and the shirt hanging out, with buttons either torn off or undone. On one
memorable night, I got back to Douglas with only the one
shoe! Not bad for a guy who never drank or smoked!

I danced, I laughed, I cried, I shifted, I ate fish and chips in
Lennox's and I went home, but I never took a drink or smoked.
People ask me why all the time. Sometimes they'll get that
sympathetic note in their voice: 'Have you a problem?'

The truth is that drink just isn't for me. I'm not against it,
but I never developed a taste for alcohol. Maybe it was a control thing. Maybe being a publican's son during those vital
teenage years was a factor, and through my life I've seen the
impact of alcohol abuse. The peer pressure to drink was
relentless for a while. I would give in and order a vodka and
coke but my inner circle of pals would know me well, and
they'd catch me sneaking to the bar to replace it with a simple
coke. After a while, people stopped caring what was in my
glass. Am I anti-drink? Absolutely not. I love pubs, and to
this day I'll nearly always be the last one out.

Cork is special to me for another reason as well. Through
my aforementioned social activity, I had met a Corkman
whose company I thoroughly enjoyed. He was working for
an insurance company at the time, and one day he called in to
me in Union Quay to say hello. I was just going out the front
door on my way to City Hall to get the Lord Mayor's itinerary
for an event that was to take place the following day, so we
walked together. We had a lot in common. We both loved
broadcasting, and he was looking to see how he could get a
start. I think maybe he reckoned that if I could get a gig, then
any gobshite could.

When we got to the back entrance of City Hall, this

gorgeous blonde woman was locking up and going home. I told her what I was looking for, and she very kindly turned around and we went back into her office to get the itinerary. Right from the off, we got on well. She hadn't a notion about GAA, local radio or broadcasting, and she looked at me, I thought, with a lack of interest. Her name was Liz Kidney, and over time she eventually began to appreciate my undoubted charm and positive assets. And so our journey through life together began. Over the years we have travelled around the world and shared many experiences. She has been my rock, but hates the limelight with a passion and so lets me off to do my own thing. And as for the friend that came with me to City Hall? It was Michael Corcoran, who today is an excellent rugby commentator on RTÉ Radio 1. Now he's my colleague and is still my friend.

Today, RTÉ 89FM is no more. It was closed down in 2000, six years after I left. It saddens me now to look across the river and see the place where the building on Union Quay used to be.

Time doesn't stand still. The arrival of commercial radio stations like 96FM and later Red FM changed the broadcasting landscape beyond recognition. The new kids on the block sounded younger, fresher and were on air twenty-four hours a day.

RTÉ local radio survived as long as it could, thanks in no small part to the presence of strong Cork voices at management meetings in Dublin 4; in particular those of Kevin Healy, who was head of radio for a while, and Joe Barry, who was director general of the station from 1992 to 1997. The station had survived various cull attempts, but once that local interest was lost, and then that Cork presence in Donnybrook was gone, a business decision was made. Listenership figures had fallen dramatically and the prospects of recovery were slim to nil. Alf McCarthy had a great line: 'We knew our time was up when we knew each listener by their first name.' After Union Quay was closed down, Alf went on to present *The Irish Collection* from 2 a.m. to 6 a.m. on RTÉ Radio 1. This was a synopsis of all that had happened on the station during daytime hours, but eventually, the costs of editing and manpower saw that terminated too.

RTÉ Cork local radio belonged to a different time. In its heyday, it was hugely popular, its programmes resonating with the people of Cork for almost a quarter of a century. Alf McCarthy, Donna O'Sullivan, Barraí Mescal, Caimin Jones and Stevie B were the foundation touchstones, as were the producers Aidan Stanley and Pat O'Donovan. But broadcasting from 11 a.m. to 1 p.m. and returning from 2.45 to 6 p.m. would not work in the twenty-first century.

I will always be grateful for the opportunities I got in Cork. There's no way I would have been exposed to that vast spectrum of experiences in Dublin. In a single week, you could be presenting on local radio, providing reports and packages for Radio 1 programmes, compiling a TV news report for *Six-One* or *The Nine O'Clock News*, doing interviews for *The Sunday Game* and, at the weekend, be on commentary duty somewhere in Ireland. It was hectic but exhilarating.

Today RTÉ Cork is a thriving hub of activity, with the *Nationwide* team led by Eoin Ryan and Shirley Murphy running the show. Paschal Sheehy does brilliant work as the southern editor, with Jennie O'Sullivan as reporter for the newsroom. *The Today Show*, presented by Maura Derrane, Sinead Kennedy and Dáithí Ó Sé, is broadcast from Cork, while on radio, John Creedon presents his show from the southern studio every evening.

I have often felt that RTÉ should set up the Cork Academy of Broadcasting on Fr Matthew Street, and require all up-and-coming talent to spend at least six months learning their trade there. Graduates may be academically gifted, but too many, through no fault of their own, are inexperienced when it comes to the reality of either live or recorded broadcasting.

In Cork, it's possible to learn and make mistakes, and yet still impress the programme makers with what you have to

At the Marty Party, on my departure from RTÉ Cork: (back row) Olan O'Brien (Radio Engineer and TV News Cameraman), Stevie Bolger (aka Stevie B, presenter), Pat McAuliffe RIP (sports reporter), Alan Short (actor), Rosarie Ryan (sales & marketing), Alf McCarthy (presenter), Shirley Murphy (nationwide co-ordinator), Jennie O'Sullivan (news reporter), Mick Fitzgibbon RIP (manager facilities TV & radio), Deirdre O'Grady (broadcast co-ordinator), Deirdre McCarthy (Managing Editor, Radio Programmes and Regions), Juliette Coughlan (broadcast assistant); (front row) Tom McSweeney (Southern Correspondent), Gerry Reynolds (Head of RTE Cork), myself, Aidan Stanley (RTE Radio Cork Producer), Tony O'Donoghue (Soccer Correspondent), Colm O'Callaghan (Editor Specialist Factual)

offer in either radio or TV or both. In Dublin you are boxed off and labelled. And that doesn't matter if you are on air or behind the scenes. It's the nature of the business and the structure that's employed, and it's one thing that bothered me when I first arrived in Dublin. Marty Morrissey now equalled sport. It was suddenly as if that was all that defined me. So I concentrated on sport for many years – possibly too many, if I'm honest. In any case, I knew as I left the banks of the Lee that I now had to work hard in the job I had been working so hard to get.

With total modesty I can say my going-away party was the best ever produced by RTÉ Cork. The speeches were incredibly witty, as many of the stories I have told here were enhanced and embellished by my great friends and colleagues. The *Cork Examiner* and RTÉ Cork came together and blew up the photo which was on the front page of the paper the morning after myself and Tony Leen chased Paul McGrath around Cork Airport. It takes pride of place in my home, though that bloody awful T-shirt still annoys me.

It was April 1994. Goodbye Cork, hello Dublin.

10. The Big Smoke

Like any decent culchie heading for the Big Smoke, I looked around to see where I might bed down for a couple nights during the week. I was useless with money, and hadn't a penny saved, so I rang my buddies Tony O'Donoghue and Mary Wilson, who were now married and living in a beautiful house in Dalkey. I asked if I could stay a few nights of the week, just for a few weeks until I could find a place to stay. Of course the few weeks grew into months – probably about six of them in all. Looking back, I really shouldn't have stayed as long as I did.

There was one night I went out for pizza, but decided on my way to the chipper in Dalkey that I would keep going and drive to Clare, as I was filming in Galway the following morning. Tony is still waiting for his pizza.

With no money saved, getting a mortgage was proving challenging, to say the least, but eventually the bank manager gave in and I got my first house in Pier View, in Wicklow town. Pier View is a row of charming two-bedroom detached bungalows built on the side of the hill. When they came on the market in 1994, they cost £38,000. In euro, that comes to just over €48,250.

I loved the place, and indeed I came to love Wicklow town and its people.

The climb up the hill to home was so steep that I never fancied the walk, but my word, when you got to the front door, the view was spellbindingly beautiful! Many a time I

stood there on Sunday evenings after a match in Thurles or
Clones and absorbed the scene spread out before me. The
lights of the capital city shimmered in the distance, with the
Dublin and Wicklow mountains to the west, and to the east,
the golden coastline of the Irish Sea, which was dotted with
the lights of huge cargo ships making their way slowly to and
from the port of Dublin to the north.

By the time I arrived in the TV sports department, it had
moved from Montrose House, which stands just inside the
gate when you enter the Donnybrook campus from the Stillorgan dual carriageway, to the main TV building. My new
department consisted of two offices upstairs at the back of the
building. Next door was the young people's department where
Ray D'Arcy hung out, while dubbing, where sound engineers
recorded voice-overs, was just down the corridor. Further
down again, you had the small studio where Zig and Zag entertained the nation, and the weather studio was right at the back.

When Tim O'Connor offered me the job that day in

Killarney, I asked him if there would be a review after twelve months.

'If you don't hear from me for fifty-two weeks of the year,' he said, 'you're doing well. If I call you into the office, consider yourself in deep shit.'

And that, more or less, was how he managed us.

My preconceptions about the sports department turned out to be totally different to the reality. In my naivety, I thought that household names like George Hamilton, Jimmy Magee, Michael Lyster, Jim Sherwin, Fred Cogley, Brendan O'Reilly, Brian McSharry and Tracey Piggott would all have their own offices, but that wasn't the case. You'd be doing well to have any desk at all.

Tim O'Connor held court every Wednesday, when the previous week's programmes would be reviewed and analysed. He was very fair and honest. If he liked what you did, you got credit for it. A word of praise from Tim meant the world. He could also be acerbic in his comments. Many's the unassuming producer or presenter who went to the Wednesday meeting assuming they had done a great job the previous weekend, only to discover that they actually hadn't. It was not the place to be if Tim was unimpressed.

Bill Lalor is a native of Ballyskenagh in County Offaly, and was a brilliant TV producer/director. He got a bit fed up of turning up for the Wednesday meetings, and so he developed two great excuses for giving them a miss. The first was that he was attending a meeting in Croke Park. This worked brilliantly, for no other reason than the relationship with the GAA was always seen as important in RTÉ. But of course there weren't half as many meetings in Croke Park as Bill suggested. His second excuse was that he was gone to a funeral, as a member of the Lalor family had suddenly passed away.

On one particular Wednesday meeting, some issue relating to GAA coverage arose and Tim looked around the room. 'Is Bill Lalor here?'

'No.' The response came from my friend and colleague Joan O'Callaghan. 'He's at a funeral.'

Everyone tried to hide their smiles, but Tim must have sensed the mood. He was blessed with impeccable comic timing, so he allowed a few moments to pass before saying, 'Jaysus. Surely every fucking Lalor in the country must be dead by now.'

Cue uncontrollable laughter.

The message got back and Bill was at most Wednesday meetings after that. *Most.*

Joan O'Callaghan was a production assistant, or BCO as production assistants are called now. That stands for broadcast co-ordinator, but even that term doesn't capture just how good she was at her job, or just how important she was in keeping RTÉ Sport going for many years. From Solloghodbeg just outside Tipperary town, Joan was always great craic. She also copped on to me very early on, telling me to 'stop my waffle' as she would call it – and that was when she was being nice. When she was in full flow, it would be, 'Marty, that's it now, cut out the bullshit.'

I'm mad about Joan.

Sports Stadium started on September 22nd, 1973 and went out every Saturday, fifty-two weeks of the year, for the next twenty-four years and three months. Its final broadcast was on December 19th, 1997.

This was a monster of a programme. Some Saturdays, it would start at twelve noon and would not come off air for six hours. The initial hour or two would usually be pre-recorded packages covering a variety of sports, including the

GAA, badminton, boxing, greyhound racing, handball, pitch and putt, rallying, tennis and even the world championship tug of war at Oriel Park. Once we got to 2.30 p.m. or 3 p.m., we would cross over live to whichever soccer match we had the rights to show, and join either George Hamilton or Jimmy Magee in Old Trafford, Anfield, Stamford Bridge or wherever they were. In hindsight, it was an amazing achievement. RTÉ did not have the financial capabilities or huge staff numbers that the BBC had at the time, and yet week after week they produced hours of top-class sports coverage.

Sports Stadium production teams were led by some wonderful but very different personalities. Mike Horgan knew his television and had a wonderful grasp of the English language. Many a *Sports Stadium* running order was dramatically changed at the last minute after one of Mike's eureka moments. Inspirational? Maybe, but it gave everybody else working on the programme palpitations.

Brian McSharry, affectionately known as Brian McShaggy owing to his beard and flowing locks, was a different individual. A kinder man I have never met. And I won't forget his heartbreak when Tim O'Connor, who could be ruthless, took Brian off his one on-air gig, the Dublin Horse Show. To his great credit, Brian took that hit on the chin, but the truth was that he loved describing the action at the RDS and I'm not sure he ever quite got over it. That little episode taught me that this broadcasting game could be tough, and that staying the distance would not be easy.

Stephen Alkin was an excellent producer/director. His great passion was domestic soccer, and later, he transferred from behind the scenes to soccer commentary. Maurice Reidy was a quiet man from Kerry who was also a terrific editor. It was Maurice and Mick Dunne who made *Gaelic*

Stadium a part of *Sports Stadium*. Mick was also the man that came up with the idea of the Top Ace handball series that was so popular at the time.

From the moment I started in the TV sports department, I was travelling the length and breadth of the country during the week, filming championship previews for *Sports Stadium*. There were many presenters, but Brendan O'Reilly was the main man at the time. He was of course a wonderful athlete in his own right. He was also a great singer, and I can honestly say he was much loved and admired, not just by his audience but by his colleagues as well.

The production team loved playing pranks on Brendan. On one occasion, one of the lads ran in holding a piece of paper with a result from Scotland.

Brendan, live before the nation, read out, 'And in the Scottish football league today we have a full-time result. Hearts 1 Lungs 0.'

My other favourite one is the day he was announcing the racing results towards the end of the programme.

'Here are the results of the five o'clock in Leopardstown. First was No. 12, 'Dundrum Boy' at 12/1. Second was No. 4, 'Here We Go' at 8/1. Third was No. 16, 'Whistletown Rover' at 25/1. Numbers 17, 18 and 19 were non-runners and *all* 24 ran.'

In his day, Brendan was in the Top 10 in the world at the high jump, and was considered a world-class decathlete. There is a story told that when he was competing in Ohio, and had already knocked the bar twice, an official suggested that his approach was a bit sharp, and encouraged him to consider changing his style slightly. He took the advice, despite the fact that changing your style in the middle of a competition was unheard of. In any case, Brendan flew over the bar. He later discovered that the friendly official who had advised him was the legendary Jesse Owens, winner of four gold medals in the 1936 Olympics.

One Saturday, Michael Lyster was presenting what he described as an easy *Sports Stadium*. This was because there was going to be several hours of golf from the Irish Open. As Michael was about to hand over live to Fred Cogley, he saw on his monitor that Fred was holding an umbrella. With a terrible sinking feeling, Michael heard Fred say that golf was suspended for the day due to inclement weather.

They had nothing lined up to fill the space. There was no place to go, no place to hide. When it came back to studio, producer Max Mulvihill told Michael to keep going, but there was nothing to keep going with. By chance, Michael had picked up an *RTÉ Guide* on the way into the studio and so, with nothing else to do, he opened up the magazine and started previewing the following week's schedule.

'Here's a programme you might be interested in at 8.30 on Tuesday night on RTÉ 1. That's *Landmark*.' Michael turned the page. 'And on Wednesday night at 7 o'clock, Michael Ryan will present another exciting edition of *Nationwide*.'

Meanwhile Brian McSharry was tearing down the corridor to the TV Library looking for a tape, any tape, to fill the gap.

By the early 1990s, Sky had entered the sports rights arena and consequently RTÉ lost the live games which had been a staple of Saturday afternoon TV. Coverage was now deferred to 3.30 p.m. Showing recorded games greatly added to stress levels because it brought tapes into the equation. This was in the days before digital recording. At the time, it took at least four tapes to record a game, which meant that when it was time to broadcast the match, you had to get the sequencing right. Inevitably, the worst eventually happened.

It was Newcastle United vs Aston Villa at Newcastle. The

first half went fine, and the score at the break was one-all. All good so far. But instead of putting on the third tape at the start of the second half, the fourth tape went in, which showed the last twenty minutes of the game. Unfortunately, the two teams scored three goals between them in the missing third quarter, so that viewers tuning in at the start of the second half were confronted with a scoreline of Newcastle 3, Aston Villa 2. It was as if there had been three goals scored during the half-time break. As you can imagine, that was a hard one to explain to an angry public.

It was nerve-jangling stuff most Saturdays. If there was an All-Ireland League (AIL) rugby match in Clontarf, three or four motorbikes would be needed to get the tapes from the pitch to Donnybrook in time for broadcasting. A runner would be waiting at reception for the first tape to arrive. They would dash up the stairs to the VT (videotape) operator, who would rewind the tape and set it up just as Brendan O'Reilly was saying to the nation, 'Now let's go to Clontarf for the crucial AIL clash between the home side and their visitors, Cork Constitution. There's just three minutes gone and there's still no score. Your commentator is Jim Sherwin.'

That essentially gave the next motorbike eighteen minutes to get from Clontarf to Donnybrook with the next quarter of the game. There was no room for a traffic jam or for the East Link bridge to be up, or, worse still, a crash. It was seat-of-the-pants stuff. An adrenaline rush like no other.

I mentioned earlier that when *The Sunday Game* started in 1979, it was purely a highlights programme. Apart from the All-Ireland semi-finals and finals, there was no live coverage until 1989, when the Munster hurling final between Tipperary and Waterford was broadcast live for the very first time. Games in Croke Park, Navan and even Thurles were a

The 1997 launch of *The Sunday Game*, with Michael Lyster and Ger Canning

challenge in the early days, as the tapes had to be motorbiked or sent by taxi back to the RTÉ campus in Donnybrook to be edited and ready for the 9.30 p.m. transmission time. If that was difficult, Páirc Uí Chaoimh in Cork was a different matter entirely. Anyone who has been to the Páirc on Lee-side can tell you how difficult it can be to get in and out of on the day of a Munster hurling or football final. A match start-ing at 3.30 p.m. back then would normally be over some time after five o'clock, but by the time the post-match interviews were recorded, it might be nearly six o'clock before the tapes were ready to go. The massive traffic jams would be at their worst at that stage, so someone hatched a clever plan. To avoid the traffic, RTÉ Sport hired a boatman and kept him on standby beside Páirc Uí Chaoimh, ready to speed across the River Lee when the time came. Once the recordings were done, a highly stressed staff member rushed from the ground with a load of big, awkward beta tapes and gingerly climbed into the waiting boat. There was at least one occasion when there was no speedboat to be had and *The Sunday Game* tapes, together with the stressed-out RTÉ staff member, had to be rowed across the river to the waiting motorbike or taxi man.

I really have to laugh when people ask me about what it's like to work for the national broadcaster. Some of the more popular questions include:

Do you have a driver?

Does a limousine pick you up?

Does somebody do your research ahead of the game?

The answer to all of these questions is a resounding, emphatic, unequivocal 'NO!'

What's the commentary box like in, say, Pearse Stadium in Galway or Páirc Tailteann in Navan?

Basic . . . but effective. Despite what you might expect, they're little more than boxes with Perspex windows perched on scaffolding. If it rains, you have to ask your colleagues from the outside broadcast (OB) unit to take out the window so you can actually see the match. Otherwise, all you'll see are shimmering colours running after a ball.

In some counties, the GAA never really thought about TV or radio commentary positions when they were building or even redeveloping their grounds. So I was consoled a little when I heard what happened to George Hamilton in Shepherd's Bush in London.

George was commentating on one of those live three o'clock games on a Saturday afternoon at Loftus Road. You would expect a ground in London to have a top-class TV commentary facility, wouldn't you? Well, they don't, or at least they didn't! The ladder leading up to the commentary box was actually on the footpath on the street at the back of the stand, and

at 2.45 p.m., regardless of whether the commentary team was
in position or not, the ladder was hauled up. Unfortunately, at
2.50 p.m. John Giles arrived to co-commentate with George.
No amount of Irish charm could persuade the London 'maors'
to lower the ladder for that legend of Irish sport. Consequently,
George had to do the first half on his own, until, at half-time,
the ladder was lowered again to allow Gilesy to climb the steps
and finish out the game in the commentary position.

Caroline Murphy was a trailblazer in RTÉ Sport. She presented a variety of TV programmes over the years, commentating on Wimbledon every year with Jim Sherwin, and producing and directing both recorded programmes and live football and hurling matches at a time when women just didn't get those opportunities. Caroline is exceptionally bright and very assertive. I remember arriving late for a pre-All-Ireland final report from downtown Dublin on the morning of a final and getting the mother and father of a bollocking from her.

'Who do you think you are? Do you think you are more important than those of us who got here on time?'

She was absolutely right, and I was never late for a Caroline Murphy shoot again! And that little incident didn't stop her and her husband Sean O'Rourke – another colleague – from

With Mícheál Ó Muircheartaigh in 2000

inviting me to be godfather to their youngest son, Fergus. I was truly humbled by that wonderful honour.

As far as I was concerned, Michael O'Carroll was the king of the sports department. He directed more than forty All-Ireland finals, and also revolutionized how motor sport and cycle racing were covered. He was and is an extraordinary talent and has always lived life to the fullest. He was a scholarship student at the Cistercian College Roscrea before becoming a bus conductor in London, and then a pastry chef with the merchant navy. In 1959 he jumped ship in Havana, Cuba, to report on the Cuban revolution. He suffered a heart attack at forty-two years of age and almost lost his life in a helicopter crash in 1974, shooting the gallops at Ballydoyle for a piece on a Derby horse called Celine. Michael was one of the first wave of studio trainees to join RTÉ when he returned from New York with his wife, Philomena, and his work as a producer – from the sixties through to the millennium – left an indelible mark on the station. He has provided the lens through which so many of us have witnessed the dramatic changes Ireland has experienced in those years. Michael directed Queen Elizabeth's visit to Ireland, together with many funerals, including C. J. Haughey's.

Despite being a Tipperary man, he never lost his slight American twang. He was the only one in RTÉ that called me 'Marty' like the Americans do; rolling the 'R'. By contrast, the Irish always put the emphasis on the 'Mart' part.

Michael would get very excited when directing a Munster hurling championship match, but he would go through the roof altogether when Tipperary was playing. There is a story told – fact or fiction, I don't know – about a Cork/Tipperary Munster final in front of a sell-out crowd in the old Semple Stadium in Thurles. These were the days before live television;

the match would be recorded for broadcast later that evening. It's important to emphasize at this point just how important the relationship between a TV commentator and their director is. While the commentator is in full flow, following the events on the pitch, the director is picking shots from the various cameras peppered around the ground in order to create a sequence of shots which combine to give the viewer a coherent experience of what's happening at the game. The commentator's headphones are tight around their ears so that all they should hear is the director's voice issuing instructions and cueing shots.

On this occasion, Mick Dunne was commentating on the hurling and Michael O'Carroll was directing.

Mick was describing a Tipperary attack as only he could, reaching new decibel levels as the drama ramped up. 'Babs Keating going through with the ball . . . And out comes the Cork defender! AND BABS IS GONE DOWN! He's been fouled!'

At the same time, Michael was outside in the OB truck shouting directions to his camera crews: 'Camera 1, keep it wide, camera 2, move in, move in. Go on, Babs! Camera 4, I'm on you. Camera 2, let me see his eyes . . . In tight . . . tighter.' It's at this point that Babs, bearing down on goal, gets hit by the Cork defender. Michael now forgets all about his cameras. 'That fucker should be sent off! Put him off, ref!'

Mick Dunne, completely in the zone, heard all this in his headphones and so without even thinking about it, he roars into the mike: 'THAT FUCKER SHOULD BE SENT OFF! PUT HIM OFF, REF!'

These men seldom used bad language, but the simple truth is that in the heat of the moment, they momentarily lost control. From my own experience, I can so easily see how it might happen. In any case, that little segment never went to air. When the tapes came back to RTÉ, it was edited out ahead of the evening's broadcast.

In addition to bringing GAA stories to an audience that lapped them up, and shining a rare light on handball, Mick Dunne was one of the journalists who initiated the GAA All-Stars in 1971. It was Michael O'Carroll that started and produced *Know Your Sport* with George Hamilton and Jimmy Magee, the show which gave away the infamous *Know Your Sport* umbrellas each week. You have no idea how many people asked me to try to get them one of these when I started working in RTÉ.

When Michael retired, Bill Lalor became the main director of All-Ireland finals. He was brilliant and he too got an adrenaline rush when his county were playing. Not Tipperary this time, but Offaly. While I was trying to do my commentary, I'd hear a whole other commentary from Bill through my headphones. Not easy to focus in these circumstances!

Marty on commentary: Not too sure that's a free, I'd question that one.

Bill in the headphones: That referee is diabolical.

Marty: This could be a red card for the Offaly defender.

Bill: He didn't lay a finger on him. You and the referee need to go to Specsavers. (*Big laugh.*)

Then the Offaly defender is sent off.

Marty: So Offaly are down to fourteen players.

Bill: Disgraceful decision. We'll have to protest on the pitch again. We are being ridden here.

This was a reference to the 1998 All-Ireland semi-final, when Offaly supporters protested on the pitch after referee

Jimmy Cooney blew the final whistle early, giving Clare the victory. I'm Clare, he's Offaly, and he's married to a woman from Cooraclare.

Linesmen were the bane of Bill's life. Camera 3 was always the one down at ground level, just to the right or left of the tunnel. This was the camera that brought you the lovely shots of the teams running out on to the field, of Ger Loughnane directing the moves, Jim Gavin sitting motionless and Davy Fitzgerald going berserk. While the cameraman went about his business, the linesman would of course be going about his: running up and down the sideline, following the game and waving his flag when required.

But somehow, week after week, the linesman would end up standing right in front of Camera 3, blocking close-ups of the action.

Bill on talkback: Tadhg, Tadhg (the late, great Tadhg de Brún, the floor manager).

Tadhg on walkie-talkie: Yes, Bill?

Bill: Will you tell that linesman to sit down or at least stop standing in front of our camera?

Tadhg: The linesman? (*Winking at me.*)

Bill: Yes Tadhg. The fella dressed in black.

Tadhg: Leave it to me, Bill.

Tadhg would immediately sit down beside me. So I'd ask: 'Are you going to say anything to the linesman?'

'I am in my arse.'

*

On the weekend of the All-Ireland finals in September, Kilmacud Crokes GAA Club in Stillorgan host a most wonderful event: the All-Ireland hurling and football club 7s. I had always wanted Kilmurry Ibrickane to take part in this tournament. I felt passionately that playing clubs like Bryansford in Co. Down, Errigal Ciaran in Co. Tyrone and Ballymun Kickhams from Dublin – to name just three – would be a wonderful learning experience for our players, who, in the normal course of events, wouldn't get the chance to play against clubs of this calibre. In 1994, I got a call to say that our application had finally been successful. We had made the cut and were in the 7s for the very first time. I was thrilled.

The team stepped up their training programme ahead of the tournament, and then, one evening, I got a call from my great friend Michael 'Moose' Talty, who was chairman of the club. He surprised me by asking if I'd be available to play on the day. I said that I'd be delighted, and I was. I was down to present *Gaelic Stadium* that morning, but this was usually recorded early, and by twelve noon at the latest I'd be free to go. I figured I'd make it out to Stillorgan, which is only down the road from Donnybrook, in plenty of time. On the Friday, Moose rang me again to make sure I was still OK to play, and to remind me that I needed to have a pair of white togs with red trim, which is what we wore with our red and green jerseys. I was driving from Dalkey into Donnybrook the following day when I thought of the togs, so I pulled up across the road from a shopping centre. As I ran up the steps into the building, one of them came loose under my foot. I heard a snap and went flying forwards towards the sliding doors.

I will never forget the pain, and, like everyone who has ever fallen in public, I was also severely embarrassed. I tried to get up quickly, but I realized that I couldn't. I knew from years of playing that this injury was neither an ankle twist nor a sprain. I told myself that I would walk it off, but as I got gingerly to my feet, I realized that the injury was not on the side of the ankle, but at the back. It was the Achilles tendon. I was sure of it. I dragged myself up and I will admit I shed a few tears because in my heart I knew that I wouldn't be playing with the lads later that day.

Silly, I know, but it would have meant a lot to me. I had given up playing football in 1992 to concentrate on my career. This was the year before we won the Clare senior championship, and while I was delighted that we had won, I was heartbroken that I hadn't been a part of it. The truth was that with all the travelling I had to do in my new job, I just couldn't give the right level of commitment to the team. I saw the 7s in '94 as a chance to wear the jersey again and just maybe rekindle that dream.

I got the white shorts with the red trim and limped into RTÉ. The minute the recording was over, I hobbled to the car and drove to Stillorgan, but my right foot was now throbbing and swollen. I grabbed my bag out of the car and as I headed to the narrow gate leading out to the playing fields, I saw a little hut with a sign over the door: 'Doctor'. I knocked and the door was opened by Dr Pat Duggan, the Dublin football doctor at the time. Great, I thought, he'll sort me out.

But within seconds, Pat confirmed my worst fear. A ruptured Achilles tendon. There was no question of playing. He told me I needed to go straight to St Vincent's hospital. I was heartbroken. Despite Dr Pat's recommendations, I stayed to watch Kilmurry play their games before I headed to A&E in St Vincent's.

It was late afternoon by the time I was X-rayed and had seen a doctor. Suddenly, playing football became the least of my worries. In my first year with the sports department, I was assigned to be the sideline reporter for the All-Ireland football final between Dublin and Down the following day. And I was also down to be the reporter in the winners' hotel on the Sunday night. But now a nurse told me that I would probably have to stay in and have surgery. I remember saying, in my best John McEnroe impersonation, 'You can't be serious!' The minute the nurse left me, I thought about doing a runner. Head for the car, do the gig and come back on Monday if I had to.

Just as I was about to do a limping 100-metre dash, a new doctor appeared. He introduced himself as Dr Aiden Devitt and explained that because it was a Saturday afternoon, there was no chance of getting the surgery done until Monday or Tuesday, and that he would have to find a bed for me. As I was digesting this news, he told me he was from Moy just outside Miltown Malbay. This, I felt, was a good omen, so I explained that I had to be in Croke Park the following day, and asked if there was any way he could bandage me up and let me off? He said that my injury was too serious, and that he couldn't release me, but added that he would ask his consultant what he thought.

I didn't hold out much hope at that stage, but when Dr Devitt eventually returned, he said, 'You're a lucky man. My consultant knows you, so I'm going to bandage you up and let you go, but you are to be back here on Monday morning for surgery.'

I was delighted, and I asked who the consultant was.

'Mr Kevin O'Rourke.'

'I don't know any Kevin O'Rourke,' I said.

'But you might know his brother,' said Dr Aiden.

'Who's that?'

'Colm O'Rourke.'

'Sweet Jesus! Thank God for Colm O'Rourke!'

Only for Colm O'Rourke, his orthopaedic surgeon brother Kieran and a good word from Dr Aiden, I wouldn't have made it to the All-Ireland football final in my first year working full-time for RTÉ.

My entire right leg was put into a heavy plaster, which was about as awkward as it sounds. The following day, twenty-four hours after had I ruptured my Achilles tendon, I scrambled out of a taxi on Jones Road and hobbled into Croke Park on the crutches that I would have for the next three months.

All-Ireland final days are both incredibly busy and incredibly exciting days for everyone working on the radio and TV coverage. Typically, there would be interviews with former All-Ireland winners to get their thoughts on the chances of the teams in the match that afternoon. We would go down O'Connell Street to meet the fans outside the Gresham Hotel, or Drumcondra to talk to those outside Quinn's pub. It's their smiles that I won't forget, the horns that would deafen you, the questions that I would be asked: 'What do you think, Marty? Who'll win?'

When they asked this, I would always ask, 'Where are ye from, lads?'

'Down.'

Then I'd say, as straight-faced as possible, 'I have thought about this in some detail, lads, and I am absolutely certain that Down will win today.'

The response was always the same. A massive roar of approval. 'Go on Marty, ye boyo! You know your football!'

Then we'd move location and find a group of Dublin fans, who'd ask the same question.

'Marty, go on. Tell us who's going to win, you mad culchie.'

'I have thought about this in some detail, lads, and I am absolutely certain [pause for effect] that Dublin will win today.'

The response of course would be deafening. They'd break into a chorus of 'Come on ye boys in blue, come on ye boys in blue . . .'

Just what we needed for the camera.

Anyway, thanks to the ongoing redevelopment of Croke Park, the crowd in 1994 was one of the smallest crowds ever to attend a final. Only the lower tier of the Cusack stand was complete and the official attendance was given as 58,684; about 22,000 less than normal.

I had some good friends on that Dublin team: Keith Barr, Jim Gavin, Dessie Farrell, Mick Galvin and Charlie Redmond.

But I also had friends in Down, who were the victors on the day, on a scoreline of 1–12 to 0–13. One of my favourite places in Northern Ireland is Rostrevor, Co. Down. It lies at the foot of Slieve Martin on the shores of Carlingford Lough near Warrenpoint. The Kilbroney River flows gently through the village and the lush Rostrevor Forest stands nearby. They'll tell you in Down that this is God's country. Pete McGrath, the All-Ireland winning manager in 1994, has told me many of the stories linked to the area. The bell of Bronach in the church dates from around 900 AD, and was found among the branches of an oak tree that had stood in the churchyard until it was felled by a storm some time in the late 1800s. As you come into Rostrevor from Warrenpoint, you'll see a row of small, picturesque semi-detached cottages on the left-hand side. This is St Colman's Gardens, where Pete

McGrath lives. Pete was a teacher in St Colman's College in Newry when I got to know him first, and we quickly established a great friendship. In the months leading up to the '94 final, we filmed a gruelling training session with Pete and the team in Rostrevor, and I got to know many of the Down players: Wee James McCartan, Ross Carr, Mickey Linden, Michael Magill and D. J. Kane, who captained the team. I didn't realize what great company goalkeeper Neil Collins was until twenty-five years later when we celebrated the anniversary of their historic win with a great night in Newry in 2019. Neil saved a penalty off the boot of Charlie Redmond in the final, and that night, Charlie, to his great credit, travelled to Newry to meet Neil and the Down lads once again for hours of banter and craic.

The Down team that had won the All-Ireland in 1991 lost to Derry in 1992. Worse was to come the following year, at a game dubbed 'The Massacre at the Marshes', when Down lost again to Derry on a scoreline of 3–11 to 0–9. Derry would go on to win the All-Ireland that year. The following May, the two teams faced up to each other once again in the Ulster quarter-final in Celtic Park in Derry. Playing in their own backyard, the Oak Leaf county were the hottest of favourites.

Down almost never got to the game. As the team bus travelled through the Sperrin Mountains, the bus driver collapsed over the wheel. Luckily, Terry Lalor, who was sitting in the front seat, had spotted him wavering a little and leaped from his seat to grab the wheel as the man slumped forward. Terry managed to get his foot to the brake and bring the bus to a safe stop as the players helped the bus driver on to the floor. They thought about calling an ambulance but decided they would be quicker to keep driving to Derry, so Terry Lalor took control. The bus driver was brought to Altnagelvin Hospital in Derry, while the Down team concentrated on the challenge before them in Celtic Park. There, they dethroned the All-Ireland champions with a scintillating performance. That victory earned the team an Ulster semi-final meeting against Monaghan. The night before that clash, two members of the loyalist paramilitary organization, the UVF, entered the Heights Bar in Loughinisland and shot six people dead with assault rifles. It was horrific. Loughinisland is the home club of Down footballer Gary Mason. In those days, as Pete would say himself, they were nearly anaesthetized to violence.

Down went on to beat Monaghan, then Tyrone in the Ulster final. They beat Cork in the All-Ireland semi-final, before securing the biggest prize in football and beating the Dubs on the third Sunday in September.

Conor Deegan picked up a nasty knee injury late in the game and was brought to the Mater hospital for treatment. In A&E, he found himself in a bed beside a fanatical Down supporter who had tried to climb the fence in Croke Park at the final whistle, but somehow managed to get himself entirely entangled upside down in the wire, and had sustained a broken ankle. He couldn't believe his luck when Deegan arrived in beside him, and immediately began pleading for Conor's jersey. To shut him up, the Downpatrick man gave him his togs and socks, leaving him lying in the bed with nothing on bar his jocks, his Down jersey and a smile.

My job on the night of the All-Ireland finals was always one of my favourite gigs of the year: the winners' hotel. The tensions of the day have dissipated, the families, wives and girlfriends are out in force and it finally begins to sink in that the county's dreams have come true.

One particular interview I did that night must have looked rather strange. Conor Deegan had been discharged from the Mater and was now using crutches like myself. It must have looked as if James McCartan was the presenter because he was the only one of the three of us that was able to stand on his own two feet. Two had played in an All-Ireland football final and were winning their second All-Ireland medals in three years. The other lad was me. No All-Ireland medal to show for myself but relieved to be there and to have got through the day unscathed.

Early the following morning, I checked into St Vincent's hospital, where my ruptured Achilles tendon was operated on by Kieran O'Rourke. I particularly remember the great care and professionalism of the medical team – especially the nurses. Whatever they're paid, they deserve every penny and much more.

For the next three months I manoeuvred, or should I say struggled, between Dublin and Clare. I couldn't drive, and travelling anywhere by train or bus was an ordeal, especially getting on and off. The gap between the platform and the lower step of the train was often far too wide for comfort. It took quite a while for me to find the easiest way to board and disembark, and I learned a new respect for wheelchair users, and anyone who has to negotiate public transport with a disability. It made me value what I had.

My first year working full-time in RTÉ Sport had been both hugely exciting and hugely varied. By Christmas, I was off the crutches and was looking forward to 1995. Little did I know what lay in store. Clare, Loughnane, Dalo, Fitzy and the gang were about to move centre stage. The Banner roar was about to be heard.

11. On a Clare Day

In the early hours of January 4th, 1996, I was travelling on icy roads from home in West Clare to Shannon Airport to meet Brendan Frawley, who was the RTÉ cameraman in Limerick at the time. We were going to see the Clare hurlers heading away on holidays. The final chapter in a remarkable year.

Apart from Jim McInerney from Tulla, Ken Morrissey from Clarecastle and Cyril Lyons from Ruan, the rest of the Clare squad were bachelors, and many of them were bringing either their long-term or their newly acquired girlfriends with them on their team holiday. No Clare team had travelled abroad as All-Ireland champions before. There was a buzz of excitement as everyone gathered at check-in with management and Clare county board officials.

The year 1995 had been an unforgettable one. It was the year the people of Ireland voted to allow divorce following a referendum, the ban on the sale of *Playboy* magazine had been lifted and the Prince of Wales had visited Dublin for the first time. John Bruton was Taoiseach and Mary Robinson was President of Ireland.

Dublin had won the football but the real sporting story was Clare hurling. The Banner had won Munster for the first time in sixty-three years and the All-Ireland for the first time since 1914. That's a gap of eighty-one years. Clare had been awarded eight All-Stars and Brian Lohan declared Hurler of the Year. It was all simply magical. This was dreamland.

The attitude at airports was different back then. The

security people at Shannon welcomed us warmly and allowed us out on to the tarmac, and even on to the plane. Manager Ger Loughnane spotted me as he took his seat at the back. He gave that Loughnane laugh: 'Ha ha ha, well, Marty, are you coming with us?'

'Sadly, not today.'

Brendan was right behind me with the camera, and we were closely attached by a short microphone lead as we shuffled down the aisle to Ger.

'Why did ye decide to go to Thailand?' I asked him.

'Well now,' says Ger, looking around, 'it's like this, Marty. We wanted to go somewhere where they knew absolutely nothing about hurling. So it was a clear choice. It was either Thailand or Tipperary. So we're going to Thailand. Ha ha ha.'

For me, the Clare hurling journey began three years previously in Semple Stadium, Thurles on July 15th, 1992. I was commentating on the Munster under-21 hurling final, a match which Clare lost to Waterford on a scoreline of 0–17 to 1–12. It was a Waterford team that contained Tony Browne, Johnny Brenner, Paul Flynn, Ken McGrath and Fergal Hartley. It was a great game of hurling and not alone did the Déise win the provincial title, they went on to beat Offaly in the All-Ireland later that year. I became friends with these and many other Waterford players as they graduated to the senior ranks: guys like Dan Shanahan, John Mullane and Stephen O'Keeffe. Maybe it's because I have a load of cousins in Tramore, but I do love the Waterford crowd, their great attitude and their love of hurling.

Despite the fact that they lost, I immediately recognized the potential of that Clare team. It included goalkeeper Davy Fitzgerald, full back Brian Lohan and corner back Brian

Quinn. Colin Lynch was at centrefield and Jamesie O'Connor was wing forward.

Ger Loughnane brought Brian Lohan home that night. Lohan was convinced he would not play for the county again, as Sean Daly had scored five points off him. The night after that match, the Clare county board met and, without leaving any time for reflection or to get some perspective on the team's performance, sacked Loughnane both from his position as under-21 manager and also as a selector with the Clare senior team. It was, to say the least, a disgraceful decision.

Before long, Loughnane was back as a selector with the Clare senior team, which was now being managed by Len Gaynor. Years later, he would tell the *Irish Times* that he believed he only got the selector's job because they couldn't get anyone else. At the time, he thought that it would take three years to develop and gel the team. He felt they had some rough edges and greenness: 'I couldn't wait to work the living daylights out of those fellas.' And he soon got his chance, being appointed senior manager for the 1995 league and championship after Gaynor stepped down. He set out his stall and brought Tony Considine and Mike McNamara from Scariff on board.

Many people forget that Ger Loughnane had been involved in twelve Munster finals as a player and selector at various levels down the years, and that he'd lost every single one of them. Yet his belief, passion and spirit were unquenchable. He loved Clare. He loved hurling. He was Loughnane before he became Loughnane. That might seem a strange statement but people around Feakle, his home place, will know what I mean. The Loughnanes were good people, but beautifully obstinate, focused and seldom wrong. That was the DNA. Ger Loughnane was and is a born leader. Like him, love him or loathe him, you can't ignore him.

The Banner got to the national hurling league final against Kilkenny and lost again. Having also lost the Munster finals of 1993 and 1994, most people saw this as yet another blow to the team and their confidence. To all appearances, it looked like it was game over.

Loughnane, McNamara and Considine knew they had three or four good players in the panel who hadn't played in the league final but who were showing well in training. They believed that with coaching, Ollie Baker, Fergal Hegarty, Stephen McNamara and Fergie Tuohy would contribute significantly to the Clare cause.

Most managers, after losing a league final to Kilkenny, would congratulate the opposition. Most managers would say that Kilkenny were the benchmark to which the rest of us must aspire. But Loughnane, in his post-match interview, went one step further. He predicted that Clare would win the Munster hurling championship. A championship the county hadn't won since 1932. Did I say 'game over'? Correction: it was game on.

There is no manager that I know of before or since then that would be courageous enough to say what Loughnane said. It was then that the country learned what we all knew in Clare. Loughnane had balls.

Just over 14,000 supporters were at the Gaelic Grounds in Limerick to see Clare defeat Cork in the 1995 Munster semi-final. Seanie McMahon's collar-bone injury after fifty-five minutes was a huge blow. Clare had already used up their three substitutes, which meant that though he could barely move his arm, Seanie had to keep playing. He was moved to corner forward where somehow he managed to win a line ball. As the ball dropped in, his club-mate from St Joseph's Doora Barefield, Ollie Baker, arrived to smash the ball past Ger Cunningham in the Cork goal.

Clare were in the Munster final. But was there any great excitement in the Banner? No. Two Munster final defeats and the loss in the league final had drained the county of confidence. But among the players, however, there was belief, belief in the Loughnane doctrine. They were calm, they were relaxed. While most of the county had given up, they knew what they were capable of.

On July 9th, 1995, Clare hurling changed for ever. Davy Fitzgerald's brilliant penalty just before the break, followed by his high-speed dash back to his own goal, is now an iconic moment in hurling history. P. J. O'Connell, better known as 'Fingers', did an outstanding job on one of my favourite hurlers, Limerick's Ciarán Carey, and scored four points from play. Jamesie O'Connor also scored four from play, with a further two from placed balls on a day when Ollie Baker overshadowed both Mike Houlihan and Sean O'Neill.

Matthew McMahon, who I had asked to help me out when I was appointed news editor of Clare FM in 1989, was the commentator for the station that day, along with John Minogue and Michael Gallagher. Matthew couldn't help but get emotional. Just after Davy Fitzgerald made a fine save down at the Killinan end, he said, 'Oh Jesus, Mary and Joseph, how are we going to keep going?'

And when things were getting even more tense: 'The cigarettes are being lit here in the commentary box, the lads are getting anxious. It's a line ball down there to Clare and who's to take it? Will ye put em out, lads? Ye'll feckin choke me!'

And at the final whistle, after Clare had won, Matthew was

almost speechless with disbelief. 'It's all over. Clare are . . . Jeessus!'

And it's no wonder it was hard to say. Nobody had said it in sixty-three years. Clare were Munster hurling champions.

Even now, as a Clareman, it's very hard to explain it. For decades it was what Clare people dreamt about. The team of the 1970s should have won a Munster championship. The national hurling league successes of 1977 and 1978 had brought great joy and hope only to have the county's dreams shattered once again in Munster finals, by a Cork team of outstanding players, men like Jimmy Barry-Murphy, Charlie McCarthy, Ray Cummins, Seanie O'Leary, Tom Cashman and Dermot McCurtain. And there was always drama when Clare was involved. They still talk about Jim Power being sent off for head-butting Ray Cummins in the 1977 Munster final in Semple Stadium. It happened just before half-time and the Banner never recovered from being reduced to fourteen players. That same day, a group of thieves wearing balaclavas robbed £25,000 of gate receipts from the old stand while the game was going on. That Clare team, of Seamus Durack, Jim Power, Jackie O'Gorman, Sean Hehir, Sean Stack, Mick Moroney, Johnny Callinan, Colm Honan, Jimmy McNamara, Martin McKeogh, Pat and Enda O'Connor and of course Ger Loughnane himself was outstanding.

Truthfully, the Munster title was all we wanted in 1995: to win Munster just like the Clare footballers had done three years previously. It was like finally getting to the peak of Mount Everest. The view from the top! There was an incredible feeling of success. We were finally rid of the burden of defeat. As far as most of us were concerned, it was mission accomplished. But that wasn't Loughnane's way. There was more to come.

In the meantime, there was partying to be done, and that's one thing we're really good at in Clare. The town of Ennis stayed awake all night. Fiddles and tin whistles could be heard on Abbey Street, on Parnell Street and on O'Connell Street. The Queens was the only nightclub in town and we rocked that place till 4 a.m., before finishing the night bleary-eyed, eating fish and chips on the kerb outside Enzo's.

For the following few days, the cup was brought to clubs and villages around the county. I filmed a piece for TV on the arrival of the Munster hurling championship trophy to Tulla. The Tulla pipe band marched down the hill, with young children holding the cup, and there outside Minogue's pub on a hot summer's evening the pipe band played and the people danced Clare sets on the street. Do you know what? As I think back now, it was absolutely heavenly. Ear-to-ear smiles, saffron and blue jerseys shimmering in the glorious sunshine, beads of sweat glistening on brows after giving it loads on the make-shift dancefloor, laughter reverberating around the streets.

Eventually, Loughnane called a halt to all such festivities, as there was now an All-Ireland semi-final against Galway to be played. It might be a strange thing to say but I never had any doubt that Clare would beat Galway in that match. The Banner totally respect their Connacht neighbours, but the reality is that the rivalry is not as fierce as it is between Clare and Limerick or Clare and Tipperary, so they didn't fear the Tribesmen in any way. The Banner had momentum, we had self-belief and an appetite for further glory. Over 54,000 people attended Croke Park on August 6th, 1995, as Clare wobbled a little but deservedly booked their place in the final with two goals from Ger 'Sparrow' O'Loughlin and one from Stephen McNamara, to beat Galway 3–12 to 1–13. Clare were in the All-Ireland final and the county went mad.

Mannequins dressed as Eric Cantona, the Manchester United footballer, and Dr Ian Paisley, the DUP leader, appeared in Ennis dressed in Clare jerseys. Signs hanging from their necks said 'Up the Banner!'

Kieran McDermott produced the song 'The Banner Roar', which would become the anthem of a season that nobody will forget. Dysart's Dick Cronin penned the lyrics and Raise the Rafters played the Tulla reel in the middle of the song. At the Rocks Bar in Ennis, they held auditions to find bodhrán players, and there was no shortage of volunteers, some of whom had never seen or held a bodhrán before. This was long before either CDs or downloads, so Kieran McDermott ran off 200 cassette tapes and brought them around to local shops for distribution. They sold out in days. The lads then took a punt and got 2,000 more done. As Kieran told the *Clare Echo*, he had just got married, had no money and now he was chancing it on a cassette tape! Thankfully, all 2,000 sold like hot cakes.

Their appearance on *Up for the Match*, which was presented by Liam O'Murchú back then, was hilarious. A wide-angled lens makes the studio in Donnybrook look a lot bigger than it actually is. The producers told the group they could only bring twelve of their many bodhrán players. RTÉ went apoplectic when nearly forty band members showed up.

In the week leading up to the final, I filmed Bishop Willie Walsh, who had taught me physics for my Leaving Cert in St Flannan's, quietly praying for a Clare victory, despite the fact that parts of Offaly (our opponents in the final) were in his diocese of Killaloe. Bishop Willie was a native of Tipperary but had been a Clare hurling selector, so his slight inclination towards the saffron and blue would surely be forgiven by God. In Sixmilebridge, Pat Fitzgerald, Davy's father and county secretary, was run off his feet fielding requests for tickets. I went around the county filming the madness as Clare flags, bunting and head gear were displayed on every street corner or bush, and old cars were done up, re-sprayed and pushed to the crossroads where they could be seen by all and sundry. There mustn't have been a can of blue or saffron paint left in the county.

The 1995 All-Ireland hurling final was played on September 3rd. At the time, Croke Park was half new and half old. The new Cusack stand with its shiny blue and grey seats had just been unwrapped. The upper deck alone had capacity for 27,000 people. The Hogan stand meanwhile was just as it had been for years. The dressing-rooms at the time were down where the Hogan met the Canal end, and the teams ran out on to the pitch from the tunnel which was located right in that corner. Anyone who has seen archive footage will know that so many great teams of the past had run out on the hallowed turf from that same tunnel.

The match referee was Dickie Murphy from the Rapparees Club in Wexford. He and his wife Jackie have been close personal friends since that time, though I've told him several times that if Clare hadn't won the All-Ireland in '95, it's unlikely our friendship would have blossomed at all. The attendance was 65,092, the atmosphere electric, the tension unbearable.

Daithí Regan of Offaly got the first point, but Clare, despite the lack of All-Ireland final experience, never panicked. They stayed calm, stayed focused. Michael Duignan scored a goal that Davy Fitzgerald should probably have saved. The shot trickled over the line to give Offaly a half-time lead of 1–6 to 0–5. I was sideline reporter at the time, so I was hovering just outside the tunnel as the teams trooped off the pitch. The body language said it all. Offaly were walking tall. Davy was clearly disappointed at having conceded a soft goal, but Anthony Daly, Seanie McMahon and Jamesie O'Connor were sending out positive signals, giving words of encouragement and clapping colleagues on the back.

Part of my remit was to grab a manager or selector on the way back out on to the pitch, to ask if they had made any changes to personnel or to the plan during the break. You would very rarely get valuable information, especially on All-Ireland final day, because people are under ferocious pressure, but I was always grateful for any little nugget of information. Once in a blue moon, you might get a beauty of a response. That day, Ger Loughnane was the last man out from the Clare dressing-room. He strolled out on to the pitch, wisps of blond hair blowing in the breeze, his white An Clár shirt clearly drenched with sweat.

I pounced. 'What did you say to your team at half-time?'

'Well, we haven't played as well as we could have in the first half, however we've been against the wind, so now the game is going to be won in the next thirty-five minutes, and I have just asked them to give their last ounce now for Clare in the next thirty-five minutes.'

As he moved away, I asked one more question.

'Do you think ye are going to do it?'

'We are going to do it,' came the immortal reply, 'we're going to do it.'

That little cameo between Loughnane and myself has been resurrected and shown time and again on various platforms down the years.

I honestly think these half-time interviews, which were later discontinued by RTÉ, should return to our coverage, especially for provincial and All-Ireland finals. You won't always get something worthwhile, but occasionally, you'll strike something special and memorable.

Offaly proved what great hurlers they were, not just on this day but in years to come. In the second half, Johnny Pilkington scored the Faithful county's second goal to make it 2–7 to 0–10. Though Clare weren't playing with the same fluidity as they had against Limerick and Galway, they never gave up. Ollie Baker had a horse of a game in centrefield and Seanie McMahon was fantastic at No. 6, while Fergie Tuohy had the game of his life, scoring four points from play. Like most teams who win championships, a little bit of luck is needed, and it fell to Clare with four minutes to go. A high dropping ball came off either the crossbar or the Offaly keeper's hurley, and Eamon Taffe was on hand to strike the ball to the back of the net. Clare now led by a point, but only for a very short period as Johnny Dooley quickly equalized. The tension was almost unbearable. Every puck out was now a potential funeral, every touch of the sliotar could mean joy or despair. It was time for leadership, and up stepped Clare captain Anthony Daly. Dalo pointed a 65 with time almost up, and Jamesie O'Connor added another from a free.

As the match drew to a close, I stood where I had watched the game, outside the tunnel, and looked up at the faces of Clare people – so many of whom were crying with happiness and disbelief. Was this really happening? Were Clare about to be crowned All-Ireland champions for the first time since 1914? Next thing Dickie Murphy blew the long whistle and the Croke Park pitch was submerged in a sea of saffron and blue. I cried. We all cried. Liam MacCarthy was coming to Clare for the winter for the first time since 1914. Just think about that. Planet Earth had experienced two World Wars, Neil Armstrong had walked on the Moon and we Irish had

fought for our independence. Eighty-one long years had passed. Clare people had lived and died without witnessing this. This was history happening before our eyes.

Anthony Daly's speech was up there with Joe Connolly's in 1980.

'In Clare, we love our traditional music, but we love our hurling as well. There has been a missing person, and that person is Liam MacCarthy.'

So much time has passed and yet I am emotional, tearful even, as I write this. The feeling never leaves you.

The winners' hotel is a crucial part of All-Ireland final

night for RTÉ Sport, because it's a great opportunity to meet the players and the people involved. I found it especially poignant to be among my own people on this most historic of nights. Michael Lyster was presenting from the studio, while Ger Canning, who has strong West Clare connections, and I were dispatched to the Berkeley Court Hotel. I remember having the craic with Brian and Frank Lohan about who was the boss, and if Brian gives out to his brother if he isn't doing his job. I also interviewed Davy Fitzgerald, his father Pat, and Bishop Willie Walsh. To end our contribution from the hotel, Clare selector Tony Considine sang 'My Lovely

Rose of Clare', just as he had done on the steps of the Hogan stand earlier that day.

Clare people don't need much of an excuse to party but now we had the most legitimate reason in the world to go crazy. The following afternoon the team bus headed to Dublin Airport with a Garda escort. People gathered on the route with Clare flags and banners as the team sped along.

We accompanied the team on the short, packed flight to Shannon. Ger Loughnane sat with his wife Mary. Sean O'Leary from Inagh, who won a Harty Cup with Ennis CBS and worked in Croke Park, was on board, as was the legendary commentator Mícheál Ó Muircheartaigh. Kieran McDermott sang 'The Banner Roar' as we whizzed through the skies before touching down in Clare. As Davy Fitzgerald would often say, 'This is unreal, boy.'

Getting through the terminal building was difficult, because an army of supporters, who had been dancing Clare sets all afternoon, surged forward on seeing Anthony Daly and the Liam MacCarthy Cup. From the terminal, we boarded an open-top double-decker bus just as dusk was falling. I remember seeing Jackie Gorman, one of the greats of Clare hurling, and a member of those great Clare teams that won back-to-back national league titles in the seventies. Cars were parked perpendicular to the road out of Shannon and families stood on bonnets of cars cheering and waving flags as the bus passed by.

On board the bus, video man Joe Fenwick, a native of Mayo who lived in Scariff, was having panic attacks as hurlers tripped over microphone leads, or a tape change was needed just when something exciting was happening.

It was cold on top of the bus as we made our way north, but our hearts were warm. The sky was still bright, with a luminous moon and some stars twinkling overhead.

When we got to Newmarket-on-Fergus, the crowds rushed towards us and the bus slowed almost to a standstill outside Dermot Halpin's garage. One lad had somehow managed to climb up the stop sign and perched there wrapped in a Clare flag and a Clare hat. As we passed, the hurlers waved from the top deck and your man sitting up on the stop sign started crying uncontrollably.

In Newmarket-on-Fergus, the makeshift stage was the back of a lorry, and there among the crowd was Liam Griffin, the Wexford manager at the time. His father was from the Banner county and at one point in his career he had got a call up to the Clare under-21 panel. I remember Liam had a brief conversation with Ger Loughnane as he got down off the stage. 'It could be you next year,' said Ger.

The homecoming to Newmarket-on-Fergus had a profound effect on Liam Griffin. He drove to Clare to experience the atmosphere because he knew it would be special. And as he drove back to Wexford that night, he went through his own Wexford squad, from goalkeeper Damien Fitzhenry to Liam Dunne to George O'Connor, Martin Storey and Tom Dempsey, and realized that man for man he had as good a team as Loughnane. He spent the following day on the phone, ringing every hurler that he wanted in his squad for the 1996 championship. And incredibly, twelve months later, on September 1st, 1996, Wexford were doing the same thing as Clare, celebrating and dancing at the crossroads as they beat Limerick in the All-Ireland final, to win their sixth title and first since 1968.

From Newmarket-on-Fergus, the next stop was Clarecastle, and if ever a village loved its sport and its hurling in particular, then this was it: magpie country.

Johnny Callinan had been the local hero, and another local

legend, Paschal Russell, had done his thing for club and county in the 70s. Now the club could boast that they provided the All-Ireland winning captain. Anthony Daly was understandably emotional as he looked down on a sea of people waiting for the Magpie Six, the six great Clarecastle hurlers: Dalo, Sparrow O'Loughlin, Fergie Tuohy, Alan Neville, Ken Morrissey and Jonathan Clancy, whose father Michael was from Mullagh and had won a Clare under-14 football championship medal with me in 1972. Bonfires toasted us, horns blew our ears off, and there was no leaving the parish until the Clarecastle boys got off the bus and were carried through their village.

It's estimated that 40,000 fans greeted the Clare team in Ennis that night, and as we looked out from the stage it was a sea of people wearing saffron and blue or waving flags of

the same colour. Despite the lateness of the team's arrival, nobody complained. This was history and we were living and breathing it. As long as I live, I will never forget Ennis on that Monday. Pubs stayed open all night and music poured out of every second one on O'Connell Street, Abbey Street and Parnell Street. Nobody closed. The Gardaí were fantastic. They allowed everybody to enjoy the night and kept a watchful eye just in case there was a hint of hassle. But there was none. In the disco in the Queens, Blur, Take That and Boyzone made way for Kieran McDermott and 'The Banner Roar', which was played over and over again. In smoke-filled pubs, we wondered would Clare ever be the same again? Would we ever recover?

I was so tired that I couldn't face driving the twenty odd miles home to West Clare, so I decided to move my car to the corner of the Abbey Street car park just as the first rays of the sun appeared in the east. I put down the seat, closed my eyes and had the finest of sleeps till 10.30 on the Tuesday morning. When I woke there was a young fella asleep on the bonnet of my car. Clearly us Clare lads can sleep anywhere.

A month later I got a call from Pat Fitzgerald, who asked me to meet himself, Ger Loughnane and officers of the Clare county board to discuss how we would celebrate our All-Ireland victory officially, and how we were going to present the team with their medals.

The meeting was in the West County Hotel in Ennis, which I was more familiar with as the venue for Club Oasis – now closed, sadly. I bopped many a night away in Club Oasis, pretending to be cool and difficult to get. It was a strategy that never worked.

At the meeting, Ger Loughnane was adamant about one thing. The night would be about the players. This was noble of him, but the truth was he was the big attraction. The people of Clare didn't call him 'God' for nothing. In full flow, Ger was as good an orator as JFK or Barack Obama. That's not an exaggeration. And he didn't have an autocue. The words just flowed outwards to his captive audience. His one problem? Time. I used say to Ger, 'I'm giving you ten minutes to deliver your speech, is that enough?'

The reply was always the same. 'Not a problem, Marty, not a problem.'

Then he'd give a speech that lasted somewhere between forty and forty-five minutes, every single time.

To be fair, if Ger liked your ideas, he would back you 100 per cent, so I always enjoyed working on gigs for him. I was at that meeting to figure out how we could stage an event to match the magnitude of what the Clare team had achieved.

'This needs to be brilliant now, Marty,' said Ger. 'No messin'. Think big! Ha ha ha!'

My proposal would have to be creative, and it would have to encompass video packages, speeches and a touch of light entertainment too.

In the lead-up to the event, I called my great friend Matt Purcell, who I'd worked with in Clare FM. I knew he would be honoured to be involved because not alone was he a Clareman, he was a Feakle man, and a neighbour of the Loughnanes.

My buddies from Limerick and Tipperary, Errol Reeves and Ian Hourican, were next on my hit list. They would provide the facility to play the video tapes, or VTs, on the big screens dotted around the room. Tom Walsh from Bruff was brought in to do the lighting, and with Tom, both the craic and the lighting were always of a very high standard. When he swung like Tarzan on his lighting rigs, I often worried that he would fall, but Tom always knew what he was doing.

The cameramen were all Clare lads: Paschal Brooks, Dave Fenwick and Noel Vaughan, who was a former student of mine.

There was so much wonderful footage to choose from; each VT had to be different. My favourite was the homecoming, which started off outside Croke Park with a Clare fan taking out his false teeth and trying to do 'The Banner Roar' only to be interrupted by a young guy coming out of nowhere to look down the lens of the camera and shout 'Up the Banner'. He, it would turn out, was Colm Collins, who is today the Clare football manager and father of Sean and Podge Collins, who would win All-Ireland hurling medals in 2013.

I visited the West County Hotel on my own several times to get an idea of the layout of the building, in order to make my proposal to the Clare county board delegation and Ger Loughnane. I believed that we needed to start with a 'wow'. A piper parading the players into the room would not be good enough.

I clearly remember the meeting with Ger and the county board at which I presented my ideas. I suggested we cut a hole in the ceiling of the ballroom and bring the players down from what was essentially an attic area on an Aer Lingus mobile passenger staircase, like those used on the tarmac at Shannon Airport to embark and disembark passengers. As soon as I explained all of this, silence descended on the room. Nobody would say anything until 'God' spoke.

Loughnane looked at me, his eyes sparkling. 'Fucking brilliant, Marty. Totally mad of course, but I love it. Can we do it?'

'Yes, we can.'

Mickey Lynch was the owner of the West County Hotel, but he was also a prominent builder. I'd always really liked him, and maybe too I had the slight advantage of having been in school in St Flannan with his son Seamus. The other positive was the relationship between the West County and the Clare county board. The hotel was the venue for county board meetings and other related GAA affairs. So we approached him and Mickey had no hesitation.

'Cut the hole,' he said.

The Aer Lingus mobile staircase was driven to Ennis by a group of Sixmilebridge lads who worked at the airport. We had thought that cutting the hole would be the big challenge, but actually, getting the staircase through the doors at the side of the ballroom turned out to be a bigger one. The doors had to be taken off, then the frames of the doors, then the air had to be let out of the tyres of the staircase. Eventually, it was squeezed through. Now we had to decorate it with saffron and blue cloth so it was totally encased and hidden from the 1,000 people who would be attending. I wanted to make sure that there'd be a sense of mystery and anticipation on the night.

Once the show began, we played the VT of the unbelievable year we'd had, just to get the audience into the mood, before introducing the All-Ireland champions to the room.

Cue fanfare! Smoke! Flashing lights! We gave it everything as the curtain rose and the players appeared overhead, then, to deafening applause, they came down the steps of the mobile staircase in a ballroom in a hotel in Ennis. They descended into a cauldron of emotion, as people shed tears of joy to see their loved ones: their sons, brothers, heroes descend from on high.

It was Hollywood, Clare style.

12. The Tide Turns

The following year was expected to be another great year for Ger Loughnane and his team, but Ciarán Carey's great catch from Davy Fitzgerald's puck out in the last few moments of the Munster semi-final on June 16th, and his subsequent scintillating, point-scoring run, ended the All-Ireland champions' reign. Limerick had some outstanding hurlers that year, men like goalkeeper Joe Quaid, Stephen McDonagh, David Clarke, Mark Foley, Mike Houlihan, Gary Kirby and the versatile T. J. Ryan, so it was no surprise that they went on to win Munster and get to the All-Ireland final.

Clare bounced back in 1997, the first championship played with the back-door system, beating Cork, Tipperary, Kilkenny and Tipperary again. To beat Tipp twice in the same championship was special from a Clare perspective, and to beat them in the All-Ireland final was even better. No All-Ireland for eighty-one years, and now we had two in three years.

I was sideline reporter again for the 1997 final. Croke Park was still under redevelopment at the time, and the dugouts for the Clare and Tipperary substitutes, officials and management had been relocated to the front of the new Cusack stand between the two 45-metre lines. There was no seat for either myself or the RTÉ floor manager Tadhg de Brún, so we threw ourselves down on the grass halfway between the two dugouts in order to keep a close eye on who would be coming on and off during the match. It was a wonderful day for Clare, who won by a point on a scoreline of 0–20 to 2–13, and yet it was a strange day too. On several occasions during that summer, I sensed something new and peculiar in the air, something I couldn't quite put my finger on. The attitude within the Clare camp – and maybe even the attitude to Clare outside the county – had changed, though perhaps it didn't change till that day, All-Ireland hurling final day, September 14th, 1997.

The official photograph of the Clare team taken moments before the start of the match is unique in that it includes sixteen players: the fifteen who had been named in the team during the week, plus an extra man at the end of the front row – Sixmilebridge's Niall Gilligan. As the two teams fell into line behind the Artane Band and the parade began, I saw Fergal Hegarty – who had been named in the team and stood for the photo between Conor Clancy and Ger O'Loughlin in the back row – head to the Clare dugout, while Niall Gilligan took up a spot just behind Anthony Daly in the parade. I ran

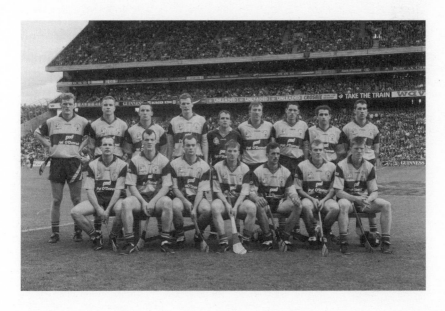

to the Clare dugout but Ger Loughnane roared at me to clear off. While he was watching the parade, I sneaked down again and talked to a county board official.

'Gilligan is starting,' I was told. 'Fergal Hegarty has the flu.'

This was said with a wink and a smile, so I knew it was a cock-and-bull story. Ger Canning was doing the match commentary. He handed down to me, so I gave a quick synopsis of what I had been told, describing it as sensational news.

Niall Gilligan went on to score three points, giving Tipperary defender Paul Shelly a torrid time. Gilligan's performance and the fact that Clare won meant that what happened to Fergal Hegarty was largely forgotten. It would turn out that Hegarty had been told during the week that though he wasn't starting, he should pose for the team photograph in order to keep the planned switch secret right up until the throw-in. To his credit, I don't think Fergal has ever spoken about this experience, but I never really liked that call.

Two benches had been placed in front of each dugout – one for Tipperary manager Len Gaynor and one for Ger Loughnane – in the hope that this might help to keep them from roaming. It didn't work. Loughnane was behind the goals as Jamesie O'Connor scored the winning point. The Clare manager was understandably on an adrenaline rush during the game, walking on to the pitch, patrolling the sideline as the play ebbed and flowed. At one stage I could see Clare were going to introduce a substitute so I sneaked down the sideline, keeping my head down so I wouldn't obstruct the view of those in the lower tier of the Cusack stand, or attract Loughnane's ire. I made it as far as county secretary Pat Fitzgerald at the corner of the dugout before Loughnane

turned and saw me. Despite the 65,575 people in attendance, I had no trouble hearing that distinctive Loughnane roar: 'Marty, what are you doing in there? Fuck off!'

The outburst brought an audible moan from those in the lower Cusack who had heard him, but this was not a time for discussion, so like a scalded cat I ran back to Tadhg de Brún. Though he couldn't help laughing, he shook his head. 'That was appalling.'

Pat Fitzgerald, to his great credit, passed me by as the substitution was being made and muttered discreetly who was going on and who was coming off.

Later that night on *The Sunday Game*, Eamon Cregan was critical, as is his right as an analyst, of the quality of the match. Tomás Mulcahy agreed that it wasn't the epic that Ger Loughnane had suggested it was earlier. In the winners' hotel – this time the Davenport on Merrion Street – Ger

Canning interviewed Loughnane, who responded live to Eamon Cregan's analysis.

'Today was a red letter day for Clare hurling as we won both the minor and senior All-Irelands, and I know we are after listening to a ten-minute whinge from Eamon Cregan.'

This was greeted by rapturous applause, and was, I think, a sign of things to come.

The following day, Loughnane told the media: 'I thought the analysis on RTÉ last night was totally unfair to both teams. It was totally inaccurate and nobody outside the man that made that analysis would have done anything like that. We all know in Clare that he doesn't like us. He made that clear on many occasions since being a player and a manager.'

He went on: 'He wasn't an appropriate person to make an analysis of that game because of other interests. He wasn't a neutral person. There should have been a neutral person. For us at the team reception, it took from the enjoyment of the night.'

In Loughnane's view, Eamon Cregan's analysis had to be answered. From the outside, it seemed that Ger was taking any criticism of the team personally, which is, I suppose, understandable when you have a close bond.

I think, however, that the change in atmosphere I had sensed in the run-up to the 1997 All-Ireland was now a tide slowly turning against Clare. The county was about to see its popularity ebb over the coming year.

The homecoming was as spectacular as it had been in '95. And then, at the All-Ireland medal presentation show two days after Christmas, we borrowed one of those carousels used to display cars in a showroom and used that to reveal the players. It worked brilliantly, and contributed to another unforgettable night. Our production values were improving, and our guests that night included Tommy Fleming, the Kilfenora Ceili Band, Sharon Shannon and the late Gerry Lynch.

If 1995 was ecstatically joyful for the people of Clare, then 1997 was probably more in the satisfying zone for players and supporters alike. Little did we know then that 1998 was going to be at the other end of the emotional spectrum. There would be drama and controversy, and at one point I would find myself dead smack in the middle of it. By the end of '98, most Clare people were exhausted. I actually believe that that great team was reaching its peak in 1998, but that everyone got distracted by things happening both on and off the pitch. There were replays, referees blowing early, referees not blowing enough, referees' reports, provincial council meetings, red cards, yellow cards, local radio rants, on-field demonstrations, overheard conversations and even high-court actions.

And then there was me and Colin Lynch's grandmother.

There was never any great rivalry between Clare and Waterford. The players come from similar stock, always pressing their noses up against the window and looking in at Cork, Tipperary and Kilkenny enjoying all the success.

But the Clare and Waterford players got to know each other in that Munster under-21 final in 1992, so every clash between the counties since then had a bit of an edge to it. The Munster final of 1998 saw the two teams meet again, and the match ended in a draw: 1–16 to 3–10.

In the replay, Referee Willie Barrett delayed the throw-in due to an unfortunate Munster council instruction that all officials had to be in their dugouts before the game began. This was neither realistic nor feasible, but while he was trying to implement the instructions, the four midfielders – Tony

Browne and Peter Queally for Waterford, Ollie Baker and Colin Lynch for Clare – started jostling each other, to put it mildly. This is quite normal, but the delay made the jostling a little more protracted and energetic than usual. When the ball was eventually thrown in, that strong physical element that you'll always get in a Munster final was deemed to have crossed the line.

Colin Lynch did pull a bit wildly, but he hit his own team-mate Ollie Baker more times than he hit Peter Queally or Tony Browne. And no player complained. This, after all, was the Munster championship. It's not for the fainthearted, and nor should it ever be. In any case, Clare won.

Willie Barrett is a very honourable man and always wrote up his report on Sunday nights before *The Sunday Game* so he couldn't be influenced by the analysis on the TV. On Monday morning he posted his report to the Munster council. He never mentioned Colin Lynch, which was a clear indication that the Clare midfielder had done no wrong in the referee's eyes. End of story, normally, but not this time. The Munster council retrospectively reported Lynch for striking with the hurley, an infraction which would ultimately lead to a three-month suspension. As a result, Colin missed the rest of the championship.

This was blatantly wrong. It seemed to be based on evidence supplied by some guy in the stand. Ger Loughnane went on Clare FM to give an interview that went on for an incredible ninety minutes, and included allegations that Loughnane ultimately had to withdraw.

It was around the same time that some anonymous Clare donor offered £10,000 to fight Lynch's case in the High Court. Wexford manager Liam Griffin came on RTÉ's *Morning Ireland* to talk about it.

'We should get hold of this guy and tell him to go away and cop himself on. We don't need fellas like that. If he has that kind of money, why doesn't he give it to us for the development of the under-age games? We don't need barristers at GAA meetings.'

Griffin was also critical of Loughnane's outburst. 'He's showing all the signs of a man under tremendous pressure. It's as if his ego, and that of his players and of every man from Clare, is on the line. And really it isn't.'

On the afternoon of Friday August 7th, 1998, Colin Lynch failed to secure a High Court injunction against the Munster council's games and activities committee. Lynch claimed that the committee had no jurisdiction on disciplinary matters and that it had proceeded unfairly against him. Mr Justice Kevin O'Higgins heard that during the replay Lynch had repeatedly struck Waterford player Tony Browne with his hurley. In the end, the judge ruled that the Munster council hadn't exceeded its jurisdiction.

O'Higgins said: 'There is no evidence relating to Mr Lynch's fears of being deprived of a fair hearing and there is existing legal authority that the courts must not interfere officiously in the affairs of private associations and must only do so to prevent or remedy matters of manifest injustice.'

The Munster council meeting that evening was held at the Limerick Inn. There was a huge media presence, as well as a big crowd of Clare supporters. The Clare delegation consisted of the chairman of the Clare county board, Robert Frost, secretary Pat Fitzgerald and Ger Loughnane, but there was no sign of Colin Lynch. Instead, he had sent his solicitor, Jim Nash, to represent him. The Munster council wouldn't allow Nash to stand in for Lynch. After the council refused to allow Loughnane to be part of the Clare delegation, Robert

Frost and Pat Fitzgerald declined an offer to hear the council's explanation for its decision. The Clare officers refused to tell the Munster council why Colin Lynch wasn't there unless Ger Loughnane was allowed into the meeting. The irony of all this was that the waiting media knew exactly why Colin wasn't there. Ger Loughnane had told us when he arrived that Colin couldn't be there because his grandmother was seriously ill.

I was part of that media group that night. The difference between me and my colleagues from the print media was that I was broadcasting live from outside the hotel on a TV programme called *Sideline View*, which was hosted by Des Cahill.

This is what Loughnane said on arrival at the Limerick Inn: 'Last Monday, Colin's grandmother, whose pride and joy Colin was, sadly had a stroke and unfortunately a few hours ago, she was taken off a life support machine. So you will understand that Colin cannot be here tonight. Whatever happens here tonight pales into insignificance [compared] to what has happened to his family over the last few weeks.'

So, a few minutes later, I stood in front of the camera and went live, telling the nation that sadly Colin Lynch's grandmother had died after coming off a life support machine. I sympathized with Colin Lynch and his family and gave an update about the Munster council meeting. I remember coming off air and taking out my earpiece, thinking to myself that I might go home to Clare tonight and call down to Lissycasey in the morning to sympathize with Colin personally. But then came the shocking news that Colin's grandmother had not died at all.

A member of the Lynch family had called RTÉ to tell them of my mistake. Glen Killane, who was the producer of the show, immediately picked up the phone and rang me. 'Marty,' he said, 'she's not dead at all.'

I froze on the spot. I could hardly breathe. As I write this over twenty years later, I can still feel the dismay. I was mortified. I was so embarrassed and so sorry that I had caused the Lynch family hurt and distress. And I wondered how the hell I had got it so wrong.

To his great credit, Des Cahill rang me and said I should try to meet the family. I had already made that decision and was in the car heading to the county hospital in Ennis.

Meanwhile, back at the Limerick Inn, Ger Loughnane, with his entourage of Clare supporters in tow, was thundering through the corridors of the hotel, roaring his head off.

'Where is Marty Morrissey? Where is Morrissey?' In the car park he confronted RTÉ Sport producer Maurice Reidy.

'Your station announced that Colin's grandmother had died tonight. That was never said to you. We said she was taken off a life support machine. It was an absolute disgrace that your station would put out a statement like that. Hasn't his family suffered enough? You have a lot to answer for. Nobody ever said she was dead. You have no respect for Clare. Most of all you have no respect for the Lynch family.'

While all that ranting was going on at the Limerick Inn, I arrived at the hospital worried sick. I parked near the back door, where the ambulances normally pull in, and found the Lynches just outside the main doors, drinking teas and coffees. I approached nervously but was so relieved that despite their worry and anxiety about their mother and grandmother, they accepted my apology and told me not to worry about it. Can you believe that incredible goodness and kindness? That's the Lynch family, that's Colin Lynch. I will never forget their warm welcome, their great forgiveness and incredible graciousness. They understood what had happened. You just can't beat good people.

Mary Ann Clohessy, Colin's grandmother, died a few days later. Unfortunately I never knew her, but by all accounts she was a lovely, kind woman. May she rest in peace.

The following week, Sean Moran of the *Irish Times* wrote this in his column: 'Everyone who heard the statement [by Ger Loughnane on his way into the hotel] assumed that she had passed away. In response Loughnane jumped up and strode through the hotel demanding: "Where's Morrissey?" In fact, the RTÉ man should have been heading in the opposite direction wanting to know "Where's Loughnane?"'

He went on: '. . . after Sunday's semi-final at Croke Park, [Loughnane] absolved Morrissey, who on Friday night had been distraught at his error and rushed to the hospital where the Lynch family were. Loughnane was reported as saying: "Now I wasn't entirely blameless either because when I made the statement going in, I should have said she was gone off her medication instead of saying she was gone off her machine."'

From 2011 to 2016 I was honoured to be assigned the RTÉ Radio 1 commentary on the All-Ireland hurling finals. Each year was different, each one unique, but the 2013 final was especially significant as it involved two counties with which I have very strong emotional ties: Cork, the county of my birth, and Clare, the county I call home. I remember the closing minutes of the drawn game as if it was yesterday.

It was September 8th, 2013. Kilkenny's D. J. Carey was my co-commentator on that afternoon in Croke Park. Clare looked to be on their way to All-Ireland glory, but Cork's spirit was unquenchable and they fought back magnificently to draw the game, then go one in front in injury time with a great Patrick Horgan point. With a single minute of injury time left, it looked like game over. Clare goalkeeper Patrick Kelly took the puck out quickly from the Hill 16 end, dropping it inside the Cork 65-metre line just in front of the Hogan, where it was gathered by Newtownshandrum's Cathal Naughton who went off on a brilliant diagonal run. Clare captain Pat Donnellan gave chase and eventually knocked the sliotar off his hurley. The ball came to Stephen Moylan, but his shot dropped short. Patrick Kelly was forced off his line and slightly to the left of his goalposts as the Cork forwards came rushing in. He gathered the sliotar and tried valiantly to get his clearance in but Luke Farrell gave chase, and putting tremendous pressure on the Inagh-Kilnamona man, he forced him to concede a sideline cut just outside the 20-metre line on the Cusack stand side. It looked all over. All Stephen Moylan had to do now was either put it over the bar or even send it wide. He did the latter, and that looked to be the final action of the 2013 championship.

All eyes were now on referee Brian Gavin. Would he blow the full-time whistle? Was there time for one more chance? One more effort from the Banner? Clare keeper Pa Kelly took the puck out as quickly as he could. The sliotar fell on the Cusack stand side. Clare's Pat O'Connor got it and hand-passed to Tony Kelly. Referee Brian Gavin almost got in the way as Kelly hand-passed to the only man available: corner back Domhnall O'Donovan from Clonlara, out on the sideline in front of the Cusack stand. Now just pause your memory there for one moment. Let me write this as a Clareman. Around Croke Park, and in every home in Clare, and in fact anywhere in the world where Clare people gathered, at that precise moment, they all said exactly what was going through my head.

'Ah Jaysus! Not Domhnall O'Donovan!'

Why wasn't it Tony Kelly, Podge Collins, John Conlon, Colin Ryan, Conor McGrath or Darach Honan? Any of them would have been a safer bet. It really was a case of ABOD: Anyone But O'Donovan! He was a great, tight-marking corner back, but he had never scored a point in the championship. Never.

Domhnall took the hand pass from Tony Kelly and took a few steps towards the Cork goalposts at the Davin end and then, from out there on the sideline, he let fly. The noise levels at GAA Headquarters rose off the scale as the Clonlara man sent the ball sailing over the bar from a ridiculously tight angle; the greatest pressure shot any hurler could have taken. It was a stunning point. So brave. It made him a hero for life.

Meanwhile, back on the radio I searched for words in my brain. There is no prepared script. You just have to react to what happens before your eyes. It's instinct. I rarely use bad language, and never in broadcasting. But in all honesty the first reaction in my head was, 'Holy fuck! Did Domhnall O'Donovan just do that?'

I knew, however, that if I had gone with that comment, I'd be out of a job within the hour.

So in that split second, I went biblical. In my hour of need, I found God, and said 'Holy Moses!' It's a phrase I never used before or since, either in broadcasting or away from the microphone. I thought nothing of it until that Sunday evening when I realized that it had made an impact among the public.

To this day, I often get the 'Holy Moses' comment as I walk down the sideline to record an interview, or when I go into a shop in Tipperary or Carlow or anywhere.

'Well, holy Moses, 'tis yourself!'

With Domhnall O'Donovan, hero of the drawn 2013 final, after Clare won the replay

In the replay, Clare prevailed 5-16 to 3-16. That 2013 All-Ireland success was a huge achievement for a group of young hurlers who were emerging from the under-21 grade. Expectations within the county were high at the time, despite the fact that Limerick had shown at the turn of the century that under-21 All-Ireland success doesn't guarantee the same level of achievement when players graduate to the senior ranks. They had won three under-21 titles in a row from 2000 to 2002, but that Limerick squad never fulfilled their full potential. Anybody involved in sport appreciates how difficult it can be for some players to transition from top-class under-age players to being good or even adequate senior hurlers or footballers.

The Clare under-21s were superbly coached and managed

With the team in the dressing room afterwards, as a Clareman rather than a journalist

by Donal Moloney and Gerry O'Connor, and would win three All-Ireland titles in a row in 2012, 2013 and 2014. Nor should we forget John Minogue's great achievement in 2009, when he managed the Banner to their very first under-21 All-Ireland title. So the raw material was there.

Davy Fitzgerald must be given credit for bringing those players through to the top level so quickly. He put together a top-class backroom team that saw two relatively unknown Limerick lads, Paul Kinnerk and Seoirse Bulfin, cross the border into Clare and contribute significantly to the Banner cause.

Davy Fitzgerald has proven himself to be an outstanding manager with his own club, Sixmilebridge, and then with LIT Limerick, Waterford, Clare and more recently Wexford; winning two Fitzgibbon Cups, two provincial titles in two different provinces, an Allianz league and of course that amazing All-Ireland title in 2013. By any barometer, that's impressive.

What was disappointing from a Clare perspective was that from the evening of September 28th, 2013, when Clare beat Cork in the All-Ireland final replay, to 2018, Clare hurlers never saw the inside of Croke Park again. Why? What happened? How come Clare couldn't win the Munster championship in those years? Especially considering the talent that seemed to be available from the winning under-21 sides?

The reasons are complex and varied. Brian Lohan, another legend of the Banner, is known throughout the county as 'Lohan', but in this instance, being called by your surname is a badge of honour. He has now entered the inter-county management arena, having previously taken charge of Patrickswell in Limerick and guided the University of Limerick (UL) to a Fitzgibbon Cup in 2015.

Davy Fitzgerald and Brian Lohan were goalkeeper and full back respectively on the Clare team that brought unbridled joy and happiness in 1995 and 1997 not just to Clare people but to a nation that loves hurling. Twenty-five years later, they have sadly fallen out with each other.

Sadder again is the list of controversies Clare has experienced in recent times. The truth is that there has been a negative vibe in Clare for a long number of years. In 2007, the *Clare Champion* awards began and ended very quickly after the lifetime achievement award went to Fr Harry Bohan and not Ger Loughnane. Fr Harry is a wonderful priest and a kind man who has been a true friend to us all. He was the Clare manager when they won national league titles in 1977 and 1978, but there was general surprise and much controversy when Ger Loughnane, who guided the county to two All-Ireland titles, didn't receive the award.

Tony Considine's management career with Clare lasted just eight months and was dogged by bad decision-making and controversy at every turn. In more recent times, the Clare centre of excellence at Caherlohan has been ridiculed and criticized as not good enough, and some officials have conceded that it's an embarrassment. Training for the Clare senior hurling team has had to take place in a neighbouring county at the University of Limerick.

The social media campaign against Pat Fitzgerald, the Clare county secretary, over a number of years was truly terrible. Nobody should be subjected to such an awful experience, nor is it right that so many hurtful comments should be available for public consumption without any editorial control at all.

I am not taking sides in this argument. There are rights and wrongs on both sides, and ego clashes too, but as a Clareman, it breaks my heart to see GAA people tearing each other apart. There must be respect, even if you disagree with a person. I don't believe it's right to wash your linen so publicly, especially when we were all one big family back in 1995 and 1997.

And we need perspective. Look where other counties are and then look at ourselves. Since 1995, Clare has won three All-Ireland hurling titles, three Munster senior championships, an Allianz league title in 2016, four under-21 All-Irelands, four under-21 Munster titles, a minor All-Ireland in 1997, Munster minor titles in 2010 and 2011, Munster intermediate hurling titles in 2011 and 2016 and an Ireland intermediate in 2011. For a county with an earlier history of constant failure and disappointment (in comparison to most other hurling counties) we have done very well. Honestly, we need to draw breath. Some protagonists need to be told, 'Stop!' I, for one, am sick of it all. Come together and go forward as one. There is no other way. We must restore peace in the Clare GAA world. Surely Covid-19 has taught us that family, community and respect for each other are among the most important things in this life.

The Clare I know and love is a county that loves to smile, to dance, to sing, to talk, to laugh, to save the hay, to do the silage, to milk the cows, to enjoy Willie Clancy Week and to play hurling, football and camogie. That's Clare. That's the Banner.

13. Friends in the North

Broadcasting is a wonderful profession. I've always valued the rare privilege of being beamed into homes around the country and around the world. What's more, I've been very lucky in that throughout my career, I've been welcomed into people's homes and business premises. The kindness shown to me will last for ever in my heart and soul.

This is particularly true of the people of Ulster. Whether it's the Bogside in Derry, the Falls Road in Belfast, Ballygawley in Tyrone or Drumintee in South Armagh, I've always enjoyed a wonderful, warm welcome from the many people I've met covering our games north of the border. Any time I travelled outside the Dublin 4 campus, I was always conscious that I was representing RTÉ, and I think that maybe because of what people in the North had been through, and were still going through in the 1990s, they appreciated that the national broadcaster was as interested in their community and their county's progress as any in the South.

When I was assigned my first match in Casement Park in Belfast, I remember travelling through British Army checkpoints and coming up the hill, passing the shopping centre on my right as I headed towards the Falls Road. My only knowledge of the city up to that point was what I had seen on TV. Rioting, car bombs, murders and violence dominated my visual memory. I was genuinely apprehensive at the continuous purring of the British helicopters overhead and the presence of their army colleagues on the street.

But then, as I drove towards Casement Park on the Andersonstown Road, the blowing of the horns, the throngs of supporters on the road, and the smell of the burgers and chips emanating from the vans made Belfast on match day just like any GAA venue down south. I turned left down Owenvarragh Park Road, passed the main entrance on the Falls Road and arrived at the gate. After a few trips, the lads on the gate got to know me and they always greeted me warmly with that lilting Belfast accent.

'Ach Marty . . . how are youuuu? Welcome to Belfast. Drive in there and park anywhere you like to your right.'

It's probably a strange thing to say but when I started travelling north during the Troubles, I always felt safe – both emotionally and physically – once I got inside the ground.

As I grew in confidence, I used drive around Belfast after matches, exploring the city and beyond. I thought I'd be nervous driving through Loyalist areas, where every flagpole had a Union Jack blowing in the breeze, and the pavements were painted red, white and blue, but I was more fascinated than anything else, and wanted to know more about the Protestant people, their culture and how they saw us.

I remember being in the pub in Quilty in West Clare on January 30th, 1972, Bloody Sunday, when fourteen civilians were shot dead by the British Army during a civil rights march in the Bogside area of Derry. I remember all of us looking at the black and white pictures on RTÉ in total shock and horror. I can still see Fr Edward Daly bravely waving his bloodstained white handkerchief as he escorted a group of local people carrying a mortally wounded boy through the streets. This was the year we won the Clare under-14 football championship. I was living in a different world down the road in the Republic.

Nine years later, in May 1981, I was doing my final exams in UCC when Bobby Sands died on hunger strike. Belfast seemed almost to be on a different continent.

It would be 1997 before I got a more detailed perspective on life in the North. This was when the Sigerson Cup was being played in Coleraine and RTÉ commissioned Donovan Ross, an outstanding cameraman from Dungannon, Co. Tyrone, to work with me on the tournament. Donovan was an intriguing man with whom I loved working. I visited his beautiful home and family many times. He introduced me to his colleague, Stephen McCoubrey. I clicked with Steve immediately – we seemed to have similar senses of humour.

At the time, the Sigerson was run off over a single weekend, with games on a Friday and Saturday and the final on Sunday. It was the first year that the Regional Technical Colleges were allowed play in the prestigious universities championship, and in that first year, IT Tralee, or Tralee RTC as it was back then, won the title, beating UL in the final. Tralee had an incredible team. Seamus Moynihan was magnificent at centre back, while the squad featured other Kerry stars of the future: Mike Frank Russell, William Kirby and Barry O'Shea. As if that wasn't enough, there was also the Galway pair, Michael Donnellan and Padraic Joyce, who would go on to win a senior All-Ireland the following year. And in among these household names was Donegal's Jim McGuinness. Fifteen years later, he would manage his own county to their second All-Ireland title. IT Tralee, meanwhile, would go on to win three Sigerson titles in a row, the only IT to achieve that accolade. When you look at the team, it's hardly surprising.

By the time we had post-match interviews done after the final on the Sunday evening, it was quite late, so we decided that instead of heading into the RTÉ Belfast studios, we would go back to Steve's house to edit the highlights.

I knew Donovan had produced and filmed reconstructions of incidents for people who were facing criminal prosecutions for alleged IRA activities, in much the same way that *Crimecall* reconstructs incidents for broadcast. On that basis, I assumed his colleague Steve was also a Catholic – not that it mattered a hoot to me what religion he was. It was only on the way back to Belfast, as we drove in convoy, that Steve called me on the mobile to tell me that it would be best to drive my car into his driveway first and that he would park outside me.

'I'll be going home to Dublin when we're finished, Stephen,' I said, 'so wouldn't it be better for me to park outside you?'

With a smile in his voice, he told me that he was from 'the other side'. He lived in Glengormley in north Belfast, and in that neck of the woods, it would be best if a Dublin-registered car was not clearly visible from the road. I remember gulping loudly, but I wasn't going to back out now, and I trusted Steve, so there wasn't a problem. Furthermore, if we didn't edit the package, there would be a gaping hole in *Sunday Sport* that night. The job had to be done.

The first thing I noticed when we arrived into Stephen's house was the number of bolts and locks on the front door. His girlfriend, Maggie, welcomed me warmly as Stephen picked up the land-line. He was ringing a friend who was part of the neighbourhood security patrol which kept an eye out for suspicious activity and potential attacks.

We edited the report and I was fed, watered and treated like a king. Afterwards, we spoke at length about the Troubles. I found out that Donovan and Stephen also did reconstruction video work for people accused of being loyalist paramilitaries. This sort of dual mandate came about because they were hired by Legal Aid, which didn't discriminate no matter who required their services. The work itself involved going back to the crime scene with a full production crew and reconstructing the incident frame by frame using lookalikes.

Donovan told me that when he started out, he might give evidence in the defence of an IRA person on Monday and a UVF person on Tuesday. By bringing their individual skills together, the two lads from opposite sides provided evidence in some of the most notorious cases, involving prominent loyalists like Billy Wright, as well as many INLA figures. Their stories both enthralled and horrified me.

That evening, Steve very kindly drove ahead of me until we got across town and on to the M1 out of Belfast. Sadly I never met Steve and Maggie again but I was delighted to hear they got married afterwards.

Four months after my weekend in Coleraine covering the Sigerson, Donovan Ross was shot by a plastic bullet fired by a female RUC officer. He was working for ITN News, covering a riot on the Garvaghy Road. The bullet broke his shoulder and the camera he had been holding fell and smashed into smithereens. Though he was compensated for that loss, he was told by the RUC 'that he shouldn't have been where he was'. I disagree. He was there as a news cameraman and was simply doing his job.

The only time I felt intimidated personally during my early trips to cover Ulster championship matches was coming back from a game in Healy Park in Omagh. I was heading to Clare rather than Dublin, and met a British Army checkpoint on the border in Aughnacloy, Co. Tyrone. The checkpoint consisted of a galvanized hut built at the bottom of a steep incline as you came out of the village. You had to veer off the road and follow a track around the lookout platform that they had built. At other border crossings, a British soldier in full gear would wave you to a stop and then come round to the window to ask your name and look for ID. Up to this point, they had always been smiling, unfailingly polite. But on this Sunday evening in Aughnacloy, the mood was different.

The soldiers were in full uniform, with their berets on their heads and their rifles strapped across their chests. What really made the encounter intimidating, however, was the fact that they were in war-zone mentality and had blackened faces.

'Will you get out of the car please, sir?' said the man in charge. As soon as I climbed out, he went on, 'Will you open the boot please, sir?'

I complied immediately.

Now the metal detector – which looked like one of those big trolley jacks they use for fixing flat tyres – was rolled under the car, and another guy went around the underside of the car with a mirror on a pole, checking for bombs.

The soldier who had taken my RTÉ identification card was scrutinizing it carefully. He looked at me, then looked at the card, then looked at me again. After a prolonged silence, he said, 'What exactly do you do, mate?'

'I'm a sports commentator. I was in Healy Park in Omagh commentating on an Ulster championship match between Tyrone and Derry.'

'That's Gallick football, isn't it, sir?'

'Yes, it is.'

'Only republicans play Gallick? Is that true, sir?'

'Ah no, not at all. The GAA and Gaelic football are about pride of place and community. Everybody gets involved.'

Suddenly someone bellowed behind me. 'Do you know where the IRA are today?'

It was a female soldier in full combat dress, with the war paint streaked across her face.

'Not a clue,' said I.

She turned, looked towards the surrounding hills and roared so loud I almost jumped. 'Come on IRA, where are you?'

Then she looked me straight in the eye. 'Will you tell your friends when they stop playing football, we will be waiting for them?'

I didn't respond. The soldier that appeared to be in charge asked me if I was returning to Dublin. I didn't want to get involved in any more explanations, so I told him that I was.

'You are free to go, sir.'

I just got the hell out of there.

I know others have experienced far worse at various checkpoints along the border over the years, but I never forgot my experience at the British Army checkpoint in Aughnacloy.

When I travel north now, it is so different. You no longer see British Army soldiers sheltering in bus shelters and ditches, there are no helicopters buzzing overhead, and the absence of checkpoints is a welcome relief. But will it stay that way? As I write, Brexit and the Northern Ireland protocol dominate the news, and once again we have scenes of violence in Loyalist areas.

Nobody wants to go back to those awful days.

14. Access Denied

Do you remember Mick Dunne in winning All-Ireland dressing-rooms? You'd see some players with fags hanging from their lips, others swigging out of milk bottles, bare-chested and emotional after victory? Do you remember after the 1979 hurling final, Kilkenny's legendary corner back, Fan Larkin, was back in his suit minutes after winning the last of his five All-Ireland medals? Fan was eating an apple in a packed Kilkenny dressing-room when Mick asked him why he got dressed so quickly.

'I have to go to mass,' Fan replied.

The sight of two great Dublin footballers, Jimmy Keaveney and Brian Mullins, in Kerry jerseys after Dublin won the 1976 All-Ireland football final has always stayed with me. Dublin manager Kevin Heffernan was sandwiched between them while Mick asked the questions. Five years later it was the Kerry captain, Jimmy Deenihan, being interviewed after the Kingdom had completed their four-in-a-row.

Mick Dunne set the bar, and although some will argue it was mayhem, and that having everybody including the bus driver in the dressing-room didn't look good, there was an innocence and a beauty about it that I loved. Quite simply, it captured the moment. It pulled the veil of mystique aside and for ten minutes we were there, in a very special place that few ever see: an All-Ireland winning dressing-room. This was unique to the GAA, this was unique to Ireland.

In recent years, however, we have lost that magic.

Mick Dunne interviewing Cork county board chairman Derry Gowan as he congratulates Kilkenny and their captain Brian Cody after the 1982 hurling final

I remember being in the Down dressing-room in 1991 after they had beaten Meath in the All-Ireland final, and interviewing Liam Austin, Peter Withnell, Paul Higgins, Gary Mason, captain Paddy O'Rourke and manager Pete McGrath live on *The Sunday Game*. The next time I was back in a winning All-Ireland dressing-room was in 2013, following Clare's victory over Cork in the replay of the hurling final. That was more personal, of course, because it was my own crowd.

Dr Padraig Quinn, a great Clareman, has been the Clare doctor for years. He rang me the week of the 2013 final and told me that if Clare won, the lads were going to surprise Brendan Bugler in the dressing-room with his own button accordion and get him to play. I asked Davy Fitz was it OK if we filmed it?

He said, 'No problem, Marty, as long as we win.'

The match ended in a draw, of course. So the plan was shelved for two weeks. But when the Banner won the replay, the button accordion was produced, Brendan Bugler's eyes lit up, and Bugs, as we call him, pulled the straps over his shoulders and the brand new All-Ireland champions let rip in the Croke Park dressing-room. I was dragged into the middle of them by Podge Collins and Tony Kelly, and the Clare lads danced the Clare set (or something like it). Afterwards, John Conlon sang 'My Lovely Rose of Clare'.

From 1991 to 2013. That's twenty-two years with no live action from an All-Ireland winning dressing-room.

What happened in between? 'Change' and 'evolve' became the in-words – in sport and in corporate life. Yes, we should change and evolve, and if that equates to improving the way we do things, I applaud and celebrate that. But not all change is positive. In recent years, we've seen the climax of the championship become a little sanitized in terms of media access. It's lost some of its natural emotion and glory. To me, the GAA is about passion, it's about the love of the game. It's about community and belonging. It's about amateurism in the very best sense of the word, and all that that stands for. It's about the ability to reach out and touch your heroes, something you don't really get with other sports. You might see Cristiano Ronaldo and Lionel Messi on the TV, but you can meet Aidan O'Shea, David Clifford, T. J. Reid and Cian Lynch because they will be walking down the street or having a coffee in your local café. I'm not saying for one moment that we need the madness that we saw when Mick Dunne was broadcasting in dressing-rooms in days gone by. I'm suggesting that it's possible to control the euphoria for ten minutes so that a snapshot of the atmosphere in the dressing-room can be captured, thus allowing the people of Ireland – those who support the games – to see what it really means to be crowned All-Ireland champions.

Richie Bennis, the All-Ireland winning Limerick hurler, managed the county team between 2006 and 2008. He was old school and I loved him for it. When the door of the Limerick dressing-room would open after big games, a journalist would ask, 'Who can we talk to?'

Richie's response was, 'What do you mean, who can you talk to? Talk to whoever you like.'

Michael Moynihan in the *Irish Examiner* quoted Richie Bennis's take on post-match interviews: 'We have no problem with it. I think it's silly to ban access at this stage. We're an amateur sport with a professional outlook and that outlook should include access to players. I don't think it affects the players to talk immediately after a game, what harm can they do? And the publicity helps to give the game a bit of profile and it's badly needed.'

I heartily agree.

Donal O'Grady employed a closed-door policy when he became Cork manager in 2003. In his view, the dressing-room was a sanctuary, and by excluding the media, it brought a professionalism to his set-up. I can see and understand his point.

But I'm pretty sure that ten years, twenty years or forty years after the All-Ireland is won, the players and the people involved would relish the opportunity to see those scenes and relive those memories. Like the day Cork county board chairman Derry Gowan came into the Kilkenny dressing-room to congratulate the victorious captain Brian Cody on winning the 1982 All-Ireland.

There are so many media outlets today that it's physically impossible to allow all members of the press in. That's a fact.

But perhaps after provincial finals, and certainly after All-Ireland finals, broadcast cameras should be allowed into the winners' dressing-room, even for a limited and controlled period of time. Let us get back a little bit of that raw emotion!

There's one other Richie Bennis story I want to mention.

Since 2004, former Limerick hurler David Punch, a Patrickswell man like Richie, has been by my side for all my championship assignments, both on radio and TV. He provides invaluable statistical information on numbers of frees, wides and all of that sort of thing. David played centrefield for Limerick in the 1980 All-Ireland final against Galway, so his knowledge and reading of the game is top-class. He has been a great and a loyal friend over the years, and like most great friends, we don't always agree.

Anyway, it was June 24th, 2007 and Limerick had just beaten Tipperary in the infamous trilogy of Munster hurling championship games at the Gaelic Grounds, on a scoreline of Limerick 0–22 Tipperary 2–13 – after extra time. The Limerick team bus was parked outside the Woodfield Guest House Hotel on the Ennis Road as Punchy and myself made our way to where our cars were parked in the grounds of the old Ardhu Ryan Hotel. Next thing we heard shouts from the team bus. It was the indomitable Stephen Lucey.

'Punchy! Marty! Come with us into town!'

David had been a selector when Limerick won three under-21 titles in a row at the turn of the century, and Stephen was a key player on those teams, so there was a strong bond there.

Punchy looked at me, eyebrows raised. I said that we couldn't go on the team bus, but that we would meet them inside.

Stephen was now joined by Niall Moran, Brian Geary and

a few more. Before I knew it, I was lifted up and dropped on the floor beside the bus driver.

'Go back to the back!' instructed Niall Moran. So I scrambled back to the last row of seats at the very back of the bus, with lads giving me high-fives and slaps on the back as I struggled down the narrow passageway. The craic was mighty. Then manager Richie Bennis arrived on to the bus.

'Right, lads,' he called, 'have we everyone?'

He began a seat-by-seat head count. I was at this stage crouched down in the back, my head more or less between my legs, hoping to God he wouldn't see me, while Punchy had taken up residence in the corner seat. Richie came halfway down the aisle before turning back to his seat without spotting me. Stephen Lucey, who was beside me, gave me a clap on the back.

'You're grand, you're grand,' he says, so I straightened up and right at that moment, Richie turned around and spotted me.

'What the fuck are you doing here?' he bellowed.

'He's coming for a drink with us!' Niall Moran shouted. 'Now drive on!'

Richie smiled and muttered something like, 'You're probably the only fuckin' Clareman we'd let on to this bus. Now keep your head down 'cos we'll be mortified if anyone finds out.'

We had a great night, even though Limerick had only qualified for the Munster final. Another occasion that I remember with great fondness involved the Monaghan footballers. I have their then manager Malachy O'Rourke to thank for allowing me into their dressing-room after they won the Ulster championship in St Tiernach's Park in Clones in 2015. It was a radio recording for that evening's *Marty*

Squad on RTÉ Radio 1, which I was honoured to present along with my great colleagues Brenda Donohue and Damien Lawlor. By the time I got all my post-match interviews for *The Sunday Game*, as well as my 'as live' piece for the *Six One News*, the celebrations had died down a bit in the new Ulster champions' dressing-room. To make the live action piece work, I had to call for quietness, then ask them, on my cue, to restart the roaring and shouting and singing. This they did with great relish. It was fantastic. To say I have a great grá for the Monaghan footballers would be putting it mildly.

One other thing I want to mention before I leave Monaghan. That evening at 6 p.m. we went live from the Roadcaster in the square in Clones. This has a glass front, so you can see right into the studio. Everything was going great until a hen party showed up. On seeing me sitting inside, the hens went wild with emotion and passion. This is not my ego talking here. This is fact. They started by waving in the window. I waved back, but they wanted more. While some of them

The Marty Squad in full flow in the Roadcaster

banged on the glass, two more started climbing the ladder at the side of the Roadcaster. Then the whole vehicle began rocking back and forth. Coffee mugs and pens went sliding on to the floor, while outside, they started chanting: 'We want Marty! We want Marty!'

Eventually our producer, Barry O'Neill, persuaded them to come down by promising that he'd let me out to meet them. I interviewed the girls on air, they showered me with kisses and left. Never will I forget the Monaghan hen party.

Anyway . . .

Professional basketball and baseball teams in America open their dressing-rooms after every game. In basketball the media has access-all-areas until forty minutes before tip-off, and the dressing-rooms must be open to the media within fifteen minutes of a game finishing. A major league baseball pass works much the same way. As well as locker-room access, reporters can stand outside the cage during batting practice and chat away to players. The NFL is a little different, but they still allow access to players at specified times each week, when the locker-room is open to journalists (though often players don't turn up). Covid-19 has changed all this, of course, but that level of access is expected to return after the pandemic.

Once upon a time, and not that long ago, I could call any hurler or footballer in the country to do an interview. These days, the more successful counties have press officers that you have to go through. Sometimes all you'd want is a short interview for the news. But it's becoming increasingly difficult to get access to players, especially during the championship season. I would love for our audiences to get to know their stars. When I started, you could film a brilliant hurler or footballer farming his land, milking his cows, walking into his office, teaching his class or driving his car to work. You'll hardly ever get that now. I'm not saying that we should do this every week but it could be facilitated on special occasions like provincial and All-Ireland finals. It's also great for the player himself and projects a positive image for his employers.

In contrast, when the spotlight is thrown on a less successful county, the reaction is entirely different. The doors are thrown open immediately. The players are always delighted to get some coverage – never for themselves, I have to say – but for their team and county. They are just so proud to have secured a win in the league or the championship. Getting featured on the *RTÉ News* or *The Sunday Game*, or indeed any newspaper, is acknowledgement of that success and they welcome it warmly.

It is the prerogative of players to choose what they want to do, and I would never put anybody under any pressure in these situations. But I lament the fact that some of these young, talented players, who can perform before 82,000 fans in Croke Park, are not allowed to participate in a short sequence which would enhance their profile and their connection to their supporters. Why is this happening? Because management is afraid they'll say something stupid. In reality, these are bright young people, most of them graduates or postgraduates, and they know the game. They are all media savvy. And if they did say something stupid, I'd probably get them to redo the piece. Trust. It's the single most important thing in the relationship between me as the interviewer and the player as interviewee. If it's the player's choice not to talk because it puts him under pressure or he doesn't feel comfortable with a big game coming down the track, I get that. I totally accept it. But a GAA fan simply wants to know about the players and the managers, and in so many ways, talking to the media is a win–win. It also opens up huge marketing opportunities for the player both short term and in the long term. So we need to move with the times and let the reins go a little, particularly as the GAA competes for media coverage with extravaganzas like the European Football Championships and the Olympics.

After Tipperary beat Cork to win the 2020 Munster football title – their first in eighty-five years, and in the Rebels' own back yard too – I went to Killenaule in South Tipperary the following day for the *Six One News* and did a piece on the family farm with full back Jimmy Feehan and his brother Paudie, who had come on as a substitute in Páirc Uí Chaoimh the previous day. The public and social media response to that piece was staggering, it was hugely positive. But did it prompt other counties to allow similar access? Sadly, no.

My father often spoke highly of a man that he absolutely loved meeting: Jimmy Gavin from Cooraclare. Jimmy, who moved to Dublin as a young man, loved to tell stories and sing songs. Jimmy's son is Jim Gavin. Like our fathers before us, we also became friends, and got to know each other really well when Jim won his All-Ireland football medal in 1995. Jim never forgot his West Clare roots (his mother is also from Clare, from the village of Moy, just outside Miltown Malbay), and later that year, he brought Sam Maguire to Martin Noel Tubridy's, O'Doherty's and the Dangenelly Tavern as part of his world tour of Clare. I remember filming a lovely piece with Jim in Baldonnel as he was preparing for the All-Ireland championship that year. At that stage he was already flying the government jet to different parts of the world, while maintaining an inter-county football career at the highest level, which must have been very difficult.

So my friendship with Jim Gavin has history. So many times I encouraged Jim to give a little more of himself in interviews when he became Dublin football manager, but no amount of persuasion would ever work. When he was in charge, Dublin football press conferences usually began at 8 a.m. in the Gibson Hotel on Point Square in the North Dock, which officially became the Dublin footballers' hotel. It's a beautiful hotel, and is well known to TV viewers as the venue for *First Dates*, but the layout of the main reception room is fragmented and full of angles that hinder cameras, which makes filming the sequence from the winners' hotel a little challenging.

I used often joke that the interviews I did in 2013 with the newly appointed Jim Gavin stood the test of time. He gave so little away that I could easily have used the same interviews for the next six years, right up to and including the five in a row, completed in 2019. Jim was tight on discipline and always felt that Dublin players had been too

media-accessible in the past, a situation compounded by the fact that there were so many journalists working in the capital and the players often met them socially. From the perspective of management, they were in the papers far too often.

That 'access denied' policy started with Pat Gilroy and continued with Jim. Jim's right-hand man, and press officer for six years, was another pilot from Jim's Air Corps days: Seamus 'Shep' McCormack. I got on great with Shep, who was always accessible, always smiling, always in sexy shorts and always beautifully tanned – which I was jealous of. We got on great until I asked the question:

'Can I talk to Diarmuid Connolly?'

'No!'

'Stephen Cluxton?'

'No!'

'Brian Fenton?'

'No!'

'Jack McCaffrey?'

'No!'

'Who can I have?'

'You can have Jonny Cooper?'

Jonny was great, I loved Jonny, and we have become great friends. But on occasions, for the sake of the audience, we need to hear and see someone else. I understand why that control was thought necessary, but it still disappoints me that in this modern era of mass communication, we know so little about players from the greatest team that I have ever seen.

If Dublin was unenthusiastic in this area, Kilkenny was not far behind. Whatever about the inter-county footballers, getting to know the hurling stars is much more difficult since hurling helmets – very rightly – became essential gear. Instant recognition is no longer possible, so being available to the media and the platform that it provides has to be a positive for any hurler who is happy to speak or meet the press. But every request for a Kilkenny hurler to do a media interview has to go through the PRO, who then checks with the manager. For the last few seasons, I haven't spoken to many Kilkenny players apart from Colin Fennelly or T. J. Reid. Both great guys and fantastic hurlers, it has to be said, but if I hear the phrase 'They are keeping their heads down' again – from any county – I will crack up!

I think Croke Park should encourage inter-county players to be available to the media once they – the players – are happy to oblige. Managers should have the right to say 'No' if the request is for a new, young player, so that he's given time to mature and deal with the situation. It's about management of your resources and giving the players a chance to benefit from their success on the football and hurling fields.

The other strategy I dislike is when the media is offered a player who has absolutely no chance of playing in the forthcoming game. This is too cute by far. I was relieved to read Tomás Ó Sé's thoughts on the matter in his *Irish Independent* column in June 2021:

> *I was saying to someone recently that it strikes me the GAA are missing a beat in not having a mid-week TV programme, a show familiarising us with different personalities from around the country. But when I thought about it after, I realised that in today's culture of almost institutional secrecy there would be next to zero chance of getting current players to participate in such a programme. Put it this way, when I was doing my own podcast last year, it was suggested that I should maybe try going that route, but just imagine me ringing one of today's stars, asking them to come on for a chat? They'd probably wonder if I had a screw loose.*

I texted Tomás to say well done and to have a little rant of my own. Finally, somebody with huge gravitas in the game acknowledged the reality of the situation.

The funny thing is I've yet to meet a player that cost his county a provincial or an All-Ireland by what they said. The match is always won or lost on the field of play.

The contrast in attitude to player availability between men's and women's sport is massive. The Camogie and the Ladies Gaelic Football Associations are incredibly helpful when it comes to providing players for interviews. Everyone involved greatly appreciates the coverage from all media outlets.

This is not just about access to post-match celebrations or pre-match packages, it's also about the way we present our big matches. The GAA has an incredibly valuable product that continues to attract a variety of sponsorship partners. In 2020 and 2021, Covid revealed the financial precariousness of the GAA when gate receipts disappeared.

Do you remember when it was the Bank of Ireland football championship? The Guinness hurling championship? Each code had its own clearly defined sponsor. Today, however, there are multiple sponsors. So how do sporting organizations give each of the many sponsors value for their sponsorship? A plastic backdrop covered in logos is wheeled out on to the pitch as soon as the final whistle blows.

The sponsorship wheelie board is the broadcast industry standard worldwide in many sports, but I'm not a fan of it. To see it being pushed awkwardly on the sideline as the match approaches the full-time whistle at Croke Park or Páirc Uí Chaoimh is unsightly. I would much rather see John Kiely or Brian Cody or Dessie Farrell or Peter Keane standing in front of the camera answering questions against the magnificent backdrop of Croke Park bubbling with emotion. Whether accidental or not, the wheelie board seems to dilute and sanitize those vital moments when victory is achieved.

Don't get me wrong here, I know the value of money. The primary purpose of the wheelie board is to give some value back to the companies that invest in the GAA. I don't expect it to change any time soon.

Peter McKenna, the stadium director in Croke Park, is brilliant. He and his team have done a remarkable job bringing Croke Park and the GAA into the twenty-first century by establishing financial opportunities that were either unknown or unrecognized before his arrival, and I'm sure if there was another way of doing this and giving value, Peter and his team would have thought of it.

I love the association with all my heart. Sometimes, however, it can frustrate me. The GAA is to be applauded for the efficient staging of the club and inter-county championships during the Covid pandemic, but I really think there was a massive opportunity missed. With Ireland under successive lockdowns, and with no possibility of crowds attending games, it would have been the perfect opportunity to think outside the box and try something new and exciting. In my humble opinion, it would have been worth running the football championship on an open draw basis, or perhaps a Champions' League-style competition with teams divided into groups. This could have been done on a trial basis for one year. If the traditionalists were upset about the loss of the provincial system, the administration could easily have blamed Covid.

The reality is that as it stands, the provincial football championship is unbalanced and has lost some of its glory. Dublin are too strong for Leinster. In 2021, they won their eleventh Leinster crown in a row. Munster is essentially a two-horse race, even acknowledging Tipperary's wonderful achievement in 2020 and the fact that Clare and Limerick are working very hard to reach the standard required. Sligo, Leitrim, New York and London will always find life difficult in Connacht, which leaves the western title between Mayo, Galway and Roscommon. By contrast, the Ulster championship is a great competition, as Cavan proved by beating hot favourites Donegal in the 2020 Ulster final, bringing the Anglo-Celt cup back to Breffni country for the first time since 1997.

Despite these occasional successes and the historical weight of the provincial competitions – which I do appreciate – I still feel strongly that under the unprecedented Covid restrictions, a brand new championship with a new direction and a new feel would have thrilled TV audiences at home and abroad.

I appreciate that provincial councils do not want to lose control or income, and nor do they want to damage the infrastructures that have served the association well, but this was the perfect opportunity to level the playing field and balance the football championship even on an experimental, short-term basis. Whether we like it or not, it is in need of oxygen, if not open heart surgery.

All that being said, the football and hurling championships remain unique and will continue to intrigue us. The long evenings, the smell of the cut grass, the sun shining, the birds singing, the boots clattering on the concrete, the smell of wintergreen, the clash of the ash, the whistle blowing, the ice cream cones, the fish and chips, the chat, the gossip, *The Marty Squad*, Pat Spillane and Sean Cavanagh, Davy Fitz and Brian Lohan, Donal Óg, Dalo and King Henry, *Sunday Sport* on RTÉ Radio 1, *The Sunday Game* and the roar of the crowd.

I really wouldn't want to be anywhere else!

15. Dad, Páidí and Me

The sharp, shrill ring of the telephone awoke me so suddenly, bedclothes went flying everywhere. For a moment I didn't recognize the room. Then the neurons began firing. New York. Fitzpatrick's Hotel on Lexington Avenue in midtown Manhattan. I had arrived from Kennedy Airport seven hours earlier on a flight from Shannon. As I reached for the phone, three possibilities arranged themselves in my head: a wake-up call that I hadn't asked for, a wrong number, or bad news.

My mother was on the phone. She was very upset. In between bouts of crying, she told me that my father was dead. She had got up that morning and told him she was going to make a cup of tea. When she got no response, she thought he was asleep, but when she came back to the bedroom Dad was cold. He had passed on. The husband to whom she had been married for fifty years the previous September, and my much loved father, was gone.

He was my best friend – more like a brother than a father. And yet, if we had been Taoiseach and Tánaiste, no policy would ever have been implemented because we had very different views on almost everything. He was the bright one. I was the slogger who would get there eventually. When I was doing my Masters in Education in NUIG, Dad was an invaluable resource, and an enormous help when I was writing my thesis. The funny thing is, he always helped in such a way that I never felt stupid.

That day, December 19th, 2004, was and is the saddest day of my life. It was only when my father died that I truly missed not having a brother, sister, aunt or uncle. For the first time, I really felt alone.

I rang Aer Lingus at JFK to try to get on the next flight home, but all I got were the automated choices: *Press 1 for ticket desk, press 2 for baggage, press 3 for economy* . . . I had a great friend, Colm Dunne, in Aer Lingus in Dublin at the time, so I called him and told him my situation. Between Colm and a colleague of his, Brendan Singleton, who was a duty manager at Kennedy Airport, I was on the next flight home to Dublin, then on to Shannon.

That shamrock on the tail fin of an Aer Lingus jet is very important, as it symbolizes our country parked there on the tarmac among the big boys, like American Airlines, British Airways, Qantas, Japan Airlines, Emirates, Etihad, KLM, Alitalia, Air France and a host of others. We hold our place in that transient world and declare: 'Hey, we are Irish and this is us.' When your father has died and you need to get home quickly, that shamrock on the aircraft means a lot.

The journey home seemed to take for ever, as I tried to make sense of what had happened.

Six years earlier, Dad had got a heart attack as he cut the grass in a house I had bought on the Watery Road in Ennis. I was in the Hotel Europe in Killarney, filming a preview package for *The Sunday Game*, when I got that first panicked phone call from my mother. On that occasion, an ambulance arrived at the house and brought Dad to the hospital. They had just got him into intensive care when he suffered a second heart attack, and only for the incredible work of the medical team, the nurses and the cardiologist, Terry Hennessy from County Westmeath, we would have lost him. I drove as fast as I could to the hospital, calling every twenty minutes to know was he still alive. I was told that he was 'stable' and 'comfortable', then they would add: 'Come as fast as you can.' That put my own heart crossways.

His years of smoking Consulate cigarettes had obviously done damage, despite the fact that he would always claim Consulate were harmless.

When I got into intensive care, he had all sorts of tubes and wires hanging out of him, with a large oxygen mask covering his face. He looked pale. But his heart was beating: we could hear it and see it on his monitor. Subsequently, he was transferred to the Mater Hospital in Dublin, where he had a triple bypass. A few months later, a pacemaker was inserted into his chest.

Over the next six years he had been fine. He had seen us off at Shannon Airport the day before. I had given him a hug and waved goodbye before heading up the escalator towards passport control.

I would never see him alive again.

To see your father lying in a coffin is never easy, but when you have travelled across the Atlantic twice in seventy-two hours and you are exhausted mentally and physically, it is especially difficult. For my mother's sake, I did my best to hold it together.

I don't know what other people do when they experience the loss of a beloved parent, but when I was left alone with him where he had been laid out in the sitting room, I cut some of his beautiful grey hair and put it in an envelope, which I have kept to this day.

I was only home an hour when a knock came to the front door. It was about noon. No local would ever knock on the front door. Everybody came to the back door and either walked straight in or gave a gentle knock before walking straight in. There was a second knock, louder than the first, followed by the buzz of the doorbell, so I went out to the hallway to see the shape of a man through the frosted glass. I assumed it was some friend of my father's, so I found the key and opened the door.

It was Páidí Ó Sé. There he was, standing in the misty rain looking back at me with his hands in his trouser pockets and his coat collar wrapped high around his West Kerry head.

'Marty boy, I heard your father had passed away so I came up to sympathize with you.'

I couldn't believe it.

Páidí Ó Sé, the man who had won eight All-Ireland medals, eleven Munster championship medals, four national leagues and five All-Stars in a row, was in my yard in West Clare having driven all the way from Ventry to share some time with us. What a great friend. I gave him a big hug and welcomed him into our home.

He sat down beside the gas fire in the kitchen and though he took a cup of tea, he wouldn't eat anything.

'I'm already pointing towards the home of football,' he said. I glanced outside and saw the car pointing southwards, in the direction of the Killimer–Tarbert car ferry thirteen miles away.

My heartbreak was that Dad would have loved to have been in the kitchen talking to Páidí Ó Sé about football, winning All-Irelands, the Miltown Massacre and, most of all, his interview with me twenty-three months earlier in Cape Town, South Africa. More about that in a little while.

Our friendship began when Páidí was appointed Kerry manager in 1995. We would record so many interviews over the next ten years. Páidí believed in *piseógs*: folk-beliefs about how to avoid bad luck and attract good luck. We could only do interviews in certain places in Kerry: Páidí's own place in Ventry, Fitzgerald Stadium, and the garden of the Killarney Park Hotel. When he became manager, the Kingdom hadn't won an All-Ireland since 1986: a rare famine. In his first year in charge, Páidí guided the green and gold to a Munster championship, but lost to Mayo in the All-Ireland semi-final. In 1997, Kerry won the national league and added a second Munster title when they hammered Clare in the provincial final. That year, Sam Maguire travelled south to Kerry when they beat Mayo 0–13 to 1–7 on a day when the great Maurice Fitzgerald scored 0–9. Páidí entered the history books as one of only a handful of men who had both captained and managed his county to an All-Ireland title. In 1998, Kerry retained the Munster title but Páidí lost that year's All-Ireland semi-final to Kildare, who were managed at the time by Mick O'Dwyer, a man whom Páidí adored.

Kerry lost their provincial title in 1999, but they bounced back in the millennium, and faced Galway in the All-Ireland final. Because Ger Canning was in Sydney for the Olympics, I was appointed to commentate the match on TV. Páidí was delighted because he believed that I brought him good luck. Despite the fact that Kerry led by seven points at one stage, Galway fought back to level the game and force a replay. Ger was back home for the replay, and, as I've said before, I was broken-hearted that I wasn't picked for that match. In any case, Kerry won the replay.

After all their victories down the years, you might expect cool heads and calm hearts when Kerry win an All-Ireland. Are you joking? They go crazy. The scenes in Tralee and Killarney in 2000 were wild. The bus, with its Garda escort, inched through the delirious crowds, the Sam Maguire perched proudly on the dashboard. You'd swear Kerry hadn't won an All-Ireland in decades. It had been three years.

Páidí sat with his bright yellow geansaí, as he used call his Kerry shirt, glued to his body in the front passenger seat, proud as a king returning to his Kingdom with the ultimate prize. Every now and then – just like a king – he would wave to his people. King Páidí was much loved and admired, for he was, after all, a good king.

Sam Maguire was back after being away for thirty-six months. By Kerry standards that was too long. The following summer, Kerry won Munster again but got badly burned by Meath in the All-Ireland semi-final: 2–14 to 0–5. In 2002, Kerry won the provincial title again but failed by a single point against Armagh who were winning their first All-Ireland title. It was the day Oisín McConville scored a cracking goal in the fifty-fifth minute. Sadly, from Páidí's perspective, the King-dom failed to score in the last seventeen minutes.

Four months later, just after Christmas of 2002, Kevin Kimmage got in touch with Páidí. Kevin was a brilliant sportsman and cyclist, but by then he'd become a journalist and was writing for the *Sunday Independent*. He'd called Páidí to ask if he could interview his nephew, the great mid-fielder Darragh Ó Sé. Páidí was assertive enough when he had to be. His response was this: 'Interview me instead.'

A few years earlier, just before Páidí's first championship match in charge of Kerry, Kevin had spent the day with him, from early afternoon to the small hours, in Páidí's pub in Ventry. Apparently, Kevin got wonderful material, including some great quotes and anecdotes. But at 2 a.m., just after everyone had gone home, Páidí brought down the shutters and said, 'Everything that's been said before this is off the record.' He then proceeded with the official interview. Kevin would have been able to do an outstanding piece based on the hours of earlier material. The piece he ended up having to write was as dull as ditchwater.

Kevin interviewed Páidí again early in 1997 and got even less. That, however, was the year Kerry won the All-Ireland. When contacted in 2002, Páidí remembered the 1997 interview and his superstitious nature rose to the surface again. He began to see Kevin Kimmage as he saw me: a lucky omen. At the time he was under pressure locally, as some within the Kingdom were quite critical of Kerry's performance in the All-Ireland defeat to Armagh.

Kevin travelled to Páidí's house for the interview. After a little while, talk turned to the insatiable appetite for success in the county. Here's what Páidí said: 'We didn't win the All-Ireland last year so it didn't matter whether we lost by one point or 50. That's not acceptable to Kerry supporters … Being a Kerry manager is probably the hardest job in the world because Kerry people I'd say are the roughest type of fucking animals you could ever deal with. And you can print that.'

The following week, the *Sunday Independent* did just that. And there was war.

By Tuesday, the Kerry county board had disassociated themselves from the comments. From a PR perspective, they should have pointed out what he really meant. Because of their incredible history in Gaelic football, Kerry people demand success. That's what he meant. No offence intended. It was just Páidí's way. If you had heard it, you wouldn't have noticed, but on paper it looked bad. The Monday papers reprinted extracts from the article, it made *What it Says in the Papers* on Radio 1, and it was debated on *Liveline* later that day.

I read the interview on a flight from London to Cape

Town, where I was looking forward to a week's holiday, and had no idea that I'd get dragged into the escalating drama.

Before I get to that, I want to mention two other episodes from that South African trip.

Earlier, I talked about Michael King, one of my best friends at home in Quilty, and today the principal of the primary school in Annagh, which he has built into one of the best schools in Clare. His Aunty Annie, or Sr Marie Therese King, to give her her full title, was very good to me growing up. She was a member of the Sisters of Nazareth congregation in Port Elizabeth in South Africa, so I said I'd drop in to see her when I was there. She told me that she'd be sitting outside the convent keeping an eye out for me. I drove up and down the streets in Port Elizabeth all afternoon before I eventually spotted her, sitting in her white Sabbath robes on a simple wooden chair in the blazing sunshine. She was intent on the prayer book open in her hands and so didn't notice my arrival. As I pulled up, I tooted the horn and the smile that broke across her face stretched from South Africa to West Clare. She rose with arms outstretched, tears of joy in her eyes.

Quilty was meeting Quilty, neighbour meeting neighbour, adopted nephew meeting adopted aunt thousands and thousands of miles away in the country of Nelson Mandela. She treated Liz and me like royalty, filling us with food and drink. Aunty Annie herself ate little. She was too excited, she said.

Aunty Annie died a few years later, and was buried in South Africa, the country to which she had devoted most of her life. I will always remember her with great fondness and love.

In writing this, I couldn't remember what order Aunty Annie was in. I still had the number of the convent on my phone, so I chanced ringing the number. A woman with a strong South African accent told me she was a nurse and didn't know much about the nuns. But she gave me a different number in Port Elizabeth, and so I rang that.

'Hello,' says I.

'Hello.' A woman's voice.

'How are you?'

'Grand,' came the response.

My ears pricked. 'Are you Irish?' I asked.

'I am indeed, and who are you?'

'This is Marty Morrissey from RTÉ in Dublin.'

'Are you the fella who does the talking about the games?'

'I am. Where are you from?'

'I'm from near Magherafelt in County Derry,' she said warmly.

'What's your name?'

'I'm Sister Brigid, but they call me Bridie at home.'

'Great to talk to you, Sister,' I said, and explained that I was writing a book and that I wanted to check what order Sr Marie Therese King had been in. We talked about her work as a nun and the many years she had been living in South Africa, and then she floored me with a question.

'Have you heard of Jim McKeever?'

'Of course I have, a legend in Gaelic football.'

She laughed. 'He's my brother.'

I couldn't believe it. To check a fact for this book, eighteen years after I had visited Port Elizabeth, I rang a number that I figured was either disconnected or no longer in use, got another number and ended up talking with Sr Brigid, sister of Derry's Jim McKeever, the man who Kerry footballer Mick O'Connell once said was the best catcher of a ball that he had ever played against. McKeever was named in the football team of the century, comprising players who had never won an All-Ireland. He was captain of the Derry team that had lost to Dublin in the 1958 final.

That's the extraordinary thing about GAA people. You never know where we're going to turn up.

Over the years I had kept in contact with Sr. Cecelia, who gave me my first job teaching in Spanish Point. She had been transferred at different times to Ennis and Nenagh, where the Sisters of Mercy had convents and schools. Over time we fell out of contact, but shortly before the South Africa trip I had met Harry Hughes, a former vice principal at Spanish Point, and heard that Sr. Cecelia was now teaching in the township of Soweto in Johannesburg. I eventually got her number, and we agreed to meet at Johannesburg Airport, from where she'd take us on a tour of Soweto.

Unfortunately, the flight to Johannesburg was delayed, so all there was time for was a cup of coffee and sandwich in a nearby hotel. Seeing her there, in civilian clothes, brought back memories of the days when she was Principal in Spanish Point and she would come down to the house at nighttime to chill out, veil discarded, and we picked football teams till the early hours of the morning.

After our lovely chat over coffee, we walked back to her car, a small van with a rear door that opened upwards. There she began a clearly well-practised routine: she removed her navy veil from a bag and placed it gingerly on her head, followed up by a large cross which she kissed before hanging it visibly over her blouse.

Then came the surprise. Out of a leather bag emerged a very large double-barrelled gun, which she brought into the car with her and placed down between her seat and the door. I looked at her in disbelief.

'What's that for?' I asked stupidly.

She explained that Johannesburg was not a safe place, and while usually the veil was a great protection, it was helpful to have the gun in the car in case anything unexpected happened. She laughed out loud then and with a twinkle in her eye told me the gun 'was only a deterrent' and was not loaded. I couldn't get it out of my head for weeks. Sr. Cecelia is now back in Ennis, thankfully.

Anyway, back in January 2003, one of the first things I did when I arrived after the long flight from Heathrow was go for a stroll in the Victoria & Alfred shopping centre on Victoria Wharf. As I was walking along, I saw a crowd of familiar-looking lads coming towards me. It was the Kerry footballers, who by complete coincidence had come to Cape Town on holidays. Among them was Páidí's great friend Mike

McCarthy, better known as Mike Larkin because of a family connection with Larkin's bakery.

'Páidí is very bad, Marty,' he told me. 'Will you talk to him?'

'I will, of course,' I said, and told him that I was staying next door in the Radisson Blu. 'Tell Páidí to call me in the morning, but leave it after eleven. I'm on holidays!'

When the phone went off at 8.30 next morning, waking me from a deep sleep, I nearly fell out of bed with the shock. I fumbled for the receiver and with eyes still closed, I brought it to my ear.

'Marty? Is that you? Am I fucked?'

It was Páidí.

'Well,' I cleared my throat. 'You are in a bit of a storm . . .'

'Will you come up to me?' he asked. 'I need your help on this one, boy.'

He told me that himself and the Kerry team were staying in the Cullinan Hotel 'up the road', and to come up as soon as I could.

So, after breakfast I made my way to the hotel and asked at the reception desk to be put through to Mr Ó Sé's room. I was told that he was expecting me, so I took the lift to the sixth floor, found his room and knocked.

That familiar Kerry voice sang out: 'Coming Marty, coming . . .'

The door swung open and there was Páidí. He was stark naked. Not a stitch.

'Come in,' he said, 'and close the door.'

All I could see as he walked away were two bare cheeks of an arse that wobbled back and forth as he made his way towards the table and chairs in one corner of the room.

I closed the door as he sat down and began rubbing his tummy – something I had seen him do so many times before.

Then, still naked, he asked the same question he had asked on the phone an hour earlier.

'Am I fucked?'

'I don't honestly think you are,' I told him. 'This is a storm that will pass. It's January. There's nothing on except McGrath and O'Byrne cup games. It will pass, I promise you. I understood what you were trying to say, it's just on paper it looks a bit harsh.'

'But Jaysus, Marty, I meant it as a compliment. The Kerry people demand results. Nothing but Sam Maguire every year or every second year will keep them happy. That's what I meant . . . They ARE fucking animals.'

'Páidí,' I said, 'maybe you shouldn't use that phrase any more.'

He nodded. 'Probably not, no.'

I told him it would probably all be over by the time he got home, and that he could apologize then.

'Will the media be waiting for me at Farranfore Airport?' he asked.

I thought they might be, but advised him to just apologize and let the whole thing die.

'Marty!' He sat up straight, as if he'd been struck by a lightning bolt. 'I want you to do a piece with me. I need to be on the *Six One News* tonight back home. I need to kill this.'

I laughed. 'Páidí, we're in South Africa, not South Kerry. I'm on holidays. It's my first day here and I don't have a cameraman.'

But he had already made up his mind that I could save the day.

'Marty boy, we are great friends and you have always been a lucky omen for me, so organize it. Call Dublin. I need this to be done. I'm getting dressed.'

And off he went into his bedroom while I picked up the phone and started making calls.

Tony O'Donoghue was the TV sports news editor at the time. His immediate response was extremely positive. Tony got in contact with Ed Mulhall, who was then head of news, and a brilliant one at that, and he too was delighted that we were about to have an exclusive that evening on the *Six One News*.

I told Páidí that we would only get one shot at this and that he needed to prepare for the questions I was going to ask. I gave him an outline of what I had in mind, emphasizing that we were not going to get any more than two minutes on the news, so he needed to be precise. At this, Páidí jumped up and asked me for my phone.

'I must talk to the boss,' he said. He went off, dialling a number, then returned a few minutes later saying that he couldn't get the boss. I assumed he was talking about his wife, Máire. We turned again to the job at hand and he started making notes.

After twenty minutes, he reversed his chair suddenly, making a loud grating noise on the tiled floor.

'Give me your phone again.'

Ten minutes elapsed before he returned, saying, 'The boss says to go ahead with the interview.'

This was a relief, because RTÉ was expecting the interview and we'd already booked a cameraman and editing time in a Cape Town TV studio.

I had to ask. 'I assume it's Máire you're talking about,' I said, referring to Páidí's wife. 'It's nice to see that you think so highly of her that you call her "the boss".'

'Máire is not the boss,' he barked, almost angrily. 'There's only one boss in Ireland, Marty boy.'

'Who's that?'

He cocked his head, just like he used to do back in his playing days when he was lining up to take a fifty. 'Charles J. Haughey,' he said.

'Are you telling me you just rang the former Taoiseach to ask him if you should do this interview with me?'

'I sure did, and Charlie told me I should do this fucking thing. He thinks you're the right man in the right place, so come on, let's do it, Marty!'

Páidí was one of the greatest and most lovable rogues I was lucky enough to know. I never suspected him of telling me a lie, but curiosity got the better of me, so when I was on my own a little later, I flicked through my phone and dialled the number he had called. A woman answered.

'Hi . . . ah . . . is this the Haughey residence?'

'Yes it is,' came the immediate response.

I said that I was just checking the number for Páidí Ó Sé, and she replied that he had been talking to Charlie a little earlier.

'Thank you,' I said, 'Sorry for disturbing you.'

I had decided that we would do the interview down on the Waterfront Pier at the Radisson Blu, where I was staying, as I had learned from my visit to the Cullinan Hotel that not only were the Kerry footballers staying there but so too were the Kilkenny hurlers and, wait for it, the Dublin footballers! We got a taxi down to the Radisson Blu, and had to go through the bar to get down to the pier area. Time was ticking on. South Africa was only two hours ahead of Ireland, and I had to record this interview, edit it and send it back to Dublin well in time for the evening news.

There was still one further twist in the tail. As we were walking through the bar, Páidí sang out, 'Jesus Christ, Mick . . . how are you, boy?'

'Not bad, Páidí, how are you, mate? What the hell are you doing here?'

I knew the voice well, but because the cameraman walking behind us was so tall, it took me a moment to see the face. It was Mick McCarthy, the Republic of Ireland soccer manager. This was getting surreal. Páidí Ó Sé and Mick McCarthy in the same hotel in Cape Town at the same time. The two lads hugged each other. I had interviewed Mick a few times, so we knew each other a little.

'I'm in a bit of shite at home so I'm doing an interview with Marty,' Páidí explained.

'I know that feeling,' said Mick, in clear reference to the Roy Keane saga in Saipan the summer before. He went on, 'I read about your fucking animals in the papers on my way over here.'

'Do you think I should do the interview?'

'Absolutely, Páidí, you should. It's clearly a misunderstanding. Do you know what, mate? I should have done an interview with Marty and told him about my controversies in Saipan with Roy Keane. I should have talked more. So Páidí, do your interview.'

With the clock running down, I got Páidí out on the Waterfront Pier ready to rock. Just as we were about to start, he asked me for my sunglasses, which he took and placed on his head, saying that this was where the Kerry footballers wore their sunglasses these days. As we started, the sunglasses fell off, so he hung them in the top pocket of the jacket of his rather dashing white suit. As we set up, you could see Robben Island, where Nelson Mandela had been imprisoned for twenty-seven years, in the distance. It must have been the most exotic location for an interview on a GAA controversy ever.

We started with his clarification that the interview had taken place in his home in the afternoon, and not in the wee small hours in the pub. No one had taken any alcohol.

Then he apologized. 'I regret very much if in part of the interview, I offended some or all of my Kerry supporters. Kerry supporters have been very loyal to me both as a player and as a manager over the last thirty years and I say if I offended them in some parts of the article, I'm sorry. I apologize and I want to continue on from here.'

He continued: 'I suppose you could say, Marty – and I won't use the four-letter word – but I suppose we used to have the 'Horse' Kenneally, we used to have Tim 'Tiger' Lyons, and now I call Kerry supporters, without the four-letter word, "animals". I regret that, but they are animals, because they look for high standards because they want to camp in Croke Park every year. And I appreciate them for that and they are my driving force.'

He said that he had the full support of the county chairman, but most particularly, he had the support of the players. We talked a little more about the reaction to his comments and I asked him if he would resign.

He pointed to a dinghy bouncing in the harbour, laughed and said, 'No more than that boat out there will I resign.'

He went on, 'I have the full support of Kerry, the hard-core supporters. Nelson Mandela spent twenty-seven years in Robben Island. I played my first game with Mick O'Connell in 1973 above in Tuam Stadium. That's thirty years ago and I'm still involved with Kerry football. Every hour and minute of the day that I wake up, Kerry football is the first thing that comes into my mind. And, well, that's the people's choice. Far be it from me to be praising myself. Self-praise is no praise.'

'But you will be the Kerry manager for 2003?'

'I should hope so.'

I felt he could answer that question a little better, so after a brief chat I pointed out that there were lots of people who thought he should resign, and asked again if he would remain on.

'Well, my intention is not to resign. First of all I feel I have the Kerry county board support. I was misinterpreted. It was a compliment to the people of Kerry I paid. They took it up totally wrong. I have no intention of resigning. I'm taking it like Páidí Ó Sé always did, on the head, and I love to be leading Kerry into the All-Ireland championship in 2003 and hopefully we will win.'

We filmed a few more questions, but the essence of what Páidí wanted to say was in the can. He walked up and down the pier a few times so we could get a few shots of him. This time he flung the jacket over his left shoulder and wore my sunglasses perched on his head. I did a piece to camera to finish off the package: 'With Páidí Ó Sé clearly determined not to resign, his view and indeed the view of the players here in South Africa is that the controversy should now be concluded. The question that now remains is will the Kerry people and the Kerry county board forgive and forget? Marty Morrissey, RTÉ News, Cape Town, South Africa.'

Páidí wanted to come to the TV station where we had to edit the package. By that point we had spent so much time filming that we were under severe pressure to finish the job on time. Long story short, we got it out and it aired as planned on the *Six One News*. While the interview got widespread coverage over the following days, it did not eradicate the anger in the Kingdom.

I do believe that, in his own inimitable way, Páidí had been paying the people of Kerry a huge compliment. It was just that those words in cold print had a different effect than if you'd heard them coming out of his mouth. Make no mistake about it, and no matter what he said to me on camera, Páidí was upset by the whole experience. He guided Kerry to a seventh Munster title in eight years, but failed to get past Tyrone in the All-Ireland semi-final. And so his reign came to an end. Two All-Ireland titles and seven Munster crowns in eight years was an impressive haul. Now, with the gift of time and hindsight, I wonder would the people of Kerry be more forgiving and more patient?

Páidí was unique. He was valuable to Kerry for a multitude of reasons, many of them beyond football.

In 2004 he took the bizarre decision to accept an invitation to manage Westmeath. Dessie Dolan, one of their star footballers, has regaled me, and many others, with more Páidí stories.

In the autumn of 2003, six Westmeath players had come to Des Maguire, the vice-chairman of Westmeath GAA, to say that they felt they were operating on 85 per cent of their ability and that they needed a big name to bring them to the next level. Earlier that year Mick O'Dwyer had guided Laois to a Leinster final victory, and so Des thought that maybe it was time Westmeath had their own Kerryman. He rang Páidí and told him that there was a job for him in Westmeath if he wanted it. At the time, the final act of his tenure as Kerry manager was still playing itself out.

'Thanks for thinking of me,' said Páidí, 'but I'm not gone yet.'

The following evening, Des was busy preparing Mullingar Shamrocks' minor team for a match when his mobile rang. He didn't recognize the number.

'Des, it's Páidí.'

Des was focused on the training session and was clearly a little distracted. 'Páidí who?'

'Páidí Ó Fucking Sé, that's who. If that job is still going, I want it.'

Des never made the same mistake again.

Páidí arrived in Westmeath, naturally enough, by helicopter. The scenes in Mullingar, where thousands came out to greet him, were quite simply unbelievable. You'd swear they had won the All-Ireland.

The rumour went out that he was getting paid a fortune, but the truth was that he never took a penny. Páidí told me many times that he didn't want money, and I know too that he told the county board that he would walk if they mentioned it again.

All he wanted was that the players be taken care of. He was there purely to prove a point. And Kerry were watching closely.

More than 15,000 turned up for the O'Byrne Cup final in Cusack Park, Mullingar. I don't think they've got a bigger crowd since. Westmeath would go on to lose the opening six games of the league. Des and Westmeath were a bit concerned at this stage. There was a running joke that Páidí would be awarded an OBE: Out Before Easter.

But Páidí had no time for winter football, whether he was in Kerry or Westmeath. He would often ask, 'Who won the league last year? Who won it the year before?' The implication being that no one remembers anything but the championship. 'Winter football is not for us, but when the swallow comes, we'll be singing.'

Early in his tenure, he brought the Westmeath panel to Sunderland football club, then being managed by Mick

McCarthy. They went out on to the manicured training fields and, giddy with excitement, they started heading the ball to each other. Páidí was not impressed and put a stop to it immediately. 'We didn't come here to play that sport!'

He loved training on the beaches of West Kerry, but of course there were no beaches in Westmeath, so he got a sand track organized in Ballinagore. This became a massive attraction in the county. But in the overall analysis, the best move of all was to persuade Tomás Ó Flatharta to train and coach the team. Westmeath won their first Leinster title with Páidí that year. It was an immense achievement and a resounding endorsement of his ability as a manager.

It was also during his time with Westmeath that I saw him change a little. There were times when I thought he wasn't himself. Westmeath wasn't Kerry, and he did not enjoy the game against Kerry in the league. It felt wrong to him to be trying to beat the Kingdom. Losing to Derry in the All-Ireland series after winning that elusive provincial title also hit him hard. I think he felt he had brought the team as far as he could, but more importantly, he had proven a point to himself and Kerry by winning that Leinster title. He was a winning manager, but it didn't feel right when he wasn't surrounded by the green and gold of the Kingdom. The following year was far less successful for Westmeath, and Páidí departed after a series of defeats, the last one to Clare.

He called me a few weeks before Christmas of 2006, asking me to go down to him in Ventry as he had an exclusive for me. He had accepted Clare's invitation to become their football manager and he wanted me to announce it on the news.

I told him I'd be down the following day around four o'clock in the afternoon, and we agreed to meet in the Dingle

Skelligs Hotel. On my way to Kerry I rang the Clare county chairman, Michael 'Malty' McDonagh, to congratulate him on getting Páidí to cross the Shannon and take charge of Clare. Malty was shocked to say the least. While they had travelled to Kerry to have a chat with Páidí about the possibility of him joining the Banner, nothing had been confirmed. He hadn't even rung them back with his decision.

It was a cold, wet, blustery afternoon in Dingle and the hotel was in total darkness when I arrived. The wind was howling as I squeezed the front door open. Páidí was waiting inside for me, but we decided to leave the TV interview until the following afternoon, so that he could plan what he wanted to say. He went home to Ceann Trá. By the time the next day's *Six One News* was over, he was the Clare manager.

Páidí brought Vincent O'Connor with him across the Shannon and invited Barry Keating from Éire Óg in Ennis and Kieran Kelleher to join him as selectors. But somehow the chemistry was never right. Nothing clicked.

There were funny moments, like the July evening in Ardfinnan when Clare played Tipperary in a Tommy Murphy Cup match. Páidí arrived into the dressing-room full of gusto and guff. There was a player lying on his stomach on a table in the middle of the room getting a massage from the physiotherapist.

'Jesus Christ,' said Páidí, 'are you injured? Are we missing you?'

'No, I should be OK,' came the response.

'Fear mhaith,' said Páidí and started undressing in the corner of the room.

Now the player slowly got up and turned to him. 'Páidí, you're in the wrong dressing-room. This is Tipperary's.'

The Banner beat the Premier that evening but lost a week later to Antrim, and soon after that, Páidí Ó Sé resigned as Clare football manager. He would never manage at inter-county level again.

But he had nothing to prove. He had done it all. All-Ireland-winning Kerry footballer, All-Ireland-winning Kerry captain, All-Ireland winning Kerry manager, Leinster-winning manager with Westmeath. What a legend.

Five and a half years later, at the age of fifty-seven, Páidí Ó Sé died suddenly. I miss him, his great character and his wonderful sense of fun. The Ó Sé family's loss was West Kerry's loss and Ireland's loss. The place is quiet without him. Dull even.

16. The Cody Interview

On the evening of September 6th, 2009, Kilkenny beat Tipperary to win the All-Ireland senior hurling title and achieve the remarkable four in a row – equalling what Cork did in the early 1940s. Kilkenny had beaten Cork in 2006, Limerick in 2007, Waterford in 2008 and now their greatest of all rivals, Tipperary.

In naming his team for the final, manager Brian Cody had omitted his 2008 All-Ireland winning captain, James 'Cha' Fitzpatrick, in favour of Derek Lyng. Richie Hogan started at wing forward, with Henry Shefflin moving to centre forward. Martin Comerford was the player to lose out.

Tipperary were leading by two points on the 62nd minute when Kilkenny's Richie Power received a hand pass between the 13-metre and 20-metre lines. Paul Curran, who was marking Richie, moved in to tackle him. They met initially outside the large rectangle, but by the time a foul was adjudged to have been committed, they were inside the large rectangle. Referee Diarmuid Kirwan blew his whistle and stretched out his arms, indicating a penalty. It was a major decision, a crucial call in an All-Ireland hurling final with just eight minutes to go and very little between the teams. Personally I thought it was either a free in or a free out for over-carrying. I felt the penalty decision was harsh.

Henry Shefflin, one of the coolest and greatest hurlers that I ever saw, stood over the penalty. Facing him was Brendan Cummins, up there with Damien Fitzhenry and Davy

Fitzgerald among the best goalkeepers that I ever saw. Conor O'Mahony and Padraig Maher stood either side of Cummins on the Tipperary goal line at the Hill 16 end, but not one of the three could stop Henry's shot. Martin Comerford, who had been introduced, scored a cracking goal less than a minute later to prove a point and to secure victory for Kilkenny. Full-time score: Kilkenny 2–22 Tipperary 0–23. The result confirmed that Kilkenny team as the greatest of all time.

Black and amber flags fluttered in the wind, 'The Rose of Mooncoin' could be heard echoing around GAA Headquarters, Brian Cody leaped around like Istabraq at a champion hurdle with Charlie Swan on his back. It was magical. It was special and it was historic.

In 2009 the Liam MacCarthy Cup was presented to the winning captain on the steps of the Hogan stand. Despite numerous appeals beforehand, the pitch was once again invaded by thousands of supporters. Afterwards, GAA President Christy Cooney spoke of his disappointment and concern over the safety of fans.

I was sideline reporter that day. By now, the post-match interviews that used to be held on the pitch had moved indoors, down the corridor past the dressing-rooms on the Hogan stand side. After the presentation to Michael Fennelly, the Kilkenny team went down the tunnel and celebrated their great victory together in the privacy of their dressing-room. I should say that even when things began to change and media became less welcome in and around dressing-rooms, I always got a warm welcome in Kilkenny's.

I've already mentioned the floor manager, the late Tadhg de Brún, who was always by my side on the sideline. A very special man, a kind man. The softness of his approach taught me to be patient when others are getting their knickers in a twist looking for a winning manager or man of the match interview. We on the frontline have to resist the adrenaline rush and treat the winning and losing dressing-rooms with respect at a time when emotions are running high. On this occasion Tadhg, with his big headphones and crackling walkie-talkie, went off to find Brian Cody and ask him to join us in the newly built but far-from-complete TV interview rooms. When Brian arrived, he was clearly in good form and why wouldn't he be? Kilkenny had just won the four in a row, and the county's thirty-second All-Ireland title. It was also the week his autobiography was to be launched.

He looked at the monitor showing the studio conversation ongoing between Michael Lyster, Cyril Farrell, Ger Loughnane and Tomás Mulcahy. Though he couldn't hear what was being said, I remember him passing a comment about the so-called experts, in a tone that suggested that he didn't always agree with them. Next thing we got the instruction from the director that they were going to come to us, so Brian got into position and off we went.

Things went fine at the beginning. Brian talked about how the spirit of the team came through when the going got tough.

'I've always said it,' he said. 'The team is built on spirit, and spirit brings you just anywhere you want to go really. Our spirit was tested to its limits there but came shining through . . . It's difficult to win one, to win two, madness to win three, but to try to come back to do it again should be impossible really . . . and you can't do it with just skill, you can't do it with a decent panel, if you don't have the thing that binds the whole thing together . . . it will fall apart.'

He talked too about Henry standing up and taking what he described as the toughest penalty he ever had to face.

This was my cue.

'And was it a penalty, Brian, do you think?'

'Well, Diarmuid Kirwan certainly gave a penalty.' He laughed. 'If you were to start wondering about all the frees in the course of a game, you'd have a fairly busy time. Did you think yourself it was a penalty, Marty?'

'Well, I wasn't too sure, but it just seemed a little bit dodgy in the replay.'

'I have no idea, Marty. Did you check all the other frees as well to see if they were dodgy as well? Maybe you should, maybe you should.'

'In terms of the referee, were you pleased overall? I'm sure you are now since you have won the All-Ireland, but did you think he left a lot go?'

'Ah Marty, please! Give me a break, will you? The referee? We are supposed to say nothing about referees. I have a habit of saying nothing about referees. Diarmuid Kirwan, I'm certain, went out to do the very best he possibly could. You seem to have had a problem with him. You tell me.'

'No,' I said, 'I had no problem with him but it's obviously a point of debate after the game.' I was about to go on but Brian interrupted.

'I can't understand, Marty, how this discussion with me is turning into a debate about a referee. It started off about the four in a row, now all you want is to talk about the referee, it sounds a bit silly.'

'Well, it's a talking point. The point is, and this is the most important point, Brian Cody, is that you have won the All-Ireland for the fourth year in a row and nothing should take away from that.'

'Well, I wasn't taking nothing away from it for certain except sheer pride and absolute joy.'

'And we are all sharing in that joy and success. Well done, Brian Cody.'

And we shook hands.

The pictures cut back to a wide shot of *The Sunday Game* studio upstairs and there was a second or two of absolute silence before Michael, being the professional that he was, broke the ice.

'Yeah, Brian Cody being interviewed there by Marty Morrissey. I don't know if Marty will be buying the book after that.'

There was an explosion of laughter from the boys, Cyril Farrell, Ger Loughnane and Thomas Mulcahy. 'He'll get a free one,' said Cyril.

Ger Loughnane, of course, couldn't hold himself back. 'Will someone please pick up Marty off the floor there?' Followed by that contagious Loughnane laugh.

Meanwhile, down in the media zone in the bowels of the Hogan stand, Brian Cody headed briskly back to the Kilkenny dressing-room.

Tadhg looked at me perplexed. 'What the fuck just happened there? What was wrong with him?'

'I don't know,' I said, but I couldn't leave it at that, so I took off after Cody.

'Brian,' I called after him, 'what was that about? When you mentioned the penalty, I had to ask you about it.'

'It was totally inappropriate, Marty. We had just won the four in a row and you wanted to talk about the referee. I felt your questioning was inappropriate.'

That was that. He continued on to the dressing-room.

Very soon after that, my phone began to light up with calls from journalists asking for a comment about the interview. Ryle Nugent, then head of sport in RTÉ, asked me if I was

OK and told me that I had done a great job. 'You asked the question that the people at home would love to ask if they had the microphone.'

Social media was relatively new at the time, but it still went wild. For a while the Cody/Morrissey interview was as big a topic of conversation as the match itself.

I got several texts from ex-Kilkenny players who said, 'You know what Cody can be like. If you poke the bear . . .' A few Kilkenny hurlers who had played that day also called to see was I alright, which was very decent of them.

The following morning I was on a very early flight to Milan to report on the world boxing championships. It was a funny morning at Dublin Airport. When I checked in at the Aer Lingus desk, the woman behind the counter asked, 'Where's Cody?'

At security, there was a gang of Dublin lads: 'Ah Marty, I'm glad somebody went down to pick you up!'

Best of all, the beautiful flight attendant at the front door of the aircraft said, 'Oh Marty, we love you in Tipperary. We all shouted "Go on, Marty!" when you asked Cody about the penalty. I'm glad to see you're alive. Welcome on board.' And she gave me a massive hug and a kiss on the cheek. At that point I began to wonder if the Cody interview was the best thing that ever happened to me. As I turned to go down the aisle, the passengers gave me a round of applause. Maybe they were all Tipperary supporters.

I bought every newspaper, and there was something about my post-match chat with Brian in all of them. And as he was interviewed by my print media colleagues later that day, the story ran on into Tuesday as well. In quiet moments in Milan, when I had no one else to talk to, I worried that I had been wrong in my line of questioning, but hand on heart I didn't set out to be controversial. I simply had to ask the relevant questions on one of Ireland's biggest sporting days. In my heart I felt I did my job as sideline reporter, but you're always wondering, or at least I'm always wondering, what are they thinking back at base? As sideline reporter, you're the first port of call for a manager or a player who is going through extreme emotions – either positive or negative. Negotiating that can be difficult at times.

Two weeks after I returned from Italy, I decided to call Brian Cody. I had given him enough time, I thought, to cool off, and I also wanted to say a couple of things privately to him.

He answered the phone himself and we had a good chat. I explained where I was coming from and he was equally honest by reiterating his opinion that he felt the direction of my questioning was inappropriate. I told him I had nothing but the height of respect for himself and for Kilkenny and reiterated my own view that I wouldn't have done my job properly if I hadn't asked about the penalty.

We agreed to differ. He was firm and assertive but also quite respectful and warm. Has it affected our relationship? I don't think so, to be honest. I can only speak for myself. Over the intervening years, we have done loads of interviews.

In 2021 I was reporting on a league game in Nowlan Park between Kilkenny and Laois. The only way I could get a post-match interview with the two managers, Brian Cody and Cheddar Plunkett, was to invite them to the radio commentary position in the new stand, which meant a walk across the pitch and up the steps of the stand. Considering our history, I was hesitant about asking Brian. But apart from an initial 'Ah Jesus, Marty', he did it without hesitation. I didn't realize anybody was watching, but several Kilkenny

officials got a great kick out of seeing Cody going across the pitch with me and up to the radio position. They couldn't stop slagging me or laughing, as they hadn't seen him do that for years. In fact one said he had never done it. For them, it was a signal that 'Cody and Marty are back on track'.

I still love Kilkenny hurling. Their massive work ethic, their hooking and blocking, their passion, their physical presence and fabulous skill set marks the person wearing a black and amber jersey as someone special. In so many ways a Kilkenny hurler is just a mirror image of their wonderful manager.

I remember many years ago we decided to do a different type of piece as a preview for yet another All-Ireland final appearance by the Cats. We planned to ask Brian about his other hobbies. Going to the cinema maybe? Going for long walks in the countryside? So we asked about Monday evenings. On Monday evenings, he told us, the juniors were training in James Stephens. Tuesday night was Kilkenny training. Wednesday was the James Stephens under-16s. Thursday evening was also hurling, as was Friday and most of Saturday. So we abandoned the idea. The man eats, drinks and sleeps hurling.

Since 1998, when he took over as Kilkenny manager, he has won eleven All-Ireland titles, seventeen Leinster championships, ten national leagues, and seven Walsh Cups. Uniquely, he was RTÉ's Man of the Match for the 2008 All-Ireland final, something that had never been done before, nor since. I've seen him achieve what he's achieved up close and personal. He is a legend of the game and is, without doubt, the greatest hurling manager. A school principal by profession, he is authoritative and assertive. It's either his way or the highway.

Many years after our tête-à-tête, I was lying by the pool in hot Dubai when my phone rang. I squinted at it through the hazy sunshine: Brian Cody. I jumped up out of the deckchair like T. J. Reid leaps for a dropping ball, wondering what the hell he wanted me for.

'Hello Marty, sorry for disturbing you but we're running a big fundraiser in the Lyrath Estate and I know you are good at that old stuff. Will you MC it for me?'

'I will of course, Brian. I'd be delighted to.'

That was as close to a compliment as I ever got from Brian Cody. And for the record, we had a great night in the Lyrath Hotel, where over 1,000 people attended.

I was asked several times over the years to be MC at Kilkenny's All-Ireland medal presentation nights, and I'd have to assume that I wouldn't have been asked without his blessing. Unfortunately, the call from Kilkenny was always a bit late and I was always booked for some other event around the country. This was always a great disappointment for me, as I would have considered it a great honour, a great compliment to be there. I would have loved to slag Cody off from the stage.

'Well Brian, did you think it was a penalty?'

I'm hoping even he would laugh at this stage.

17. Me, Pope Francis, Eid and Knock

I know this will shock you, but once upon a time I wanted to be a priest. Fr Morrissey, I thought, had a nice ring to it. I even went to the point of saying mass in the house. I was only eight or nine at the time. My vestments consisted of a towel, the host was a Marietta biscuit, the chalice was a flower vase, lemonade was the wine and Fr Marty was at your service. Somewhere in my homily I prayed for the souls of two neighbours, Joe Flynn and Patrick Clancy, who were alive and well and sitting in the front row in the kitchen attending my first mass.

To be honest, I don't think my childhood desire to be a priest had anything to do with spiritual awareness, but it may have had something to do with being the centre of attention. Only-child syndrome I call it.

I served mass in St Ann's Church on Bainbridge Avenue in the Bronx, and also in Mullagh Church in West Clare, where I was once photographed holding the paten as Fr Michael O'Keeffe was giving out holy communion during his first mass. The picture appeared in the *Clare Champion* and became the most talked-about photo in our house.

In 2014, ten years after my father died, I decided to organize a once-off Christmas concert to raise funds for a new heating system in that same church. My main motivation, however, was to raise the spirits of the community, which had been through quite a bit of tragedy and loss that year. I asked the parish priest, Fr Anthony McMahon, for the loan

of the church, and he readily agreed. A few of the locals were disgruntled at the prospect of a concert in a place that, in their view, should be reserved as a house of prayer. We respected their perspective, but I also knew that the church could accommodate a larger crowd and would create a wonderful atmosphere.

We sold out within days, but then look who we had coming to Mullagh: Phil Coulter, Mike Denver, Sandy Kelly, Tommy Fleming, the Galway Tenors, the Kilfenora Céilí Band, the Eugene Donnellan set dancers and the great P. J. Murrihy and his family. P. J., if you remember, had sung at the medal presentation in St Joseph's Spanish Point thirty-one years earlier. There was also the incredibly talented Micheál Sexton, brilliant local musicians Caroline Tubridy and Brid Donoghue and her family, and the Mullagh church choir. A wonderful committee came together to work on the project: Beatrice O'Dwyer, Tim Donnellan, Therese Doohan, Rita O'Dwyer, and many more. John Joe Hassett built a magnificent stage around the altar while the GAA club organized parking in and around the village. It was a wonderful night. For the first time in decades, Mullagh buzzed with excitement, and the whole thing culminated in us earning over €20,000. The benefits can be seen today, particularly on a cold winters' morning when the heating system makes it a little bit more comfortable to pray.

It was spring 2018 when my phone rang and the name Tom McGuire, who was head of RTÉ Radio 1 at the time, appeared on the screen. He said something that I didn't quite catch but it sounded like he was asking me to commentate on the Pope in Croke Park.

'Tom. Did you say "the Pope"?'

'Yes I did,' said Tom. 'It's been confirmed he's coming in August, so get the finger out and start doing your research. Eileen Heron will be your producer. Talk soon.'

I was delighted. A new challenge! We had several production meetings, and as usual Eileen had everything organized to a tee. Her only source of apprehension was Croke Park. She had never worked there before, so I suppose that's where I came in. I knew every door and window in GAA Headquarters. Joining me on the radio that Saturday night would be a friend of mine, Alison O'Connor, a great journalist from Bantry. We had started our careers around the same time on Leeside. Alison did a lot of work for the *Cork Examiner*, as it was at the time, while I was in RTÉ Cork Local Radio. Fr Joe McDonald, from the Falls Road in Belfast, who was at the time the parish priest at St Matthew's in

Ballyfermot, would be the third member of the broadcast team. We would be stationed in the commentary position on the seventh floor of the Hogan stand, which, by now, was like a second home to me.

I was nervous to be honest, but maybe on reflection it was probably more an adrenaline rush. After all, how many times would I get the chance to commentate on a pope visiting Croke Park? Anyway, I told myself, it was radio. Everybody would be watching it on TV. But as I followed the reaction on social media, I very quickly copped on to the fact that a great many people were listening in their cars and in their homes around the world.

The Pope was in Ireland for the World Meeting of Families, and the event in Croke Park was seen as one of the key moments in his short visit. A crowd of about 80,000 had gathered in the stands and on the pitch, with clear avenues between groups so the Popemobile could navigate the venue speedily and safely. We were chatting live on the radio when suddenly the crowd erupted into spontaneous applause. There was no announcement, no fanfare, just a kind of spiritual vibe that rippled through the crowd.

I began: 'So this is it. This is the moment. This is history. A pope, spiritual leader to 1.3 billion Catholics on Planet Earth, has travelled across Europe from Rome to be with us and to witness the church's World Meeting of Families and is about to enter Croke Park, home of the GAA, the Gaelic Athletic Association. We are reaching out to you tonight from the third largest stadium in Europe . . . This is Croke Park, Dublin, Ireland. Wherever you are in the world right now, from Donegal to Dingle, from New York to Sydney, let me tell you that the 266th Pope is now entering Ireland's most iconic stadium. The scene is spellbinding. The man in all white has arrived from Rome. The reaction from his flock is jubilant, emotional, spiritual . . . magical even.'

There was a tremendous roar as the Popemobile arrived from the corner of the Nally and Hogan stands. Flashes flared all around the stadium as everyone strained to catch their first glimpse of Pope Francis. The Popemobile moved slowly up past the 13-metre and 20-metre lines, with Pope Francis waving and smiling as he came, his black-suited security detail walking briskly alongside.

I went on: 'There's a magnificent stage built in front of Hill 16, while on the pitch are thousands of people sitting or standing on thousands of seats. The Hogan, the Cusack, the Davin stands are all packed. It's like a mega rock concert on All-Ireland final day, but the main man is Pope Francis. It's unforgettable. It's surreal. It's fantastic.'

I talked about the history of Croke Park, about Bloody Sunday in November 1920, and about the many legends of the game who have graced that sacred ground. There was the famous boxing match between Muhammad Ali and Al Lewis in 1972, and of course the list of megastars who'd performed on stage, from Tina Turner and Garth Brooks to Elton John, U2 and Bruce Springsteen.

'Pope Francis in his Popemobile is now gone past the Davin and is heading down to the Cusack stand, still waving, still smiling. He's gone past the 45 and heading towards the 65 . . . The Pope is now in front of the stage. The circle around Croke Park has been completed. An amazing sight to behold. For the people in Croke Park, their faith is alive, vibrant and real. Meeting the Pope up close and personal is a life's dream fulfilled . . . Tonight for the concert, he will not sit on the stage, as he did in Philadelphia a few years ago, when he was a Caesar-like figure at the back of the stage, but will sit amongst the people with Cardinal Kevin Farrell and Archbishop Diarmuid Martin on either side of him.'

As he arrived into the stadium, Patrick Bergin sang Leonard Cohen's 'Anthem'. Once seated, he was treated to a short performance from a Riverdance troupe, Daniel O'Donnell sang a song, and Sr Bernadette led a band of children in a rousing Dingle polka. There was a performance from the High Hopes choir and African dancers, and Andrea Bocelli and Celine Byrne performed 'Ave Maria'. At the end of the night, Andrea Bocelli returned for an incredibly rousing version of 'Nessun Dorma', which had many in the crowd in tears, and everyone on their feet.

It was a night I will never forget. For a few weeks afterwards I'd been asked, 'Where is the Pope now?' My response was, 'He's in Rome – but a week ago he was between the 45 and 65 on the Cusack stand side!'

Almost two years later, in July 2020, I got a call out of the blue from Roger Childs, commissioning editor and executive producer of religious content in RTÉ. His beautiful, soft English accent was touched by a smile as he came to the reason for his call.

'We're going to broadcast Eid live on *RTÉ News Now* and I'd like you to commentate on it.'

I was both bewildered and flattered by Roger's invitation. I asked him to give me a day or two and let me think about it. But I have to be honest: when he said that there were those in management who weren't sure it should be me doing it, that decided me. I would do it, and do it to the very best of my ability. As my close friends and colleagues will tell you, I can be pig-headed and stubborn sometimes! The fact that

Kathy Fox was going to produce the event for RTÉ also swung my decision, as I think she's brilliant.

Diversity is so important for our society, and with that openness comes understanding, acceptance and respect for the other person's views and traditions.

We shouldn't forget that not so long ago, when our ancestors were forced to leave Ireland to look for work, we suffered the ignominy of seeing signs that said 'No Irish need apply.'

So I began my research and learned that Eid al-Adha is known as 'The Great Eid' and is considered the holier of the two Eids, the other being Eid al-Fitr. The festival is marked with Salat (Prayer) followed by the Khutbah or Sermon by the imam. At the conclusion of the prayers and sermon, Muslims embrace and exchange greetings and give gifts, so it's a bit like Christmas. Many Muslims also take this opportunity to invite non-Muslim friends, neighbours, co-workers and classmates to festivities to better acquaint them with Islam and Muslim culture. In normal years, it's also a time of pilgrimage. Muslims are encouraged to go on a five-day Hajj, or pilgrimage to Mecca, once in their lifetime. In 2020, because of Covid-19, pilgrimages were almost impossible, so Muslims had to find other ways to celebrate.

Shaykh Umar al-Qadri is a Sunni Islamic scholar and sheikh who arrived in Ireland in 2004 after completing his religious studies in Pakistan, and founded the Clonee Mosque in a residential estate. Four years later, he founded the Al-Mustafa Islamic Cultural Centre Ireland in Dublin.

Umar sees no conflict between being Muslim and being Irish. His daughter in primary school is helping him learn Irish. He deliberately preaches in English to his Blanchardstown congregation as a signal that Islam is not a 'foreign' faith. It's also a unifying language for Muslims who have roots in Indonesia, Malaysia, Nigeria, Pakistan and the Middle East. He was critical of his own father, a Pakistani cleric who worked as an imam in The Hague for over twenty years but never learned Dutch. He wants to send a message that Muslims are not in Ireland to take over, but to enrich an increasingly diverse and mutually respectful culture.

RTÉ's live broadcast of the event was seen as historic. So no pressure then!

There was clearly huge interest from many Muslims who would have liked to have been part of Eid at GAA Headquarters. Within two hours of the event being announced, 500 people had registered on Eventbrite and another 500 on Facebook. The problem was that because of Covid, no more than 200 people could attend. This made the live broadcast all the more important. It's important too to acknowledge the GAA for allowing Eid to take place in Croke Park, and RTÉ for deciding to broadcast it for the very first time.

It was a very small crew that morning in Croke Park, with satellite engineers Tom Drury and Davy Ebbs, cameramen Paul Deighan, Owen Corcoran and Colm Hand, while the sound engineer was Steve Farrell. Jarlath Tierney directed and Kathy Fox, as I've said, was the producer.

My main job – much like my main job during matches – was to let the audience know what was happening, to let the sound and pictures tell the story. Lorraine O'Connor from the Muslim Sisters of Éire joined me on commentary. She is a native of Dublin who converted to Islam. We had one meeting a couple of days before Eid, and considering that broadcasting was a totally new experience for her, she took to her new role with great grace, bringing a deep knowledge of what was happening during the ceremony.

The Eid Prayer and Eid Sermon were given by Shaykh

With Lorraine O'Connor

Umar Al-Qadri. This man is one of the finest orators I have ever heard: powerful, succinct and sincere. Other faith leaders spoke, and there was a most wonderful uplifting speech by Abood Abdullah Aljumaili, who travelled to Dublin with his family in 2008 to escape the war in Iraq. He was just nine years of age when he arrived in Ireland and couldn't speak a word of English. What helped him to make the transition and settle in Ireland? The GAA. He couldn't even hold a hurley at the start, but he practised every evening and now plays with his club, Ballinteer St John's in south Dublin. He provided a wonderful end to a unique and memorable day.

The warm welcome I received from everyone involved in Eid will stay with me for ever. When Shaykh Umar Al-Qadri saw me walking down the sideline in front of the Cusack stand, he shouted, 'Ah, Marty Party! How are you? What do you think? Will the Dubs win six in a row?'

The phone rang one Monday lunchtime in 2017. I recognized it as an RTÉ number and answered, expecting someone from the news or sports departments. Instead it was a member of the *Liveline* team, letting me know that I was about to become the topic of conversation on the programme when they went on air.

'What? Why?'

'Because of your sermon at the Knock Solemn Novena last Wednesday.'

'My what?'

It turned out that a piece had appeared in the *Catholic Voice* under the headline, 'Inappropriate "Speech" at Knock Novena'.

'Have a look at it if you can,' I was told, 'and if you wish to comment, call me back.'

I had no intention of commenting, but I did turn on the radio.

Now, I don't know Anne Keeling, the journalist who wrote the piece, but I'm sure she's an excellent journalist. Her points were well made and of course I respect her view, but I don't have to agree with her criticisms. In her two-page analysis of my 'speech' in Knock the previous Wednesday she wrote:

> *Are RTÉ personalities now our religious guides? Or have our congregations become so feeble minded that this is the only calibre of homilist that will draw us in our thousands and entertain us, as we seem to need to be entertained not with the Higher teachings of the Church but with amateur psychology? A joke from Mr Morrissey about thinking Fr Gibbon's call was to ask him for tickets to the All-Ireland football final between Dublin and Mayo elicited a burst of laughter. From then on there were regular peals from the congregation who seemed to be delighted as a typical Friday night* Late Late Show *audience.*

She also said:

I noticed that he had for reasons best known to himself, chosen to leave the top buttons of his shirt undone.

Now, Joe Duffy is a masterful broadcaster as we all know. He dealt with the matter fairly and objectively, eliciting opinions both in my favour and against.

I think Tom Shiel, writing in the *Irish Times* the day after I spoke, understood what I was about better than Anne Keeling. He said:

Gaelic games broadcaster Marty Morrissey received a standing ovation in Knock Basilica yesterday when he outlined his advice for living a happy and fulfilled life. Addressing several thousand pilgrims at the annual novena, he spoke for almost 30 minutes on the theme of living life to the full. His 3 p.m. address was interrupted by several outbreaks of applause.

Tom also went to the bother of talking to a native of Knock, Joe Rattigan, who said, 'It was a great idea for Fr Richard to ask Marty to speak at the novena. We need more lay speakers like him if the popularity of the nine-day novena is to be continued.'

The whole thing started a few weeks earlier when I got a phone call from Fr Richard Gibbons, the parish priest in Knock. When he introduced himself, my first thought was that he was looking for tickets for the All-Ireland. My second was that it was one of the lads from home – Butcher or Rabbit or Moose – pulling my leg (that happens a lot). This guy had a more distinguished accent, however, so I heard him out. But when he asked me to speak at Knock novena, I was gobsmacked.

'Are you joking me?'

He wasn't. He told me that my colleague Bryan Dobson

had spoken at the novena in the past and that the people in Knock really wanted me to speak this year.

OK, now I was convinced this was a joke.

Right at that moment, who came around the corner only Bryan Dobson. I called him over, thinking, I have this guy now. So I handed the phone to Dobbo. The joker on the other end of the phone introduced himself, and Dobbo goes, 'Oh hello Richard, how are you?'

Good God, I thought, this Fr Richard is real. I felt I couldn't say no at that point.

When the day finally arrived and I sat on a stool behind the altar, near where the candles are lit, I suddenly experienced a strong sense of cold feet. The basilica was thronged. Jammed. Standing room only. At this point, however, there was no going back. When Fr Richard introduced me, I walked forward with great nervousness and trepidation but pretending – of course – to be super cool. I asked the Blessed Virgin Mary not to abandon me, even if she didn't like any of my broadcast work; and if my late father was around, he would be a great help too.

I introduced myself to the crowd and told them that they were not about to hear a sermon, that I was no preacher. 'I'm one of ye, an ordinary Joe Soap trying to do his best here on Earth, trying to live life honestly and use whatever gifts God gave me. I'm certainly no holy Joe, in fact I'm no holy Marty!'

Fr Richard had asked me to speak on the topic of 'living life to the full'. In my view, love is number one. Love is the greatest power on earth. To live life to the full, we must love life to the full. Whatever we give in life is what we receive in return. I genuinely find that if you give positivity, you receive positivity. Feelings of enthusiasm, excitement and passion come from love, and when we feel any of them consistently, they give us a life filled with exciting and passionate things. And love can be many things, not just romantic love. It might also be your love of set dancing at the Willie Clancy week in Miltown Malbay, or the jazz festival in Cork, or One Direction or U2. It might be watching Aidan O'Shea catching a high ball in the middle of Croke Park. It might even be watching *The Sunday Game*. It's that feeling of love and passion that excites and thrills you.

If love is an important element of living life to the full, then so too is communication. Isn't a hug a wonderful thing? Isn't the spoken word fantastic? Of all the creatures on this planet, only us humans have the ability to communicate through the spoken word. What we say and how we say it is crucial. The throwaway remark, the critical comment, can cause so much damage, damage that you mightn't even be aware of. I often think of that Dale Carnegie quote: 'Perhaps you will forget tomorrow the kind words you say today, but the recipient may cherish them over a lifetime.' Kind words cost nothing but they accomplish so much. What we say can increase the sum total of this world's happiness.

I talked about that amazing moment at the end of the All-Ireland semi-final replay between Waterford and Kilkenny in 2016. Pauric Mahony from Ballygunner in Waterford had the last free of the match, 65 metres out from the goal. Had the shot gone over, it would have drawn the game and possibly forced extra time. But the sliotar dropped short and was caught by the Kilkenny goalkeeper, Eoin Murphy. Game over. Waterford beaten. Pauric Mahony was devastated. He curled up on the ground distraught and inconsolable, his dream of playing in an All-Ireland final shattered. Then, from the crowd, a young girl in a Kilkenny jersey made her way straight across to Pauric and, despite the jubilation around her, she put her arms around Pauric to console him. The moment was captured by a photographer and it was on every front page of every newspaper on Monday morning.

Jennifer Malone, from Kildare in Co. Kildare, has Down Syndrome. She's had meningitis. She's had open-heart surgery. She's on her second pacemaker. She nearly died several times when she was a child. Her great love is sport. It excites her, it thrills her, it identifies her. She spent a bit of time in Kilkenny preparing for the Special Olympics and while there, she became a huge fan of Henry Shefflin – hence the Kilkenny jersey. Despite being non-verbal, Jennifer Malone managed to say more in that simple gesture than you could communicate in a book full of words.

Speaking in Knock that day was without doubt one of the greatest honours of my life, and I was especially humbled by the standing ovation I received when I finished – and it happened twice! I spoke in the afternoon and again at the evening session. As I stood there looking down on the sea of beaming faces, I thanked the Blessed Virgin Mary and my dad at least ten times. I couldn't believe it, and every time I think of it now, it sends shivers down my spine.

This was actually my second solemn novena of 2017. Two months earlier, I had been invited by Fr John Dunphy and Cem Crowe to speak at the solemn novena in St Clare's Church in Graiguecullen, Co. Carlow. The theme that time was 'A time to pray, a time to heal'. When I finished my talk, I was asked to meet the Poor Clare Sisters, an enclosed order living right next door to the church. Mother Abbess Sr Rosario welcomed me warmly, as did Mother Francis, Sr Dominic, Sr Canice, Sr Paschal, Sr Mary and Sr Ann Marie, who was almost 100 years old. We took selfies together

through the barriers and they asked me all about *The Sunday Game*. What was Michael Lyster really like? Who did I think would win the All-Ireland? When was I going to be on the radio again and could we organize a Marty Party in Graiguecullen? For a group of women living in an enclosed environment and who had devoted their lives to God, I was impressed by how up to speed they were with my world. They told me that when their prayers allow, they listen or watch my commentaries, and they had a particular love for the 'Holy Moses' exclamation of 2013. My buddy Fr Eoin Thynne took a lovely photo of the nuns and myself and I asked them would it be OK if I put it up on Twitter. My guess is that some of them hadn't a clue what Twitter was but I got a unanimous 'Yes', so I posted it and to my great surprise, it went viral.

The life of devotion and prayer that they lead is incredible in this day and age, but not one of them would have it any

other way. Their warmth, hospitality, humility and spiritual presence, as well as their promise to say prayers for me, has always stayed with me. I got an invitation to call any time. I haven't got round to it yet, but one fine day, we'll organize a Marty Party with the Poor Clares in Graiguecullen!

18. Leadership and Passion: The Rise of Women's Gaelic Games

It was the first week of October 1986. I got a call from Paschal Brooks asking me what I knew about ladies' football.

'Very little. Why?'

'Some babe wants to meet us to discuss whether we're up for filming a match in Dublin in two weeks' time.'

Typical Paschal. Always willing to do the gig, but always vague on details.

'When are you free to meet her?' he asked. 'How about Friday evening, or better still Saturday? If we meet her on Saturday afternoon, we could stay the night and hit Leggs on Leeson Street and you never know, Morrissey, we might get the shift!'

'Paschal,' I said, 'you had me at "hello".'

We travelled to Dublin the following Saturday and met Helen O'Rourke, a primary school teacher who had recently been appointed PRO of the Ladies Gaelic Football Association. Our mission, if we chose to accept it, was to film the All-Ireland senior ladies' football final on October 12th, when Kerry, aiming to win their fifth All-Ireland in a row, would face Wexford in Croke Park. The junior final between Waterford and Wexford would also be recorded.

We got the gig. My guess is that Helen had her doubts about the two gobshites from Clare, but she took a chance on us. Not that she had much of a choice. Few others were doing what we were doing. It was VHS time. Internet was a word nobody knew. RTÉ was the only shop in town, and in

1986 ladies' football wasn't seen as big enough to warrant any sort of coverage by the national broadcaster.

Ladies' football in its earliest form was little more than entertainment at summer festivals. According to the LGFA, Tom Garry from Clonreddin outside Cooraclare set up a parish league in 1926, but it faded into oblivion. In 1969, the female staff of Clonmel post office played the Tipperary county council office at the Clonmel Sportsfield. The admission price was one shilling, with all proceeds going to the Biafra relief fund. Now, in 1986, the ladies' inter-county final was to be played in Croke Park for the first time, and I was thrilled to be there.

The day itself was dull and cold, but despite the fact that Croke Park was 90 per cent empty, the crowd noise was deafening. Kerry won on a scoreline of 1–11 to 0–8. That Kerry team was special. Mary Jo Curran was just spellbinding to watch as she soared into the clouds to gather the ball. When I think of that Kerry team, the Lawlor sisters, Margaret and Eileen from Ardfert, immediately come to mind. Also goalkeeper Kathleen Curran, defender Nora Hallissey, flying wing forward Marina Barry and the goal-scoring star, Del Whyte.

Wexford had great players at the time as well: Joanne Codd, Catherine Murphy, Mary and Kathleen Moore, Mary Thorpe, Anne Whyte, Angie Hearne and Christine Harding.

The gig must have gone well, because we filmed the next few All-Ireland finals in Croke Park on behalf of the LGFA and saw the Kerry team go on to win an incredible nine titles in a row.

Much has changed since those early days, and I have been privileged to witness ladies' football take its rightful place in the hearts and minds of the people of Ireland. It's a tale of leadership, passion, and a voluntary movement that has been simply unstoppable.

The 1986 finals were recorded on VHS with a few hundred watching from the Hogan stand. In 2019, the ladies' football All-Ireland finals were broadcast live by TG4 with a staggering 56,114 people in attendance. That's incredible growth in a relatively short space of time.

There are many things that underlie that success: good under-age structures, high-quality volunteers and of course leadership. The latter ingredient is the most difficult to get. One thing I have learned is that some can manage but only a few can lead. Oprah Winfrey put it best when she said: 'Leadership is about empathy. It's about having the ability to relate and connect with people for the purpose of inspiring and empowering their lives.'

Today, Helen O'Rourke is chief executive of the LGFA. That first meeting with her initiated a close relationship that has lasted for over thirty-five years. I now consider Helen one of my closest friends. Although she has always stayed in the background and shuns the limelight, she deserves to be recognized for her role in making ladies' football the formidable force it is today.

Helen grew up on the north side of Dublin, the eldest of six children born to a Leitrim father and a Limerick mother. (Sadly, Helen lost both her parents in 2021.) While she played basketball in school, she was always drawn to the GAA. She became secretary of the Dublin ladies' football board, and being a primary school teacher, her instinct was to get more children involved in playing games. Though there were those who laughed at what she was trying to achieve, she succeeded in bringing more and more schools into the fold. So many young girls were encouraged to try it, and when they did, they found that they loved it.

Getting national press coverage and generating awareness of the association was really challenging. Helen was told that football wasn't ladylike, that it wasn't healthy for footballs to be hitting off women's chests. Another difficulty was the fact that camogie players wore skirts while the footballers had the audacity to wear shorts.

Seán Óg Ó Ceallacháin, who used to read GAA results from around the country every Sunday night at 11 o'clock on RTÉ Radio 1, declined to include ladies' football on his list. It was persistence from Helen that eventually prompted him to change his mind.

In the mid-1990s, she stood for election to become the next president of ladies' football. Both of her opponents were men. On the night before the election, one of them asked her if she thought she was really up for the job, and suggested she'd be better off standing down and gaining more experience.

She was thirty-one years of age at the time. The following day she was elected and became the eighth president of the LGFA. She held that office from 1994 to 1997, during which time she had neither an office nor full-time employees. And she kept meeting resistance from the establishment. At a meeting with my boss Tim O'Connor, the group head of sport, he told her that people would be more interested in watching tiddlywinks than watching women playing football on TV. To be fair to Tim, ladies' football was nowhere near where it is today, but understandably that comment didn't go down well with Helen at all. When her presidency came to an end, there was a feeling in the association that a full-time CEO was needed, and so she became the very first chief executive Officer of the LGFA.

In 2000, TG4 began their sponsorship of the ladies' Gaelic football championship and that relationship has been hugely positive for both parties. Today the LGFA employs fourteen people full-time at national level and eight at provincial level, which gives you an idea of the phenomenal rate of progress.

Achieving this kind of growth took a lot of innovation and creativity.

In the 1997 All-Ireland senior ladies' final between Waterford and Monaghan, referee Finbarr O'Driscoll added no fewer than eighteen minutes of injury time. There was outrage, and calls to *Liveline* on Radio 1. What was the referee thinking playing that amount of injury time? Later, when the game was analysed frame by frame, it emerged that Finbarr was actually correct in his decision. But rather than do nothing at all and wait for the media storm to fade away, the LGFA brought in the clock and the hooter system, which continues to this day. It's a great system. It takes a key pressure out of the referee's hands and lets everybody know exactly how much time is left on the clock.

Ladies' football introduced the sin bin before the men's game, and it's been a great success. The 'Ref Cam' experiment, as it was called, wasn't as successful. In more recent times, a 'score assistant' was employed at all live TG4 ladies' football matches. They sit in the Outside Broadcast (OB) unit and if there is any doubt about a ball going between the posts or crossing the goal line, the score assistant reviews camera footage and gives the referee their view. Unfortunately, Covid-19 and the need to maintain social distancing in the OB unit sidelined that new dimension. The score assistant probably won't be used again until 2022, when it's hoped that the health crisis will have abated.

I have commentated on nearly every All-Ireland senior ladies' final since I joined RTÉ, and I am deeply honoured to have seen such wonderful footballers reach the peak of their sporting talents during that time. In the early days, I got to know the Waterford, Monaghan and Laois teams that emerged to take their place in the sun. Waterford won no fewer than five titles between 1991 and 1998, powered by an incredible group of women from beautiful Ballymacarbry. Michael Ryan, their manager, is an extraordinary man who later became the Waterford and then the Westmeath hurling manager. Marie Crotty, Catriona Casey, Fiona Crotty, twins Geraldine and Martina O'Ryan, Aine Wall, Julie Ann Torpey and Noirin Walsh were outstanding talents.

Monaghan had Jenny Greenan, Niamh Kindlon, Margaret Kerins, Edel Byrne, Christine O'Reilly and of course the legendary Brenda McAnespie who – amazingly – played in an All-Ireland final when she was pregnant. And in time, her twin daughters Aoife and Ciara, who are simply brilliant footballers, also played for Monaghan.

I remember with love and admiration the wonderful Lulu Carroll, who is sadly no longer with us. Sue Ramsbottom was one of those extraordinary players that electrified the crowd when she got on the ball. Mary Kirwan and Tracey Lawlor were exceptional players whose company I thoroughly enjoyed.

Mayo produced the awesome Cora Staunton, who won four All-Ireland medals and shares the distinction, with Mary Jo Curran, of being an All-Star recipient eleven times. Although Cora will be forty on December 13th, 2021, and despite a horrific quadruple leg break two years ago, she is still producing the magic down under for her club, Greater Western Sydney (GWS) Giants. Such a severe injury at thirty-seven years of age would have signalled the end for the vast majority of athletes. But not Cora. In April 2021, she was named in the AFLW team of the year, in a sport she only took up three years before.

I love the Heffernan sisters, Christina and Marcella, not just for their football ability but for their great sense of craic and loyal friendship. Martha Carter, Claire Egan, Diane O'Hora and Fiona McHale were great Mayo players. Galway had quality footballers too, like Emer Flaherty, Annette Clarke and Sinead Burke. Tyrone play a lovely brand of football, and there is no doubt that Gemma Begley, Lynette Hughes, Neamh Woods and Eilish Gormley were very special players and would get their place on any team in Ireland.

And what about Armagh's Caroline O'Hanlon? I think I'm busy, but Caroline's schedule is truly intimidating. She somehow manages to play football with club and county *and* play professional netball in Manchester with Manchester Thunder *and* practise as a GP in Newry. All at the same time!

With the Lidl Ladies Team of the League, Division 1, in 2016

She played in the 2006 All-Ireland final, has won three All-Stars and was Northern Ireland's sportswoman of the year in 2010.

Between 2005 and 2020, the Brendan Martin Cup (the women's equivalent of the Sam Maguire) was shared between just two counties: Cork and Dublin. It's remarkable, but maybe not so remarkable when one considers the incredible talent that both counties have featured over that period.

Briege Corkery, Rena Buckley, Angela Walsh, Bríd Stack, Juliet Murphy, Nollaig Cleary, Orla Finn, Geraldine O'Flynn and Valerie Mulcahy are legends of the game. In full flow, Cork were simply unbeatable, and along the sideline they had a great manager in the late Eamon Ryan. He was a gentleman, and knew his football better than anybody else, and yet he would listen to you as if he was hearing something for the first time. That's class. That's respect. A lovely man whose positivity I loved and whose gentleness and company I treasured.

Dublin under Mick Bohan have also proven to be worthy All-Ireland champions. Their style of play is very much like their male counterparts: a great cocktail of good defensive work and wide, expansive football when they go forward. Siobhan McGrath – named player of the year in 2019 – is exceptional, but then so too was her father John, who comes from Shannon Gaels country around Labasheeda in the parish of Kilmurry McMahon in Clare. I played alongside John on the county minor football team. He was so good in his day, he could easily have worn the Dublin or Kerry jerseys.

Lyndsey Davey, Carla Rowe, Sinead Ahern, Denise Masterson, Angie McNally, Mary Nevin, Niamh McEvoy, Sinead Finnegan, Niamh Collins, Olwen Carey and the brilliant Sinead Goldrick, who has now been recognized as an All-Star on seven occasions, are all individually and collectively out-standing footballers who richly deserve their success.

The Dublin/Cork monopoly was finally broken on September 5th 2021, when Meath won their first All-Ireland senior title to deprive Dublin of five in a row. New stars emerged, like Emma Duggan, Vikki Wall, Niamh O'Sullivan, Emma Troy and captain Shauna Ennis.

The thinking and strategy of the LGFA has always impressed me. They are always experimenting and implementing new ideas. During the Covid lockdown in 2021, in partnership with Lidl and the youth mental health organization Jigsaw, they introduced the 'One Good Club' initiative, which was based around a five-step mental health awareness programme. It ran over a ten-week period, with twenty-five clubs participating.

I visited seven clubs around the country, and I was overwhelmed by what they had done in their communities, in a wide range of circumstances. That's the spirit at grassroots level that has catapulted ladies' football to a new level and made it one of the fastest growing sports in the world. Some of the new activities organized and encouraged by the clubs during Covid included learning how to play the spoons and the brush dance, treasure hunts that could be done in cars, litter clean-ups and putting compliment cards and chocolate bars on people's doorsteps in their local village, painting and Pilates classes, and overall getting everybody involved in something fun while maintaining social distancing and wearing masks during a pandemic. I also enjoyed producing and presenting the Lidl One Good Club Awards remotely, using Ger Kilkenny's state-of-the-art virtual studios in Pallasgreen, Co. Limerick. The show that we produced was broadcast on the LGFA's Facebook Live page and got over 20,000 views.

The Ladies' All-Star tours are now legendary, and I am so lucky to have been part of most of these wonderful and memorable journeys. Dubai, Singapore, San Diego and Hong Kong have all been on the LGFA hit list. The first All-Star tour was held in 2004, when the Big Apple survived the ladies' visit. We were all much younger then, but in all honesty it took me two weeks to recover from the madness and mayhem. I missed out on the trip to Singapore two years later, but was back for the trip to Dubai in 2008. We had a ball. I always smile at the memories of going on safari and camping out with the girls in the desert. Trying to ride a camel is not easy, but once I threw the leg over and got into the saddle I thought I was a great little jockey! But then all men think that, don't they?

Cameraman Cormac Downes travelled with us on most of these trips so that we could film a report for *Nationwide*, one of the best and most successful programmes on RTÉ 1.

During these trips, we met and interviewed several international stars, including John Smit, who was the Springboks' captain when they beat England in the Rugby World Cup final, golfer Ernie Els, and the wonderful tennis player Martina Navratilova, who won Wimbledon nine times and the US Open on three occasions.

These tours were always great craic. I loved the way the girls would mingle well with each other despite being from different counties. There were never any cliques.

My lasting memory of Toronto in 2012 was the welcome we received from Sean Harte and an army of volunteers. I was particularly delighted to meet a fellow Clareman, Eamon O'Loghlin from Ennistymon, who had emigrated to Canada three decades earlier. He had been executive director of the Ireland–Canada Chamber of Commerce for many years and had helped countless Irish emigrants get a job when they landed on Canadian soil. I was shocked to hear of his sudden passing eight months after our visit, in January 2013.

We stayed in the Sheraton Centre Hotel, a block away from the Eaton Centre mall, where we all spent some time browsing around the shops. Two days after we flew home, that same shopping centre was all over the news following a shooting in which two people died.

During the All-Stars tour to Hong Kong in 2014, there was a tripleheader of matches: a ladies exhibition game between a Hong Kong and an Asian selection; a Jim Stynes Cup compromise rules game between the Hong Kong Gaelic Dragons and the Hong Kong Aussie Dragons; and the main event – the ladies All-Stars 2013 v. the ladies All-Stars 2014. My abiding memory, as the light faded among the 4,000 skyscrapers of a city far away from home, is the sight of a group of women with absolutely no connection with Ireland playing ladies' Gaelic football. There were Chinese, Japanese, Australians, Filipinos, Taiwanese, South Koreans, English and a few Europeans playing with an O'Neill's size 4 football in GAA jerseys and shorts. You have to wonder. How the hell did this happen?

In San Diego in 2016, I had a puck-around on the deck of the *USS Midway* with my friend Lieutenant Commander Declan Hartney. Back in 1986, Declan had watched *Top Gun* in a Limerick cinema and realized his calling in life. He emigrated to Philadelphia in 1994 and joined the US Navy as a maintenance technician on the F/A-18 Hornet strike fighter aircraft. It must have been some transition for a young lad from the rural village of Kildimo. Since 1999, he has travelled the world with the Blue Angels, the flight exhibition and demonstration team of the US Navy.

Back at home, one of my great honours and undoubtedly greatest challenges is the presentation and production of the annual TG4 ladies' football All-Stars, which we put together every November. It's a very special night for the footballers and their families, and Helen O'Rourke's request is the same as Ger Loughnane's in 1995: make it different and unique. The team that came together back in 1995 for the first of these productions has remained much the same over the years, with a few additions.

There are VTs reflecting the year gone by, live guests on stage, fabulous artists and a 'hall of fame' recipient. The big announcement at the end of the night is that year's All-Star team, as well as the players' player of the year. This is one of my favourite nights of the year, and thankfully every single one for close to twenty years has gone off without a hitch.

Not even the LGFA staff are aware of who's going to be there until the artists appear on stage. I presented it on my own for a few years, then Roisin Ni Thomain and Aoife Ní Thuairisg joined me on stage in different years. They were brilliant. Eventually a lad from West Kerry called Dáithí Ó Sé got the gig to co-present with me. I figured he wouldn't last long, but so far I haven't managed to shake him off! The truth is we are great friends and I always thoroughly enjoy the banter. When the event began, there were 500 in attendance. Today, it's grown to 1,500.

There have been so many wonderful highlights over the years. Pat Egan of Pat Egan Promotions has supplied us with some wonderful acts, including Mary Black, Frances Black, the Saw Doctors, Eleanor Shanley, the Kilfenora Céilí Band, Mike Denver, the Tullamore Gospel Choir and Sharon Shannon, to name just a few. The reaction to Nathan Carter launching into 'Wagon Wheel' is something I will never forget. All I could see from the stage was a sea of black tuxedos dancing between tables, while the women rolled up their elegant dresses, kicked off the high heels and leaped up on to the tables. It was a fantastic moment in time.

For a very different reason, I remember another moment. Helen suggested that I interview Clare Clarke on stage at the 2014 TG4 event. Clare was an exceptional woman who worked for the LGFA for eleven years. She was hard-working, loyal, vivacious and witty. Everyone connected to ladies' football knew her well from phoning LGFA headquarters or meeting her when they called into the office.

She was diagnosed with cancer in 2010, then got the all-clear, but was then diagnosed with secondary cancer. She initiated the 'Climb4Clare' programme when she learned that there was no support to help her children deal with the news.

She said, 'I am just a normal person and I don't have the words or the vocabulary for what is happening myself. How do I explain to my children in a vocabulary that they will understand and allow them to answer any questions they are asked?'

Through the Irish Cancer Society, she was introduced to CLIMB, which stands for Children's Lives Include Moments of Bravery. Joining up with the LGFA, Clare raised funds so that CLIMB could be rolled out through all cancer care centres in Ireland and help children understand what's happening to their loved ones and how to cope and prepare for the worst possible outcome.

On the night of the 2014 All-Stars, I surprised Clare by inviting her on to the stage to join me for a chat. She lit up the room with her bubbling personality and the genuine love that people felt for her. Despite her illness, I remember her as being stunningly beautiful inside and out, and always frank and honest.

'A year and a half ago,' she said, 'it came back to my spine and since then, it's gone to my liver and lungs in the last eight weeks. There's good days and bad days. Some days you can't get out of bed, you're not well, and then other days, you're sitting on the stage with Marty Morrissey having a great time.'

I can still hear her laugh as she said those words. At the end of our interview, Clare got an emotional and lengthy standing ovation which was richly deserved.

Three months to the day later, on Saturday January 31st, 2015, Clare Clarke died peacefully in her home in Dublin, aged thirty-five. She is survived by her husband Ciaran and her two beautiful daughters, Ava and Katie. She is a huge loss to her parents, Peter and Carmel, and to her colleagues Paula Prunty and Fiona O'Grady, who started working with Clare and Helen around the same time, as well as her dear friends

Lyn Savage, Rose Mary Coyle, Máire Ní Mhaoilchiaráin and William Harmon.

My relationship with the Camogie Association is very different. No tours and no All-Stars, but I'm very proud to say that I have commentated on nearly every senior All-Ireland final since I joined RTÉ.

For the laugh, I once asked a former president of the Camogie Association why I was never asked to MC the Camogie All-Stars.

'You are way too close to the ladies' football crowd,' I was told. That put me in my box!

Camogie is a truly wonderful game that has steadily got better over the years, as rule tweaks have allowed more physical contact. I have witnessed some major milestones in the game, including Lynn Dunlea's hat-trick of goals in the 1993 final and Linda Mellerick's last-minute goal in 1995 to secure a Cork victory over Kilkenny. Then there was eighteen-year-old Denise Gilligan's two goals to signal Galway's arrival on the big stage as they won their first All-Ireland in 1996. Three years later Tipperary won the first of their five All-Ireland titles in six years, when fourteen-year-old Claire Grogan was superb, as was Deirdre Hughes, who got the vital goals. One of the best games of all time had to be the 2012 All-Ireland final when Wexford achieved their dream of three All-Ireland titles in a row, defeating Cork to retain the O'Duffy Cup. It was also the day Ursula Jacob scored a whopping 2–7. Today, Ursula is of course a colleague of mine, and works as an analyst on our GAA coverage, as does Anna Geary, who captained Cork to their twenty-fifth All-Ireland victory in 2014.

The biggest camogie crowd ever was in 2007, when 33,154

were in Croke Park to see Wexford, captained by the great Mary Leacy, captivate the attendance and the TV audience with a marvellous display against Cork.

The camogie players and ladies' footballers I have seen are just outstanding athletes, bubbling with skill. They give a huge commitment to their chosen sport, and have such a positive attitude to health and training. They are superb role models for the generation coming up behind them. These players put in the same massive effort as their male counter-parts, and I am so delighted to have been assigned to cover their sports long before they became fashionable. I have been privileged to see Angela Downey and her sister Ann play in Croke Park. I have become great friends with both. And it's wonderful too to see Angela's son Conor Browne play for the Kilkenny hurlers.

Each county produces its own stars. Cork's Linda Meller-ick was a genius with a ball, as were Rena Buckley and Briege Corkery. What Rena and Briege achieved is mind-boggling. Rena won seven camogie All-Irelands and eleven football All-Irelands. In addition, she received five camogie All-Stars and six football All-Stars. Briege also won seven camogie and eleven football All-Ireland medals, while she also picked up six camogie All-Stars and ten ladies' football All-Stars. I don't think we will see their like again, to be honest.

In Tipperary, goalkeeper Jovita Delaney was a special tal-ent. Una O'Dwyer and Ciara Gaynor were among my favourite players. Add in Sinead Nealon, Jill Horan and Emily Hayden from the Premier county and you have three of camogie's brightest stars.

Mags D'Arcy was a brilliant goalkeeper for Wexford, and played a huge role in their four All-Ireland wins, while Kate Kelly was a fantastic player with huge support from Aine

Codd and Michelle Hearne. The O'Connor sisters will always have a special place in my heart.

When the West awoke, the maroon and white was worn proudly by Therese Maher, and that family tradition is continued today by her niece, Carrie Dolan. I loved watching Veronica Curtin and Molly Dunne in action as they headed towards their opponents' goals, while the McGrath sisters – daughters of Michael 'Hopper' McGrath – are incredible talents. Ann Marie Hayes was a great wing back, while Niamh Kilkenny is in a different league altogether. The Kilkenny team that won the 2020 All-Ireland had some brilliant performers: Davina Tobin, Meighan Farrell, Denise Gaule, Ann Dalton and the Walshs, Miriam and Grace.

Camogie is growing in popularity all the time, and I'd like to think RTÉ is helping to spread the gospel. On June 20th, 2021, we broadcast the league final between Galway and Kilkenny, but because it had a 7.30 p.m. throw-in on a Sunday evening, there were complaints aimed at the Camogie Association and RTÉ Sport. It was claimed that it was too late in the evening, making it difficult for players and supporters who had an early start the following morning.

A legitimate and reasonable point. So here's the dilemma: do camogie officials play the game early in the afternoon and keep their own constituents happy, or do they look at the bigger picture and seek the biggest TV audience possible? If you want to spread the word that camogie is a great game, then the most powerful medium is unequivocally television. Furthermore, if you are advised by RTÉ sports management that this is a great slot in the schedule – and it was – then Sinead McNulty, the chief executive of the Camogie Association, and her officials made the right call. And here's the proof. The peak viewing figure of 222,000 people watching was outstanding. That's an invaluable reach. If the game went ahead as suggested at 2 o'clock in the afternoon, the numbers watching would probably have been much lower.

I have always believed that a doubling-up of fixtures with the men's game is the way forward, especially if that game is a hurling match and TV cameras are at the venue anyway.

The two-year 20 x 20 campaign was about creating a cultural shift in our perception of girls and women in sport. It had three targets: 20 per cent more media coverage of women in sport, 20 per cent more female participation at player, coach, referee and administrative level, and 20 per cent more attendance at women's games and events. The catchphrase was a good one: 'If she can't see it, she can't be it.'

When the campaign ended, there had been a 13 per cent increase in female participation at all levels and a 17 per cent increase in attendances at women's games and events. But while awareness has also risen, the campaign found media coverage still lags behind men's sport. So while there's a lot done, a lot more needs to be achieved.

Declan McBennett, the group head of RTÉ Sport, has been a leader in this area since his appointment to the top job in 2018. He is clearly determined to give opportunities to women sports stars and broadcasters in an effort to have gender balance. Since he took over, the philosophy in the department has been simple: there's a first time for everything, and if she *can* see it, she *can* be it.

In 2019, Cora Staunton was the first woman to co-commentate on an All-Ireland football final on RTÉ Radio 1. Ursula Jacob is today an established analyst, and speaks on both camogie and hurling. RTÉ Sport has always been to the forefront of providing opportunities to female broadcasters, and Caroline Murphy was a leader in that, as was Tracey

Piggott. Clare McNamara is a fine broadcaster and has proven her skills in radio and TV news as well as presenting mainline sport programmes. Today our department has many great female presenters: Jacqui Hurley, Evanne Ní Chuilinn and Joanne Cantwell. Siobhan Madigan is an excellent reporter and, in another first, provided commentary on Euro 2020 during the summer of 2021. Marie Crowe from Sixmilebridge has worked so hard to seize any opportunities that have come her way. She's a grafter, has earned her spurs the hard way and I admire her for that, probably because she reminds me a little bit of myself in terms of relentless determination. She has made *Game On* her own on 2FM, where her knowledge and love of sport shines through continually.

One thing that saddens me is the personal abuse that women get online, especially those with a high profile in politics or sport. I am flabbergasted at what I see on occasion: nobody deserves such terrible treatment. In a 2020 survey carried out by Plan International, 67 per cent of Irish girls have experienced some form of abuse or harassment online. The average age for the abuse to start in Ireland is thirteen. Globally, girls as young as eight years of age are targeted. It is quite clear to me that social media companies need to put policies in place that prevent and respond to online harassment, and hold the offenders to account. Being involved in sport is a healthy, positive experience and the GAA family, which includes the Camogie Association and the LGFA, is vital in giving that feeling of belonging and inclusiveness that we all crave.

The message must go out that sport is all-inclusive and that there is a role for everyone. Nobody must be excluded.

That's camogie, that's ladies' football, that's the GAA.

19. Francie, Katie, Bernard and Me

On July 19th, 1996, the opening ceremony of the XXVI Olympiad began with the parade of nations at the magnificent Centennial Olympic Stadium in Atlanta. Teams from 197 countries emerged from the tunnel on to the running track in what is a hugely prestigious part of the razzmatazz that signals that the Olympics we all love and cherish is starting. This parade was a little different from an Irish perspective in that the flag-bearer was a nineteen-year-old from the Galway Travelling community called Francis Barrett. Francie for short. I always feel a great sense of pride during that opening parade, to think that our little country, an island on the periphery of Europe, can take on the Americans, the Russians and all the other nations of the world.

Francie Barrett's presence at the Olympics, and his role carrying the tricolour, meant an awful lot to the Travelling community. Francie's coach, Chick Gillen, a barber on Dominick Street in Galway City, saw something special in Francie. They had converted a lorry container on the Hillside halting site where he lived into a gym. It had a ring and a few punchbags, but neither electricity nor running water. Francie's achievement is truly heroic when you think of the facilities available to our elite athletes today. You have to wonder what he would have achieved if he had arrived on the scene in the last few years.

Francie Barrett fought his first Olympic bout in the light welterweight division against the Brazilian Zely Ferreira dos

Santos at around 3 a.m. Irish time. Niall Cogley was the executive producer of RTÉ's Atlanta Olympics coverage. He decided to send a crew and a satellite van to Francie's home place that night. I was to be the reporter.

We arrived at Hillside some time after one in the morning. Margaret and Frank, Francie's parents, invited us into their homes. We were fed and watered and overwhelmed by their welcome. They asked me about my love of boxing and I relayed the story of my dad's friend Patrick Clancy, pretending to box with me as a child, and how my grandfather from Doneraile in north Cork taught me to jab and use my right hook. One night, while we were messing around like this, he knocked me over. I hit the corner of the table and split my forehead open. They recalled similar stories. So when I spoke to Francie's mum on air, we chatted about being proud, being nervous, if they thought he would win, what was he like as a young lad, was he always pretending to be boxing and so on. When I asked if she had ever suffered at his hands, I meant in the context of my own playing around with my grandfather. I knew as soon as the words were out of my mouth that I had phrased the question poorly, but I hoped people would understand the context. Margaret Barrett knew exactly what I meant – she made nothing of it. She said 'No', but that he loved the boxing and was always pretending to be moving like a boxer as a child.

We filmed the Barretts around the campfire as they and their neighbours watched Francie beat his opponent 32–7 in an impressive display of southpaw boxing nearly 4,000 miles away across the Atlantic Ocean.

A couple of lads in the halting site sang a song for us and it was after 5 a.m. before we left. Because of the euphoria surrounding Francie's win, and the tsunami of Olympic events that keep coming at you in that first week, it was a few days before my interview with Francie's mother became the subject of *Liveline*. Some callers accused me of insulting Mrs Barrett, though that was never my intention. I wanted to explain the context of our conversation to Marian Finucane, who was presenting *Liveline* at the time, but Niall Cogley thought it best to say nothing at all.

I was upset by all the criticism, and concerned about what the Barretts would make of it, so I rang Margaret Barrett and apologized profusely for my poorly phrased question. She said I had nothing to apologize for. She understood the context and said that some people wanted to cause trouble.

'Marty love,' she said, 'you are always welcome to Hillside and always welcome to our home.'

And suddenly, what was being said on *Liveline* didn't matter to me any more.

I will never forget Margaret Barrett and her family for their great kindness on the night we were there, but even more so when the controversy arose. My admiration and respect for the Travelling community is built around my night on Hillside, when my colleagues and I were so warmly welcomed. The Travellers are an indigenous minority ethnic group with a long-shared history, identity, language and value system. They should be treated with dignity, respect and non-discrimination.

Two nights after beating the Brazilian, Francie Barrett took on a Tunisian, Fathi Missaoui, in the second round of the light welterweight division and lost, 6 to 18. Missaoui went on to win the bronze medal. Six weeks after competing, Francie Barrett was back working on a building site in London. We never met, and I never met his mother and father again either. But I salute them and I salute what Francie achieved against the odds.

I learned a valuable lesson: prepare your questions, phrase them properly and avoid *Liveline* if at all possible.

I didn't get to go to the Sydney Olympics, but my luck was in for the next three Olympiads, as I was part of the away team in Athens, Beijing and London. There might be no medals for the journalists or broadcasters who cover the Olympics, but we bring the same sense of pride, determination and passion for those two weeks that the athletes do. We all want to be at our very best. I know I am biased, but I believe that RTÉ Sport do a fabulous job at the Olympics, and with modest resources too.

During the early months of 2004, there were lots of rumours going around that Athens would not be ready for the Olympic Games, which were due to open on August 13th. It was decided in May that executive producer John D. O'Brien, cameraman Eamon Taggart and myself would travel to Athens to see – some might say investigate – whether the various venues and stadia would be ready in time. We could plainly see that they weren't ready, and it seemed unlikely that they would be ready by August. Many of those whom we had lined up to talk to about the situation actually declined to be interviewed when we got there.

To be fair to the Greeks, they came up with a great plan. They erected miles and miles of beautiful, bright blue barriers festooned with the Olympic logo, and used these to hide everything they had dug up in erecting the various stadia. Unless you looked behind a barrier, you thought, this place looks great! It cost the Greek government €8.954 billion to run the Games, but for that money they got a great tram system, a new international airport and upgrades to their expressway and metro systems.

A total of forty-two Irish athletes travelled from Ireland

to Greece to compete in nine different sports. But it was a forgettable Olympics. My role was poorly defined. I was told to get 'colour', but there wasn't too much excitement for the Irish.

My personal highlight took place at the Olympic Aquatic Centre, where we were filming interviews. Just as we were leaving, there was a flurry of activity at the door, the sound of flashbulbs popping, and who should arrive, surrounded by security guys in black suits, only the American supermodel Cindy Crawford. I always had a fancy for Cindy, so here was my chance to make an impression.

I shouted, 'Cindy! Cindy! Marty Morrissey here from Irish television!'

I figured she mightn't have heard of RTÉ but was secretly hoping that our eyes would meet and she would say, 'Oh Marty! I have always wanted to meet you!'

That didn't happen. I went on, 'We're from Ireland!'

Now Cindy looked at me directly, or at least that's what I felt, despite the fact that she was surrounded by hundreds of people. And then she said, 'Oh hi! I love Ireland!'

And that was it. She disappeared into the throng. Cindy and I were finished before we ever got going. Clearly it was the worst chat-up line ever. I never used it after that and sadly, Cindy and I never met again.

In the end, it was left to a horse to get us all excited in Athens. Waterford Crystal and Cian O'Connor won our only gold medal in the individual show-jumping event. But you know the luck of the Irish is running out when the horse fails a drugs test. Two months later, Cian O'Connor was stripped of his gold and it was presented instead to the silver medallist, Rodrigo Pessoa from Brazil, on a horse named Copacabana Beach.

*

Glen Killane was appointed group head of sport in RTÉ in the year of the Athens Olympics. He would be my boss for six years. Glen was always positive and always thought outside the box. He had served his time as series editor of *The Sunday Game*, *Champions League*, *Rugby World Cup* and other big sporting programmes that were essential to RTÉ's output, so he knew how the place worked. He had been elevated to the top job in sport when Niall Cogley announced he was leaving us to join Setanta Sports as CEO – which came as quite a surprise.

I was on holidays in Miami Beach in 2006 when the phone rang and Glen's name appeared on the screen. He was aware that I was getting restless, that I wanted to do other things and challenge myself a bit more.

He got straight to the point. 'I'm going to expand our boxing presence a bit and concentrate on this lad Bernard Dunne from Tallaght, and the other Irish boxers at the Beijing Olympics. So would you be interested?'

'Would I what?' says I. 'Count me in and thank you.'

And so my boxing broadcasting career began. I loved boxing, and those involved in the sport at the time were good people who took great care of me and guided me along. My first outing was at the Irish National Finals at the National Stadium on the South Circular Road. I sat beside the great Jimmy Magee, and learned so much from listening to him. Now, in addition to doing post-bout interviews, I also supplied the TV commentary on recorded fights.

The atmosphere in the stadium on those Friday nights was electric. Dominic O'Rourke from St Michael's Club in Athy was, and still is, the Irish Amateur Boxing Association (IABA) president. Gary Keegan was the high-performance director, while Billy Walsh and Zuar Antia were the coaches.

Gerry Hussey was the team psychologist while Jim Moore, Jim Walsh and Des Donnelly managed the team.

For the next six years of my life I travelled the world, to Olympic qualifiers and world championships, and to Olympic Games in Beijing in 2008 and London in 2012. The windy city of Chicago in Illinois, the beautiful Italian city of Pescara on the Adriatic Sea, Baku in Azerbaijan and Moscow in Russia were all places that I would never have seen if I hadn't been working for RTÉ Sport.

Neilus Dennehy is a great and trusted colleague of mine, a proud Kerryman normally based in Waterford. Neilus was one of the first people who was capable of shooting all we needed on camera, editing it on his laptop and sending it back across the globe via FTP to Donnybrook. No need any longer for a satellite feed.

I remember Moscow in 2010 for high levels of black-market activity, visible everywhere. We had both an interpreter and a driver on the trip, and transported ourselves and the large amount of gear we needed around the city in a van. On one occasion, as we approached a set of traffic lights, two policemen directing traffic came over to the van and started talking to the driver. Though we couldn't understand a word of Russian, we could tell that the driver was apoplectic with rage. We asked our interpreter, Dimitri, what he was saying.

'Marty, I'm not sure how to translate, but I think, "holy fuck".'

'What? Why? What has he done wrong?'

By now the driver, Alexander, had climbed out of the van, crossed the road and had sat into the passenger's seat of the police car. Meanwhile the traffic was building up behind us. Horns were blaring angrily and drivers were going ballistic over the delay.

'Has he been arrested?' I asked.

'No, he's just paying the fine.'

'What fine?'

'They know that he's probably driving tourists and so he must pay because they know he now has money.'

'How much?'

Dimitri shrugged. 'One hundred, maybe two hundred euros.'

When Alexander returned, he was still in a rage. He never stopped talking as we took off down the street, and he'd bang the steering wheel for emphasis from time to time.

'What's he saying?' I asked.

'It's holy fuck time again,' replied Dimitri, laughing.

They wanted €200 but he got away with €150 – and this kind of thing, we were told, happens all the time.

Ultimately, five Irish boxers qualified for the Beijing Olympics: light flyweight Paddy Barnes, bantamweight John Joe

Nevin, light welterweight John Joe Joyce , middleweight Darren Sutherland and light heavyweight Kenneth Egan. Paddy Barnes secured a bronze medal in the quarter-final, and faced the Chinese boxer Zou Shiming, who had beaten Paddy in Chicago 22–8 in the quarter-finals of the World Championships. That day in Beijing, the Chinese boxer scored a 15–0 victory. The scoring was impossible to comprehend, as Paddy had found the target six times during the fight, and yet the judges hadn't given him even one point. The margin was outrageously flattering to the Chinese boxer on home soil. There was a theory that the points for Paddy were given to Zou Shiming by mistake.

When I interviewed Paddy after the bout, he was raging. He acknowledged that his opponent was a great boxer, but said that the judges must be on drugs to miss what he had done. I tried to console him by telling him he had still won bronze, but he kept saying something that I couldn't understand.

'Sorry Paddy, but I can't hear you with the crowd roaring. Could you repeat that?'

But it wasn't the crowd at all, it was Paddy's strong Belfast accent. Between that and his anger, I found it impossible to make out what he was saying, until it dawned on me.

'I don't want it, I don't want it, I don't want it,' he roared.

Paddy was normally a quiet, warm, witty individual, so this was out of character.

'What don't you want?'

'The bronze medal.'

I pointed out that it was a great honour and a huge achievement to win any colour medal at the Olympics, and that Ireland was proud of him. Eventually he cooled off and accepted his medal.

Funny enough, when the two boxers met again at the London Olympics four years later, the contest ended 15–15, with Zou Shiming winning on a countback. Paddy had lost again, but he'd made his point: what had happened in Beijing was highly questionable.

Darren Sutherland, a fabulous boxer from the St Saviour's Olympic Boxing Academy in Dublin, stopped the Algerian middleweight Nabil Kassel in his opening bout. He was then drawn against the powerful Venezuelan Alfonso Blanco in the last sixteen. Blanco had beaten Darren at the AIBA World Championships in Chicago and was the favourite entering the ring. But the Dubliner produced a brilliant performance at the Workers' Gymnasium Arena to beat him 11–1, win a bronze medal and qualify for the semi-final against Great Britain's James DeGale. DeGale won in the end: 10–3.

A little over a year later, on September 14th, 2009, Darren Sutherland died unexpectedly in London. He was a really lovely guy. He is a massive loss to his family and to his wider boxing community.

Kenneth Egan was Ireland's great hope of another medal in Beijing. He met China's Zhang Xiaoping in the light heavyweight final, and the Asian fighter was handed a controversial 11–7 decision. It ended Kenneth Egan's dream of winning a gold medal in the same division in which Muhammad Ali had won his at the Rome Olympics in 1960. Kenneth fell to his knees after the bout, convinced that he had won.

'I genuinely thought that I had won that fight by two or three points,' he told me afterwards. But Kenneth was now a silver medallist, which was a huge achievement, and Ireland came home with its biggest haul of medals since the 1956 Games in Melbourne.

In 2012, I was very lucky that Declan McBennett, who was then head of RTÉ sports news, suggested I should go to the London Olympics, to provide radio commentary on any Irish bouts, to do pre- and post-bout reports for TV news, and to interview Irish athletes for TV. Ireland sent sixty-six athletes to compete in 2012. In the end, we won six medals – one gold, one silver and four bronze – in our most successful Olympics to date. I was very busy at the Games, but I loved every minute of it. Jack McGouran, the media officer for the Olympic Council of Ireland, was a massive help to me at every Olympics but especially in London, as was Paul McDermott from the Irish Sports Council.

Paddy Barnes defended his bronze medal and became only the second Irish athlete in eighty years to win medals at two consecutive Olympics. Michael Conlan won bronze in the flyweight division, while John Joe Nevin became a silver medallist as a bantamweight. Cian O'Connor proved to be an outstanding showjumper and Olympian when he came back after the heartbreak of Athens to win bronze in London in the individual jumping. Rob Heffernan walked into history with a bronze medal in the men's 50-kilometre walk. He would later become a close friend when we did *Dancing with the Stars* together in 2018. Katie Taylor was of course the gold medallist and, with great respect to everyone else, she was the story of the London Olympics.

Once she entered the London Olympic Stadium on the evening of Friday July 27th, 2012, as the flag-bearer for the Irish team, Katie Taylor, who already had four world championship gold medals, became a lightning rod for both the national and international media. This was the first time women's boxing was a part of the Olympic Games, and Katie was the overwhelming favourite in the lightweight division. The pressure was enormous, the expectation huge.

The fact that Katie got a bye in the first round added to the tension; it wasn't until ten days after the opening ceremony that she got to fight. It's a long time to be waiting. The ExCeL Arena in East London was the venue for all the Olympic boxing. A capacity crowd of 10,000 people arrived to witness Katie Taylor of Bray and Ireland taking on Natasha Jonas of Liverpool and Great Britain. Some boxing officials say it was the fight that cemented women's boxing on a global scale. Taylor won, 26–15.

What was striking was the incredible noise reverberating around the arena. Our commentary positions were very different to anything we'd seen before. In the National Stadium we were always ringside, but to use a GAA analogy, in London we were located at the Davin end: up on elevated ramps with tiered seating for the VIPs beneath us. The noise was deafening. I could not hear myself speak, despite turning the volume as low as possible on my headset and using a lip ribbon microphone rather than the one attached to my headset. I looked at my colleague Jimmy Magee, who was commentating for TV, and when I got his attention he just rolled his eyes to heaven.

But this was special.

Two days later, Katie comfortably won her semi-final joust with the Tajikistani fighter Mavzuna Chorieva. Again, the Irish sang their hearts out. 'The Fields of Athenry' bounced off the walls.

The final, against Sofya Ochigava from Russia, was beyond description. A sellout crowd, most of them Irish or pretending to be Irish, arrived early to the arena. Long before the fighters entered the ring, you'd hear the odd burst of *Olé Olé!*

And then, when Katie appeared, the roof nearly came off. I have never experienced anything like it before or since.

Taylor in one corner, Ochigava in the other corner. These two had history. It needed to be sorted here and now. In my headphones I could just about hear a voice in Dublin saying, 'And now let's go over to the ExCeL Arena for the Olympic women's lightweight 60kg final. Come on, Katie! Let's join our commentator in London, Marty Morrissey.'

The bell rang. Round one. Keep calm, Marty, and describe everything you see. Every jab, every right hook, every left hook, every swerve, every point was painted as best I could. It was 2–2 at the end of the round.

Round two: the Russian southpaw slowed the pace, playing her well-established defensive game, which included lots of holding. And it was working. At the end of the round, she led Katie 4–3. Sweet Jesus, I thought, this is not going to plan.

Round three: the bell rings and away we go again. Right hook not once but twice, left jab and another right hook. This is better from Katie. Ochigava's equipment needs attention, and that kills the momentum Katie was building up, but she now leads 7–5. Here comes the fourth and final round. The Russian has to go for it now and throws a haymaker which Katie does well to avoid. A booming right causes Katie to stumble but she looks OK. It might be deemed a slip. She must have scored with a great left just before the bell. Did she? Bout over. Fight over. Dreams either broken or fulfilled.

The wait was unbearable. Could this go to a countback? Then, finally, the result came: Katie had won the gold medal for herself and for Ireland, by 10–8. Tight enough but who cares? I could hardly say the words: Katie Taylor, Olympic gold medallist 2012. I'm not ashamed to say that I cried, we all cried. Seán Bán Breathnach bawled his eyes out on Raidió na Gaeltachta.

It was not until 2009 that the International Olympic Committee decided to add women's boxing to the Games. A young woman from Bray had had a dream to win a gold medal at the Olympics at a time when female boxers weren't even allowed to compete – and now here we were watching history being made. There would never be a first gold medal in the women's lightweight division again. That honour belongs to Katie forever. We all participated in a journey that we will never forget. The worry, the crying, the joy, the ecstasy over those fifteen minutes will stay with me forever. Our little country had taken on the might of the world and won gold for the first time since Michael Carruth won in Barcelona in 1992.

It surprises me a little to say this, but Katie Taylor winning the gold medal, and the privilege of commentating on the fight on the radio for RTÉ, is and will always be my No. 1, despite commentating on All-Ireland finals on TV and radio.

Now we had a new challenge. Up to this point, we hadn't disturbed Katie Taylor, her father Pete or coach Zuar Antia. We felt we needed to allow them to prepare quietly and diligently for the monumental task ahead of them. Now that the gold medal was won, Ireland needed to celebrate and RTÉ needed the new Olympic champion on Bill O'Herlihy's Olympic programme later that night. The programme producers reached out to Irish boxing officials in London. The word came back that this wasn't working, and not because the officials wouldn't co-operate. It appeared that Pete Taylor had other plans.

Now I started to get messages from Ryle Nugent, Glen

Killane, who was now head of television, and even Noel Curran, the director general of RTÉ, asking me to see if I could get a word with the Taylors and ask them to make themselves available later that night.

I went down to what they call the 'mixed zone', which is an area designated for the athletes and coaches to walk through after the competition so that broadcasters and print media can meet them to discuss what happened. While Katie talked to the print media, I had a quiet word with her father Pete about joining Bill O'Herlihy later that night. He said it wasn't logistically possible. Katie was tired, and in any case they were already booked to go to the Irish House in King's Cross. I pleaded with him. I said that while it was a great night for the Taylor family, Katie's gold medal was not just for herself and her family but for Ireland as well. But he wasn't for budging. I rang Billy Walsh to ask for his help, and as always he was brilliant, but his pleas also fell on deaf ears.

I reported back to Dublin that it didn't look like we were going to get Katie for the programme, and as you can imagine there was huge disappointment and concern. I packed up my notes from the commentary position and walked out into glorious London sunshine. Despite Katie's amazing victory, I felt despondent. I had failed to get the Taylors on the show with Bill, despite the fact that we had built up a great relationship with Katie and Pete over the years. I genuinely believed that if I could get to Katie herself, she would trust my explanation of why this was so important.

So I turned around and went back into the ExCeL Arena. They were closing up, but I still had my accreditation and when challenged I said that I had left my briefcase upstairs. I found one of the Irish officials, who told me that Katie was being drug-tested. I didn't know where the testing area was, but I found another official, who directed me down into the bowels of the building. When I got there, the testing area was empty. Someone had left their white coat, complete with an accreditation tag, hanging on the back of a chair. Through a crack in the door, I could see a number of Irish boxing officials down the corridor. Now I was faced with a dilemma. Do I shout at them, draw attention to myself and risk being thrown out? Or do I don the white coat and take a chance?

I swiped the white coat.

I was now where no journalist should be, deep inside the medical test centre. I had hardly got inside the door when a big security guy – he must have been six foot five – suddenly appeared.

'Where are you going, mate?'

I flashed the accreditation card, with my thumb covering the photograph. 'Medical,' I said. Hadn't I been a medical student in a former life?

He gave me the thumbs-up.

When Dominic O'Rourke and the lads saw me, they burst out laughing. 'What are you doing here, Dr Morrissey?'

But Pete Taylor didn't exactly welcome me with open arms. Once again I explained to him how important it was that Bill get to talk to Katie that night.

'This is not happening,' he said. 'We are going to the Irish House later and after that we're going for a family dinner. Katie is very tired.'

By then Katie had joined us so I pleaded my case with her. Once again, I explained that the country needed to see her with Bill that night. We were all so proud of her. It was a night of celebration for our country.

She turned to her dad and said, 'I think Marty is right. A lot of people have supported me, so I think we should go with Marty.'

To his great credit, Pete said, 'If that's what you want.'

Deal done.

The Taylors went off to get their clothes from the dressing-room while I called Peter Nicholls, a lovely Englishman who drove TV crews, commentators and reporters like myself around the various venues of London. In a world of varied venues, strict deadlines and tight schedules, a driver who knows his way around the Olympic city is absolutely essential.

Peter and I brought Katie, Pete and Zuar Antia back to the Olympic village. The Taylors arranged to rejoin Peter after a shower and a change of clothes, and he would bring them to the Irish House for their arranged meeting.

I went back to the nearby International Broadcast Centre (IBC), a massive temporary media centre. Everybody in RTÉ was delighted that I had persuaded the Taylors to join us live, although I was a bit concerned that their visit to the Irish House might go on a bit, and that we would be cutting it fine.

I hadn't been in the centre long before my phone rang. It was Pete Taylor. There was an awful lot of noise in the background. Big crowd at the Irish House, I thought.

'Could you send Peter and the car to the same address to pick us up again?' Pete said. 'We want to get out of here.'

'No problem, Pete, but I think he's waiting outside.'

I rang Peter Nicholls and he confirmed that he was waiting just where he had dropped the Taylors. I was still a bit worried about getting Katie on air, so I just asked him to bring the Taylors to the IBC, and said that I would go with them to where we had our 'live point'. This was a derelict apartment building which we shared with the BBC and which had a spectacular view of the Olympic Stadium in the background.

When I got to the car, the Taylors were in the back seat, so I hopped into the front passenger seat. As the car started to move, I turned around to face the new Olympic champion and her coach, and I asked them how the Irish House had been. I'd been assuming that the Irish House was something like the ambassador's residence, and that Katie had been the guest of honour at a VIP reception. It turned out that, at each Olympic Games, the Irish House is Ireland's primary party destination. In London, it was located in a large pub. The Taylors left as quickly as they could.

I was aware that Gary Lineker and the BBC were mad looking for Katie to go on their Olympic programme, but they couldn't find her. Nor could anybody from the international media. I'm delighted to say she was with us, but it took an extraordinary effort.

The Taylors appeared on *The Olympic Show* with Bill O'Herlihy that night and all was well in the world. Katie had fulfilled her dream of winning a gold medal at the Olympics, I had commentated on her great victory on RTÉ Radio, and I'd avoided getting arrested for impersonating a doctor into the bargain. It was a special time and a special night for a very special woman called Katie Taylor.

There was another great night for Ireland three years earlier, when Ireland's rugby team won the grand slam for the very first time since 1948. It was Ronan O'Gara's drop-goal in the Millennium Stadium in Cardiff that won the day and gave Ireland a 17–15 victory that will never be forgotten. In addition to that piece of O'Gara magic, there was also Brian O'Driscoll's and Tommy Bowe's brilliant tries in the space of two minutes, and Ryle Nugent's superb commentary on RTÉ television.

Later that night Irish eyes turned to the O2 Arena, where Bernard Dunne was facing the Panamanian Ricardo Cordoba for the WBA super bantamweight title.

In the years leading up to that night, boxing promoter Brian Peters had asked me to be ringmaster and warm up the crowd ahead of big fights in the National Stadium or City West. But nothing quite compared to the O2 that night, as I looked from inside the ring to the sellout crowd in tiered seating all around me, from ground level to just under the roof. To be fair, I didn't have to do too much to whip up the crowd. For one thing, they were already on a high after Ireland's Grand Slam win. For another, Bernard Dunne had by now become a household name, much admired and loved. The connection that Bernard had with the people of Ireland was helped enormously by a television deal that Brian Peters had struck with the then group head of sport, Glen Killane. Boxing hadn't been on our screens for years, but Glen had a good feeling about Bernard, and he deserves credit for taking a calculated risk that was now paying off with a world-title fight.

I called out to the crowd: 'Good evening ladies and gentlemen. Are you ready to rock?'

It was a phrase that I often say to pals if we're heading to a party somewhere, but I also used the line in the National Stadium when starting out with Peter and Bernard back in 2006, and so it became part of my warm-up routine. The response was overwhelming. A surge of energy and noise as over 8,000 boxing fans roared back at me, 'Yes we are!'

There were some great boxing fans among the VIPs there to support Bernard: Brendan O'Carroll, aka Mrs Brown of *Mrs Brown's Boys*, Keith Duffy from Boyzone, former RTÉ presenter Brian Ormond and many others.

Boxing fans will remember Bernard's battle with Sean Hughes in the National Stadium for the IBC super bantamweight title, and the European super bantamweight title fight in 2006 against Esham Pickering, when the Dubliner won on points. He defended the title twice, first by defeating Reidar Walstad from Norway by unanimous decision. The EBU made Kiko Martinez the mandatory challenger for Dunne's European title, and Kiko left Spain for the very first time in his life. I was there to warm up the crowd that night. Things did not go according to plan, however. Kiko had Bernard on the canvas with a beautiful right early in the first round. Worse was to come. The Spaniard floored the Dub twice more before the referee stopped the fight after only ninety seconds.

The Martinez camp had travelled to Ireland full of confidence and had placed bets with Irish bookmakers that Kiko would have a first-round victory. They got odds of 66/1 and left Ireland with bulging pockets. Happy days for Kiko and Spain, but a disaster for Bernard Dunne and Irish boxing. We all thought, 'game over'. And this is why I admire Bernard Dunne and his management team of Brian Peters, trainer Harry Hawkins and Mike McGurn so much. Bernard got back off his backside and worked even harder, and on the night of the world title bout against Ricardo Cordoba, he looked like a man transformed.

This was the first world championship fight in Dublin in thirteen years and would become ESPN's Fight of the Year in 2009. In my view, it was probably the greatest ever fight on Irish soil.

Round three: Dunne knocked Cordoba to the canvas with a deadly left hook.

Round five: Cordoba had Dunne on the canvas not once but twice.

Round eleven: Cordoba was knocked to the canvas three times, first with a right, then with a left hook and a deadly left–right combination. When Cordoba fell for the third time, the referee stepped in and stopped the fight. The Panamanian left the O2 Arena on a stretcher and Bernard Dunne was now a world champion after one of the greatest fights Ireland ever saw. The capacity crowd of 9,000 went wild. A Grand Slam win for the first time in sixty-one years and a world boxing champion crowned. No day quite like it before or since. Simply unforgettable.

*

Getting an Olympic or a European football championship venue ready for a major fixture takes a huge amount of organization and an intense logistical effort. Every TV station needs somebody on the ground. On October 20th, 2004, I was sent as George Hamilton's producer to Donetsk in the Ukraine for a Champions League match between Shakhtar Donetsk and Glasgow Celtic. As I knew only too well, George would be busy preparing his match commentary and getting his notes together, so it was my job to ensure that everything was in place for a smooth broadcast that night.

Heading off to a Champions League game with George and Jim Beglin during my quiet season was a real treat. Over the years, I've been to games in Madrid, Barcelona, Paris, Milan, Rome, Oporto, Monaco and of course London, and each has its own special memories. Madrid and Barcelona for the majestic surroundings of the Santiago Bernabéu Stadium and the Nou Camp; Paris for the exquisite restaurants, and to hear George converse in fluent French while Jim Beglin and myself struggled to speak English at 4 a.m. Milan for the beautiful Italian women I met, Rome for praying for forgiveness for sinning in Milan. Oporto for its beauty and narrow cobbled streets, Monaco for the helicopter ride from Nice and the magnificent boats in the bay.

My buddy David Punch had often said he'd love to come with me on one of these football trips, but it wasn't until the trip to the Ukraine that he finally walked the walk. The Limerick man was going to pay his way and go with me to Donetsk.

Before we headed off to the Ukraine I remembered the three pieces of advice, or, more precisely, the three sets of instructions that Tim O'Connor, then head of sport, gave me when I first started at RTÉ.

'If Clare win a Munster championship match tomorrow, Marty, would you hit the right tone?'

'I hope I would.'

'Would you say you'd be at 100 per cent or 90 per cent or 80 per cent capacity?'

'100 per cent,' I said immediately, thinking that this must be the right answer.

'Wrong answer, you culchie,' he said, with that cynical smile of his. 'You have nowhere to go if you are at full capacity and it's only the first round of the championship. Hold back. Do not over-reach. Wait for the right moment. It will come, I think, if there's a brain there between those two ears.

'Next. If you are ever representing RTÉ abroad, always bring two bottles of Paddy with you.'

'What? Why? I don't drink.'

'You don't drink? I knew I shouldn't have given you this gig.' He went on. 'It's not for you, but you might need it some day. Trust me. And finally, Marty, my last piece of advice is this: don't fuck it up.'

George and Jim were travelling separately, so myself and Punchy went off together. Two Paddies on the plane to the Ukraine and two Paddys in my luggage.

After the aircraft came to a stop outside the terminal at Kiev Airport – within touching distance of the building – we disembarked and boarded a bus which did two laps of the plane, then pulled up beside the terminal. Bizarre. We went through passport control, came back out the same door to the tarmac again and then walked about a mile to the aircraft which would bring us to Donetsk. To say we had doubts that this plane would ever fly was an understatement. It was a ramshackle DC11 with the two engines at the tail end. We boarded through the front door and passed through first class, which was completely empty. I pulled back the pink plastic shower curtain that separated first class from economy and saw that the latter was packed. All eyes turned to the two Paddies emerging from behind the curtain. None of the overhead luggage holders had doors, so dozens of straps and handles dangled over the heads of the passengers. It was like a scene from *Airplane!*

Our seats were the last two at the back, right beside the engines. The smell of aircraft fuel was stifling, so I asked could we move. The air steward obliged, but only moved us up four seats. I love flying, but this was the first time that I felt genuinely nervous. Thankfully, however, we got there safely.

The terminal building in Donetsk was essentially a massive hangar. A tractor and trailer loaded with our baggage pulled up just outside it and we picked our luggage from the pile. I needed the toilet, but decided against it when I saw that the toilets were embedded in the ground, and that the little doors on the cubicles didn't hide much from those passing by outside.

At all of the other Champions League games I'd been to, there was always a representative waiting at arrivals with 'Mr Morrissey' written on a white card. He would then whisk me off to the hotel or to the venue. But nobody was waiting in Donetsk. When we got outside the 'terminal', it was like something from an old movie: foggy and run-down, with street lights flickering in the dusk. There was no public transport, and no sign of a taxi.

We spent half an hour searching for some way of getting to the hotel, without success. Next thing a fancy coach pulled up at the far end of the car park, and we quickly realized it was there to pick up the Glasgow Celtic players. I decided that we had no option but to ask the Glasgow lads for a lift. Martin O'Neill was their manager at the time, and I felt confident the Derry man wouldn't say 'No'.

Just as we took off towards the Celtic bus, a pair of dim headlights came shining through the fog and a Fiat Uno emerged out of the gloom, its horn blaring. We could make out a dimly illuminated 'T', but the 'AXI' had been broken off at some point. The car itself looked like it had been around since 1962. It was light blue in colour, and the wing and front passenger wheel cover were completely gone, revealing the engine inside. It didn't look safe, but we were tired and we decided that it was grand.

When I pulled open the door, the driver beamed up at me, the light glinting off his gold tooth. We bundled in and headed for the city. Suburban Donetsk was as colourless and bleak as the airport, but the city? It was like driving into Las Vegas. Crowded streets, bright lights and everybody dressed up and looking fabulous. It was such a sudden and a bewildering transformation.

The following afternoon around four, I rambled down to the magnificent Donbass Arena, which was only a ten-minute walk from the city centre. I had brought a hard suitcase with me, which contained an ISDN box with microphones and headsets for George and Jim. Kick-off was scheduled for 10 p.m. local time, so there was no rush.

I found our commentary position and plugged in all the gear, but no lights lit up, there was no sound and the TV monitor remained blank and dead. I disconnected everything and tried again. Nothing. Then again and again. Still nothing. I could hear George's voice in my head. 'A nation holds its breath . . .' – but this time it would be because there were no pictures, and no sounds emanating from Donetsk. I ran off and found a sound engineer, but he didn't speak a word of English. Then I found another, but he didn't speak English either. Both set to work with the gear in the commentary position, but nothing they did seemed to make any difference. Eventually, with two hours to kick-off, the studio in Dublin called to ask why they couldn't see or hear us. Even George had arrived, and he's never early! The two sound engineers were working away at the equipment, but I was far from convinced that they were actually trying to do anything. One of them would hardly look at me and the other thought the whole thing was a big joke.

'You have football in Ireland? Guinness?'

It was then that I remembered the two bottles of Paddy. So I turned and ran back through the thickening crowd to the hotel and grabbed the two bottles of whiskey. It was now just an hour to kick-off and I still had to get back to the stadium. My mobile phone was hopping at this stage as the studio in Dublin 4 began panicking about the live broadcast that lacked both pictures and sound. Back at the stadium, I found my two sound engineers and presented them with the Paddy 'to thank them for all their great efforts'. The sullen one cracked open the bottle and took a massive slug. He smiled for the first time that evening and gave me the thumbs-up. Then he turned back to the equipment and within seconds, Dublin had both picture and sound and George and Jim were up and running.

Were the two lads going to switch us on anyway? I'm convinced that the two bottles of Paddy saved the day.

I must have lost a stone between the stress and running back and forth between the hotel and the stadium. And ever since that time I have always been keenly aware of Ukrainian affairs.

In 2009 that same stadium was officially opened, but five years later, in August 2014, it was damaged by artillery shelling as the Ukrainian armed forces clashed with pro-Russian separatists for control of the town. It was further damaged by shelling in October 2014 and has been closed ever since. Sadly, thousands have lost their lives since the war started, and it is still unsafe to visit Donetsk.

The Ryder Cup came to Ireland for the first time in September 2006. It was a great opportunity to see the best golfers in the world up close, but also to let the hair down and have a bit of craic as well. That's the way I saw it, anyway!

For RTÉ's coverage, my job was to go around the Arnold Palmer course at the K Club in Co. Kildare in a golf buggy with a cameraman – either Eamon Taggart or Cormac Downes – and interview the golfers and the many celebrities in the gallery.

I decided our first port of call would be the buses that were bringing spectators to the K Club from various locations in Dublin. Lo and behold, we made a few interesting discoveries. On one bus we met Ben Dunne of Dunnes Stores fame. On another, in the very back seat with a peaked cap pulled low, was Shane Filan of Westlife – who, despite my best efforts, wouldn't sing one bar of a song for our viewers. Mind you, it was about 8.30 in the morning to be fair to him.

Colin Montgomerie beat David Toms in the first singles match on the Sunday, and while I had heard the Scot could be a bit grumpy on occasions, he certainly wasn't with me. Phil Mickelson was another very approachable guy, while Tiger Woods was more distant but very mannerly. Among the spectators I talked to were tennis great Boris Becker, and basketball superstar Michael Jordan, who I found to be an absolute gentleman. Europe won the Cup by an incredible nine-point margin that matched the record they'd set two years previously. The Irish were well represented by Paul McGinley, Padraig Harrington and Darren Clarke, who had lost his wife Heather only six weeks previously to cancer and was obviously heartbroken and emotional.

Paul McGinley has always impressed me. He showed a touch of class when he offered a handshake and conceded a twenty-foot putt on the 18th to J. J. Henry to halve their singles match, because he thought his opponent might have been put off by a streaker running across the green. The Europeans were well in front at the time, but it was still a nice gesture.

At one point that weekend, I returned to the OB truck with a tape to be told that Bill Clinton had arrived at the K Club and was out on the course somewhere following the golf.

'Go on Marty, go get him,' was what a producer told me. There was much laughter in the OB, because the consensus had already been reached that nobody was going to get near him. He was on a day off, and off limits. But I relished the challenge of getting a few words with Mr Clinton.

Finding the 42nd President of the United States was easy: the crowd were following him as much as they were Tiger Woods or Padraig Harrington. Clearly the only option was to 'doorstep' him: just be courageous and have the balls to walk up and approach him. What was the worst that could happen? Well . . . the US Secret Service could go ballistic and arrest me, as they don't take too kindly to people approaching a former President.

As I spotted him in the distance, wearing a red short-sleeved golf shirt and a pair of well pressed black trousers, he looked relaxed. His entourage consisted of five Secret Service officers, four men and one woman, with three of the five wearing dark sunglasses, clearly armed and ready to pounce: exactly what you see in the movies. As the group walked from the 16th green to the 17th tee, surrounded by thousands of golf fans moving in the same direction, cameraman Cormac Downes and I positioned ourselves in Mr Clinton's path.

Cormac had tested the camera and the microphone beforehand, as he always does. But as Clinton approached, Cormac exclaimed: 'Shit – the sound is gone. I can't hear you.' I tested the microphone again. Nothing. Blankety blank.

Cormac put the camera on the ground and fell to his knees to install new batteries. Bill Clinton was now 50 yards away . . . 40 yards . . . 30 . . . . the blood drained from my face. But Cormac is brilliant and got the batteries installed just in time. The former President of the United States was now right in front of me, so I put out my hand to shake his and he did the same. I said, 'Hello Mr President, I'm Marty Morrissey from RTÉ, very nice to meet you, sir.'

The Secret Service agents moved a little closer, but Clinton's response was warm and he was clearly happy to engage with me, so they backed off.

'Nice to meet you,' he said, still walking. 'It's a wonderful course. I've played it before. I like it a lot.'

I asked him, 'Is there any hole you like in particular?' What was I thinking? Could I not have come up with a better question?

President Clinton looked down at me wryly, with a little smirk which turned quickly to laughter. He had now stopped walking.

'No . . . I find them all difficult. I like this course for this

tournament, though the most interesting one is the 15th where the US had two balls back to back in the water. A little bit of local knowledge stood the European team in good stead here.'

I asked him what he thought the long-term effects of hosting the Ryder Cup would be for Ireland. He said, 'I don't know, but I hope it will cause more people to come here to play golf.'

And with that he shook my hand, and also Cormac's hand, and moved off with the five US Secret Service officers right beside him.

One wit in the crowd shouted, 'Mr President – have you met Marty Morrissey?'

Another roared 'Marty for President!' and it got a round of applause in among the howls of laughter. 'Four more years, Marty!'

20. Mayo, Cluxton, Marriage and Jail

I'll make no apologies for this statement: I love the Mayo crowd. They are just great people who have a passion for Gaelic football like no other county, and that includes Kerry and the Dubs. And I'm not writing this to be nice to them but because I can be in McHale Park in Castlebar on the most awful night in the depths of winter, with wind howling and rain cascading down, and they will be packed into the stand and the terraces, roaring and shouting as if it was a summer's day.

'Will ye kick it in for Christ sake and let the ball do the work!' (To be roared in a strong Mayo accent.)

Over the years, they have produced some fabulous footballers, including T. J. Kilgallon, who is married to my wonderful colleague Eileen Magnier. For the record, Eileen is a proud Kilkenny woman. Willie Joe Padden is still an idol in Mayo and a man I love meeting. Other great footballers I've loved watching in action include Maurice Sheridan, John Casey, David Brady, Anthony Finnerty, Keith Higgins, Andy Moran, Lee Keegan, Tom Parsons, Cillian O'Connor, Cora Staunton and of course Aidan O'Shea. In 2021 Aidan played his 150th match for his county, which is simply incredible.

One of my favourite Mayo stories unfolded on Saturday May 4th, 2019.

A few years earlier, I had asked the powers that be to consider broadcasting, on radio, the opening game of the championship between New York and the visiting team from

Connacht in Gaelic Park in the Bronx. I thought it would be good for both RTÉ and the GAA, because it would show explicitly that we had not forgotten the thousands of Irish – like my parents – who had emigrated and sought a new life for themselves on the other side of the Atlantic. To the great credit of RTÉ, I got the go-ahead. Larry McCarthy, who is today the president of the GAA, had served as chairman and county secretary for New York GAA and was a massive help in ensuring the broadcast happened. Larry and I have some mighty laughs together. We have a similar sense of humour, and like to keep each other well grounded too.

No words of mine can describe what it was like for me to go back to Gaelic Park in New York and commentate on a Connacht championship match live from the Bronx. On a personal level, I felt it brought me full circle. I played in Gaelic Park as a child, and to return to the same venue as a broadcaster to commentate live was very special to me.

There was such a good reaction to that first broadcast that we did it every year until Covid grounded us. My hope is that those happy days will return and we can resume that public service soon again.

To the cynics reading this, well done in getting this far into the book – and if you're thinking *It got Morrissey a free trip home to New York*, well, you're dead right!

So it was Mayo's turn to travel to the Big Apple in May 2019. Rónán Ó Coisdealbha, the head of sport in TG4, is a great guy. We have travelled around the world together, along with one of the best cameramen I know: Mikey Ó Flatharta. I've often been in their company when they launch into some intense conversation *as Gaelige*. They talk so fast that I have no hope of following them, and the two boyos know this, which is quite annoying. They'll look at me intently and they keep using the word 'bollix' until they get my attention, then make it clear they're talking about me. We have a great laugh together.

When Rónán and Mikey are done with their work for TG4 in New York, Mikey comes with me around the city. Over the years we have done a large number of news reports and *Nationwide* segments for RTÉ. Eoin Ryan is the man in charge of *Nationwide*. From Clonmel in Co. Tipperary, he is one of the great guys in RTÉ. With the bare minimum of staff and resources, he produces a wonderful programme three times a week the year round, and his viewing figures are always impressive. Eoin operates out of the Cork Studios, where himself and Shirley Murphy make a great team.

On this particular day, the Saturday before Mayo were due to play New York in the Connacht championship, we were filming a full *Nationwide* programme. We had stopped for coffee and a hot dog in a Manhattan diner when I spotted a

Twitter notification from John Madden, a former Mayo goal-keeper. He was asking all Mayo fans to gather in Times Square at 6 p.m. that day to sing 'The Green and Red of Mayo'.

Later that evening, we were there to see no fewer than 6,000 people, in Mayo jerseys and waving flags and banners, flood on to Times Square. Funnily enough, access was denied to the viewing area here; it was cordoned off with yellow police tape. The Mayo crowd weren't that well organized and were standing around aimlessly, so I jumped up on a low wall and asked for quietness. I explained that Mikey the camera-man was from Connemara in Galway. This, I'm delighted to say, got him the biggest boo ever heard in Manhattan. When I said I was from Clare, that got a massive roar of approval – Clare offering no threat to Mayo football. I told the crowd I wanted to do a piece to camera with the crowd behind and beside me, and when I finished (with the words, 'Marty Mor-rissey, RTÉ News, New York'), Mikey would pan over the crowd and they would give 'The Green and Red of Mayo' everything they'd got.

It took a few takes but the 6,000-strong choir was fantastic.

At that precise moment, unknown to me and my new friends, we were all being watched on surveillance cameras by the New York Police Department, and they did not like what they were seeing. From their perspective, this was a large unruly mob, and to make matters worse, the media (i.e. Mikey and me) were on the scene as well. The riot squad was hastily assembled in expectation of trouble. As the orders were being issued, a detective was called in to look at the gathering crisis in Times Square. This was Pat Donohue, a native New Yorker born to a Laois mother and a father from Connemara – who just happened to be my co-commentator on RTÉ Radio 1 the following day in Gaelic Park!

Pat looked at the bank of monitors and started to laugh.

'Cancel the riot squad, guys, they're the fucking Mayo football supporters.'

On September 18th, 2011, Kerry played Dublin in the All-Ireland football final. It was a repeat of the quarter-final two years previously, when Kerry hammered the Dubs by 17 points. This final had history written all over it. It was Dublin's first for sixteen years, and manager Pat Gilroy had shown exceptional skills in guiding the team to the biggest day of the GAA year.

People are inclined to forget what football was like before Dublin's rise to power. Just a year before, in 2010, Meath put five goals past Stephen Cluxton. No mean feat, as we now know.

In the 2011 final, Kerry started strong. In the first half, Darren O'Sullivan ran through the heart of the Dublin defence and laid off a ball to Colm 'Gooch' Cooper, who beat Cluxton to score a great goal.

Pat Gilroy brought on Kevin McManamon in the 51st minute. Twelve minutes later, with Kerry up by a goal and a point, Declan O'Sullivan lost possession, and Cian O'Sullivan gathered the ball in midfield and found Alan Brogan. Alan hand-passed to Kevin, who sent a powerful shot past Kerry goalkeeper Brendan Kealy to score a brilliant goal. It was now Kerry 1–10 Dublin 1–9.

Wing back Kevin Nolan, who would get the Man of the Match award afterwards, scored a fantastic point to level the match after receiving a pass from Diarmuid Connolly. It was Kevin's first ever point in championship football.

Kerry lost possession again and Dublin worked it towards Hill 16, with Michael Darragh MacAuley giving it to Bernard

Brogan who scored a great point with the clock on 68 minutes. But Kieran Donaghy produced an incredible shot from 35 metres out in front of the Cusack stand to score the equalizer.

Game over? Not quite.

Kevin McManamon was judged to have been fouled by Barry John Keane as he was running towards the Hill 16 goalposts. Bernard Brogan signalled to Stephen Cluxton to make the long journey up from the Davin end goal to the spot of the foul: 45 metres from the Kerry goalposts, a few metres in from the sideline on the Cusack stand side. Cluxton placed the ball on the ground, took five steps back, then two to his right, paused, took the run up and stroked the ball beautifully between the posts. He then turned and ran calmly back to his goalposts, while 82,300 people in Croke Park went ballistic. The final whistle blew and Dublin were All-Ireland champions for the first time since 1995.

Stephen Cluxton, the goalkeeper. Stephen Cluxton the hero.

For decades, it had been the norm that supporters from the winning team ran on to the field to congratulate their players at the end of an All-Ireland final. But this particular year, the GAA were anxious to halt that tradition on health and safety grounds. In the rush to get to the field, people could easily get crushed or injure themselves. I was on sideline duty for RTÉ that afternoon, and the GAA asked me to make a number of public safety announcements in order to try and help keep fans in the stands.

When the final whistle blew, I moved swiftly on to the pitch with cameraman in tow, so that everything we saw and did would be shown on the big screens around the ground. I headed for the Dublin players, while simultaneously encouraging the 82,300 crowd to stay where they were.

One of the first footballers I reached was Michael Darragh MacAuley, who was my neighbour in Rathfarnham at the time.

I grabbed his arm. 'What does it feel like to win the All-Ireland?'

'Unbelievable, unbelievable, unbelievable, unbelievable, unbelievable, unbelievable, unbelievable, unbelievable.'

Seriously. He said it eight times, and got a desperate slagging about it for months afterwards.

Two months later, we played against each other in a charity match in Croke Park. Afterwards, Michael Darragh told the *Irish Star*: 'I was dying to get him with a tackle but he went into goal so I couldn't get my hands on him. So Marty, if you are out there, I'm looking for you!'

Though there was some resistance to the pleas to keep off the grass, the fans eventually accepted the argument and now it's become standard practice after an All-Ireland is won.

On the steps of the Hogan stand, as GAA president Christy Cooney was presenting the Sam Maguire to the Dublin captain, Bryan Cullen, I couldn't help but notice the hero of the day, Stephen Cluxton, slip unnoticed through the crowd and retreat down the tunnel towards the Dublin dressing-room.

On impulse, I followed him.

I gingerly pushed open the Dublin dressing-room double doors and made my way down the short passageway before turning right into the main dressing-room area. As I approached I could hear the sound of studs moving across the floor over the muffled cheers from the blue army of supporters over our heads. Stephen already had one boot off and was unlacing the other when I turned the corner. I didn't know what kind of a reaction I'd get, so I was relieved when he looked up and smiled.

'Are you OK?' I asked.

'I'm grand.'

'Look, I'm not here as an RTÉ reporter but just a GAA man. What you did out there was truly fantastic, Stephen, so well done. Congratulations.'

'Thanks very much,' was the shy response.

'Why are you not outside with the lads?' I asked.

'I'm grand here. I'm not into all that stuff at all. Let them enjoy it. I just love the football part,' he said.

'Fair enough, but I think you should be out there with them. What you did to kick that winning point was brilliant. Congratulations, Stephen.'

'Thanks,' said the greatest goalkeeper in Gaelic football.

I walked back down the passageway, through the doors, and was about to turn left down the tunnel and out into the glare of light and noise when Tomás 'Mossy' Quinn and Bernard Brogan came running down the tunnel towards me.

'Where is he?' said Mossy.

'He's in the dressing-room. You should try to get him out.'

'We will,' said Bernard as they continued down the corridor. Minutes later, the two lads returned and clearly their powers of persuasion were better than mine because Stephen Cluxton was with them.

This amazing goalkeeper, who had the talent, the skill, the courage, the temperament, the balls to kick that winning point, wanted none of the attention. He only wanted to play football.

Most weddings are held at weekends, and many times, because of work commitments, I've been unable to attend, and so missed out on the special days of friends and relatives. In hindsight I deeply regret that.

But I wasn't going to miss the wedding of my great friends Davy Fitzgerald and his now wife Sharon O'Loughlin. The happy couple have always been loyal to me and vice versa. Which isn't to say that I agree with Davy on everything. Every now and then we will disagree fundamentally about something involving hurling, but it will always be forgotten by the end of the discussion.

Davy Fitzgerald's record as manager is hugely impressive. An All-Ireland and National League success with Clare; a Munster championship with Waterford; a Leinster championship with Wexford; Fitzgibbon Cups with LIT and success too with his own club, Sixmilebridge.

Sharon comes from a brilliant sporting family in Clarecastle and was a fine camogie player with her native Magpies, and with the Banner. Her brother Ger 'Sparrow' O'Loughlin played corner forward on those great Clare teams, while another brother, Fergie, is a highly thought-of coach and has been involved with Kilmoyley in Kerry and Clooney-Quin in Clare.

So, on Friday October 4th, 2019, I headed to Dromoland Castle just outside Newmarket-on-Fergus to the wedding, which turned out to be one of the best weddings I was ever at.

But not before I broke an embargo that I knew nothing about.

I decided to go a bit later than the time on the invitation, timing my arrival for the start of the dinner. Unknown to me, Fr Harry Bohan, parish priest of Sixmilebridge and a great friend to all who are lucky enough to get to know him, had given the couple a special blessing witnessed by the invited guests. He spoke afterwards, and on behalf of the couple he asked people to keep any photographs private and not to put anything up on Twitter or Instagram.

I knew from other events in Dromoland over the years that the best way into the area where wedding receptions were held was through the back door, near the golf club. As I pushed open the door, who was standing there in his tux only the groom himself, smiling from ear to ear.

'Jaysus Marty, about time for you to arrive. If I wasn't standing right here, you'd be telling me in a hour's time that you were here from the beginning when I know you fucker you weren't. So I'm glad I caught you!'

This was followed by howls of Davy laughter.

'Would you like a photograph with me and my new wife?'

'I would love one, Davy, of course!'

I kissed Sharon on the cheek and gave her a big hug. Syl O'Connor, one of my best friends, was there with his wife Mary Ann, so I asked him to take the picture.

'No bother,' says Syl, taking my mobile phone.

Afterwards, I picked the best one and up it went on Twitter and Instagram.

Delighted and proud to be at my great friends' wedding today. Got one of the first photos with Davy and Sharon. They are a great team together and we all wish them much happiness. Dinner is at 6.30, then the party begins!

I pressed send at 5.46 p.m.

Not long afterwards, Davy came over to the table and gave me the nod to indicate that he wanted a private word.

'Hey buddy, I don't give a fuck but Sharon is bulling.'

'Why? What happened?'

Davy started to laugh. 'We're already on Independent.ie, the *Sun*, the *Star* and it's not even 7.30! You obviously put up the photo that Syl took. We'd asked that there would be no

social media but typical you, you bollix, you arrive late and mess it up!'

I apologized right away.

'My advice now, Marty, is to keep your head down and say nothin'.'

But sure within minutes Sharon found me and gave me a fully deserved bollicking, though with grace and laughter. She then dragged me up on the floor and we danced the night away. The speeches were great, the entertainment fantastic and it truly was a most memorable wedding.

The following morning I woke up to the photograph of myself, Davy and Sharon in all the papers. You couldn't avoid it. We were everywhere.

I decided not to contact the Fitzgeralds for a few days.

A week later I was at another wedding. This time it was my Cork camogie buddy and *Dancing with the Stars* colleague Anna Geary's turn to walk down the aisle with her husband-to-be Kevin Sexton. Kevin is a proud Dublin man who used to work in the ticket office in Croke Park and is undoubtedly one of the soundest guys I know. Anna has been a very loyal and positive friend to me since we got to know each other during her playing career. Her transformation from a camogie star to a TV star is all down to her great natural talent and her determination to succeed in what can be a tough business. She was a vital part of *The Marty Squad* on RTÉ Radio 1, and hopefully will be again when things get back to normal after Covid. She also shone brightly on *Ireland's Fittest Family*, a brilliant TV concept originated by our mutual pal Davy Fitzgerald, together with James Sexton from Shannon and Animo Productions.

Anna had very kindly requested that I introduce the wedding party to the guests gathered at the reception at the magnificent Castlemartyr Hotel Resort in Co. Cork. I was very proud to oblige. She gave me the details and I put a few words together for my debut as a Wedding Party Introducer. I based it on my introduction to the All-Ireland hurling final in Croke Park in 2016:

Just in case you are walking on 5th Avenue in New York, jogging around the Corniche in Abu Dhabi, late-night dining in Shibuya in Tokyo or just chilling out on Long Street in Capetown, South Africa, let me tell you, this is Croke Park, Cork style! It's October 11th, 2019. It's 6 p.m. and this game is about to get under way. The Sunday Game for the first time is today called 'The Friday Game' and we are broadcasting around the world.

It's Cork and Dublin in the final and thousands have come from New Zealand and Texas, from Donegal and Galway, from the Kingdom of Kerry to the People's Republic of Cork and of course the Jackeens from Dublin's Fair City. You can easily pick out the Jackeens, ladies and gentlemen, they all have red noses from nose bleeds once they got beyond Clondalkin! Welcome to Culchie Land!

I introduced all of those sitting at the top table before it was time to bring in the bride and groom:

Between them, Anna and Kevin have twenty-four All-Ireland medals. Anna has twenty-three and Kevin has one Féile medal, the most prestigious of them all. They have been involved in many All-Ireland finals together in Croke Park. Anna playing in them, Kevin working at them.

Did you know that Kevin once got a trial for the Dublin hurlers when Anthony Daly was manager? A few weeks later Kevin injured his knee, but to this day he still refers to himself as a former Dublin hurler!

Anna is a special woman. I knew her as a great Cork camogie player and an All-Ireland winning captain. We became quite close when we did Dancing with the Stars *together, and in my humble opinion she is a star and I'm very proud to call her my friend.*

Ladies and gentlemen, the bride and groom, Anna Geary and Kevin Sexton. Mr and Mrs Sexton!

Both weddings were days to remember and nights that were unforgettable. They made me appreciate what family and good friends mean.

Five months later, the coronavirus arrived on our shores and we all had to forgo these great occasions to limit the spread of the virus and keep the vulnerable safe. I haven't been at a wedding since, but it would be hard to beat the last two I was at for sheer craic and enjoyment.

Before Covid put an end to it, I played football on Tuesday evenings on the astro pitches in UCD with a large selection of footballers who were legends in their own minds. They hailed from a multitude of countries, and despite our different cultural backgrounds, we managed to convince ourselves that we were still eighteen and could run as fast as ever. It was of course an opportunity to get some invaluable exercise and move the body a bit after a stressful weekend. I also looked at my Tuesday nights in Belfield as an educational experience, as I learned curse words in several different languages as balls hit the post, or there was a tough tackle, or the ball ended up in the next field despite the fact that the kicker faced an open goal.

It used to amuse me how Conor Faughnan, formerly of AA Roadwatch, could be on the radio on Wednesday mornings telling the nation about driving between the white lines, staying within the speed limits, wearing your seat belt and generally being careful, while twelve hours earlier the very same man was the Speedy Gonzales of the Astroturf. He was like a man possessed, burning up opponents with speed, gusto and strength. He was one of these lads who would go through you rather than around you. Michael Lyster presented *The Sunday Game* from 1984 to 2018, but is better known to the Tuesday night gang as the Iron Man from Barnaderg, Co. Galway. He played full back and abided by the 11th commandment, well, his 11th commandment: Thou Shalt Not Pass. Another Galwayman, Paul Byrnes, was a great friend of mine who was an excellent and an integral part of the RTÉ Sport team until 2017. We've played football for twenty years on and off, and I swear neither he nor Michael ever played a match without wearing the maroon and white of Galway.

Then there was Geoff Power, a former colleague of mine in the RTÉ sports department, who had left broadcasting to travel the world. He's now a playwright and an independent documentary producer with Midas Productions. Many of his programmes have been broadcast on RTÉ and TG4.

One night after football, Geoff and I were chatting and he asked me if I would meet his creative writing class. I said I'd be delighted to. As the time drew nearer, however, Geoff seemed hesitant to give me any details about this class. I couldn't figure out if he was just having the craic with me, or if there was something else going on. He didn't reveal the venue until the day before.

'It's the Midlands Prison.'

I laughed. 'You can't be serious! I'm not going to any prison.'

'That's why I didn't tell you!' said Geoff.

We talked about it for a little while and in short, he convinced me to come. I didn't want to let him down, and I will admit I was also a little curious.

The following morning, I arrived at the gate at the Midlands Prison on the old Dublin Road in the town of Portlaoise. A barrier lifted and the security man in the glass hut gave me a warm welcome and asked the perennial question: who did I think would win the championship?

'Good start,' says I to myself.

The large gates before me rolled slowly open and I drove through to the car park as directed. Geoff met me and we walked together towards the massive front door. The security reminded me of what happens at an airport: jackets off, belts off, shoes off; all were piled on to a tray on rollers and passed under the X-ray machine. My much-loved mobile phone and I were separated and were not reunited for over an hour. I then had to walk through a metal detector to ensure that I wasn't carrying any weapons before finally being given the all-clear to enter.

Two uniformed prison officers were then assigned to keep me company. So off we went. Our footsteps echoed off the bare but brightly painted walls, while huge sets of keys jangled from their belts. Some of the keys were gigantic antique things that must have been close to a foot long. We stopped at a huge door and one of the guys selected one of the huge keys, slotted it home, then rattled it around a little before it turned to release the door, which swung open to reveal another corridor. The door was locked behind us before we moved on.

Some of you may recall an American TV programme called *Get Smart*. During the opening credits, bungling secret agent Maxwell Smart would walk through a series of doors that would open for him then close again behind him. That's just what it was like in Midlands Prison that morning. The doors and corridors went on for ages before I saw a prison cell, let alone a prisoner.

The cells themselves are spread over three floors. The top floor is reserved for the best-behaved prisoners who require the least supervision. If trouble breaks out, the prison officers can leg it there, where resistance is considered unlikely.

Eventually, I began to hear voices. My two-man escort now changed formation: instead of walking either side of me, one walked ahead and the other behind. I was struck by the cleanliness of the place, and the strong smell of disinfectant. Midlands Prison houses 800 male prisoners, divided between sex offenders and regular prisoners – 'ordinary decents', they called them. I had vaguely expected them to be wearing special prison gear, but the first prisoners I saw were wearing tracksuits and runners. Many were heavily tattooed and muscular. One of these saw me and shouted, 'Jaysus, Marty, how long are you in for?'

'Two weeks,' says I.

'You'll love it, the grub is great.'

We kept walking, meeting more and more prisoners, until we arrived at the centre of a large circular zone from which four very long corridors of cells radiated. This actually looked like my idea of a prison. I looked up to an abundance of artificial rather than natural light, and what appeared to be endless rows of iron bars.

Suddenly there was a huge commotion. Roaring and shouting emanated from a cell upstairs – the sounds of a vicious row. There was bad language and I heard feet thumping at speed towards the source of the disturbance. Within seconds a siren ripped through the building, so piercing that you felt like closing your eyes and putting your hands over your ears. Suddenly, my two new prison officer friends were doing a lot more than simply keeping me company. I was grabbed and led speedily down the corridor. I didn't protest. I can move when I have to and this was undoubtedly one of those situations when I had to. We came to a room, went inside and locked the door after us. My heart was thumping, but once inside the room, I felt fine.

The two boys told me that outbreaks of violence are fairly common. Overcrowding is an issue in all prisons, and there was also a serious drug problem. My respect for prison officers was sky-high after this. They work in a very difficult environment, but the banter and connection they have with some of the prisoners is an effort to make a difficult situation just a little bit more tolerable for everybody, including themselves, and that is admirable to say the least.

Order was quickly restored and we were back outside, heading to where Geoff ran his creative writing class.

It was just an ordinary room, with desks like those you would see in any school. When I arrived, the prisoners – about ten in number – nodded hello. Geoff introduced me in his usual eloquent style and asked me to speak about what I did and how I did it.

One thing I had learned over the years was that short is beautiful, so I spoke for just fifteen minutes about how good sport, the GAA and RTÉ have been to me. Then I stopped and invited questions.

The silence seemed to go on forever, until eventually the questions began. Someone asked how I knew the name of everyone on the pitch. I shrugged and told the truth, which was that it was really just about having an interest in and a passion for the sport that I loved. 'I would spend a full day putting all my notes together, sometimes a day and a half. I'm with the Roy Keane motto: fail to prepare, prepare to fail. I would probably only use ten per cent of what I've gathered together but I'd rather have it than be looking for it.'

'Are you ever stuck for words?'

'All the time. Especially around four o'clock on a Sunday afternoon.'

They got a kick out of that.

Before I knew it, a full hour had passed. Geoff thanked them for their engagement and me for giving my time to come and talk to them.

Education is an option at all prisons, and it's needed. Many of these prisoners left school without completing second-level education. The Midlands Prison school allows prisoners to sit both the Junior Cert and the Leaving Cert, and other QQI examinations, while some will do Open University courses. This can be quite challenging, because internet access is not allowed. There are also classes available in metalwork, woodwork and pottery as well as creative writing.

I would condemn and abhor what these prisoners did to their fellow human beings when they were in the outside free world. And yet my innate Christian belief is that if they serve their time, regret their actions and take advantage of the opportunities they're offered in prison, then surely that must be a positive thing.

They thanked me for visiting them and I knew immediately that the expression of gratitude was genuine. I think they enjoyed the hour they spent talking to me and asking me questions.

And so we began to walk. Door after door. I was Maxwell Smart again. But it was different this time. The long key went in, rattled around a little, before turning to unlock the door, bestowing on us the freedom to move forward to the next section. My head was rattling with all I had seen.

The prison officers showed me the canteen and the meeting place where prisoners' families and loved ones come to see them. The room was divided in two by glass barriers. No touching allowed.

And so we walked to freedom. I emerged into glorious sunshine and clean, fresh air. Portlaoise never felt or smelt so good. Passing through all those doors and corridors felt like being in another world. Not a world I would ever want to experience. It must be awful to be a prisoner. But then you must do something pretty awful to become one.

I was glad that Geoff invited me but I had no desire to go back. One visit was enough.

21. The Wireless

I always seem to be away when one of my many bosses calls to offer a gig. I was in a hotel in Times Square in the run up to Christmas 2010 when the phone rang and Paddy Glackin's name came up. Paddy is internationally renowned as one of Ireland's greatest fiddle players, but I know him as a kind, pragmatic and honourable man who would always give you a fair hearing. He was then the head of RTÉ radio sport, and he asked if I'd be interested in presenting *Countrywide* on Radio 1 on Saturday mornings for a few weeks in January and February, when regular presenter Damien O'Reilly would be away. I said yes, of course, but truthfully, I hadn't a notion what *Countrywide* was about. Back then, Copper Face Jacks was always a great spot on a Friday night, so Saturday morning was chill-out time. As the programme was going to air, I'd usually be tucked up in the sack snoring my head off.

I very quickly learned what a smashing little show *Countrywide* was (as it still is). It's like *Nationwide* on the radio, though with a slightly more agricultural feel. It's been called 'the farmers' programme', which is partially true. It has its roots in a programme called *Farm Week* which used to be broadcast every Saturday morning between 8.30 and 9. These days, it's more an audio snapshot of rural and urban life. In presenting *Countrywide*, I worked with top-class producers like Ana Leddy, Brian Lally, Sinead Egan and the incomparable Ian Wilson, all of whom were a joy to work with. More recently,

Eileen Heron produces the show, and her love and care for the programme is obvious.

Going out with my radio recording device has always given me great joy, whether it's hopping up on to a massive combine harvester as dusk falls on the barley fields of Kilkenny, or going to the great food markets around the country, like the one in Cahir, Co. Tipperary. I once joined the crew of Irene Hamilton's boat in Kilrush before heading out across the blue waters to Scattery Island with a group of tourists. These days have been so memorable, not alone for giving me great material for the show but also for keeping me grounded. Meeting and talking to people who are following their passions reminds me of what is important in life. *Countrywide* has also given me the opportunity to meet and interview people that I would never have met otherwise: singers like John Spillane and Mags McCarthy, to name just two, have lit up the airwaves with their personalities as well as their beautiful songs.

My link with Tom McGuire goes back a bit. He is a native of Longford but resident in beautiful Mount Temple in Co. Westmeath. When I left RTÉ Cork to come to Dublin, he got my old job, then went on to climb the management ladder to eventually become head of RTÉ Radio in January 2014. I told Tom on my many visits to his office (which probably annoyed the poor man beyond belief) that I would love to do more presenting on the radio. A year later, he gave me a most wonderful opportunity. Derek Mooney, who presented an afternoon programme on Radio 1, was moving on to new challenges and Ray D'Arcy was transferring back from Today FM to take his place. But there would be a gap. Would I fill in?

Would I? The initial period was two weeks, but that grew into three and ultimately ended up as four. Five days a week in the afternoon slot on Radio 1 between 3 and 4.30.

I absolutely loved it. It was the best four weeks I ever had.

I worked with the great production team of Olan McGowan, Peter Hegarty, Sheila O'Callaghan and Pat O'Mahony. At our first meeting, they asked me what I had in mind for my stint. I felt that it should be positive, interesting and as much fun as possible, avoiding anything too serious or downtrodden. The programme is sandwiched between *Liveline*, hosted by the great Joe Duffy, and *Drivetime*, which was presented by Mary Wilson at the time. She's easily one of the best journalists that I know. Getting the right mix of content for a programme that sits between these two would be a serious challenge. I felt that people needed to smile a little, to be stimulated during that afternoon hour and a half. I was very conscious that many listeners were in their cars at that time, picking up children from school, and that during a hard day, positive content and a bit of a laugh are so important.

My very first guest was comedian Dara Ó Briain, whom I greatly admire for his intelligence and wit. Any man that played football and hurling for Bray Emmets and togged out for the Wicklow minor hurling team, speaks fluent Irish and loves science is my kind of a man. But there's another, more personal reason for my affection for Dara. In December 2004 I flew to New York for some Christmas shopping, and rang home as I was waiting for a taxi at Kennedy Airport. My father answered the phone and started telling me about this great Wicklow comedian who had been on *The Ryan Tubridy Show* earlier. He must have relayed every single joke that Dara told, while myself and Liz stood there in the freezing weather with that terrible wind-chill factor that I've only ever found in New York. When I told him I knew Dara, he couldn't believe it. This, it would turn out, was my last proper conversation with my dad.

On other days, Donny Osmond spoke to me on the phone and Chris de Burgh, whom I really like, came into studio for a ten-minute interview and then stayed for the whole programme, chatting away to every other guest we had on. The response from the listening audience was hugely positive. With each passing day, we seemed to gain traction in the papers.

One of the greatest treats in my life occurred during the last days of my four-week stint, when I was asked to play a small part in John B. Keane's *Moll* at the Gaiety Theatre. I was Ulick: a bit of a gombeen with a habit of scratching himself. He's the potential love interest of the priest's housekeeper, who was played by Mary McEvoy, who will of course always have a special place in people's hearts as Biddy from *Glenroe*. To be on the same stage as Mary, Des Keogh, Clare Barrett, Damian Kearney, Pat McDonnell and the late, iconic Frank Kelly was truly an honour for me. And I had only one

With Frank Kelly when we did *Moll*

line: 'There's no fear of a fall. I'd say she was often saddled before.' (Exit Ulick.)

To walk on to the Gaiety stage with such luminaries of Irish theatre was beyond my wildest dreams. The rapturous response from the audience still rings in my ears and sends a tingle down my spine. Did I really do that? It was almost like an out-of-body experience as I think back on it now, and all I had was one line! I'd love to take acting lessons and perform once again in the Gaiety. At the break, I was like a goggle-eyed fan, taking selfies with the cast and getting Frank Kelly, aka Fr Jack, to say those immortal words: 'Drink! Feck! Arse! Girls!'

Frank died thirteen months later, on February 28th, 2016. May he rest in peace.

During the London Olympics in 2012, some unidentified person had started sending me cards. The writing was big and spread across both leaves of the card. Then I got this one:

B Grace anseo!
    Hey Marty . . . you just brought out beads of sweat on me on the first Katie fight . . . I thought you were going to have an organism! What a commentary!!!

There was a small circular on the card which read 'Schedule Doctor's Appointment', and he wrote beside it: *Especially for the Larynx. Well held, Brendan x*

I couldn't believe it. Brendan Grace was writing to me. One of the greatest talents this country has ever produced had reached out to me and I was so chuffed, so delighted, so proud. He still makes me laugh even though he's gone to his eternal reward. After an All-Ireland hurling final commentary on the radio, Brendan wrote from his home in the USA:

Well Marty
Who needs TV!
There I was lying in the sun in Florida.
I was hoarse . . . I saw the match . . . on radio.
Jesus . . . Well held, Mr Morrissey . . . Great,
Brendan Grace

When I was filling in between Derek's departure and Ray's arrival, I rang Brendan and asked him to join me on the radio. He came on and, as usual, he got a tremendous reaction.

Our friendship grew, and about a year later I found myself performing with him in a six-part TG4 series called *Fir Bolg*. (I told you this acting bug had gotten to me!) My colleague Aonghus McAnally had invited me to take a cameo role in

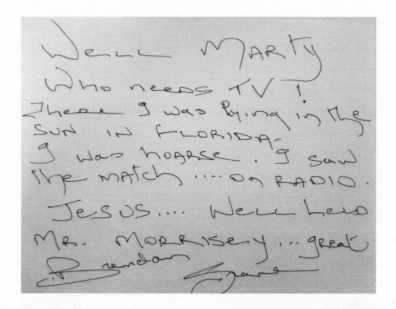

Well MARTY
Who needs TV !
There I was lying in the
SUN IN FLORIDA-
I was hoarse . I saw
the MATCH .... on RADIO .
JESUS.... WELL DONE
MR. MORRISEY ... great
Brendan

the series, which was about a disbanded traditional group
getting together for a reunion. I had my doubts about doing
it but then Brendan called me and said, 'Cop on to yourself
and get your arse down to filming next week.'

And so I did, and what a great opportunity it proved to be!
I played a rock journalist at the band's press conference,
together with DJ Colm Hayes and Lucy Kennedy. The band
included Sean McGinley, Don Wycherley, Peadar Cox,
Máirtín Jaimsie and Aongus McAnally. There were also roles
for Caroline Morahan, Amy Huberman, Patrick Bergin, Liam
Cunningham, Stephen Rea, Paddy Moloney, Conal Gallen,
Ryan Tubridy and Daniel O'Donnell. I thought I was in
Hollywood!

Just like my part in *Moll*, I had one line to remember: a
clear indication of the producers' assessment of my acting
talents! In August 2016, *Fir Bolg* was launched by the Irish
Film and Television Academy at the Sugar Club. It was the
last night that I had a really great chat with Brendan. I miss

his cards and I miss his support. He had no reason to contact me; he was the star, the legend. But he befriended me with those cards from Florida, which he sent without knowing what type of guy I was. That was a big call by a very kind, very big-hearted man, and I was all the richer for his friendship and kindness.

We all need support, we all need great friends, and by God Brendan and Eileen Grace proved to be loyal friends to me. Brendan died on July 11th, 2019. But in my heart he will live forever.

We'd had such a wonderful time over the month of doing the afternoon show that we decided to go out with a bang. The final programme would be broadcast from Studio 1, which is the largest studio in the Radio Centre. We would call it 'The Marty Party' and invite listeners to attend. So we put out the word, and the show sold out within the hour. At two o'clock on the Friday, there was a queue at the front door of the Radio Centre which stretched all the way back to the administrative building. We quickly realized that the upstairs balcony, which would normally seat 200 people, wouldn't accommodate the crowd, which was closer to 400. Extra seats had to be placed on the studio floor. The turnout was amazing to see, especially since we'd only been on the air for four weeks. I really appreciated the effort that so many people went to. They travelled from all over the country, as well as from down the road in Dublin 4.

And here's the strangest thing of all. Normally, broadcasters will seek media attention when an event is planned, and send out invitations to journalists hoping that they will give some positive coverage. For the 'Marty Party' show, the journalists rang up RTÉ *asking* if they could attend. They were of course most welcome.

Oliver Callan, who is such a brilliantly talented mimic, pretended to be me at the top of the show, so it was the fake Marty taking on the real Marty in a quiz about, well, me!

Nathan Carter sang 'Wagon Wheel', and everyone jived away up on the balcony and down on the studio floor. Later, the Kilfenora Céilí Band got the crowd rocking, with a lively set battered out by Eugene Donnellan's All-Ireland champion set dancers from West Clare. Andy Irvine played and sang beautifully, while actors Mary McEvoy, Eamon Morrissey, the late Eurovision songwriter and broadcaster Shay Healy, model and chef Roz Purcell, and Lorraine Keane, formerly of AA Roadwatch and TV3, were all there on my final day.

I was a bit emotional as I wrapped up the programme, which surprised me. I can usually contain that side of my personality.

I passionately believe in the team ethos, so I thanked all those who had worked on the show: Sinead Renshaw, Elaine Power, Ann Marie Donnellan, Edel Hynes, Michelle Brown and Karla Zambra. I wished Ray D'Arcy the very best of luck and thanked RTÉ management for giving me the chance to host the show.

Filling in for a day or two is fine, but four weeks was a huge endorsement (or a huge risk, depending on your perspective). Regardless of how those four weeks had gone, it had already been decided that Ray was coming into the afternoon slot. RTÉ tend to put 'talent', as they like to call those who are on air, into carefully labelled boxes, and it's seldom you get to climb out of that box and diversify. My box reads 'Sport'. I can understand the need for these boxes from a logistical point of view. But surely it must also be about looking at what somebody can offer. I always thought that the late

Colm Murray had a talent that really could have been developed. People loved him, and his kind of connection with the audience is very rare. It's not all about your Instagram numbers or how many followers you have on Twitter. It's about that connection to the listener, to the audience.

I'm not saying I have it. I'm sure there are people who like my style and others who think I'm an asshole. What can you do except try your very best? Nobody is going to be liked universally, it's just impossible. RTÉ's Jim Jennings and Tom McGuire showed real leadership by taking me out of my box and giving me the chance and the responsibility to present a daily programme, five days a week for four weeks.

The following Monday, I was back doing my regular job as a GAA correspondent, and was down the country filming a report for the *Six One News*. I pulled in to the side of the road at three o'clock to listen to Ray as he began his programme. To my astonishment, I felt very lonely and emotional again. After all the hype and daily media coverage, that slot now belonged to somebody else. This particular journey was done for me and I had to get over it.

Ray is a fine broadcaster, and I have been a guest many times on his radio show and on his TV show *The Den*, risking my life with those two rogues Zig and Zag, as well as Dustin the turkey. I was hoping that some day they might want me to fill in for Ray when he's taking holidays. It hasn't happened yet but I'm sure it will, some day soon. My number is 087 24 . . . Look, just call the sports department, they'll know where to find me!

For a number of years I was given the opportunity to fill in for Ryan Tubridy on his morning show, and I absolutely loved that too. This was a completely different challenge. Ryan has developed a unique style. He comes on at nine, but mightn't speak to his first guest until 9.25 or 9.30. For those twenty-five minutes, he talks off the cuff based on what he picks up from the morning papers. It's a wonderful talent. I also greatly admire Ryan for what he does on *The Late Late Show*. In particular, he was outstanding during the Covid pandemic, and I don't think anybody could do *The Late Late Toy Show* better than Ryan. He's brilliant with kids. He really connects with them.

Oliver Callan is now the preferred choice to fill in for Ryan, and I can understand why my friend is much liked in that role. He can be Oliver Callan, but he can also be Leo Varadkar or Paschal Donoghue or Mary Lou McDonald, all in a matter of seconds. That's just magical.

Every now and then, when I took the notion, I'd get out my mobile, ring Tom McGuire and straight out ask if he'd got any radio gigs for me. The answer was usually negative, but he always gave me hope. I knew that he still saw me in the box labelled 'sport', but the truth is that four-week stint in the afternoon spoiled me. I was now more interested in mainstream broadcasting and was hungry for new challenges. But I liked Tom's thinking and his positivity. He thought that maybe we could do something after matches on Sundays, and asked if I could do a radio show from six to seven. *Second Captains* had the slot previously, but unfortunately (or fortunately from my perspective) they were unable to commit to the slot. Myself and Tom discussed the proposition many times. I thought there were huge possibilities and massive potential, but there were also a few logistical difficulties that had to be overcome. I spoke about it to Donagh McGrath, the head of sports news and radio sport, and to his great credit, he was positively disposed to me taking it on.

And so, on June 7th, 2015, *The Marty Squad* was born, with

Paddy McKenna from Co. Leitrim as co-presenter and my great friend Brenda Donohue as reporter. We were backed up by three experts: former Cork camogie star Anna Geary, former Roscommon goalkeeper Shane Curran, and another goalkeeper, David Herity, who won five All-Irelands with Kilkenny. Our first producer was Barry O'Neill, a great hurling man from the Aodh Rua club in Ballyshannon, Co. Donegal. He already had enough to do putting *Sunday Sport* together without this being added to his list, but he did it splendidly and always with a smile.

I loved *The Marty Squad*, and it went really well for its first five championship summers, until Covid arrived in March 2020. It was a really busy programme, and a big logistical challenge. After completing a live match commentary on TV or radio at whatever venue I was assigned to, I would usually have to run across the pitch through the crowd to do my 'as live' interview with the winning manager or captain for the *Six One News*. I'd record the interview, then leg it back to the

mobile outside broadcast unit, better known as the Road-caster, which would be parked outside the ground. To do all that in a very short space of time was a real test of stamina, speed, time-keeping and sheer determination. Most Sundays, I got to the Roadcaster with seconds to spare. On those few occasions when I didn't make it on time, Paddy McKenna or, from 2016 onwards, Damien Lawlor was there to open the programme.

I thought it was essential that we do something different to the traditional Sunday sport programme. Meeting the players that were just involved in the game was crucial, and to be fair, county press officers like Dublin's Seamus 'Shep' McCormack were brilliant. He organized the likes of Brian Fenton, Ciaran Kilkenny, John Small, Dean Rock, Bernard Brogan and many others to come out and join me down the corridor from their dressing-rooms underneath the Hogan stand. Other counties, including Kilkenny, Cork, Limerick, Donegal and Mayo could not have been more helpful.

Most times, the lads were in their bare feet, bare-chested and still togged in their shorts, so we were capturing moments which we felt would be really interesting to the transient audience that were making their way home from games across the country. *The Marty Squad* was also built around meeting the fans as they left Páirc Uí Chaoimh in Cork or Pearse Stadium in Galway or wherever we were; and here, Brenda Donohue shone brightly. She's just great at finding fans with a connection to the team.

On September 1st, 2015, *The Marty Squad* travelled to Passage East in Co. Waterford to fulfil our promise, following an on-air competition, to do the crossbar challenge in the Déise. It was a beautiful Thursday evening in Waterford and on our arrival we were thrilled to see a huge crowd gathered in the local GAA ground. Colm Flynn, a fellow Clareman (and now the Vatican correspondent for EWTN News), travelled with us to film the event just in case any of us miraculously hit the crossbar. Each participant had to run up to the camera and say their name, then take their shot. It was one ball, one chance. No best-of-three lark for us. We hadn't the time.

Noel Connors, the Waterford hurler, was first. Back of the net. No good.

Thomas Connors from Passage was next. He hit the bar. Fair play.

Miriam Walsh from Passage tried but the ball dribbled into the net.

Pa Walsh, Passage East, hit a shot but it went straight into the net.

Eoin Kelly, the Waterford hurler, had a go but missed. Over the bar.

Paul Flynn, a former Waterford hurler, tried but missed.

James Rea from Laois also missed.

Paddy McKenna, co-presenter from Leitrim, missed. Ball still missing.

Brenda Donohue, Kildare, didn't even manage to hit the ball.

Then it was my turn.

The crowd chanted 'Marty! Marty! Marty!' And of course I played up to it. This is show business, after all! I threw down the sliotar and performed my little trick by picking it up between foot and hurley, then in one movement flicked the sliotar on to the bas. I did a few fancy steps; the crowd got even more excited. This was the moment, I decided, and I went for it. I flung the ball into the air and as it dropped, I struck it cleanly. Sliotar and ash smashed off each other in perfect harmony and the ball accelerated towards the

goalposts. In the silence that followed, the crowd watched the ball rise straight and true, and then there was that beautiful *ping!* as it struck the crossbar.

There was a massive roar. I had actually hit the crossbar in Passage East. One strike. One hit.

It was undoubtedly the greatest fluke of all time. I couldn't believe it. The crowd went wild with excitement and I danced around with the locals. I'm sure that's where Larry Bass of ShinAwiL Productions, the executive producer of *Dancing with the Stars*, first saw my raw talent as a dancer, and why he invited me to become a contender for the glitterball trophy a few years later.

At the time, and for a few years afterwards, I was MC for the Bord Gáis under-21 hurling championship games around the country, and every half-time we would have a crossbar challenge, but I never hit it again.

There were other special moments on *The Marty Squad*. In September 2017, Derry footballer Ciara McGurk scored a first-half goal against Fermanagh in the ladies' junior All-Ireland final. Later that afternoon, she was being interviewed by Dáithí Ó Sé on TG4 when she turned around to see her boyfriend Ryan McCloskey down on one knee in front of the Hogan stand crowd. We think he proposed and we think she said 'Yes'. It was hard to tell with the noise and the huge emotional reaction at that precise moment. Brenda was there to capture it all on tape and we played the whole romantic episode on our programme.

In August 2019, the Ladies' Gaelic Football Association got permission to use Croke Park for the All-Ireland semi-finals for the very first time. We spoke to the players involved, but the real highlight of the show came from a group of women that we thought we would have on the programme for about five minutes. Instead, they were still talking to me live on air twenty minutes later. The Ballybough Ladies 'GAA for Mas' was a group of women who brought humour, sensitivity, pride of place and wit to a whole new level that day. Though they lived in the shadow of Croke Park, many of them – amazingly – had never been inside the ground before, and here they were talking to me on the radio about their experiences of playing football earlier that afternoon on the pitch they had heard so much about. In glorious late summer sunshine, they relayed their stories with passion, honesty and a wonderfully wicked sense of humour. I was so impressed with them that, within a year, they would play an integral part on an episode of *Marty and Bernard: Back on the Road Again*. More about that later.

It always filled me with pride when I'd get a call or an email from the Taoiseach's office, or occasionally Áras an Uachtaráin, saying that Leo Varadkar or Michael D. Higgins would happily do an interview with us after the All-Ireland finals. They didn't have to, but they did.

We met some great characters on our journeys around Ireland, like the Roscommon barber Paddy Joe 'Ice cream meltin', flags flyin', Rossies dreamin'' Burke, who has appeared many times on *The Marty Squad*. Paddy Joe loves Roscommon and goes through the summer with primrose and blue on his head, his back and on his feet. When the Rossies win the Connacht championship, it's become traditional to bring the Nestor Cup to Paddy Joe's barber shop in Roscommon town on the Monday. There were always great photo opportunities as Paddy Joe would be perfecting the latest hairstyles, still clad in his Roscommon jersey and bandana.

Staying in Roscommon for a moment, one beautiful sunny evening after a match in the Hyde between Roscommon and Galway, we had just finished broadcasting *The Marty Squad* from outside the grounds. I was starving, so I offered to take the gang for a beautiful dinner in a classy restaurant in downtown Roscommon. And so we headed for Supermac's!

All we wanted were a few snackboxes, with the essential curry sauce for me, but what we got on our arrival was simply unforgettable. The place was packed with people in their Roscommon and Galway jerseys. The moment we came through the front door, the crowd burst into spontaneous applause. I thought either Tom Cruise or Brad Pitt had walked in behind us, but no, it was all for us. As you can imagine, it's a rather bizarre experience to walk into a packed Supermac's and get a standing ovation. When the crowd started singing 'The Fields of Athenry', the atmosphere reached a whole new level, one which I doubt was ever reached before in Supermac's. We posed for selfies, and one kind lady bought us each a 99 for our dessert. The kindness and warm welcome was unprecedented, and let me say categorically that it was very much appreciated.

In December 2019 I was back again in Tom McGuire's office to see, once again, if there was any hope of getting a slot somewhere in the radio schedule. It was well known that Tom would be retiring the following September, so I was hoping he'd give me something before he sailed into the sunset. On this occasion, he thought that there might be some room in the schedule for a radio show on public holidays, and a little while later he called to offer me the gig: two morning hours on RTÉ Radio 1 on the year's seven public holidays. It was something. It was a chance; a glimmer of light. Ana Leddy would be my producer and Brenda Donohoe would be available as well. Most two-hour shows would have a much bigger production team of researchers and producers, but I didn't complain. And, as it turned out, the small team worked out really well.

Then, suddenly, Covid arrived in Ireland and everything changed. Ana was now working from home, and for a full year and a half I didn't see or meet her at all. Though we spoke on the phone and shared ideas, it wasn't quite the same. Brenda is more than just a fellow presenter, she's an excellent ideas person and contributes hugely to the programme, while John Reilly provides invaluable technical assistance at base, as does Brian Namock, RTÉ's Tralee-based regional production engineer. I might have a good contacts list on my phone, but Brenda leaves me standing when she puts on the glasses and starts sifting through her names. The partnership works wonderfully between us. Brenda and I usually suggest who we'll have on, and I extend the invitations. Then Ana takes over, and from that moment until broadcast time, she weaves her spell and guides us through the various discussions.

Doing a live radio show while working remotely was a new challenge. I was used to Ana producing from the studio and directing me in my ear, but now that vital connection, that crucial information flow, was gone. Sheila O'Callaghan, whom I'd worked with before, came into the studio on the day to ensure things ran smoothly, and she is just superb: so calm. But Ana had an in-depth knowledge of what we had planned for that morning's programme, and we just couldn't do without her knowledge, experience and expertise. So we devised a plan. Normally I would never have my phone with me in studio, but I turned it on silent and brought it in, and while I was on the air, Ana would send me WhatsApp messages from her kitchen table.

If she was getting frustrated with anything, the phone would light up like a Christmas tree.

Marty, you have two minutes left in this. Going well.
You have one minute left, start wrapping.
Marty, you are over-running. Wrap.
MARTY! YOU ARE NOW 3 MINUTES OVER. WRAP! WRAP!
    WRAP!!! GO TO BREAK NOW!

Panel discussions were particularly difficult when nobody was allowed into studio. We had to have all our guests on audio lines, which is challenging because you can't see them and so can't tell when someone wants to say something. Over time, we graduated to having guests on Zoom calls, and the visibility factor made it much easier for all involved.

Perhaps the most challenging programme for myself and Ana happened on August 3rd, 2020. We were live on air and

I was in the middle of a really enjoyable interview with Victoria Smurfit when my phone lit up. This time it wasn't Ana. It was my boss Declan McBennett, texting to say that John Hume had died and that I needed to announce it immediately. I had to think on my feet. It helped that as soon as I had finished with Victoria, we were going to a pre-recorded interview, which would give me time to take a deep breath, calm everyone down and speak to Ana about what we would do. The programme that we had planned for weeks was now dead in the water. We had to react to this breaking news.

Declan suggested I get in contact with Tommie Gorman and Miriam O'Callaghan, both of whom had known John Hume well. I passed both phone numbers to Ana, and by the time the taped interview was finished, we were ready to announce John Hume's sad passing and have Tommie and Miriam lined up to speak to me live on air. That brought us to the ten o'clock news headlines, which gave us a two-minute window to draw breath and get ready for the next hour. A whole hour! Getting through it would require a massive team effort, and it gave me the best personal example I have seen of a group of individuals coming together in a moment of crisis to react to a breaking news story. We were not political journalists or producers, but cometh the hour, cometh the women. Sheila O'Callaghan was making phone calls frantically in studio, Ana was in her kitchen sending texts and making similar calls to her contacts in Derry, where she had worked previously with the BBC Radio Foyle service. Tommy Fleming and Diarmuid Gavin were supposed to be my guests in the hour, and I asked both to stay as the programme developed and evolved. I can't praise the two lads enough as they sat there in the studio with me for the full hour and got very little time to speak, as all of Sheila and

Ana's hard work on the phone lines began to pay off. Former Northern Ireland first minister David Trimble joined me on the line, as did former deputy first minister Mark Durkan, together with Tony Blair's former adviser Alastair Campbell, former Taoiseach Bertie Ahern, and Sinn Féin president Mary Lou McDonald.

There was no time to write introductions, so I asked John Reilly to print off the Wikipedia pages of our guests before they came on. After that, I was on my own and just hoped that my own political knowledge would carry me through, and that my questions were sufficiently intelligent and relevant on this sad day for both the Hume family and John Hume's thousands of supporters and admirers.

I got a brainwave as I was speaking to one of our guests. I scribbled a quick note to Tommy Fleming asking him if he had the backing track for Phil Coulter's 'The Town I Loved so Well', and if he knew the words. He gave me the thumbs up, then slipped outside to the production area to explain my idea to Sheila, who ran to get everything ready.

So, at the very end of our two-hour show on August 3rd, 2020, Tommy Fleming ended the programme singing 'The Town I Loved so Well' as a tribute to the late John Hume. People asked me afterwards how I came to think of it, and the truth is that it's actually my favourite song. When Phil Coulter came to perform at the concert I organized in my parish church in Mullagh a few years before, I asked him to please sing the song he wrote about his home place. The last verse is particularly poignant when you think of John Hume. Rest in Peace, John.

> Now the music's gone but they carry on
> For their spirit's been bruised, never broken

They will not forget but their hearts are set
On tomorrow and peace once again
For what's done is done and what's won is won
And what's lost is lost and gone forever
I can only pray for a bright brand new day
In the town I loved so well

At the start of 2021, I really didn't know whether the new head of radio, Peter Woods, and his management team of Tara Campbell, Penny Hart and Siobhan Haugh would invite me back to present the public holiday radio show.

I knew and liked Peter, a great and very proud Monaghan man who loved his sport and traditional music, and who was especially passionate about current affairs. His fingerprints are all over some of the brilliant programmes that have developed on RTE Radio 1 over the last number of years, like *Late Debate*, and under his guidance Radio 1 feels different and refreshed now with Claire Byrne, Sarah McInerney, Cormac Ó hEadhra and Katie Hannon, all outstanding in their field of expertise.

One day in February 2021, I got the call from Penny Hart. I'll never forget her words. 'We would like you to present the radio shows on public holidays for the year ahead.'

I was so delighted, and to be honest, I'm still on cloud nine.

Like everything else I had done in RTÉ, it has taken time. To Peter Woods and his management team, I say 'Thank you'. I will be forever grateful. They even allowed me to call my programme *The Marty Morrissey Show*. I would still love to do more on radio, but right now I'm there for seven mornings out of three hundred and sixty-five in the year.

It's a start!

22. Adventures of a GAA Correspondent

In October 2012, two months after the London Olympics, Ryle Nugent called to say he wanted to meet me. Ryle was the group head of RTÉ Sport at the time, and we had had an excellent professional relationship and a personal friendship. There was something different about this request, and to my mind it meant only one thing: trouble! To make things worse, he said he didn't want to meet me in his office or on the RTÉ campus, but suggested that we have dinner: this convinced me that it had been elevated to Serious Trouble! I just said, 'OK, whatever it is . . . I didn't do it.'

We met at Marco Pierre White Steakhouse & Grill on Dawson Street in Dublin. We spoke at length about the Olympics and Ryle was kind enough to congratulate me on my boxing commentaries and my role in the coverage generally. It still wasn't clear why he wanted to see me, but eventually we got down to business. He wanted to offer me the position of GAA correspondent in the RTÉ newsroom.

This was not the first time this possibility had arisen. Back in 2008, I had been encouraged by the then head of sport, Glen Killane, to apply for the new position of 'Gaelic Games correspondent' that was being created in the newsroom. Glen mentioned that if I took the role, I might come under pressure to give up match commentaries – though Glen didn't think I should have to do so. I told him that no matter what happened I wasn't going to give up my commentaries, and Glen reassured me that he had no desire to see that happen. He thought the Gaelic Games correspondent role was an opportunity to rubber-stamp what I was already doing on an ad hoc basis. So I applied and was called for interview. On the interview board were Cillian de Paor, acting managing director of news and current affairs; Declan McBennett, head of TV sports news; and Paul Byrnes, executive editor of *The Sunday Game*. Cillian was adamant in the interview that if I was offered the job I would have to give up my commentaries. I told him categorically that I wouldn't do that, as commentating on matches was the primary reason I had joined RTÉ in the first place.

Late on a Friday afternoon I was called down to an office in the newsroom area, where both Cillian de Paor and Glen Killane were waiting for me. They offered me the position, but on the clear stipulation that I would give up my GAA commentaries. To me it was a case of déjà vu, as I had outlined my attitude during the interview.

They asked me to think about it over the weekend, and I did. In fact I can procrastinate with the best of them on occasions, and I wasn't completely sure if I was right or if I was just being stubborn. Would I regret turning down the role? Would there be repercussions? I dissected it left and right, up and down, and in the end the result was always the same: 'No.' But when Cillian rang me to get my final response on Monday, I dithered once again.

Eventually, after some more soul-searching, I walked down the long corridor to Cillian's office and said, 'Thank you for the wonderful offer, but I have to decline and you know the reason why.' I just had to stick to my guns.

Which brings me back to October 2012, sitting across from Ryle Nugent in Marco Pierre White's restaurant on Dawson Street. The GAA correspondent role was vacant, and Ryle was essentially offering me the same job that I had turned down four years previously. But this time it was different. Kevin Bakhurst from the BBC in London was taking over from Ed Mulhall as head of news in RTÉ, and Kevin apparently saw no reason why I couldn't continue with my match commentaries while serving as the GAA correspondent. I would, however, have to give up my boxing commentaries, which I loved and which had brought me to corners of the world I wouldn't have seen otherwise.

I had just returned from London about six weeks previously so was still in the afterglow of the Olympics. I hesitated for a while, as I needed time to think, but Ryle was adamant that this job was right for me, and that I was right for it. I agreed, and in January 2013 I started as GAA correspondent, and I've loved every second of my nine years in the role. I hope I've played my part not just in keeping audiences informed of events in the Gaelic games world, but in strengthening a relationship between the GAA and RTÉ that hasn't always been positive.

That relationship hit a low point when Croke Park announced the TV deal they had struck with Sky Sports in April 2014. We had to report on the new arrangement, which meant the end of RTÉ's exclusivity in broadcasting championship games. But it was a blow to RTÉ. The public reaction was generally negative, but Donagh McGrath's advice for my news report was sound: keep to the facts.

The president of the GAA at the time, Liam O'Neill from Co. Laois, was bursting with excitement about Sky's involvement, and he and Paraic Duffy were heading for the RTÉ studios to go on the *Six One News* and *Prime Time* respectively. Paraic Duffy was an exceptional director general of the GAA, which is a massive compliment considering he took over from

Liam Mulvihill, who had guided, cajoled and directed the GAA into the twenty-first century. The GAA owe the Longford and Monaghan men a huge debt of gratitude. On this particular day in 2014, Liam O'Neill and Paraic Duffy would face two greats of Irish broadcasting and journalism, Bryan Dobson and David McCullagh respectively, and you'd want to be wide awake, well-informed and on top of your brief to be facing them any day of the week. I don't think they were ready for it, to be honest. I had tried to mark Liam O'Neill's card earlier in the day, when I met him at the front door of the Croke Park Hotel, but I'm not sure he was taking cognisance of what I was trying to tell him. It would have been wiser for the GAA officials to wait a few days, and gauge the reaction from the GAA grassroots, before agreeing to do those interviews.

Bryan and David probed the two GAA officials with knowledgeable questions. They were doing their job and doing it brilliantly. The GAA criticized RTÉ afterwards for the intense level of scrutiny.

The tension arising from the affair has taken a while to dissipate, but things are better now. The appointment of Declan McBennett as head of RTÉ Sport has helped enormously in that relationship. Declan comes from a GAA environment in Oram, Co. Monaghan, and was one of the club members that carried the coffin of the legendary country singer Big Tom at his funeral in Oram in 2018. He and his family now live in South Armagh, where he is heavily involved in Dromintee GAA club.

No matter what I say or write on the subject of sports broadcasting rights, I can be accused of being biased because of where I work and what jersey I wear. So let me speak personally here.

I can fully understand the GAA wanting to create

competition for its broadcasting rights, and generating income that will ultimately benefit clubs around the country and the running of the organization at every level. But I find it difficult to support putting any of our games behind a paywall.

There was a Saturday in 2021 when there were two Leinster hurling championship matches in Croke Park – Galway v. Dublin and Kilkenny v. Wexford – followed later in the evening by Cork against Limerick in the Munster hurling championship. All three matches were on Sky.

Hurling is a summer game and has a small window of opportunity to be shown and promoted to the largest available audience. It should not be curtailed in any way. There was huge disappointment in those counties that the games were not free to air, and the same was true for the Cork v. Clare game a few weeks later.

This is not to say that paywalls are always a bad thing. In 2020, when we eventually got games up and running in empty grounds after the beginning of the Covid pandemic, county boards across the country needed to find some way of replacing the revenue lost as a result of not being able to sell tickets for matches. So they developed streaming services behind paywalls, and many people were happy to pay to see their teams in action.

GAAGO, which is jointly owned by RTÉ and the GAA, is a fantastic service that has a worldwide impact, with games accessible globally. This is the pandemic present, but it's also the future: watching a Tipperary football championship match between Arravale Rovers and Éire Óg Annacarty as you relax in a coffee shop in Abu Dhabi or take in the rays on Bondi Beach. It's a long bloody way from the back of a tractor and trailer in Doonbeg, filming on VHS.

*

On Sunday May 24th, 2015, I was on my way to Semple Stadium in Thurles to commentate on Clare against Limerick in the Munster hurling championship: the second game we were broadcasting on that particular day. The first match was between Cavan and Monaghan in the Ulster football championship at Breffni Park. The studio for the day was in Thurles, which brought Michael Lyster and his panel of football pundits Joe Brolly and Tomás Ó Sé to Tipperary to speak about the Ulster game.

I had just passed through Drom and Inch and passed the Ragg pub and restaurant in the townland of Bouladuff between Borrisoleigh and Thurles when the phone rang. It was Maureen Catterson, RTÉ communications manager for TV, Radio and Online, who is a great and loyal friend.

'Where are you?' she asked breathlessly.

'In the car, on my way to Thurles . . . why?'

'Don't answer the phone unless you know who it is.'

'Why?'

'Joe Brolly said something about you on *The Sunday Game* on the TV and it will go viral. Trust me.'

It was great advice as usual from Maureen, but within seconds of hanging up from her, the phone rang again. It was Paul Byrnes, who was editor of the live programme being broadcast from Semple Stadium.

'Have you heard what happened?'

'I have, but I don't know the details,' I replied.

Paul explained what Joe had said. He was genuinely raging, and he told me he was going to get Joe to apologize at halftime. (Both of us agreed afterwards it was a wishy-washy apology.) As we spoke I could hear my phone going off continuously as more and more people were trying to get in contact with me, and he was editing a programme live on air, so we said our goodbyes and agreed we'd talk later.

I checked my phone, which was full of missed calls from journalists whose numbers I happened to have, or unknown numbers, or, worse still, private numbers. I very rarely answer 'private number' calls these days because unfortunately they are usually somebody who has got my number and who wants to take the piss out of me because they think it's great craic. So I kept driving and didn't talk to anybody else until Ryle Nugent called me. He asked me was I OK and that for now I needed to concentrate on my commentary, and we'd talk about Mr Brolly afterwards.

So what had Joe said about me?

In the build-up to the match between Cavan and Monaghan, Joe had said that 'I have called Cavan over the last few years the Black Death, because the football has been . . . somebody said it's as ugly as Marty Morrissey.' This shocked Michael Lyster, who extended his hand towards Joe saying, 'Oh no, no, no,' and looking away in disgust. But Joe was on a roll and said, 'Maybe I should apologize to the people of Cavan for that.' Michael responded, 'Please do, but apologize to Marty Morrissey for a start,' and he did something that I never saw Michael do ever before or since that time. He wagged his finger disapprovingly at Joe. He knew this was wrong. Michael Lyster is one of the great guys of Irish broadcasting, a gentle man who has never raised his voice since the day I got to know him, and I always enjoyed our chats and the sharing of our various stories in the office when we were in the office together. I miss that craic with him, and the likes of Bill Lalor and, more recently, Paul Byrnes and Robbie Irwin since they all left.

While I joke about being a sex symbol and looking like Tom Cruise or George Clooney, I am well aware that I fail miserably on both counts. But I am what I am. It is not pleasant to read anonymous people on social media pass negative comments about how I or anybody else looks and the hurt that can cause is unimaginable. Can you imagine the impact negative nasty comments can have on young people? I mightn't be seventeen or eighteen any more, but it still hurts no matter what age you are. Having it said on air only accentuates that hurt or doubt you might have about yourself. While we all pretend to be confident and wash it off as if nothing happened, deep down it resonates and stays with you for some time.

At half-time, Joe Brolly said, 'I want to say that what I said about Marty Morrissey was said in a spirit of affection, not literally.'

A visibly unimpressed Michael Lyster replied, 'I presume that's an apology,' before reprimanding the Belfast-based barrister by saying, 'We appreciate that, because it was out of order, Joe.'

I drove back to Dublin after doing my commentary, and I knew from the number of phone calls I was receiving that Joe's comments were gaining traction. I was also disappointed that Joe didn't call me that evening, because if I had messed up and insulted somebody on air, the first thing I would have done is pick up the phone and apologize. But nothing came.

The following day's *Irish Daily Star* front-page headline read: 'YOU'RE NOT UGLY MARTY', with a subheading, 'Brolly sorry for "out of order" jibe'.

In the *Irish Daily Mirror* on page 11, the headline read: 'Fury over Brolly's ugly jibe at Marty.' The subheading was 'RTÉ pundit sorry for criticizing colleague Morrissey's looks.'

Ryle checked in on me, as did Maureen, but I was fine

apart from feeling a bit embarrassed about the attention. The last thing I would wish for was to be headline news, and be on the front page of any newspapers.

Eventually, on either the Tuesday or Wednesday evening, Joe Brolly called me and apologized for his words. I accepted the apology readily.

People kindly wrote letters to RTÉ, and to editors of various newspapers, complaining about Brolly's comments and expressing support for me, which I greatly appreciated.

On Thursday, RTÉ issued a statement from Ryle Nugent in his capacity as group head of RTÉ Sport.

'I have spoken with Joe Brolly about the comments he made in relation to RTÉ Sport's GAA correspondent and commentator Marty Morrissey on last weekend's *Sunday Game* live broadcast. Joe is acutely aware that his ill-conceived attempt at humour was both inappropriate and extremely hurtful and had no place in any broadcast. Further, Joe is fully cognisant of the fact that similar comments in any future broadcast cannot and will not be tolerated.' He continued, 'Joe Brolly has spoken at length with and offered a heartfelt apology to Marty Morrissey which was graciously accepted. All parties now consider this matter closed.'

Now here's the thing. Despite his comments back in 2015, Joe Brolly and I have remained good friends and have done a few gigs together since. We all make mistakes.

God knows I have made a few myself, so who am I to hold a grudge? And the man after all did apologize.

Joe Brolly is essentially a good man who undoubtedly has the uncanny ability to cause mixed reactions among the public. He must be given credit for incredible acts of kindness, like what he did in 2012 when donating one of his kidneys to his club-mate Shane Finnegan.

His love and knowledge of football was there for all to see when he was with us in RTÉ, and is still there visibly every weekend in the *Sunday Independent*.

Do I enjoy his company? Absolutely. In the summer of 2021 I got a text from him at half-time during a commentary I was doing on TV, telling me he was in Clare and hanging out with a Banner County legend, Seamus Clancy from Corofin, who won Clare's only football All-Star in 1992. I have always maintained that what we do in *The Sunday Game* is not merely sport: it's a cocktail of sport and entertainment. We want to deliver illuminating analysis, but we also want to bring a smile to the viewer at home. I am not saying we always achieve that, but that's what we strive to do. Joe Brolly played his part in attaining some of those objectives over twenty years as a pundit for RTÉ while living close to the edge on many occasions.

In 2018, the Kildare footballers were having a bad time. They'd been relegated in the spring to Division 3 of the league, and then lost to Carlow in the Leinster championship. Cian O'Neill's days as manager looked to be numbered.

Then they got their act together to achieve victories over Derry and Longford. In the draw for Round 3 of the qualifiers they got Mayo, who had been All-Ireland finalists against Dublin the previous summer and probably gave their greatest display, only to be pipped at the post once again. Kildare were in no-hope zone.

The only consolation was that the Lilywhites were drawn out first, so had home advantage. St Conleth's Park in Newbridge was not the most salubrious location in Ireland and badly needed an overhaul, but it was home to Kildare. It was their home ground. Beginning and end of story.

The Irish Derby was on at the Curragh on the same day and there were rumblings from Croke Park about health and safety issues, so Kildare were invited to nominate a second venue. They declined the invitation. At 1.30 p.m. on the Monday afternoon, the GAA announced a double-header in Croke Park: Kildare v. Mayo and Cavan v. Tyrone.

It quickly became known that Kildare were not happy. Their resolve startled the GAA authorities. The issue was on *Liveline*, so was now a topic of conversation nationwide. Kildare people were talking to Joe. They were entitled to home advantage. They were first out of the bowl. I can still hear their voices.

A few years earlier, I had been a guest of Moorfield GAA club one night as they were launching Lorcan O'Rourke's wonderful history of the club. Lorcan is a brother of Sean O'Rourke, formerly of RTÉ, and was Croke Park's main man in handball for many years. The launch was my first time getting a chance to hear Cian O'Neill speaking, and I thought he was terrific. A great orator, he held the room and captivated his audience with his words and descriptions. Now, with the venue dispute heating up, I was planning to go to Kildare to meet him. Then I remembered he was a lecturer in Cork, and I got a brainwave. I rang him late in the day and invited him to go to the Cork studios on Fr Matthew Street so he could speak live on the *Six One News* and give his thoughts on the loss of home advantage for their qualifier.

The interviewer, Eamon Horan, asked O'Neill if the county's position was 'Newbridge or nowhere'. The response was emphatic: 'It is indeed. From the top, I'd like to be explicitly clear about that. We were pulled first out of the bowl. We will be in St Conleth's Park. The draw is the draw, the fixture is the fixture. Stick to the rules you created. Stick to the draw that was made in the presence of the president of the GAA, John Horan. Stick to those rules and let's go play football. We will be togged out in St Conleth's Park on Saturday evening at seven o'clock. We're going to be ready to go. That's our home venue. We earned it by winning the last two matches on the road and that's not going to be taken away from us.'

The *Six One News* is a huge platform, and very quickly the weight of public opinion got behind Kildare and their desire to play the game at home. The 'Newbridge or Nowhere' campaign was successful, and eventually Croke Park relented: the Kildare v. Mayo game was rescheduled for St Conleth's Park.

When the controversy started, I had asked Kildare county board officials to speak to me but they had blatantly refused or not answered my calls. But worse was to follow. The Saturday night of the match, my job was to report back to the studio live for the *Six One* and *Nine O'Clock News*. When I arrived in the car park outside St Conleth's Park and tried to gain access to the pitch, I was told by the 'maors' or officials at the turnstiles that I was not to be allowed into the grounds.

Those were their instructions. I had to laugh, as I felt I had contributed in a very small way to their success in getting the game back to Newbridge. Or maybe I was perceived as causing trouble between themselves and Croke Park. Nobody would tell me what the problem was. We had to file our pre-match report from the car park.

Once the game started, however, the 'maors' let me in to watch – but with the clear instruction that I was not to allow myself to be seen! For the record, Kildare won 0–21 to 0–19, knocking Mayo out of the championship, which was quite an achievement.

It shows you what can be done when people come together and unite behind a cause. I don't think Kildare have been able to re-create that sense of togetherness ever since. Knocking Mayo out of the championship was either the turning of a page and a new beginning, or it was just the pinnacle of what they could achieve.

Unfortunately for Kildare, it looks like it was the latter.

The International Rules series has had its supporters and its critics since the concept originated way back in 1967, when the Australians embarked on their world tour. The first proper series took place in Ireland in 1984, under a two-match aggregate-points format.

When I was in college in UCC I played against a touring Australian selection in Páirc Uí Chaoimh and got the mother and father of a hammering. Sean Walsh from Tralee, a member of the great Kerry team that would later win four in a row, was at midfield, and he was 'small' in comparison to the Australian opposition, which tells you how tall and muscular these guys were. That experience stimulated a huge interest in our opposition's sport and culture, so when I got my job in RTÉ Sport I was delighted to be assigned as sideline reporter for the games in Croke Park. In Australia the sideline reporter is called the boundary rider, and the boundary rider for the Seven Network in Australia was Robert DiPierdomenico, who had been a legend with the Hawthorn Club in Victoria. He had been sent off in one of the first Test series in 1986 along with Australia's Gary McIntosh and Ireland's Pat Byrne and Jack O'Shea, so he came with quite a reputation. Known as 'The Big Dipper' Down Under, he was 6'1" and 93 kg of Australian manhood with strong passionate Italian blood running through his veins. When I was interviewing him in Croke Park along the sideline, he took the opportunity to call me 'The Little Dipper' – much to the amusement of my colleagues, friends and, worse still, the audience.

In 2003 I went to Australia for the first time to commentate on the International Rules series. The Subiaco Oval in Perth had a capacity crowd of 43,500 for the first Test.

The second Test took place in the Melbourne Cricket Ground, better known as the MCG, where Ronnie Delaney won his gold medal for Ireland in 1956, and as I commentated in that historic venue I couldn't help but think of the great Irishman and of all the sports heroes who had performed on that hallowed ground.

The 2003 Ireland squad contained some wonderful footballers, like Graham Canty (Cork), Sean Marty Lockhart (Derry), Dessie Dolan (Westmeath), the late Cormac McAnallen (Tyrone), Benny Coulter (Down), Ciaran McManus (Offaly), Padraic Joyce (Galway) and Odran O'Dwyer (Clare).

It was a proud experience to commentate on an International Rules match in a faraway land in the southern hemisphere and talk about my fellow parishioner and clubmate Odran O'Dwyer from the other side of the village of

Mullagh in the parish of Kilmurry Ibrickane. What were the chances of that? In 2019 we won an over-40s All-Ireland medal together; my contribution was quite minimal but Odran was still providing the magic. Today we reminisce and reflect when I have some ache or pain and call in to see him at his performance therapy clinic in Ennis.

When the 2003 International Rules series was over, I travelled up the Gold Coast to Brisbane to work as a 'producer' for Ryle Nugent, who was commentating on Rugby World Cup matches in Lang Park, also known as Brisbane Park.

From my point of view, the International Rules tours I've covered over the years have been an opportunity to get to know some of the best footballers in Ireland and to earn their trust, and I can't count how many times over subsequent years connections made on those trips helped me in my job as GAA correspondent. I've also met lots of Irish emigrants in Australia who had left our island on the periphery of Europe to start a new life in pursuit of something that they felt they couldn't attain at home.

From the players' point of view, International Rules provided an opportunity to wear the green of Ireland. It was also a chance for someone like the Mayo footballer Aidan O'Shea, who captained Ireland in 2017, to play with Mattie Donnelly from Tyrone or Michael Murphy from Donegal or Stephen Cluxton from Dublin as team-mates rather than opponents.

There were some rough days in those series, and I remember Sean Boylan, who managed Ireland in 2006, going ballistic in Croke Park after a ferocious tackle on Graham Geraghty by Australia's Danyle Pearce. A quietness descended on the attendance of 82,127 people at GAA Headquarters as a neck brace was wrapped around the Meath man and he was driven off in a motorized stretcher. That episode – including Ireland's less-than-angelic behaviour in the confrontations that followed – came very close to terminating the whole concept. Afterwards at a press conference under the Hogan stand, Kevin Sheedy, the Australia manager, grew tired of the indignant questioning. 'Every time Australia win, the series is coming to an end,' he said. 'Unbelievable! You're the greatest conmen I've ever met.'

The competition survived that episode, but over the years there have been criticisms of the concept. In 2019 former Kerry footballer Tomás Ó Sé blasted the GAA for maintaining friendly relations with the AFL, arguing that the series was an opportunity for AFL clubs to scout emerging Irish talent. It's a valid point. Probably the most vociferous critic was former Tyrone manager Mickey Harte, who said in 2008 that tours to Australia are in essence just a free holiday for the players involved, before repeating the claim in 2011 and calling on the GAA to withdraw from the series as it does a 'total disservice to the development of Gaelic Games on the international stage'.

Whether or not International Rules promotes the game we love, the game of Gaelic football, is questionable. But then our football has also changed quite dramatically. It's totally different to what it was twenty years ago. But to see our fellow Irish people's eyes light up and to hear their voices as they cheer and shout for their country would eradicate any doubts you might have about the value of these games. Every venue where the games were played in my many trips to Perth, Adelaide and Melbourne were either sold out or close to it primarily because of the Irish in those cities. It means the world to the diaspora for the Gaelic football stars to travel so far away to play a game of football.

The last time I travelled to Australia was in 2017. This time the first Test was played in Adelaide, a beautiful city that I had never visited before. Nicholas Walsh of Cavan was my co-commentator in the Adelaide Oval, and as a result of International Rules we became great friends. Nicholas carved out a wonderful AFL career starting in 2000 with the Melbourne Demons. Injuries brought him home and on to the Cavan football team for a while before returning to the Greater Western Sydney Giants as a coach.

In 2017 I met Tadhg Kennelly, who won an All-Ireland and an All-Star with Kerry in 2009 after winning the AFL Premiership with Sydney Swans in 2005. Years earlier, in 1999, Tadhg did one of his first TV recordings with me at the back of the Listowel Arms Hotel, and I have always admired him and what he has achieved. For the first Test, in Adelaide, he was working with Seven Network next door to our commentary position, so we called in to see him.

We moved on to Perth for the second Test, and all the pubs in the immediate vicinity were packed with Irish fans who clearly considered this an opportunity to celebrate their Irishness. I was meeting the Sexton sisters, Orla and Diana, as well as Grainne Whelan from my own parish of Kilmurry Ibrickane, who had emigrated to Western Australia, and while we had a great time, we had no peace as the crowd went wild for a 'Marty Party' and a lorry-load of selfies had to be taken.

One of my favourite photographs was taken by my pals in Sportsfile inside the ground, as a group of lads from Monaghan had got masks produced with an image of my face, so it was me looking at quite a large number of me, which was a bit scary.

The bottom line is the International Rules is not just about

a game of football. It's much more than that. The 2020 series had to be cancelled because of Covid, and the planned 2022 series must be in doubt. But I sincerely hope the concept doesn't die, as the positives outweigh the negatives.

Do you remember the Ice Bucket Challenge that was all the rage in 2014? I certainly do. Many Irish people embraced the challenge, with families and celebrities alike undergoing a dunking for the benefit of the Irish Motor Neurone Disease Association, to the tune of over €1.7 million.

It was a very simple concept. It had started in America in June that year. Once you did it yourself, you had to nominate three more to experience the shock of the ice-cold water treatment. The nominated people had to accept the challenge of having a bucket of ice water poured over their head, film it, post it on social media and ask others to do the same and make a donation to the charity. Newsreader Sharon Ní Bheoláin accepted the challenge, and Jenny Greene and Nicky Byrne poured two buckets of water over her outside the front door of the TV Building in RTÉ. Dáithí Ó Sé was dunked on the Monday night of the Rose of Tralee by our colleagues Kieran McDonagh and Kim Burrows, who are great at their jobs as floor managers but mighty craic as well. Dáithí nominated Ryan Tubridy, Ray D'Arcy and Marty Whelan.

In August, I got a call from Lisa Clancy, who was then director of communications in Croke Park. She asked if I would do her a favour, and because we always got on great I said I would if I could.

Lisa asked if I would do the Ice Bucket Challenge in Croke Park the following Sunday, when Donegal were to play Dublin in the All-Ireland football semi-final.

Now, I am very happy to be involved in many worthwhile causes and I really enjoy any charity work that I do, but I had strenuously avoided the Ice Bucket Challenge many times previously. To suggest that I'd do it in front of everyone in Croke Park was ridiculous.

'Absolutely not,' says I. 'Get this idea out of your head – now.' But the following day she rang again, and so too did a few of her colleagues.

It felt like the entire Croke Park staff were in on it. So eventually I relented. That was a mistake.

I togged out under the Hogan stand. I found my Clare jersey and put it on over tracksuit bottoms and walked out the tunnel. The craic with Robbie Smith and Tom Ryan and the others that operate events around the tunnel was mighty. Emma O'Driscoll from RTÉ's Young People's Department was MC and got a great kick out of introducing me to the crowd. I walked slowly and apprehensively towards the corner of the Hogan and Davin stands, the crowds having the craic with me as I made my way to that section of Croke Park. I was a bit naive here, as I should have looked more closely at what was being planned, but I was distracted by the craic and the crowd. Waiting for me were two 'friends', Ciaran Whelan and Mark McHugh, former Dublin and Donegal footballers, all smiles and knowing damn well that this was their chance for retribution. They were obviously relishing this opportunity to drown me.

I sat in my seat facing the pitch, photographers all around us clicking their cameras at frenetic pace.

And then the lads let me have it.

I knew immediately it wasn't a bucket. It was a barrel. Two of them.

It kept coming . . . the water, the ice, the freezing effect and the non-stop laughter ringing in my ears. I bolted off my seat, drenched to the skin, nearly blind. I ran around like a scalded cat and turned around to face my two buddies, and although I was still recovering my eyesight I could see the shimmering figures of Whelan and McHugh coming after me again with a second barrel of water – and down it came again. And then Paul Byrnes, executive editor of *The Sunday Game*, came along with a small bucket of water and threw that at me as well, just to finish me off! They were all in on it. But trust me, I know where these guys and Lisa Clancy live and my day will come!

After Donegal had beaten Dublin in that All-Ireland semi-final and everybody was on their way home, I was beside the outside broadcast truck parked underneath the Hogan stand. Who comes along but Rachel Wyse from Sky Sports, who said she was now doing the Ice Bucket Challenge in front of Hill 16 and would I come out for the craic and throw the bucket over her.

Like, she had me at 'Hello'.

So out I went and joined the Sky Sports team in front of the Nally stand, and when she was ready we let Rachel have both buckets of H_2O. Overall a great and pleasurable day in Croke Park!

23. Dancing with the Stars

If you asked me what was the best thing I ever did since I joined RTÉ, in terms of craic, losing weight and taking on a challenge far outside my comfort zone, then there is only one answer. *Dancing with the Stars.*

I had my doubts about getting involved, and I procrastinated for ages after Larry Bass, the programme's executive producer, called and made the offer. It was year two of the series. My colleague Des Cahill danced in the first series, and I knew from him how much fun it was, *and* how difficult and exhausting it was to fulfil his normal work commitments during his stint on the show. I still don't know how he did it.

I met Ryle Nugent for a long chat and we both agreed that if I was to do it, I would have to be excused from duty for as long as I lasted on the show. This was the lesson learned from Des's involvement. I also talked to another vastly experienced member of staff: the director of content, Jim Jennings. I've always trusted his judgement, professional expertise and advice. Because he was so encouraging, and because I was getting so many positive vibes from everyone else about it, I eventually called Larry back and said 'yes'.

I was already being paid a salary by RTÉ, so I wasn't going to get anything extra, as the other contestants were. This was fair enough, considering they had given me the time off to become a fabulous dancer, and perhaps some hoped I might turn professional and get the hell out of RTÉ altogether!

I was in, and in for the long haul, and determined to

become the next Fred Astaire or John Travolta or Michael
Flatley. I knew I could jive and waltz Irish style, and of course
I could batter out a Clare set. I kept telling myself: this ball-
room dancing couldn't be that difficult, could it?

Larry Bass wouldn't tell me who my opposition was going
to be, and though I tried to cajole Sheila Meaney and Catherine Neylan from ShinAwiL Productions to give me a hint
about who else had signed up for the madness, they would
give nothing away. Nothing. And they thoroughly enjoyed
telling me nothing.

On Tuesday November 28th, 2017, three days after coming back from International Rules duty in Australia, I travelled
to Kilcoole to film the opening sequence. It was there that I
met my beautiful dance partner, Ksenia Zsikhotska, for the
first time. We clicked right from the off. And it was here too
that I finally met my fellow contestants: businesswoman
Norah Casey, broadcaster Maïa Dunphy, All-Ireland winning
Cork camogie captain Anna Geary, comedian and actress
Deirdre O'Kane, model and former Miss Ireland Aoife
Walsh, fitness model Erin McGregor, Olympian Rob Heffernan, Munster and Ireland rugby player Tomás O'Leary,
singer Jake Carter and comedian Bernard O'Shea. Unfortunately we lost Aoife Walsh within the first week or two due
to an injury, and for a while we didn't know who would
replace her, but eventually Alannah Beirne, who had been a
Britain's Next Top Model finalist, arrived at rehearsals. Alannah's mum, Brenda Hyland, was Rose of Tralee in 1983,
while her brother Tadhg is an Irish rugby international. That
was a great line-up by any measure, and in my view, our group
was the best of the four series!

My four fellow male contestants and myself reminded
me of country lads at the back of a dance hall in Miltown

Malbay, admiring the view and going nowhere fast. Initially, we all felt a bit intimidated by the professional dancers, who looked fabulous and could move with wonderful flexibility and dexterity. When all of us lads looked at each other (especially Bernard and myself), we knew immediately we'd be playing against the wind in both halves.

Rob Heffernan was great fun. As we sat beside each other watching the professional dancers perform their spectacular opening number on the mirrored floor, Rob nudged me gently and said, 'Marty boy, are we in heaven? If I've died and this is where we've ended up, don't resuscitate me, I'm happy out boy!'

Rehearsals took place at the Liffey Trust dance studios in Dublin's Point Village. It hadn't been announced yet publicly who was participating, so some press photographers hung around outside the Liffey Trust snapping photos of us as we entered the building. There was one particular hazy photograph, shot looking upwards through a window and supposedly showing a few of us, that one of the papers published. It was a game, and great fun. We were supposed to be avoiding them at all costs until the cast was revealed, but sure they were nice guys so after a few days we posed for them and took a few selfies with them as well.

Rob was paired off with Emily Barker from Nottingham, while Tomás O'Leary got Italian Giulia Dotta. Bernard O'Shea was with Valeria Milova, whose husband Vitali Kozmin danced with Alannah Beirne. Norah Casey was paired with Curtis Pritchard, who later became famous as a contestant on *Love Island*, where he dated Maura Higgins. Maïa Dunphy was going to dance with Poland's Robert Rowinski, while Anna Geary was paired with Kia Widdington, who is now one of the professional dancers on *Strictly Come*

Dancing in the UK. Erin McGregor hit the dancefloor with Ryan McShane, while Jake Carter danced, and fell in love with, Karen Byrne.

My partner, Ksenia, was born in the Ukraine. When she was six, she and her mother flew to London to begin a new life together. Despite being small in stature like myself, Ksenia – who became a great friend – can be quite forceful and assertive in her own unique, inimitable and loving way.

On December 4th, on 2FM's *Breakfast Republic*, Bernard O'Shea confirmed he was participating, although he meant that in the broadest possible terms. Two days later on *The Ryan Tubridy Show* on RTÉ Radio 1, Maïa Dunphy announced that she had said 'yes' to *DWTS*. And on Friday December 8th, Norah Casey, Erin McGregor and myself were guests on *The Late Late Show* to announce that we were officially participating. It was game on now; too late to turn back.

Each morning I would leave Rathfarnham to pick Ksenia up at 9 a.m. We would drive to the Liffey Trust studios to begin practising our routine, which Ksenia would have choreographed. Each dance would be recorded on one of our mobile phones, and the clip would be sent to a producer and ultimately the director of the show every week. Lunchtime was usually an hour from one to two. At the beginning, I was a chicken wings with a can of Coke man, but it's amazing what happens when you sit round a table with all these professional dancers looking slim, muscular and sexy, drinking their water and eating 'grass', as I called it: lettuce and salads. No matter how mentally strong you are, the guilt eventually envelops you. By mid December I was on lettuce and water myself! And much as I hate to admit it, I was beginning to enjoy my new lifestyle. Until about nine o'clock that night, that is. I'd be absolutely starving, so I'd get a Thai takeaway or fish and chips. But I'd never tell Ksenia! I'd always brush the teeth extra well the next morning, then I was good to go.

After lunch we would all gather in the biggest studio to rehearse the big number – there was one in every show – which brought together all the dancers. I loved these numbers, as we could take the piss out of each other, and the added benefit was that I could easily hide from Darren Bennett, who was the principal choreographer along with his wife Lilia Kopylova.

'One, two, three and four, five, six!' he bellowed, clapping his hands like a schoolmaster. At the beginning, while the professional dancers were on their best behaviour, none of the rest of us took much notice of him. We were all laughing at the back of the class. But on the second morning, the music stopped suddenly and he spoke sternly to us. 'Gentlemen, gentlemen. This has to stop. You won't be laughing in a month's time when you will be dancing live on the TV. Right now, your behaviour is unacceptable.'

I looked around at five grown men – an Olympic medallist, a rugby international, a stand-up comedian, a singer/songwriter, and me – all getting a mega dressing-down from this lad. Rob, Tomás, Bernard, Jake and myself became quiet boys after that. Well, at least until the following morning!

The cast clicked immediately. Anna Geary opened a WhatsApp group called 'The Marty Party' and all eleven of us communicated on it nearly every day. Even today, I remain close to the lads, and to Anna because of the work we do; and I feel I can call Norah, Deirdre, Erin, Maïa and Alannah any day of the week and resume our friendship, even though we mightn't have spoken for months.

My first dance was a quickstep to Joe Dolan's 'You're Such

a Good Looking Woman'. I'd always loved the song, but after three weeks of 'Oh me oh my . . .' even I began to wilt.

It wasn't easy. Ksenia would walk me through the dance first, then we would embrace and move until we got it right. I could jive and quickstep before *Dancing with the Stars*. In fact, I actually won a jiving competition in Clare years before. I had learned how to jive from Geraldine Morrissey, who came from a townland called Ballymakea between Quilty and Mullagh. Geraldine was a brilliant dancer, and though we're not related, she became part of our family when she worked in our shop and pub after we came home from New York. If the pub was quiet and some song came on the radio, she would grab me and teach me how to jive behind the counter. Eventually we graduated to the dancefloor in the Caledonian Lounge. The Morrisseys were a lethal combination when we got going.

But this was different. This was ballroom dancing. I was far out of my comfort zone, and remembering all the steps wasn't easy. Posture, I discovered, was very important, but I could never get my shoulder as high as Ksenia wanted it to go. At one stage she actually used a strap to tie it up. I still remember her words to describe what we were about to do: 'Slow, slow, quick, quick, slow, slow, quick, quick, slow.'

We'd finish between six and seven in the evening, then leave our small studio in Liffey Trust and move to the big studio, which had three walls with floor-to-ceiling mirrors. Ksenia, Emily and Giulia would have organized between themselves to meet there and perform each of our routines. Rob's first dance was a jive with Emily to a great number: 'One Way or Another (Teenage Kicks)' by One Direction, while Tomás O'Leary and Giulia danced a foxtrot to the beautiful 'All of Me' by John Legend.

Then it was my turn. As the music began, Rob shouted, 'Come on, Marty boy, do your John Travolta!'

My response was to burst out laughing, which didn't please Ksenia.

I was so bad compared to them that I felt sure I'd be the first one eliminated. But then Bernard O'Shea showed up. His and Valeria's first performance was a tango to the Buggles' 'Video Killed the Radio Star'. She was brilliant, but Bernard looked like a sitting duck rather than a moving one. Myself and Bernard bonded after that. We knew we were both in deep shit.

Ksenia was going back to London to be with her mum for Christmas, so we decided to take the holiday season off. Driving around the city during that time, it was so strange to see all of us up there on massive billboards.

We were back in the dance studio on January 1st, 2018, six days away from the first show live on RTÉ 1. Things were getting serious, so we practised and practised and practised.

Wardrobe is an essential part of the glamour of *DWTS*, and every week we'd have to take a break from rehearsing to go down to Capel Street to see the clothes that had been chosen for us and to do a fitting. Monica Ennis, Raziana Nojib and Niamh O'Connor did a fantastic job of making everyone look spectacular.

That Saturday, on the eve of the show, we had a full dress rehearsal, which began at 8 a.m. For the five preceding weeks, we'd had to visualize where the cameras and the audience would be located. It was funny sometimes, as we practised, to pivot and land, smiling at a wall that we pretended was a camera. Now we were at the Ardmore Film Factory in Bray, from where the show would be broadcast live. Now, for the first time, we could see the cameras, the impressive set, the spiral

staircase. The seats were empty, but they would be full the following night. The thought sent a shiver down my spine.

Sheila Meaney signalled to myself and Ksenia that we
were next, so we walked on to the dancefloor, and when I
turned around all I could hear was 'Go on, Marty!' from the
crew. There were guffaws of laughter, which of course made
me laugh as well.

That Saturday rehearsal scared me more than anything
else. Up to this point, we had been practising in a bubble.
Now I knew that in just over twenty-four hours, we would be
performing live. I didn't want to let Ksenia down or make a
show of myself, so that evening I went home to Rathfarnham and practised my dance routine in the underground car
park, over and over again. It's not easy to do a quickstep on
your own, surrounded by cars, with a howling January wind
blowing through the place. I hoped the neighbours didn't
spot me.

Call-time on the Sunday morning was 8 a.m. As I drove
down to the studio, I wondered how long would I last. Would
I be the first to get the P45? I consoled myself with the
thought that I would at least knock three weeks out of it, as
nobody was eliminated until the end of the third show.

Let's do this, I thought, and enjoy it.

Those Sunday morning gatherings, when everybody
involved in the show came together, were great craic. The
slagging was of a very high standard. You could order breakfast backstage and have a full Irish if you liked, with the
traditional rashers, sausages and black pudding. The contin-
ental style was also available. You can guess what the pro
dancers ordered.

A full dress rehearsal started at 9 a.m. sharp. We rehearsed
again after lunch and by the time it was done and dusted,

there was just an hour and a half to chill out before the show started. The dressing-room for the lads was quite small, and there were no separate rooms. The six pro dancers togged out alongside Rob, Jake, Tomás, Bernard and myself. At the beginning, you'd try to be discreet stripping off. When you see Curtis, Robert, Ryan, John, Kia and Vitali in all their glory, it can be quite, let's say, intimidating. But after a few weeks, those moments of inferiority you experience are forgotten as the pressure is on, and nobody takes any notice of the shape you're in. It's a case of get dressed and get out. The gallons of aftershave are equalled only by the amount of deodorant sprayed over various parts of our bodies. We mightn't be able to dance but damn it, we smelled good.

Amanda Byram and Nicky Byrne presented the show. They had their own dressing-rooms upstairs, but if Nicky heard the laughter and craic, he would often join us. Jake would usually have his guitar with him, and it was wonderful to listen to a member of Westlife and Jake Carter sing a song or two. Then Eimear Forrestal, who was the senior production co-ordinator, would appear in the door and tell us we had to be backstage in ten minutes. The craic was over. Reality was dawning. That first night, panic set in. I was convinced that I had completely forgotten my steps. I ran down the stairs and found Ksenia, who had just completed the pre-recorded group dance, which would be shown as if it was live later in the programme, and we performed our dance one more time backstage.

I have been honoured to commentate on All-Ireland finals on both TV and radio, and Olympic boxing finals. While I was nervous on all of these occasions, they were nothing compared to this. What was it that Michael Caine once said? Be like a duck. Calm on the surface and paddling like crazy underneath. That was me. As the clock ticked towards 6.30 p.m., we gathered backstage. The crowds were in. You could hear the constant chatter outside. James Patrice had warmed them up wonderfully.

Then it was cue music, lights, action!

On that first night, only the lads performed with their professional dancers, and Ksenia and I were scheduled to go last. Waiting was torture, but eventually the moment came. We had practised for five weeks. Now it was time.

The voice-over declared, 'It's Marty Morrissey and Ksenia Zsikhotska!'

The crowd applauded. The music began with a drum beat, then Joe Dolan launched into the song. When the chorus came, we finally came together and clinched. I held Ksenia in my arms as we moved together in what I would describe as perfect synchronization, although I discovered shortly

afterwards that the judges didn't quite agree with me. The crowd applauded and I sang and danced with Ksenia, although she told me to stop singing and concentrate . . .

Then it was over. The crowd exploded into applause; they seemed to love it. I hugged Ksenia in both gratitude and relief. Then we walked towards Amanda and the three infamous judges.

Lorraine Barry, from Cabra in Dublin, was World Ballroom Dance champion in 1999 and 2001, and British Open champion three times. I liked Lorraine from the moment I met her. She's a very classy lady: kind, knowledgeable and giving. She really knows her dancing. Julian Benson is a great character. Born in Adelaide, he's lived in Ireland since he was twelve years of age. A superb choreographer, he was diagnosed with cystic fibrosis when he was two, and initially given a life expectancy of thirteen. He's a brilliant performer and a hugely positive influence.

And then there was Brian Redmond. A native of Blanchardstown, he performed at the Royal Albert Hall in London and the Kremlin Palace in Moscow. In 2004 he retired from competitive dance and set up a dance school in Co. Kildare, where he now lives. He was hired to be the Simon Cowell character in the series. And he does it rather well. Brian didn't appreciate my dance moves, or maybe the lack of them. I wanted to bring ballroom dancing to a whole new level, but he was very much a traditionalist. Some of his comments and criticisms were accurate, some harsh, some unnecessary, but he was always entertaining. For the audiences if not for me. Bernard was the only one who, in Mr Redmond's eyes, was worse. Brian gave him a paltry score of two.

Out of a possible thirty points that first night, Jake and Karen got nineteen, Rob and Emily tied with Tomás and

Giulia on seventeen while Ksenia and myself got twelve. Bernard and Valeria scored ten. I felt I was marked very harshly, and still do to this day!

Now we had two weeks to prepare for the next dance, and then we would have a single week to learn the one after that.

When the lads met up in the dressing-room afterwards, we convinced ourselves we were brilliant, and that the female contestants, who were due to perform the following week, would never reach our standards. We tried to convince Norah, Anna, Maïa, Alannah, Erin and Deirdre that given our brilliant performances, they'd be better to withdraw from the competition rather than embarrass themselves. They smiled and said nothing.

And so the first *DWTS* Marty Party began. We all headed to Krystal Niteclub on Harcourt Street and had a wild night of drink, craic and dancing. This was the pattern on all the Sunday nights to come, which meant that for most of us, Monday was a washout. We considered this normal behaviour, but we would subsequently learn that, over the following two seasons, the contestants took the show a lot more seriously than we did. They hardly ever went out on a Sunday night. As John McEnroe would say, 'You can't be serious!'

The following Sunday night, the lads and myself stood on the stage with Nicky Byrne and watched our female colleagues in awe. They nailed their first performances brilliantly and the slagging stopped immediately.

The biggest fear for the third week was the elimination factor. Nobody wanted to be the first to go home. After the first two weeks of the show, Ksenia and myself were the second lowest according to the judges' scores. Only Bernard and Valeria were worse. Bernard and I knew we were crap and that we were highly unlikely to survive. That week, he was dancing a salsa to Sister Sledge's 'He's the Greatest Dancer'. It was very funny, but it wasn't just funny. He got a staggering seventeen from the judges!

Myself and Ksenia were second last to perform: a cha-cha-cha to James Brown's 'I Got You (I Feel Good)'. I knew, despite the applause, that my co-ordination had been a bit off. This was the dance where I leapt into the air from a platform at the beginning. With the great gift of hindsight I really should have moved a lot more, rather than just standing there with Ksenia weaving beautiful patterns around me. She was trying to save my ass by not exposing my limited ability, but it didn't work. As the number ended, I headed for the steps of the main stage with my back to the crowd and Ksenia draped me with a long, sparkling cape which read 'MARTY, Godfather of Dance'.

'It's like going to a party and having one glass of shandy,' Brian Redmond chided. 'That's not a party, Marty.'

I got a two from Brian Redmond, a two from Lorraine Barry and a four from Julian. A total of eight points. It was the lowest score in the history of *Dancing with the Stars*, a record that remained in place for two years, until Fr Ray Kelly scored a six in 2020 for his even dodgier cha-cha-cha. But despite my horrific score, the public vote saved me, and I was really grateful for that.

Sadly, we lost Norah Casey that night. She took the disappointment of her early departure on the chin and smiled her way off stage. Norah went back to being a very successful businesswoman while her dance partner, Curtis Pritchard, went on to become a star on ITV's *Love Island*. Today Curtis has 1.3 million followers on Instagram. He's a nice guy, a great dancer and really wanted to be famous, so I'm delighted for him.

The fourth week on *Dancing with the Stars*, movie week, was probably my favourite on the show. We were dancing what's called an American smooth to 'Pretty Irish Girl', sung by Brendan O'Dowda and Ruby Murray. The song is from the 1959 film *Darby O'Gill and the Little People*. I put my heart and soul into rehearsals, to try to ensure that our performance was much better than the previous week. Getting my ass kicked live on TV really focused my mind. My biggest problem, or really Ksenia's biggest problem, was trying to get me to stop singing. She would stop the rehearsal suddenly and say angrily, 'Marty! Will you stop singing and concentrate on the steps!' On other occasions she would say underneath her breath something that sounded like 'moichi'. She would repeat this word, steadily increasing the volume each time, but she wouldn't tell me what it meant. So I googled it, and found out that it was Russian for 'shut up'.

Bernard O'Shea danced a paso doble to 'He's a Pirate', a Klaus Badelt and Hans Zimmer number from the movie *Pirates of the Caribbean*. It was a brilliant piece of choreography, superbly performed by Bernard and Valeria. They got eighteen points from the jury. This was the night that Anna Geary gave what was, in my opinion, her best performance: a contemporary ballroom dance to 'Let It Go' from the movie *Frozen*. She got twenty-seven out of thirty, but I'd have given her the full thirty. She got a massive reaction to that performance. Anna knew the value of Instagram, and would be backstage on her phone either going live or recording herself reaching out to followers to vote for her.

That night, sadly, we said goodbye to Tomás O'Leary. We really missed his company in subsequent weeks.

Ksenia and I got fifteen from the judges: a four, a five and a six. This was almost double what we got the previous week, but we still ended up with the lowest score. Thankfully, however, the public saved us again and we weren't eliminated. There was something about the American smooth that I really loved, and the photographs that were taken during that dance are especially evocative and memorable for me.

That night, we visited one of my favourite stomping grounds, Copper Face Jacks on Harcourt Street. Word had got out about the Marty Party, and now the entire crew and their partners joined us for the craic. Blathnaid Treacy, who hosted the spin-off show *Can't Stop Dancing*, was now part of the gang and told the *Irish Mirror*, 'The Marty Party reminds me of being in college, you know those mad nights out where you don't know where you're going to end up.'

During my time on *DWTS*, I did more press interviews than I had ever done in my life before. Entertainment journalists like Ken Sweeney, Sandra Mallon, Nicola Bardon,

Barry Moran, Niamh Walsh, Siobhan O'Connor, Philip Nolan, Michael O'Doherty and Eoin Murphy were exceptionally good to me. Their positivity was very much appreciated, and I was getting about 100 letters a week, from both children and adults. People loved the vital ingredients of *DWTS*: music, dancing, glamour and of course the competitors themselves. They mightn't have a huge public profile at the beginning, but part of the enjoyment was getting to know everyone. One of the big advantages the show enjoys is its scheduling. *DWTS* comes on at 6.30 p.m. on a Sunday night, just after the news on RTÉ 1. It's the depths of winter, when it's dark by five o'clock. So many people wrote to say that they always sat down as a family and watched the dancing. Interestingly, more fathers than mothers wrote to me.

By week five, we were still hovering around the twelve-point mark, and my three amigos, Brian Redmond, Lorraine Barry and Julian Benson, started getting negative comments in the media about their negative comments about me. I have to admit I enjoyed that. This was the week we did the Charleston with 'We no speak Americano' by Yolanda Be Cool & DCUP. Jake Carter and Karen Byrne were looking good on twenty-seven points, which is why I decided I needed to change tactics. I asked the producers if I could take my shirt off like Jake. Request denied, not once but five times. They said Ireland wasn't ready for that yet.

Maïa Dunphy was eliminated that night, despite a very impressive tango with Robert. She was a little bit negative the following morning in her interview with Ryan Tubridy, but I could understand her pain. After all, she had got nineteen points and was gone, while the two gobshites O'Shea and Morrissey, on fourteen and twelve points respectively, were still in the competition. The *Irish Sun* carried a picture of the three judges, with a quote from Brian Redmond: 'I don't care if I'm Ireland's biggest b****cks.' This was inspired by one viewer's comments about the harsh feedback he aimed at me. In the interview Brian said, 'To be honest I couldn't sleep at night if I told Marty he was a great dancer. The people at home would know I was lying.'

Sometimes the media coverage was overwhelming. There was always some story, however flimsy or whimsical. I'd call to a shop in the morning on my way to pick up Ksenia and find myself on the front page. The subeditors and headline creators had a field day. 'NO CHA-CHA CHING', screamed one headline. The story explained that I wasn't getting the 'estimated €3,000 per episode' that the others were, because I was an RTÉ employee.

Getting through on week five is crucial because now you get a pass. Week six was switch-up week, which meant we all changed partners and there was no elimination. Phew!

We were brought upstairs to a large meeting-room where they told us who we were switching with. The news was good. Rob Heffernan and myself were swapping partners, so I was now going to dance with Emily Barker. Emily is fantastic in every way. A Nottingham girl, she loves Ireland and used to date Curtis Pritchard. Now, however, she would be rocking with me. That week we would be jiving to 'Crocodile Rock' by Elton John.

It was a great week. We started our jive in a boat, but getting out of the boat wasn't that easy. Each time we tried it, either we fell back or the boat tilted and tipped us out. I will never forget the dress rehearsal the following Saturday morning. In the middle of the routine, I had to grab my trousers as they were falling off me because I'd lost so much weight. Emily is a brilliant dance teacher and I really loved my week with her.

Julian's reaction to our performance was much appreciated. 'Operation Transformation. The king of rock and jive is back in the game. What a transformation. You gave it everything. We can see you worked hard and you moved up a grade.'

Lorraine added: 'You are the type of student I'd like to work with every week. You missed a little bit here and there. For me you seized the moment and I'm going to give you a gold star for effort.'

Brian of course just couldn't resist taking a pot shot, and said my dance was 'more like crocodile shock than crocodile rock', but he still conceded that it was my best dance so far. And yet we still only got fourteen from the judges, which even I thought was a bit harsh.

Anna Geary and Ryan McShane were paired together, and their dance was a Viennese waltz to 'Say You Love Me' by Jessie Ware. They were fantastic, and the twenty-two from the judges was disappointing. This prompted Ryan to voice his opinion that the marking was harsh and, worse still, inconsistent. Afterwards he told the *Irish Mirror*, 'It's not just tonight. I feel they've been under-scoring for the whole series. I just wanted them to know it's not going unnoticed.'

Here's a man after my own heart, I thought. I didn't know whether he was referring to me or not, and truthfully I was afraid to ask, but at least something was being said in a public domain.

It was back to knock-out again for week seven, and the nerves were jangling. I was now in foxtrot territory and back with Ksenia. We danced to 'Raindrops Keep Fallin' on my Head' by B. J. Thomas, and if the truth be told, this was probably my favourite dance. The fact that the umbrella came down so smoothly to me from on high always intrigued me.

Like everything else in my life, I had been slow to get going, but now I felt my movement was better, and that I was beginning to find the soul of ballroom dancing. The tension and nervousness I had felt on Sunday nights was finally leaving me and I was hoping I would survive for another week at least. Did I care whether I won or not? Absolutely not. But I did want to compete and try my best.

That week, Bernard and Valeria were dancing a Viennese waltz to 'What's New Pussycat?' by Tom Jones. I never laughed so much. Brilliant choreography by Valeria and superbly delivered by her and my new pal Bernard. In the end, however, they ended up in a dance-off with Erin and Ryan, and there was only going to be one winner there. Bernard was gone.

The fun was over and that night I really began to feel that I was in a dancing competition. Somehow, miraculously, I was still alive and heading to programme eight of twelve. Only seven couples remained.

'Guilty pleasures' was the theme for the following Sunday night's programme. Our guilty pleasure was a rumba to Chris de Burgh's 'Lady in Red'. We practised in Smithfield that week and did a major spread for *VIP* magazine. I felt good. We were second to perform and to be honest, we both thought we had done well. We got sixteen points from the judges, our highest score since the series began, and Ksenia had me convinced that we would make it to week nine. So we were both genuinely surprised when we ended up in a dance-off with Alannah Beirne and Vitali Kozmin. To put it bluntly, we hadn't a prayer. Nicky and Amanda cued a commercial break and Ksenia and I got into position.

'Now make sure you smile,' was the advice from Ksenia.

'I will.'

I shouted to Jake, who was up with Nicky Byrne and the rest of the gang on the overhead mini stage, 'Any chance you'd do the dance-off for me?'

That got a laugh.

So this was it. My last dance.

'Come on, Marty boy!' roared Rob Heffernan.

I gave it everything and probably performed better than I had the first time. But Julian Benson saved Alannah, as did my old friend Brian Redmond. Alannah was now safe, which meant that Lorraine didn't have to vote, but she too admitted that her vote was with Alannah. Brian Redmond kept his best line until the end. 'When you stand still, you have an air about you. In fact I think you are probably one of the best standing still dancers I've ever seen.'

I was out. It was over. The best three months of my life. I danced live on TV, something I never thought I would do, and found myself miles outside my comfort zone. I had nothing prepared when we walked over to Amanda to be interviewed, but I knew I wanted to thank Ksenia from the bottom of my heart for all she had taught me.

My fellow competitors were and are wonderful people who, like myself, gave up months of their lives to do this. We shared something unique and special.

It was Rob's birthday the following Wednesday, so his gorgeous wife Marian and I planned a birthday party for him that Sunday night. We hired a boat docked on a Dublin quayside and a full live band that played until the early hours. The following morning, I picked up Ksenia as usual and headed to the RTÉ studios in Donnybrook to do what our group called the walk of shame: meeting Ryan Tubridy on RTÉ Radio 1 and then Jenny Greene down the corridor in 2FM.

Nicky Byrne usually co-presented with Jenny, but he wasn't in that particular morning. He was obviously too upset about me getting my P45 from the show.

The papers had a field day.

'PARTY'S OVER FOR MARTY', roared the *Irish Daily Mail*. The *Irish Daily Mirror* had 'MARTY PARTY POOP-ERS', with sub headlines like 'Morrissey loses Alannah dance off' and 'Fab favourite fifth to make exit'. The *Evening Herald* quoted me: '"I'm sorry to go" – Marty shown red card as he loses dance off.' The *Examiner* went with 'The party's over as Marty makes his last stand.'

Each Sunday night after the party was over, Ksenia and I would treat ourselves to a snackbox in Supermac's or a chicken chilli wrap in McDonald's on O'Connell Street. Ksenia loves her sweet potato fries, and while we were diligent about what we'd eat during the week, we both got into the habit of break-ing out on a Sunday night. There was always training and rehearsing to look forward to on Monday morning. Now sud-denly that was over. I dropped Ksenia back home early that Monday morning, and as I drove south on the M50 towards Rathfarnham, I got a sudden bout of loneliness. It was rather strange. I still can hardly explain it now. What was I going to do for the rest of the day? There was no rehearsal, no ward-robe fit-out. What would I do next Saturday morning when the dress rehearsal would be on? Worse still, what would I do next Sunday night at 6.30? Could I even watch the show? It suddenly went from constant phone calls, photoshoots, press interviews and craic with Rob and Jake to nothing. The phone stopped ringing. The silence was deafening. It wasn't as if I had any notions about winning *Dancing with the Stars*, it was more the company and buzz of the whole thing. I won't lie to you, it took me a while to come back down to earth.

Ksenia and I spoke about five times that Monday, but she was much more pragmatic than me. We went out for dinner that night in a classy place that we both loved called Eddie Rocket's. She and I became close friends over our three months on *DWTS*. I can honestly say I don't think I have ever spent so much time over so short a period with anyone in my life before. It was ten hours every single day for three months. I'm delighted to say that our close friendship continues to this day. Ksenia even attended the Kilmurry-Ibrickane victory dance with me in the Bellbridge Hotel in Spanish Point at the end of January, when we put on an exclusive performance for my home crowd.

Anyway, the following Sunday Alannah Beirne was eliminated. That genuinely surprised me, as she and Vitali were outstanding. A week later Rob was gone, with Erin unlucky to lose out in the semi-final in week eleven. Only the very best dancers were left to compete in the final and that's the way it should be. Jake Carter, Deirdre O'Kane and Anna Geary battled it out, and in the end, Jake and Karen won the final and brought the glitterball home. They richly deserved it.

Dancing with the Stars is a brilliantly produced show. The cameramen and women, lighting engineers, set designers, VT editors, sound engineers, producers and directors are all incredibly talented people who make those of us in front of the camera look good and sound better. It really is a team effort.

The show opened me up to a whole new audience. Sport fans now saw me in a different light. For whatever reason, the children of Ireland really loved what I did on *DWTS*. Perhaps it was the sight of me struggling week after week, but still trying and having a laugh. So many people I don't know told me how their daughters or sons cried themselves to sleep on the night I was eliminated.

I still get letters about my time on *DWTS*. When a boy or girl asks for a photo these days, 90 per cent of the time it's because of my dancing rather than my commentaries. That says something about the power of the show.

Although Brian Redmond criticized me quite harshly on TV, his little daughter Anna loved me for some reason. Brian and I have become great friends over the last few years. When I was a guest on his radio show on KCLR 96FM, I got great satisfaction and quite a laugh for giving him a two as a radio presenter.

I remember commentating on a club match in Healy Park in Omagh in 2020, when we were all trying to learn to live with Covid-19. On my way to the stand I was walking behind the goalposts, where a group of young boys were kicking a ball around. I figured that in Tyrone these boys wouldn't know me, but they ran over and, in a most mannerly way, asked for a photo.

'We loved you on *Dancing with the Stars*, Marty. We wanted you to win it. We really wanted to party with Marty.'

We all laughed.

I had been on *Dancing with the Stars* through January and February 2018. This was September 2020 and those boys ranged in age from ten to thirteen. That meant they were between eight and eleven when I was trying to dance. But they remembered. That said it all.

24. Marty and Bernard

My friendship, or 'bromance' as they call it, with Bernard O'Shea started with *Dancing with the Stars*. Before that we had a passing acquaintance: I had been a guest several times on *Breakfast Republic*, the RTÉ 2FM show he presented along with Jennifer Zamparelli, Keith Walsh and Lottie Ryan. Saturday and Sunday were really long days for everybody involved, and between breaks and rehearsals there were plenty of opportunities for myself and Bernard to have the craic, especially when the girls were rehearsing. Nobody was supposed to leave the studio, but one Sunday morning the five lads – Bernard, Rob, Tomás, Jake and myself – piled into my car and we went down the road to the local café. It was like dodging school for an hour, but I felt we needed it to refresh ourselves for the night ahead. Of course there was panic back in the studio when they discovered their five top-class male dancers were missing. We got a bit of a finger-wagging and told not to do that again, unless we told them first, which was fair enough. I never mentioned that the boys actually wanted to go to the nearest pub for a quick pint.

Over time, Coffee Delights became our local. We always got a wonderful welcome from owner Jimmy Kavanagh and his brilliant staff.

Bernard asked me if I'd consider doing a TV programme with him. I said yes straight away, and RTÉ asked us to do what they call 'a tester', to give the decision-makers an idea of what this programme might look like. So one wet, miserable day, we met outside the radio centre and squeezed ourselves into a Fiat 500 belonging to Larry Bass's daughter Carla, which had been fitted out with cameras. Off we went around Dublin, closely followed by two camera crews in their own cars. We drove up and down O'Connell Street, visited the Zoo and ended up parked outside the entrance to Áras an Uachtaráin. We hadn't meant to stop there, but we had lost one of the camera crew cars. As we sat there, we discussed what it must be like to be the President of Ireland, and reflected on how the changing nature of the presidency reflected the changing face of the country.

I've met Michael D. Higgins and his lovely wife Sabina a few times in the past few years. Their warmth and kindness are genuine, and Michael D. always seems to be up to date on what I am doing. I love his personality, his great intellect, his linguistic ability, his wonderful sense of humour and above all else his grounding in mother earth. No airs and graces here. But then he was raised in Newmarket-on-Fergus, so he's one of ours.

'Wouldn't it be great craic,' said Bernard, 'if we could get past the gates and go in for a spin?'

'Will we try?'

Bernard laughed. 'I put a fiver on it that you won't get us in. No, make that a hundred euro.'

'You're on.'

We hopped out of the car and walked to the gate. Out of the security hut came a Garda in full uniform.

'How are you, Marty?' he said.

Going well so far, says I to myself. 'Grand, Garda, how are you?'

After a brief discussion about the Dublin footballers, I explained what we were doing and asked if we could possibly take a little spin around the Áras for a TV programme that we were trying to put together.

He laughed. 'My wife will probably kill me for saying this because she loves you, and loved ya on the dancing, but I have to say "No". It won't happen unless you get permission from the Áras.'

Bernard walked away from the gate smiling. 'I can't believe you failed, Morrissey. I can't believe you failed. Somebody has finally said "No" to Marty Morrissey.'

But the Garda on duty had actually given me an idea. I pulled out my phone and walked away from Bernard so he couldn't hear my conversation. At this stage, the two cars of cameramen, sound engineers and producers had pulled up behind our borrowed Fiat 500.

Larry Bass, the producer, climbed out. 'What are ye doing?'

'Marty is annoyed,' said Bernard. 'He can't get into the Áras.'

I wasn't annoyed at all. I was on the phone to Hans Zomer, the head of communications at Áras an Uachtarain. I had befriended him when I was editor of the GAA GPA All-Stars TV programme, and President Higgins was guest of honour. I explained my situation to Hans. He emphasized that this was not normal policy, but that he'd see what he could do. I don't know if he asked the President or not, but lo and behold, we got permission. One drive past the front door. No selfies, no photos and nobody was to get out of the car.

That's exactly what we did. And I believe now that that little achievement was what got the show commissioned. I made sure to thank Hans profusely, but I never got that hundred euro from Bernard.

In all honesty I had my doubts that this Marty and Bernard programme would ever become a reality. In the television world, you get more proposals rejected than accepted. The director of content at RTÉ, Jim Jennings, is a great and kind man who knows his broadcasting better than any of us. He calls it straight and really has done it all. When Bernard met him accidently and suggested the idea to him, he saw something in the concept. Later, when Larry Bass put a proposal together with the invaluable help of Alan Gillespie, there was a favourable response. Here were two individuals with similar backgrounds. I was from West Clare and Bernard was a Garda's son from Durrow, Co. Laois. And yet we were very different in terms of our broadcasting careers and interests. Not everyone would put a stand-up comedian and a sports commentator together on a TV show, but after much discussion and long negotiations, we got the green light to do two programmes.

I was absolutely delighted. This was a new adventure, a new challenge and a unique opportunity. To his great credit, my boss, head of sport Declan McBennett, gave me permission to do it.

In the following weeks, myself and Bernard met in the ShinAwiL offices in Sandymount with Alan Gillespie, Sheila Meaney, Larry Bass and, later, Evan Chamberlain, who was appointed director. Grainne O'Carroll, daughter of the great Michael O'Carroll, was going to be the series producer. Grainne has an awesome CV, having been series producer on *Room to Improve*, *Apres Match*, *Who do you think you are?*, *Blind Date* and many other successful TV programmes. In other words, we had a great production team.

We decided that the two programmes would each have a different feel. In the first, two traditional lads would go on a quest to make their mark on the world of the modern man. I'm talking manicures, moisturizers, make-up and being

Insta-fabulous. And as part of that, we would first set out to find out what a modern man is. The second episode was 'The Survivalist'. This would explore our ability to survive in the most difficult conditions possible . . . in Wicklow!

Because time was tight, filming was a bit disjointed. We filmed bits and pieces of the two episodes on various dates in September and October 2018 and again the following February. For 'The Survivalist', we joined the Reserve Defence Forces, who put us through a rigorous training regime at the Curragh. We ran for miles, dragged ropes, climbed obstacles, crawled through drains . . . In short, they tried to kill us under the guise of getting us fit and ready to survive in the Wicklow jungle. We spent some invaluable time with Shayne Phelan, a real survivalist, who taught us how to light fires and deal with difficult situations in the wild. We travelled to the Burren in Co. Clare and abseiled down the side of a cliff just a few miles from the Cliffs of Moher, with nothing but the Atlantic Ocean beneath us. Neither of us had ever abseiled before.

I absolutely love the sea, but only to look at or to paddle in. Despite being from Quilty, where the Atlantic Ocean plays a huge part in our lives, I have a terrible fear of the water. But one Sunday, I found myself filming at the Forty Foot in Dun Laoghaire with the Dublin Swimming Club, being coached by Caitriona Kehily from West Cork, who I later discovered to be a niece of the former great Cork foot-baller Kevin Kehily. Bernard and I had to strip again in Malahide, this time to freeze ourselves in ice baths. This is a key part of the Wim Hof method, which the production team reckoned we needed to learn ahead of our Wicklow excursion. The exercise is designed to boost the immune system, improve concentration and overall mental well-being. It was hilarious, but actually quite beneficial.

For the first programme, we got manicures and talked about what women look for in a modern man. We met Bernard Brogan, the former Dublin footballer, and found out about moisturizers, getting a facial and buying a suit. Jennifer Rock, 'The Skin Nerd', mesmerized both of us with relaxing facials – so relaxing that I fell asleep and woke to Bernard's laughter. Our next port of call was the Sugar Daddy Barbers in Exchequer Street, where Bernard got his eyebrows threaded and I got my nostrils waxed and ears syringed. Sweet Lord! Whatever about the ears, the nose job was awful.

We travelled to Co. Kildare to meet Damien Nolan, 'Ireland's Ken Doll', to find out about Botox fillers and the work he has done to make himself even more handsome. Just so he wouldn't have to look at the needle going into Damien's lips, Bernard started answering phone calls to the salon we were in. 'Hello, Marty's Hair Salon. What can we do for you?' He went on to have full conversations with clients, as if they were making hair appointments with me.

On another day, we dropped into the Assets Model Agency to meet Derek Daniels and ask him if we could become male models. He gave Bernard some hope but he ruled me out completely. I found that a little difficult to take.

The best bit was getting our portfolio photographs taken by a professional modelling photographer, Stephen James O'Neill. We put on white T-shirts that clung to our non-muscular bodies, then we struggled into tight jeans. I couldn't close the fly, so the shirt hung loosely to cover the vital components. I left the studio in pain, not from the poorly fitting clothes but from laughing continuously.

Then and there, we decided that a strict diet was urgently required. We're still working on that one.

To learn how to be a modern man, there was only one place to go: New York. This was home turf. I brought Bernard and the crew to 3095 Reservoir Oval, Bainbridge Avenue, Bronx, New York 10467: my home address when I was a kid growing up in New York. I haven't written it out since I was ten or eleven years of age, but still I remember it perfectly. It shows you how much your little brain can soak up when you're young. Despite all my trips to New York over the years, this was my very first time back at Reservoir Oval since we'd left all those years before. It was nostalgic and emotional to stand on the same block and look across to the park where my dad played ball with me.

Back in Manhattan, myself and Bernard met Dr David Shafer, one of America's leading plastic surgeons. He showed us a catalogue of procedures that he could perform in an effort to make me even more beautiful than I already am. Dr Shafer took photographs of my face and, using 3D technology, showed us what he could do with my face and chin. Bernard courageously declined to get anything done but I decided to get botox injections, purely for the sake of the programme obviously. The sight of the needle coming towards my face was very scary, but I just closed my eyes.

Bernard sat beside me during the procedure, saying 'Sweet Jesus, sweet Jesus, let him live, Lord. The women of Ireland need this man.'

The following morning we met Neil Collins, a former Roscommon footballer who had travelled to New York to experience a new world and become an international fashion designer. What he had for Bernard and myself to wear was beyond outlandish. Once we had the gear on, he took us down the streets of Manhattan to see if we would 'pop'. In other words, to see if we'd be noticed, because in New York, being noticed was king. And so the three of us walked and walked and boy did we pop. We were down near Lexington Avenue when this truck pulled up and the driver shouted out the window, 'Marty! What the fuck is wrong with you?' He hadn't seen the cameras, so I had to run over and explain to him what we were doing.

Later that evening we had a date with Anne Koch. Now here was a woman I wanted to meet. Anne started life as Ken Koch, and was a brilliant American football player and a member of the US Air Force. She said that she had always known that something was not quite right. Her Junior Prom was 'horrible', she said. 'Here's my date in a beautiful dress and I'd love to be wearing it.'

She showed us a photo of a very handsome man wearing a tuxedo and a moustache. 'When I think of Ken Koch, this

is the image I think of,' she said. 'I think of this guy as my twin brother, a different part of my life.'

The turning point came when she was diagnosed with squamous cell carcinoma. 'Death and mortality hit me like a ton of bricks,' she said. In 2013, she underwent gender confirmation surgery.

Anne Koch's message was simple. Create a welcoming environment. Be inclusive of transgender people. Treat people with respect. Our meeting with Anne Koch was informative, riveting and unforgettable.

We had so much fun in New York. We met Instagrammer Erika Fox in her beautiful apartment in Manhattan. The flame-haired Kerrywoman brought myself and Bernard down the street to teach us how to pose on a crosswalk when the traffic lights are red. How come it took a Kerrywoman to teach us that little trick? There's a skill in it, and Erika – better known to her Instagram fans as Retroflame – clearly has it. When I have this book written, I'm going to concentrate on my Instagram account, and if you see me posing at traffic lights in Ennis, Killarney, Letterkenny or Dublin, blame Retroflame.

As a final step in becoming modern men, we brought the portfolio of pics we'd taken in Dublin to Nole Marin, who was a judge on *America's Next Top Model*. Nole had been well briefed by Grainne O'Carroll, and when we showed him our photographs, he dismissed them with great relish. We then dressed in clothes he had selected and climbed the stairs to the rooftop and a spectacular view of Brooklyn Bridge.

'We want to see your raw talent,' he said, and with fashion designer Sergio Guadarrama lending assistance, they guided us through various poses, showed us how to walk properly and sell what we were wearing.

Bernard was a brilliant model – once he got out of the habit of walking like he was heading home after a long day in the bog! He's tall, with a reddish tinge to his hair, and Nole loved him.

Snow began to fall as we finished filming. By the time we had changed our clothes and emerged back on to the streets of New York, the scene had changed dramatically. The Big Apple was covered in snow. It was beautiful. It would turn out to be the biggest one-day November snowfall in New York in 136 years: 6.4 inches fell in Central Park.

It was time to go home.

We arrived back into Dublin Airport in the early hours of the morning. The instruction was go to bed, if we could, and sleep off the jet-lag because the following morning we were going to be collected early to head to our next location – the details of which were kept from us. We knew we had

457

finished the first programme, and that now we would turn our attention to the survivalist show.

The following morning, we were driven into the picturesque hills and valleys that surround Lough Dan in Co. Wicklow and told to go into the log cabin and change into our hiking and wet gear.

But I don't remember any of that. Here's what I pieced together afterwards.

Apparently, we both stood there in our wet gear – boots, waterproof jackets and trousers, warm shirts and woolly hats – while the survivalist team roared into our faces like sergeant majors in the movies. We were then blindfolded and water was suddenly thrown at us at a ferocious rate. Then our blindfolds were ripped off and we were seized, dragged down the slope, thrown into the lake and told to swim to the flag some distance away. We were fully clothed and weighed down with jackets and boots. Besides all that, I had one other major problem. I can't swim.

I'm told that I tried to swim, but lost my blue and yellow woolly hat, and then became more interested in saving that than reaching my destination. Eventually a member of the survivalist team waded in to rescue me and bring me to dry land. Bernard, meanwhile, made the target and swam back. Drenched to the skin and shaking with the cold, we were told that we had to light a fire.

Apparently, I kept asking Bernard where my phone was, so much so that he eventually lost the rag.

'Marty! I don't know where your phone is. I'm trying to light the fire!'

I was of no help whatsoever.

Next thing, Bernard stripped off his soaking shirt, trousers and boxer shorts until he was stark naked. You will be glad to hear I don't remember that. And nor, thankfully, was it ever shown on TV.

And still I kept at Bernard. 'Where's my mobile phone?'

'They threw it into the lake, Marty. It's fucking dead.'

I got very upset at this apparently, because my phone is an extension of my right arm.

The survivalist boys then began roaring at us again and put us running up the hill, laden down with logs. 'Move it, O'Shea! Come on, Morrissey!'

At some point, someone gave me a swig out of a can of Coke, and then halfway up the hill I vomited it out at high velocity. They did show that on TV, of course, to my embarrassment.

Back at the log cabin, someone gave me my phone and for some reason I started calling my friends. Again, I don't remember this, but I found out afterwards that I had called some of them up to ten times over a twenty-minute period.

Alice Daly was production co-ordinator on the show. She brought me a cup of hot chocolate to warm me up before lunch. She realized something was up when I kept asking her where I was. The only thing I remember was the lunch itself: bacon and cabbage. As I ate, I kept asking Bernard how I'd managed to get wet.

'Do you remember being thrown into the lake this morning?'

'Not really.'

'Do you remember being in New York?'

'Yes, of course.'

'Do you remember your flight home?'

'Not really,' I said, hesitatingly.

Now Bernard was worried. He thought I might have had a stroke. Arron Lynch is a really talented cameraman, and is one of these guys who can turn his hand to anything. He opened up his laptop and showed me what we had filmed that morning. I didn't remember any of it.

The medic on the crew, Mark Corcoran, tested my oxygen levels and heartbeat and found everything normal, but Sheila Meaney, our executive producer, decided to stop filming immediately and bring me to a doctor. Alice Daly drove her car with Sheila in the front passenger seat and yours truly in the back, oblivious of what was happening. They brought me to a doctor in Ashford, and she felt I should be brought to hospital for a more comprehensive analysis and observation. At the Beacon Hospital in Dublin that evening, the doctor on duty examined me fully. He was confident that I hadn't had a stroke but was suffering from something called transient global amnesia. As I lay in the bed in accident and emergency with Sheila and Alice sitting at my bedside, the phone rang.

It was Bernard. 'Are you OK?'

I told him that I was fine but the doctor thought I was suffering from transient global amnesia.

'What the hell is that?'

'I haven't a clue.'

'Stay there. I'll call you back in a few minutes.'

He hung up, then went on the internet to ask Dr Google what transient global amnesia was.

When he called back, he sounded excited. 'You'll be fine,' said Dr O'Shea. 'The causes of transient global amnesia are a sudden immersion in cold or hot water or wild sexual intercourse.'

'It's definitely the former,' I said, 'but if the press find out I'm in hospital, tell them it's the latter.'

Transient global amnesia is a sudden temporary interruption

of short-term memory. Although patients may be disorientated, and not know where they are, they're otherwise alert and attentive. You just fail to recall recent events. I stayed in the Beacon Hospital for three days and nights and was tested and retested until they were satisfied that I was ready for action again.

Almost three years after this incident I still can't remember what happened to me on that Monday morning in Co. Wicklow. I don't remember flying home from New York to Dublin, or going into the lake, running up and down the hills around the lake, vomiting on the side of the hill or asking Bernard where my phone was.

I will never forget the care and attention I got from Sheila Meaney, Alice Daly and the ShinAwiL team. Jim Jennings also rang to make sure I was OK. Likewise, I greatly appreciate the professionalism and care from the nurses and the doctors in the Beacon Hospital. I have no doubt now that my amnesia was caused by the sudden shock of cold water in Lough Dan, and that my tiredness from all the travelling and busyness was also a factor. Thankfully I've never experienced anything like it since.

A few months later, we returned to Co. Wicklow and finished filming that part of the programme. This time, I didn't go near the lake.

Thankfully, the public really seemed to like *Marty & Bernard's Big Adventure*. Audience figures suggested that we had held our own in the coveted 9.30 Sunday night slot, which was previously held by the highly rated *Room to Improve*. I was delighted when we were commissioned for a second series. Senior management laid down certain parameters, however. They wanted more of the spontaneity they had seen in the original tester. They wanted more interactions like the one with the Garda we met outside the Áras.

After many meetings and discussions, we got the green light for three programmes in the second series. Joe Edwards and Trevor Cunningham were with us again in terms of camera and sound, and so too were Arron Lynch, John Dunne and Ken O'Mahony, while Paul Magee operated the drones. Joe McElwaine and Shane Byrne were the directors. We were thrilled.

At the initial production meetings, I suggested that we meet GAA for Mas, the ladies football team from Ballybough. They had been brilliant on *The Marty Squad* a few years earlier. The second and third programmes would involve the RNLI in Kilrush, about thirteen miles from my home place, while the Durrow fire brigade from Bernard's home village in Co. Laois would also feature in the third.

The theme was simple: Marty and Bernard were back on the road. We decided that as we travelled around the country, we would help raise awareness or raise a few bob for the club or organization featured on the show. We wanted to shine a torch on communities, hear people's individual and collective stories, and have a few laughs along the way. The positivity of these communities and the work they were doing was what we wanted to highlight.

Ballybough, in the shadow of Croke Park, is an area that has experienced its fair share of gang violence, murders and drug problems, but the community spirit is unquenchable. I could happily live with the women I got to know in Ballybough for the rest of my days if they would have me. I simply love their company, wit, loyalty, trust, sense of belonging and love for each other and their home place. Tanya Behan, Joan O'Brien, Dawn Everard, Marie Farrelly, Susan Meier, Nicola Kelly, Joyce Walsh, Aisling Devine and Jackie Byrne, whose son Jack plays for the Republic of Ireland soccer team, welcomed us into their homes and simply lit up the TV with their personalities.

The concept for the show was simple. The women of Ballybough would raise money for their ladies' football club by baking cupcakes with mine and Bernard's faces on top. They would then set up a stand just inside the Cusack stand entrance to Croke Park before the All-Ireland club finals on St Patrick's Day.

The GAA loved the idea. They gave us a loan of their kitchen and corridors for a full day of filming. They also gave us the wonderful Cian Irvine, the chef in Croke Park, who taught myself, Bernard and the mothers themselves how to mass-produce cupcakes using the big ovens in GAA Headquarters. Ross Lewis, one of Ireland's greatest chefs and owner of Chapter One restaurant, was involved, and we also met Michael Darragh MacAuley, an eight-time All-Ireland medallist with Dublin, through his work in the inner city. To this day, people often ask me how the women in Ballybough are doing and when we're going back to film more.

For episode two, we had planned to go to sea with the RNLI lifeboat in Kilrush, but Atlantic storms kept thwarting our plans. We met Karoly Torok, who emigrated to Ireland from Hungary many years ago and joined the RNLI after his brother-in-law was killed after an accidental slip while sightseeing at the Cliffs of Moher. The RNLI searched the coastline for days and eventually found the body of Karoly's brother-in-law, which meant a huge amount to the family. Shawna Johnson owns a pub in Kilrush and has had serious health issues, but if there's an emergency call in the middle of a bad winter's night, Shawna will be the first to the RNLI Station at Cappa, just outside Kilrush. Then there's the Keating family, with both father and son (both called

Fintan) involved in the RNLI while Fintan Jr's son James, though still only a child, is showing signs of being attracted to the sea. It's in the DNA, and it's beautiful to see.

My mother's guest appearance in the programme, as we drove the car around Quilty and Seafield near home, got a positive reaction. She emphasized to the nation that the county of my birth was Cork. Bringing Bernard to St Joseph's in Spanish Point where I taught was also a personal highlight.

While the Ballybough women went off baking cupcakes, the challenge to the Kilrush RNLI was to record a song that Bernard wrote. It was a great little number. We booked the RNLI staff into Martin O'Malley's Miltown Malbay Studios, and got Killarney singer Gemma Sugrue to whip them into shape. David Brophy, former principal conductor of the RTÉ Concert Orchestra, joined us on the journey. Both he and Gemma were outstanding. I played a very small part in the recording by playing four notes on my old piano accordion. This took me a while to get right, but after hearing those four precious notes, David Brophy seemed to think that I had huge potential.

I have never met a more dedicated group than the members of the fire brigade in Durrow. I had never thought about what fire brigade men and women do on a daily and nightly basis for 365 days of the year, but based on my experiences in Durrow, they are beyond heroic.

I met and got to know Bernard's mother Mary and his sisters Marian, Siobhan and Caith as we dined for breakfast and lunch in Bowes Café in the square and dinner in the Castle Arms Hotel nearly every day for a week. Our fundraising project was a calendar based on photographs of the fire brigade. The night we presented the calendar was emotional, as we had secretly filmed little vignettes with their family members which I hope they will treasure for the rest of their days.

The public reaction to the two series was overwhelmingly positive, and the ratings were really good. Most TV programmes take time to grow and develop, and the truth is we really didn't know what this programme was meant to be until we got to the end of season two. We had first thought it would be comedy, but it turned out that it was more about life stories, about people, about heart and pride in that community.

We are thankful we got two seasons but I would be lying if I didn't say that I was disappointed that they didn't at least give us another. I'm not exaggerating when I tell you that I'm asked every day when *Marty and Bernard* will be returning to our screens. Another season, visiting the people on the Aran Islands or in South Kerry or North Donegal or Mayfield in Cork City, could have been entertaining, insightful and very positive.

But hey! That's television.

25. Special Moments

One of the best phone calls I ever got was from Philip Kampff, ex-RTÉ and now of Vision Independent Productions, the company behind successful TV programmes like *Operation Transformation*. Philip was putting together a proposal to televise the National Ploughing Championships and wanted Áine Lawlor and myself to present the programmes. He got the green light to produce three half-hour programmes, which would be called *Ploughing Live*. I was thrilled to be involved.

Áine Lawlor is a special woman and a special talent. We hit it off from the very start. When we started presenting together, she got a letter from a viewer who suggested she needed to stop presenting *Ploughing Live* because she was a 'serious journalist'. She loved that note.

Noel Dunne, the 'King of Bling', was also part of the team. He gave us all the information we needed on the farmers and their magnificent machines.

I never realized how big the ploughing championships were until I got there myself. Before Covid arrived, the ploughing was the biggest outdoor exhibition and agricultural trade show in Europe. It's Ireland on tour. Everybody who's anybody, or at least everybody who thinks they're anybody, is there.

The RTÉ tent was one of the most popular at the show. The public could ramble in, take a look around and get their photograph taken in a machine that gives you an *RTÉ Guide*

cover with your face on it. Alternatively, they could sit in the tent and watch as Ryan Tubridy, Sean O'Rourke, Joe Duffy and Ray D'Arcy presented their radio shows. The tent was a fabulous connecting platform between RTÉ and our audiences.

Myself and Áine were also selected to present a programme from Bloom, Ireland's largest gardening festival. If I was in my element at the ploughing, Áine was the queen of Bloom. She adores gardening and appreciated the artistic endeavour that was everywhere to be seen.

I will never forget getting a call from Áine Moriarty, chief executive of the Irish Film and Television Academy (IFTA) during Bloom 2018, asking if I would be able to make the presentation of the IFTA awards that night at the RDS. I knew I had been nominated for an award, and so had put the tuxedo in the car just in case, but getting to the ceremony on time would be almost impossible since I would be live on telly at the time.

I've never really given much thought to awards, let alone sought them. I wanted to win championships with Kilmurry Ibrickane and play for Clare. While I did get to play for Clare at minor level, and briefly at senior, I never won anything. And so pragmatism took over. You just try to be the best you can be at whatever you do.

Anyway, as soon as we were finished at Bloom, I ducked into the RTÉ caravan to tog out. It was fairly cramped. This was not Hollywood after all, but RTÉ. Once I was decked out in my finery, I headed over to the RDS, but I missed the announcement by about two minutes. This still breaks my heart, as the room was full of my peers, and their acknowledgement and acceptance is important to me. I had won the 'TV Presenter of the Year' award for 2018. I never won much in life, so this was something special – and the most special thing was that this award was decided by public vote. I feel very lucky to have that connection with the audience. I value it every day.

Three years earlier, in 2015, I had received the prestigious honour of 'Clare Person of the Year'. Being recognized by your own crowd is something I am very proud of. It was a great night. To have Liz and my mother, my colleagues, close friends and the West Clare gang all together under one roof was wonderful.

Bizarrely, in April of that same year, I was given the 'Cork Person of the Month' award, which meant I was then a nominee for 'Cork Person of the Year'. That has to be some sort of record. Just to be nominated in the county of my birth was overwhelming, and made me so proud. The overall 'Cork Person of the Year' title that year went to John Looney from

Togher, who founded the Cork City Hospital Children's Club in 1992. You feel a little bit inferior when you meet great people like John, and see the huge positive impact he and his fellow volunteers have had on the lives of young people.

In November 2019 I was deeply honoured to be awarded a UCC Alumni Award together with four other graduates of the Cork college. This prestigious event was held in the Aula Maxima, where, four-and-a-bit decades earlier, I first met Murt Murphy and Don Good, who laughed as I signed up for the UCC freshers team. As I walked from the back of the Aula Maxima to receive my award, I felt a touch of giddiness. It meant the world to me to be recognized by my college as someone who had done something worthwhile. The circle of this part of my life was now complete, and to have Liz there with me made it extra special.

I was told that I would be the last to receive my award that night, and was asked to speak on behalf of all five recipients, all of whom had achieved way more than I ever had. In my speech, I reiterated that I was a Cork-born Clareman.

'I love this city, this county and the people of Cork. UCC is a special place. There is something here for everyone . . . You can be academically gifted, or you can work your backside off, which is what I did. While you are here, you feel part of the UCC fabric. You feel that incredible community spirit, that feeling of pride, that sense of belonging that this is where I am from, this is who I am, this is my village. This is UCC and I love the place. It's great to be back and not have to do an exam!'

I have thoroughly enjoyed all the wonderful All-Ireland homecomings I've witnessed down the years. Each one is different and unique to its county. Probably the most spiritual ones for me were the Galway football victories in 1998 and 2001.

When I travelled west with the team on the Monday after the All-Ireland football final, Athlone was the first stop. Here, the team disembarked and walked across the bridge over the River Shannon into Connacht with the Sam Maguire Cup lofted high. Back on the bus, I looked around and saw brilliant footballers like Padraic Joyce, Michael Donnellan, Kevin Walsh, Ray Silke, Ja Fallon, Declan Meehan, Kieran Fitzgerald, Seán Óg de Paor and Derek Savage. What a pleasure to get to know them all.

The most strange and wonderful of all the sights I saw that night was on the road between Caltra and Mountbellew. Darkness was descending. It had just rained and in the night sky there was a flicker of blue and yellow light peeping through the dark clouds in the distance. Sam Maguire was sitting proudly on the dashboard of the bus as we sped through the football strongholds of Galway. And then it happened. As we came around a bend, there in front of us was a straight road and on either side, illuminating it like a runway, was a long row of glittering lights: sods of turf that had been soaked in petrol and lit up to welcome the All-Ireland champions. I've been to most counties after winning an All-Ireland and I can honestly say I never saw anything like this before. I asked Declan Meehan about it many years later and he said that it was a Galway tradition, often used to celebrate local weddings or a couple going off on their honeymoon.

To me it was just beautiful.

We were so late that night after stopping in towns like Ballinasloe and Tuam, that we all thought there would be nobody waiting for the Galway lads by the time we got to Eyre Square in the early hours of Tuesday morning. But they were there.

Thousands and thousands of Galway supporters had waited hours to see their team, to shake hands and clap them on the back. It was three in the morning by the time we all sat down for dinner at the Sacre Coeur Hotel in Salthill. Absolute madness but great craic.

In contrast, when the Tipperary hurlers won the All-Ireland in 2019, they were late leaving for Thurles from what used to be called the Burlington Hotel – now the Clayton – in Dublin. Due to time constraints and logistics for the *Six One News*, they did me a massive favour by staging their departure well ahead of the moment they actually took their leave from the capital. Everyone boarded the bus, which then did two laps around Burlington Road, Waterloo Road, Mespil Road and back down Sussex Terrace and Sussex Road to the hotel. I can still hear the laughter ringing in my ears as the Tipp team enjoyed going around in a circle for my benefit.

I am particularly proud that every year of the Dublin footballers' first five in a row (there was no homecoming after the sixth) and the Dublin ladies' three in a row, I've been asked to be their MC when they celebrate their incredible achievements. I have always considered this a great and unique honour, especially since I am not a native Dub.

Apart from my own crowd in 1995 and 1997, the homecoming to beat all homecomings has to be Limerick in 2018. I never saw anything like it: 90,000 fans gathered between Colbert Station and the Gaelic Grounds, where they all somehow seemed to find space on the pitch. The stage was erected at the city end, and to be master of ceremonies for that homecoming was one of the most special nights of my life. I thank Mike O'Riordan, the Limerick GAA CEO, the Limerick county board, John Kiely and the Limerick players for bestowing this wonderful honour on me. It was spell-bindingly beautiful to stand on that stage and see a sea of green and white on the pitch, and everyone so deliriously happy. I drove down to Limerick that afternoon not really knowing what to expect; but I did know I would have the added honour of working with Keelin Shanley. She was one of the finest journalists I knew, but more importantly, she was one of the nicest people I had ever met or worked with. I knew she was ill, but never heard her complain once. Eighteen months after that night, on February 8th, 2020, Keelin passed away after a heroic battle with cancer. She was and is much loved by her colleagues and we remember her with real affection. May she rest in peace.

With a combination of Cork and Clare blood running through my veins, there was only ever going to be one rugby team that I would love and support. On Saturday May 20th, 2006, after years of coming close, Munster beat Biarritz to win the Heineken Cup for the first time.

The Millennium Stadium in Cardiff was supposed to be a neutral venue, but Munster fans had gone around Europe buying tickets from other clubs and there were some 65,000 members of the Red Army there that day. At two crucial moments during the game, Sky TV pictures of the massive crowd gathered in O'Connell Street in Limerick were shown in the stadium. Nine days after the final, Biarritz lodged a formal complaint with Sky, claiming that the impact of those stirring images gave Munster an unfair advantage.

The following day, I was in Pearse Stadium in Galway to commentate on a Connacht championship match between Galway and Sligo, but the pitch was waterlogged. After the match was postponed to the following Saturday, I got a call from TV producer Paula Fahy, who asked me would I mind going to Limerick to present the homecoming for the Munster team when they arrived back from Cardiff with the Heineken Cup. I leapt into the car and headed for Limerick in atrocious driving conditions. When I got to Limerick, an estimated 40,000 people were waiting patiently in the rain for their heroes.

I can still hear the ferocious roar that greeted captain Anthony Foley and coach Declan Kidney when they brought the cup on stage. At one point, with help from Paul O'Connell and Donnacha O'Callaghan, my friend Alan Quinlan lifted me up and threw me into the air, much to the amusement of the crowd in front of us and the TV audience watching at home. It was great craic. I was proud to have played a very small role on that historic afternoon.

Anthony Foley was always exceptionally kind to me. In October 2016, in Paris, Anthony died in his sleep the night before Munster – of which he was now head coach – were set to play Racing 92. He was only forty-two. I don't know his wife Olive, but the way she handled herself at the time of his sudden passing will always stay with me. She was outstanding as she dealt with the utterly unexpected loss of her great husband while keeping things grounded for herself and her children.

I can assure her and her two young boys that Anthony Foley will never be forgotten. Rest in peace, Axel.

After Covid-19 arrived in March 2020, I spent a lot of my time in West Clare with my mother, trying to keep her safe. Like all of us, she found it difficult to grasp what was going on. She loves going to mass every morning and has a tremendous faith. She couldn't understand why some of her best friends wouldn't 'come out to play', as I referred to it.

To be honest, I felt safer in the wide-open spaces of Clare than in Dublin at the time. Working for RTÉ meant I was part of an essential service, and when there were developments in the sporting world I would travel back to Dublin on motorways that were devoid of cars. It was like driving through a post-apocalyptic Ireland. Scary.

One evening, my colleague Jacqui Hurley rang about a breaking GAA story. The TV sports news crew is a small team, and I am very proud of them: Jacqui Hurley, Evanne Ní Chuilinn, Clare McNamara, Eamon Horan, Paul Flynn, Dave Kelly, Joe Stack and Justin Treacy, with Tony O'Donoghue as soccer correspondent and Donagh McGrath as our line manager. Anyway, I told Jacqui that I was in West Clare with no facilities, so she suggested I do something on my phone. I hadn't a notion how that might be done, but following instructions from Jacqui, I went out to my shed – or office, if you want to get fancy – and eventually got something that went to air, but it was crap. The slagging started immediately. Claire Byrne had filmed segments of her own Monday night show from her shed, so people on social media wondered was Claire with me in my shed, or was I in her shed?

The whole business made me think. In order to keep myself busy, I came up with the idea of doing a live Instagram programme from my shed. Would it be possible? I called my great friend Matt Purcell and he – in his lovely Feakle accent – nonchalantly told me that anything was possible in the world we now live in. My broadband was poor, and calling Eir and waiting on the line for hours was not good for my health. So I rang my neighbour, Declan Morrissey, who works for Clare Wifi, and he and they were brilliant. Just before Covid struck, myself and head of 2FM, Dan Healy, had talked about doing a show called *The Marty Party*, so out of courtesy to Dan, I called and told him I was think-ing of doing this Instagram programme, primarily for my own sanity. It was Dan's idea to propose it to our employer for the RTÉ Player. Within a few weeks, we had been given the green light to produce *Marty in the Shed* for a four-week run. Three people were appointed to work with me: produc-ers Nigel Power and Sinéad Stimpfig, with Claire Monahan as researcher. Matt Purcell provided the technological wizardry and over many phone calls, we came up with a format.

It was a wonderful four weeks. I loved working with these great people. The show was a combination of Zoom calls recorded in the shed and VTs which were edited back at base in Dublin.

Oliver Callan was my first guest, launching it with his bril-liant impression of Leo Varadkar. Then his Marty spoke to the real Marty. Very confusing. Actress Victoria Smurfit joined us from her home in London; she was just fabulous. One of my great friends from *Dancing with the Stars*, Nicky Byrne, gave us exclusive backstage footage from the Westlife concert in Croke Park. Then he had a penalty shootout with his children in their garden, filmed by his wife, Georgina Ahern. (Nicky was a great goalkeeper and played with Leeds United before his singing career skyrocketed.) Mike Denver showed us his newborn baby while Chris O'Dowd joined us from his home in California. I have been a huge fan of Chris O'Dowd for years. To achieve what he has achieved on a global stage is truly phenomenal. I didn't know him person-ally, but I follow him on Twitter so I took a chance and asked him to follow me so I could DM him with my invitation to join me in the shed. He followed. I asked. He agreed.

I was so delighted. He's a former Roscommon minor

goalkeeper, of course, so there is that strong GAA connection, and I'll always be grateful to Chris for his great kindness in agreeing to join me in the shed. I'm looking forward to meeting him in person some day.

Rob Heffernan and Aoibhín Garrihy joined me on another day, while Mayo footballer Aidan O'Shea and his girlfriend Kristin McKenzie Vass were up for a laugh and did a kind of contortionist routine they had previously done on social media.

The reaction to *Marty in the Shed* was very positive, and the audience figures reflected that. They tell me that 5,000 streams per programme on the RTÉ Player is considered a success, and between May 10th and June 14th 2020, *Marty in the Shed* received 40,823 streams. To broadcast from my own backyard in West Clare, from a Steeltech, was such a wonderful treat. I will always be grateful to Aoife Byrne and Adrian

Lynch in RTÉ for allowing me that unique opportunity, and to the great team that worked with me.

Apart from my acting debut in John B. Keane's *Moll* at the Gaiety in 2015, there were two other occasions when I had to put on a disguise. The first was for a wonderful one-take promo of RTÉ's *Big Music Week* in 2012. I dressed up as Elvis Presley, and that great legend of broadcasting, the late Larry Gogan, teed up 'A special request from the King'. It then cut to me standing next to him in my full, white skin-tight Elvis gear. The camera moved along the corridors of RTÉ, where dozens of presenters and entertainers lip-synced and performed to 'Brewing Up a Storm' by the Stunning.

Four years later I was dressing up again for a series of photographs to commemorate the 1916 Rising, and even went on *The Late Late Show* in full regalia, glued-on moustache and all. I don't know where Maureen Catterson – the communications manager for RTÉ – gets all her brilliant ideas, but she is highly imaginative, very creative and brilliant at her job. We need more like her! In 2016, she persuaded Miriam O'Callaghan, Joe Duffy, Marty Whelan, Sean O'Rourke, Kathryn Thomas, Bláthnaid Ní Chofaigh, Liz Nolan and myself to wear what was fashionable back in 1916, and the photographs have pride of place on the mantelpiece at home.

They sit beside my All-Ireland football medal. Yes, you read it right: I have one.

In 2019 I was asked by a great friend at home, Michael Considine, if I would join the Clare over-40s squad as the championship was approaching. My club-mates Odran O'Dwyer and Johnny Daly were already involved, so, despite the fact that my time was limited and that I was the elder lemon of the squad, I agreed to have a go. I know what you're thinking. Will he ever get sense?

I attended one training session in Clarecastle and thoroughly enjoyed the banter and the craic with the lads. Tom Morrissey, one of the heroes of the Clare team of 1992, was in full forward, and as always with Tom you'd hear him before you'd see him. Quite an accomplishment considering how tall he is. 'Fong it in to me!' he'd roar.

My first match was against Galway, in Doonbeg, and I was introduced as a substitute late on. Galway had arrived in a matching maroon strip. In contrast, while we might have had the Clare jerseys on our backs, we wore a wide array of different-coloured togs and socks. On arrival to my new position of corner forward, the Galway corner back said, 'Jaysus, I don't believe it. But since I have you, any chance of an All-Ireland ticket?' We both laughed.

He went on, 'Whatever else, you can't fucking score or I'll never hear the end of it.'

I made one scintillating diagonal run in the hope the ball would be sent into the space I had run into. I got a massive cheer from the sideline, which is why, performer that I am, I took a bow. I barely had time to accept the rounds of tumultuous applause before the final whistle blew.

There was such great craic with the likes of Dessie Molohan, Ger 'Bobby' Kelly, Cathal Hill, Patsy Keyes, James Murphy, David Neenan, Mike O'Shea, Mickey Donnellan and some lad called 'Tyson' that I agreed to fly to London to play against the home side in Ruislip. The London lads told me they were looking forward to marking me, which I thought was a compliment initially. When I saw the gritted teeth and smoke coming out the nostrils, I thought maybe they had a different sort of marking planned for me. Anyway, Clare management decided not to use my silken skills to bamboozle the opposition, or indeed our own team, so I flew home without seeing any game time.

We got to the All-Ireland shield final against Kildare, which was fixed for St Brigid's home ground in Kiltoom in Co. Roscommon. I got the hint loud and clear when they asked me to tog out *and* do the commentary on the video as well. So there I was, fully togged out with jersey, shorts and boots, mike in hand, commentating on the match. And then Clare manager Michael Considine called me down from the stand, as my county needed me.

Michael Liddane, a fine footballer from Naomh Eoin country out by Loop Head, came running through. I made space by running in the opposite direction, and clearly the Kildare corner back didn't know what to do. Stick with me or go for Liddane? Michael was fouled, just to the right of the posts. Michael Considine, along with the entire Clare side-line, roared to leave the ball down and let Marty take it. This was to be my moment. History books would show that I scored a point in an All-Ireland final against Kildare, *if* I could tap it over the bar. The tension was palpable. Suddenly, one of the Clare lads decided to take a quick free, despite the clear instructions from the sideline. My moment was gone. Deleted. Seconds later, the final whistle blew and we were Over-40 All-Ireland shield champions. What do you think of that, Joe Brolly?

It was only later that I realized that I had won an All-Ireland medal without touching the ball once. That must be a record.

Mark McKenna, the executive producer of RTÉ's Olympic coverage in 2021, called to ask if I would report live from Kellie Harrington's home on Portland Row in Dublin in the early hours of the morning of her Olympic gold medal bout. Ireland was buzzing with her performances and I was delighted to be asked.

I don't know Kellie, but I am her biggest fan. Not just because of her boxing ability and her journey to that incredible moment in time, but because of her personality, her humility and the way she carried herself all the way through. Now, at 6 a.m. on Sunday August 8th, 2021, she was bidding to become our country's third ever Olympic boxing gold medallist, following in the footsteps of Michael Carruth and Katie Taylor.

The day before Kellie's fight, I was commentating on the All-Ireland hurling semi-final between Limerick and Water-ford. After the match, I left Croke Park and went down the road to Portland Row to visit the Harringtons. The street was bedecked in green, white and gold bunting, the tricolour flew from every window and telegraph pole. It was a sea of colour and you could sense the excitement in the air. I asked the locals where Kellie's house was and they proudly and excitedly pointed the way.

When Kellie's dad Christy opened the door, smiling ear to ear, he said, 'Ah Jayus Marty, it's yourself. I'm so delighted to meet you. I can't invite you in because of Covid.'

I told him that it was the other way round – I was delighted to meet him – and that I was fine at the door. People passing by honked their horns and roared 'Come on, Kellie!' Christy's reaction was as spontaneous as it was proud. He stood on the footpath and waved to everybody as if he was on a presidential campaign. Then, for some reason, I started waving as well. Two grown men acting like schoolboys. It was very funny and we enjoyed the moment.

That night, I set six different alarms on my phone to make sure I'd wake in time, but to be honest I hardly slept. Myself, cameraman Ken O'Connor and satellite van engineer Davy Ebbs arrived at Portland Row at 5.15a.m. to find Kellie's brother Christopher putting a sign on the front door asking that the family be left in peace during the fight. The two lads thought we'd get no interview, but when I greeted Christopher, he said that he was good to go. Ken and Davy were really impressed, but of course it was my visit the evening before that was the key. Before the fight, Christopher stood with us until we went live, by which time other journalists and photographers had arrived.

Davy Ebbs played a blinder. He got a chair and placed it on the footpath outside the Harrington house. He then put a small monitor on the chair, and held up a rabbit ear antenna so that we could watch Kellie's fight. As 6 a.m. approached,

Portland Row fell quiet. It was a beautiful morning. It was quite surreal, to be watching a TV plonked on a chair outside the Harrington home in Dublin as Kellie boxed for gold far away in Tokyo.

The first round belonged to Kellie's Brazilian opponent, Beatriz Ferreira, but the second and third were Kellie's. RTÉ commentator Hugh Cahill roared, 'She has it! She has it!' and he was right.

Kellie fell to her knees in the ring in Tokyo, just as the front door of the Harrington home burst open. Champagne corks popped and we were all drowned in bubbly before we saw any of the Harringtons. I will never forget the sight of the residents of Portland Row, who had been watching Kellie on the big screen that had been set up further up the road, run down the hill in their thousands to the Harringtons. They hugged and cried. They sang songs, including the national anthem. Then it was time for Kellie to be presented with her gold medal, so I grabbed Christopher's arm.

'You don't want to miss this,' I said, pointing to Davy Ebbs's TV monitor.

The crowd gathered around the chair, which was connected by wires and cables to the satellite van. I volunteered to hold the rabbit ears, but every now and then the signal would disappear and the screen would go to black. Can you imagine the reaction? The groans could be heard in Tokyo.

'Ah Jaysus, will you hold the bleedin' antenna steady Marty?'

Eventually, Davy gave me the P45 and he held the antenna himself.

We did a live interview with the family afterwards, and Kellie's mum admitted she couldn't watch Kellie fight, even in an Olympic final.

The Harrington family are very special, and as long as I live I will never forget their kindness and warmth on that historic weekend. As for Kellie herself, she is in a different league entirely. She brought tears of joy to her family, to her partner, Mandy, to Portland Row and to the people of Dublin. We all needed her spirit and determination after a torrid year. For that alone we should be forever thankful to an Olympic gold medallist and a true legend of Ireland.

And finally, one very special moment.

On Tuesday August 24th, 2021 my boss Declan McBennett called to tell me that I would be presenting *The Sunday Game* night-time programme on September 11th, the evening of the All-Ireland football final. Des Cahill, who usually presents the programme, would not be available on the day as his son Paul was getting married. I was delighted and hugely grateful for the opportunity to fill in for him.

I had been commentating on matches since 1989 and had worked as a sideline reporter for two decades, and now I was going into studio to present *The Sunday Game* on this special night. From the back of a trailer to commentating in Croke Park to sideline reporter to studio presenter: all boxes ticked. I was deeply honoured. And it had only taken thirty-two years.

The circle was now complete.

26. Reflections

Larry Bass rang me one day in February 2020 to ask if I'd speak to a friend of his who had, apparently, sent me several emails to which I hadn't replied. This isn't like me. I'll nearly always reply, though it can sometimes take a few weeks.

'Who is this guy?' I asked.

'Michael McLoughlin,' he replied.

'And who's he when he's awake?'

'He's the managing director of Penguin Random House in Ireland.'

'Ah, that's why I didn't respond, Larry. I appreciate the compliment but honestly I don't want to write a book. Nobody would be interested in reading what I'd write.'

'Will you just talk to him?' Larry pleaded. 'Have a chat and be open to whatever he suggests.'

'Grand, I will. Give him my number.'

Michael and I would go on to have many chats. He can be very persuasive. But I genuinely felt I hadn't the inclination or the time to write a book. I was just too busy.

That was February 2020.

In March, Covid arrived and sport left. By June, I had completed my four weeks of *Marty in the Shed* and Michael was back on the phone being his persuasive self. At this point, my opposition to writing began to wilt. Maybe I *should* write a book. After all, what else am I doing?

Then something strange happened.

I was in the back room of my house, which once upon a

time was my grandmother Kathleen Twomey's room. When she died, it became the place where we stored things like books, tapes, odds and ends and general junk. Anyway, I was in there looking for an old tape when I noticed one of those yellow Post-its stuck to one of the built-in presses. I'd never noticed it before. As I got closer, I recognized my father's writing. He had died in December 2004. Now, sixteen years later, here was a Post-it note that somehow I had never seen before.

Penguin Irl,
25 St Stephen's Green
Dublin 2
Michael McLoughlin

'Wow,' I said to myself. To see my father's writing *and* what he had written really shocked me. I had to sit down. How had Michael's name ended up on a Post-it in the back room in our house, and remained there unseen for sixteen years?

Dad had written two books, *Land of my Cradle Days* and *The Changing Years*, both of which were reflections on country life in Clare when he was young. They had been published by O'Brien Press. I remembered then that my father also wrote a work of fiction, *Floating Witness*, and though he never finished it, he had contacted several publishers about it. Either he spoke to Michael, or he planned to speak to him. That was the only reason I could think of for finding his name where I had found it. And now, here was I talking to the same man about writing a book. I took it as a sign, or maybe I wanted to see it as a sign. I don't know what I wanted but it certainly rattled my cage.

There were other reasons why I undertook this project.

Like so many others during Covid times I went out and bought a bike. There are so many scenic routes around home. One of my favourites takes me down the hill on the Wild Atlantic Way, past my grandparents' old home to O'Doherty's Cross. Cooraclare and Kilrush lie straight on down this road, but I like to turn right as if heading to Doonbeg, then right again just before Paddy Kelly's house, then continue past Queenie Frawley's and Clonadrum National School where my father went to school. On this particular occasion, as I cycled on through Clohaninchy, a terrier emerged from a house. He was determined that I wouldn't stop there, or else he'd have one or both of my ankles for tea. I cycled faster, but then, because I was going down a slight incline past Cooney's house, I needed to brake. I wasn't used to my new bike, however. I braked too hard and went flying into the ditch. It might have been covered with green swathes of grass, but there were hard-nosed rocks underneath which I smashed into. My back and ribcage took the brunt of the impact, and it hurt. I sat there in the ditch for a few moments, trying to gather my composure. It was probably only seconds but felt a lot longer. The embarrassment! I hoped to God that nobody had seen me.

Eventually, I dragged myself out of the ditch and hobbled home with a wobbly wheel, dented pride and fierce sore ribs.

That was a Thursday. I was working in Dublin over the weekend, but by the time I got back down to Clare on the Monday, the ribs hadn't improved at all, so I decided to call my friend Dr Billy O'Connell, who hails from Kerry. When Billy and I meet, it's football, life, philosophy, music, Kerry, Clare and everything in between. I told him about my fall and he said that as I was there, he'd better give me a quick once-over. He put on his stethoscope and began placing the diaphragm slowly around my chest. I knew him well enough to know I wasn't getting a clear round. In fact, he frowned a little bit too much for my liking.

'What's wrong?' I asked.

'Let me listen again,' he said.

Billy always spoke gently, and despite all his years in West Clare, Kerry hadn't left him. 'Marty, that sounds irregular to me. Are you feeling OK?'

'Never better,' was my response.

'We're going to do an ECG right now to check you more thoroughly, and it's your neighbour that will do it for you.'

Nurse Maire Conway is one of my best friends and one of the greatest neighbours anybody could ask for. She has a brilliant sense of humour.

'I always wanted to say this,' she said. 'Take off your shirt and lie down there, Marty.' This was followed by peals of laughter.

She attached pads to my chest and within minutes confirmed Billy's diagnosis. Atrial fibrillation. This is an irregular, sometimes rapid heartbeat that can increase your risk of stroke, heart failure and other heart-related complications. Was it the fall that caused it? I don't know, but I do know that there are plenty of people walking around not knowing they have it, so at least now I knew. It was a great get by Dr Billy.

He now needed to put me in the care of a cardiologist. I immediately thought of the man who saved my father's life way back in 1998: Dr Terry Hennessy. We had become great friends when he cared for my father and have maintained that friendship ever since. Terry thought it best to do an angiogram, which is essentially an X-ray of the blood vessels, to find out if there were any other issues or complications.

It's amazing what runs through your mind when you're sitting in a hospital bed. There was a lot of worry. Would I be OK? I felt absolutely fine. But then my father and my father's father had both died of heart attacks reasonably young (in their seventies). So family history on my father's side wasn't so hot. On the other hand, my mother's people had all lived into their eighties and nineties. So overall, the DNA wasn't too bad. I have been so lucky with my health, thank God. Apart from the odd cold or flu, I've rarely been sick.

I told nobody at work what was going on, and when the angiogram was done it came back all clear, thank God. There was then the option of getting a cardioversion done. This is essentially an electric shock which gets the heart beating regularly again. Sometimes it works, sometimes it doesn't. Luckily enough, it worked for me, and now my ticker is thumping out a regular beat again. So I can't wait for Copper Face Jacks to open up!

There had been one other health scare that gave me pause. On holidays in Thailand, a cold sore on my lip got worse in the sunshine of Koh Samui. It was a really strange experience. I found it difficult to shave because I suddenly couldn't move my lips or my face sideways. I avoid doctors as much as I can, but this was so alarming that I went to a medical centre twice on holidays. On my second visit, the night before departure, a young doctor who told me that she had only just graduated gave me corticosteroids. These, it would turn out, saved me from worse complications in the long run.

Back home in Dublin, I went to see my doctor in Rathfarnham. Dr Alex Khourie is a native of Iraq who came to Ireland to study and never went back. My face was now beginning to droop significantly, and Alex immediately decided that I had or was developing Bell's palsy. He dispatched me to St Vincent's Hospital to make sure it was nothing more sinister. I spent a night in the hospital and in the morning the drooping had stopped and the numbness had eased, so they released me. I was scheduled to commentate on a match later that afternoon so I needed to get out of there.

I never told anyone about this episode as I didn't want to complicate life for myself. But these frightening experiences forced me to reflect on where I was in life. All things considered, maybe it was time to write a few words. Maybe I could use the lockdown to do something useful.

And so I began writing in January 2021, and finished in the early hours of Friday August 27th. Eight months of nonstop thinking about writing.

The first night was a blank. The second night was blankety blank. The third night I wrote about 500 words, but decided the following day that they were all shite. How would I get to the 80,000 words Michael McLoughlin had suggested? I hadn't managed that in my Masters in NUIG. In fact, if my experience with that – which was my last big writing project – was anything to go by, this book would either fail or end up taking forever. My thesis took almost seventeen years to write.

Originally, I had intended to write a book of stories and anecdotes from my career, but when I started tapping on my battered old laptop I found that I needed to put people and events in perspective. And so it began to evolve into an autobiography of sorts. I had to go back to be able to go forward. And yet I found writing about myself quite intimidating. I didn't want this to be self-indulgent, egotistical or boring.

Nor did I want it to be a book about the greatest footballers, hurlers, camogie players or ladies footballers that I have seen. Like, who really cares what I think? Greatness moves from generation to generation. When I started, D. J. Carey was the man. Then Henry Shefflin emerged. Now it's Cian Lynch. In football it used be Peter Canavan but the hero today is David Clifford. Judgement is subjective and fame is transient. My book needed to be informative and revealing about a guy who really hadn't a clue what he was doing or where he was going when he was a teenager, or indeed in his mid-twenties.

I would love to tell you I had a great plan for my life. I hadn't. I'd love to tell you the stars have been aligned since day one. They haven't. Most things happened by accident. The rest was sheer hard work, thanks to a work ethic passed on by my parents. I didn't plan to be a teacher. I didn't plan to have a career in the media, not at the start anyway, although I pursued it with a passion once I knew that this was where I wanted to go. Once I got the bug of commentating on matches, I was hooked. There was no turning back.

Did I want to be well known? Absolutely not. I only strived to be as good a commentator as I could be. I couldn't care less if I was never seen on TV, I just wanted to go to the games. But slowly, over time, I got reporting and presenting gigs and broadened my horizons to the point where I acquired skills that only come through that level of exposure. Slowly, audiences got to know me, first in sport and later in other programming areas.

There are negatives in every job and sometimes it is difficult to get private time. But I knew that when I was trying to get into RTÉ. The arrival of social media has brought added pressure. These days, it feels like I represent RTÉ every moment of my waking life.

In the broadcasting world that I operate in, I am well aware that not everybody will like you or your style of broadcasting. Us front-of-house people hope that we don't annoy the audience. Sometimes we get it spot on. Other times not so much.

I have worked at three Olympiads and commentated on thirteen All-Ireland finals – eight on the radio and six on TV. But no man is an island. None of this is achievable on your own. Broadcasting is a team game. I have worked with some of the most talented people that anybody would wish to know, and that includes people who not only make me look and sound good, but who also cover my ass on every gig and broadcast. It's a long list, which includes cameramen, VT editors, floor managers, sound engineers, producers, directors, make-up artists, satellite van engineers, broadcast co-ordinators and news and programme editors. Nothing would have been possible without RTÉ's greatest asset, its people.

This is a challenging environment for public-service broadcasters like RTÉ, who must continue to evolve and reflect the changes in society. We all have days when we have a good old-fashioned rant about the place, but truthfully, I wouldn't like to have spent my career anywhere else. It's not perfect, but what place is? I love it, but I love the people more.

So what's next?

I absolutely love presenting my radio show on public holidays. I still have a burning ambition to have a more regular presence on the radio, be it on weekdays or at the weekend. *The Marty Party* is a TV show that I will do someday, I hope. It will be a good old-fashioned entertainment show, where we come to our audiences rather than our audiences coming to D4. It will be singing, dancing, laughing and chat. It will be about community. God knows we need something like that

Back where I started: doing commentary in 2016 on Kilmurry Ibrickane's
Munster club championship quarter-final against Dr Crokes in Quilty

now. We must get back to our grassroots audiences, be they in West Cork, North Donegal or South Wexford, and reconnect the national broadcaster with these communities.

On a personal level, I hope that by reading this book, you have gotten to know me a little better. As I finish up, let me emphasize two qualities that are vitally important to me.

The first is belief. Belief in yourself and your own talent, but never becoming egotistical. Believe that you can fulfil your dream, even though there will be days when it will look like it's never going to happen. It's not an easy journey, but it's fabulous when you reach your destination. Remember that you're never too old to learn. There's a friend of mine that loves the GAA analogy: keep togging out and you'll eventually get a game. It's actually true. It certainly applies to me.

The second quality is trust. Trust yourself to be fair and honest always, and the people you interview and the people watching will trust you. Lose that trust and you lose the dressing-room. It's game over.

People in the TV and radio world are often described as celebrities. I'm no celebrity. I'm just a lad from West Clare who had a burning desire to perform, to commentate on games, meet people and have the craic along the way.

It's been emotional, it's been fascinating and it's been great fun so far. But it's only half-time. The second half begins now.

Thank you for sharing your time with me. Thank you for believing and trusting in me and for allowing me to be in your homes through the magic of radio and television.

And thank you for reading *It's Marty!*

Acknowledgements

To the people I love and care about, and who for some inexplicable reason love me – why the hell didn't ye stop me? If you have a story to tell, you should share it, ye said. I should have stuck to my guns and said 'No' like I wanted to. What was wrong with lying on the couch watching TV every night, or bringing our new dog Sammy for a walk?

Just write, said Liz, and waffle as you usually do. So I began, with a frightening blank screen on my laptop in the shed in West Clare on a bitterly cold January night. And here I am nine months later, in my apartment in Rathfarnham in Dublin, thanking you for picking up my book.

A lot of people have helped shape me, from New York to West Clare to Cork, London and Dublin. Thanks to the people of my great parish of Kilmurry Ibrickane who gave me my love of football, sport, music and a sense of pride in community. To my wonderful broadcasting friends and colleagues in RTÉ, who guide, produce and direct me, thanks for making me a much better broadcaster. Especial thanks to those in the Sports Department, including the *Sunday Game* team led by Noel Carroll, Rory O'Neill and Wes Liddy, and many others who work passionately behind the scenes. To my immediate bosses Declan McBennett and Donagh McGrath, thank you for your continued belief in me. To the GAA and the various communities of Ireland, thank you for being there and allowing me at various times to be with you in your clubs and homes. Thank you to the great photographers – John Kelly, Kyran O'Brien, Paschal Brooks, Joe Buckley, and Liam

Hogan, and the staffs of the *Irish Examiner*, Sportsfile and Inpho – who had the gift and the eye to capture moments that were special to me and stimulated memories.

This has been a journey I never thought I would undertake, but Michael McLoughlin from Penguin Random House deserves great credit for his non-stop encouragement, and for linking me up with two new friends, John Hearne and Brendan Barrington, who were my long-suffering editors. You should see the Before and After photographs of the two boys. They have visibly aged in nine months. You can take the next nine months off, lads – I'm done!

To my wonderful mother Peggy, thank you for being so strong, although I know you miss Dad every day. To Liz, thank you for your love and support. To my great circle of friends, thank you for being who you are and being there for me.

People have asked me where I got the title for my book. It's simple, really. After I was on *Dancing with the Stars*, when the children of Ireland saw me they would shout: 'It's Marty!' I really hope you've smiled and even laughed as I've recalled my life so far.

Picture Credits

Photos not listed below are courtesy of the author.

Page 8: Pat Murphy/Sportsfile
Page 29: Paschal Brooks Photography
Page 36: Paschal Brooks Photography
Page 42: Paschal Brooks Photography
Page 74: Courtesy of Sean Malone
Page 88: Paschal Brooks Photography
Page 98: Paschal Brooks Photography
Page 99: Paschal Brooks Photography
Page 108: *The Irish Examiner*
Page 113: *The Irish Examiner*
Page 123: *The Irish Examiner*
Page 124: *The Irish Examiner*
Page 132: Liam Hogan Photography, Ennis
Page 155: *The Irish Examiner*
Page 166: *The Irish Examiner*
Page 176: *The Irish Examiner*
Page 179: Matt Browne/Sportsfile
Page 186: RTÉ
Page 188: Brendan Moran/Sportsfile
Page 189: Lorraine O'Sullivan/Inpho
Page 213: David Maher/Sportsfile
Page 214: Matt Browne/Sportsfile
Page 217: Ray McManus/Sportsfile
Page 223: David Maher/Sportsfile
Page 225: Ray McManus/Sportsfile

Page 235: John Kelly Photography

Page 236: Joe Buckley Photography

Page 248: Ray McManus/Sportsfile

Page 253: James Crombie/Inpho

Page 257: Piaras Ó Mídheach/Sportsfile

Page 293: Eoin Noonan/Sportsfile

Page 310: Keith Heneghan Photography

Page 318: Cody Glenn/Sportsfile

Page 321: Brendan Moran/Sportsfile

Page 322: Brendan Moran/Sportsfile

Page 326: Brendan Moran/Sportsfile

Page 363: Stephen McCarthy/Sportsfile

Page 382: RTÉ

Page 392: James Crombie/Inpho

Page 395: Brendan Moran/Sportsfile

Page 412: Stephen McCarthy/Sportsfile

Page 420: Ray McManus/Sportsfile

Page 422: David Maher/Sportsfile

Page 433: Kyran O'Brien Photography

Page 437: Kyran O'Brien Photography

Page 442: Kyran O'Brien Photography

Page 443: Kyran O'Brien Photography

Page 492: Diarmuid Greene/Sportsfile

Index

Page references for photographs are in *italic*

Moloney, Seanie 52–3,
57–8
Monaghan 252–4
Monahan, Claire 475
Montgomerie, Colin 358
Mooney, Derek 383
Moore, Christy 91, 156
Moore, Jim 338
Moore, Kathleen 313
Moore, Mary 313
Morahan, Caroline 387
Moran, Andy 362
Moran, Barry 439
Moran, Niall 251–2
Moran, Sean 232
Morgan, Billy 163–5
Moriarty, Áine 467
Morning Ireland (RTÉ)
164
Moroney, Billy 79–80
Moroney, Dympna 137
Moroney, Mick 207
Morrissey, Alice
(grandmother) 11,
12, 13, 15, 18, 19,
19, 21, 22
Morrissey, Declan 474
Morrissey, Eamon 389
Morrissey, Geraldine
46, 429
Morrissey, Ken 202, 217
Morrissey, Martin
(father) *25*
at McNamee Awards
98
death 9, 263–6, 384,
485
education 13
emigration 4, 14–15

father's death 23–4
and Jimmy Gavin 256
heart attacks 264–5
Hillcrest 28
*Land of My Cradle
Days* 23–4, 485
marriage 13–14, *14*
and Marty's career
45–6, 47, 101, 118
and Marty's thesis
100
mother's death 22
in New York 4–5,
15–18, *17*, 24, 26–7
in Quilty 27, 28, 34–5,
38–9
return to Ireland 22,
28
smoking 12–13
as teacher 13
as writer 485
Morrissey, Marty
Achilles tendon injury
194–7, 201
acting
Moll (John B. Keane)
384–5, *385*
Fir Bolg 386–7
amnesia episode
458–61
and alcohol 173
BBC application
141–3
birth 15
boxing 332–4, 337–52,
480–3
car 91–3
Champions League
football 353–7

childhood 9
desire to be a priest
296
first communion 22,
22
holidays in Ireland
18–22, *19*, *20*
in New York 4,
15–16, *16*, *17*, *18*, *25*,
296
in Quilty 27, 28,
31–2, 33–9, 41–4,
45–7
Clare FM 130–41, 143
and Clare Clarke
325–6, *326*
Clare Person of the
Year 468
Cooraclare
documentary 97
Cork Multi Channel
TV 84–5, 101–116,
108, *113*, 123–7, *123*,
124
Cork Person of the
Month 468
Countrywide 381–2, *382*
Crossbar challenge
393–5
cycle events 95–6
Dancing with the Stars
424–47, *photos
passim*
in Dubai 321, *321*
education
Master's 100, 263
in Mullagh 22
St Ann's, New York
24–6